FROM BOUNCING BOMBS TO CONCORDE

*To my wife Charlotte,
and in memory of my
old friend the aviation
journalist Arthur Reed*

FROM BOUNCING BOMBS TO CONCORDE

The Authorised Biography of Aviation Pioneer Sir George Edwards OM

ROBERT GARDNER

SUTTON PUBLISHING

First published in the United Kingdom in 2006 by
Sutton Publishing Limited · Phoenix Mill
Thrupp · Stroud · Gloucestershire · GL5 2BU

British Library Cataloguing in Publication Data
A catalogue record for this book is available from the British Library.

ISBN 0-7509-4389-0

Typeset in 10.5/14.5pt Photina MT.
Typesetting and origination by
Sutton Publishing Limited.
Printed and bound in England by
J.H. Haynes & Co. Ltd, Sparkford.

Contents

Foreword

by The Rt Hon. Sir John Major, KG CH

Very few people rise from the very bottom to the very top, build up achievements as they go, and leave a beneficial legacy behind them. One such is George Edwards. George Edwards was a rounded man, a man with a hinterland far wider than his genius for engineering. From his boyhood he had a love of cricket and used his knowledge of the game to help Barnes Wallis make the 'bouncing bomb' bounce in the Second World War. The dams of the Ruhr were destroyed by leg spin. George loved painting, a passion that came to him late in life, and was sufficiently good at it to have a canvas accepted for the Summer Exhibition at the Royal Academy at the age of 92. It was an achievement that gave him great satisfaction. We all owe a great deal to George Edwards, though few people will know how much until they read this biography. His life merged with history at key moments in war and peace, and his genius for innovation shaped events in the Second World War and in the general history of aviation. In wartime, apart from helping to destroy the great German dams, he designed an innovative system to detonate enemy magnetic mines to protect our shipping lanes, modified aircraft for special assignments, and was a member of the team that uncovered vital aeronautical information from Germany at the war's end. In peacetime, in his work for Vickers, he led the programme on the TSR.2 supersonic strike aircraft and the BAC One-Eleven jet-liner. He had earlier headed the design teams responsible for the Viking and Viscount airliners and the Valiant, Britain's first V-bomber. Later he was instrumental in the development of the most famous airliner of all: the Anglo-French Concorde. I first met Sir George Edwards, OM, designer, inventor and former chairman of BAC, at The Oval. An elderly, modest, undemonstrative man, a flat cap perched on his head, his vowels less precise than his remarkable mind, he sat quietly while watching the cricket. Beside him were two fellow spectators talking of their respective fathers' significant contributions to the Second World War. If only they had known . . . This biography will enable many more to know that George Edwards is part of our nation's history; and it is time his story was told.

Acknowledgements

There are many people I wish to thank for their assistance in the preparation of this biography, not least of whom is Sir George Edwards himself, who patiently spent some 30hr with me, describing his life and career. To the Edwards family, especially his daughter, Angela 'Dingle' Jeffreys, who encouraged, supported and managed the project before and after the death of Sir George in 2003; Richard and Clair, his grandchildren; Clair's husband, Gary; his relatives Grant Edwards, who researched his early years, and 'Uncle George' Thurgood, his brother-in law, I extend my heartfelt thanks for their co-operation and generous help.

I am indebted to many colleagues from my old company, the British Aircraft Corporation (BAC) and British Aerospace: Dr Norman Barfield, who was closely associated with Sir George for over fifty years, provided and researched much essential information, as well as proofreading the entire work; John Motum, whose considerable background knowledge and guidance were both illuminating and encouraging; Don McClen, who gave his expert advice on the chapter on Saudi Arabia; Brian Cookson, formerly the company legal director, who cast his eagle eye over the BAC chapters; and Bob Gladwell, who worked for the company in America for many years, and recalled the heady days when Vickers and BAC airliners filled the US skies. Special thanks must also go to Roger Steel, once the company personnel manager and personal art tutor to Sir George, and Mrs Joyce Brixey, his secretary for fifty years.

The recollections of two famous test pilots, G.R. 'Jock' Bryce of Vickers-Armstrongs and BAC, and Capt Eric 'Winkle' Brown of the Royal Aircraft Establishment, have given me much invaluable and enlightening information.

Others from the company or associated with it have also provided me with technical assistance and other help, notably Ron Hedges, keeper of the BAC heritage; film-maker Paul Drew of Communicator Ltd; Peter Gibbon of MGA

Ltd; and Barbara Ferguson, formerly of BAC. From the book world I received most helpful guidance from Neil Clayton, Nick Cook and Stephen Chalk. I am extremely grateful to them all.

This biography has been greatly enhanced by several distinguished people who were good enough to give me their time for interviews, and who have provided testimony about George Edwards. I would like to thank sincerely the Rt Hon. Sir John Major, who has written the foreword for the book; Sir Richard 'Dick' Evans, who later succeeded Sir George as chairman of the company, and who contributed the concluding chapter; and the Rt Hon. Tony Benn, who not only gave me the most entertaining interview, but was good enough to research every reference to Sir George from his diaries.

Others were able to recall Sir George's life outside the aircraft industry. From the cricket world, Sir Alec and Eric Bedser took part in the most amusing three-way conversation with Sir George for my benefit. Bernie Coleman, Derek Newton and Raman Subba Row, from the Surrey County Cricket Club, not only remembered the days when Sir George was president, but their conviviality was much appreciated. To Prof Patrick Dowling, until recently Vice-Chancellor of the University of Surrey, and Duncan Simpson, formerly Hawker's chief test pilot and neighbour, who served St Martha's on the Hill, as did Sir George, I offer my grateful thanks.

Lastly, this book could not have been written without the help of Sir George's oldest colleague and friend, the late Norman 'Spud' Boorer, whose astonishing memory and vivid description of George Edwards from the earliest days at Vickers has added the essential colour and detail to his story. I only hope I have done it justice.

Robert Gardner
March 2006

Author's Note

As far as possible, the story of George Edwards has been told through the eyes of Sir George himself, whose recall, perceptiveness and wit had not deserted him even in his nineties. It has been compiled through a series of interviews with him, together with interviews with his family, colleagues and others. To convey the immediacy of Sir George's contribution I have used the present tense, as I have with the other contemporary interviews.

The author has also been given access to Sir George's personal papers, which include correspondence with ministers and Board minutes. References from other books and papers have been fully acknowledged both in the narrative (I dislike margin notes) and in the appendices.

On Sunday 2 March 2003, the anniversary of the first Concorde flight, at the age of 94, George Edwards died peacefully at home in Guildford, Surrey, surrounded by his family. By his own wish this authorised biography has been written on the strict understanding that it would not be published until after his death. I hope it captures something of the fortitude, spirit and humour of a truly great Englishman.

CHAPTER ONE

In the Beginning

In January 1935 George Edwards, then 27 years old and working as a junior structural engineer in London's docks, travelled from his home in Highams Park, Essex, for a job interview at the Vickers Aviation company at Weybridge in Surrey. It was his second visit to the famous Vickers factory built alongside the Brooklands motor circuit, now described as the birthplace of aviation and motor racing in England. On the first occasion he had applied for a job as an aircraft stressman, and had been interviewed by the head of the stress office, Mr Pratt. But Pratt could only offer £5 a week, the same as George was already getting in the docks. 'Pratt was a decent bloke, but had been given some pretty rigid rules and regulations about pay,' Edwards remembers, adding with a grin: 'I wasn't going to go to a slum like Weybridge for no extra money!'

Shortly afterwards, Vickers wrote to him, suggesting the company might be able 'to do a bit better' if he applied for a job as a draughtsman in the drawing office. So once again young George set out for the Weybridge factory, but this time he was interviewed by Paul Wyand, the chief draughtsman. Wyand offered 5s a week more, bringing his weekly wage packet to a princely 5 guineas. Edwards needed the extra money, as he planned to marry Dinah Thurgood, his sweetheart from college days, later that year. This time he accepted the offer, which he later described as 'not extravagant'.

George Edwards had headed towards the aircraft industry and Vickers after being tipped off by a colleague in the docks, named Watts. Watts knew Barnes Wallis, who had already established a reputation as the designer of the successful R100 airship and was now designing aircraft at Weybridge. Wallis had told Watts that Vickers was cranking up against the threatening war with Nazi Germany and was recruiting people, particularly structural engineers, from outside the aircraft industry. Watts suggested to Edwards that there was not much future in the docks. 'The place is not big enough for you,' he told him, and said that if he could get a job at Vickers, or somewhere like it, he stood a good chance of 'going places'.

So, in February 1935, George Edwards went to work as a draughtsman in the drawing office at Vickers Aviation at Weybridge. His section leader was the experienced George Stannard, and his senior mentors were the gifted Barnes Wallis himself, with whom he was to have an uneasy but respectful relationship, and the less volatile but equally distinguished designer Rex Pierson.

'I had the great fortune to join Vickers at Weybridge under two very remarkable men – Barnes Wallis and Rex Pierson – and I learned a lot from both of them,' he said many years later. He added: 'They were two different people with quite different characters and approaches. Wallis was determined to achieve quality at almost any cost; Pierson was equally determined that an aeroplane should be a properly balanced product, with each specialist demand getting its fair share and no more. Rex Pierson, in my view, was a much underrated man, overshadowed as he was by Wallis's strong personality, but he was a first-class aeroplane designer.'

Thus, overseen by two of the greatest aircraft designers of their time, George Edwards began a career which, from such humble beginnings, was soon to blossom along a path of accelerated promotion. Within five years he became experimental manager, working on some of the most secret and ingenious wartime inventions. Within ten years he was chief designer, introducing the world to gas-turbine-powered aircraft. By 1953 he was managing director, and ten years later he took command of the most powerful aerospace company in Europe.

George Robert Freeman Edwards was born above his father's toyshop at 12 The Parade, Highams Park, Essex, on 9 July 1908. His start in life was poor; in fact it could not have been worse. A twin sister died at childbirth, and his mother died two weeks later from childbirth fever. His father was unable to cope on his own, and baby George was placed in the care of his mother's sister and husband, Bill and Sal Medlock. They lived 'round the corner' in a small terraced house in Handsworth Avenue, in which George was to spend all of his formative years.

Highams Park is a small suburb of Walthamstow on the north-eastern fringes of London. Through its centre runs what was the Great Eastern Railway, between Chingford and London Liverpool Street, with its level crossing, signal box (still standing) and station. The neighbourhood is full of rows of small Victorian and Edwardian terraces, and in such a building, a three-storey Edwardian house with ground-floor shop, George was born. The building is still there, now numbered 499 Hale End Road; the toy shop has gone, replaced by a solicitor's office. On the wall above is placed a blue oval Waltham Forest Heritage plaque commemorating Edwards's birth and achievements. George's paternal family were true cockneys, having been born and bred in the East End of London for generations, within the sound of Bow bells. His grandfather and great-grandfather were cabinetmakers, and it was not until 1900 that his father and uncle Charles moved into Highams Park. George Edwards has always been proud of his cockney roots, and says: 'We were proper working class, and I was born among a lot of cockneys. I talked the same language and I still do.'

His father, Edwin, was one of three brothers, and appears to have been the most enterprising of the three. From a job as a chemist's packer he went on to join industrial chemist Burroughs Wellcome as a salesman, and was sent to South Africa as a sales representative. He returned to England in 1907 and married Mary Freeman, one of ten children whose father came originally from Northamptonshire but was now working as a gardener at the Church of Holy Trinity in Roehampton, Middlesex. Her mother's family were from Cambridgeshire.

After his marriage, and with money saved while abroad, Edwin, with his brother Charles, acquired the shop in Hale End Road together with a second shop opposite. One was a newsagent and tobacconists, which Edwin ran himself, while across the road the toy and fancy goods shop, above which George was born, was looked after by his brother. The third brother was not involved and ran a bookmaker's business in Clapton, later described by his nephew as 'a bit of a racket'.

Despite the difficulties after his mother's death, George Edwards's childhood was comfortable and caring. His 'beloved' aunt had worked as a cook in a nearby big house, Beech Hill Park. His uncle was the local policeman. 'They were proper working class, and had been brought up in the country. He came from Huntingdonshire and was a copper while I was growing up. But their main job was to keep me fed and going,' he says. His cousin was Bob Gregory, a famous Surrey cricketer who toured with England and taught him to play and love the game, a passion he retained for the rest of his life.

Although Edwin was somewhat removed from his young son's upbringing, he kept a fatherly eye on him. 'My father was no fool. He wasn't well, that was his trouble, he suffered from curvature of the spine,' says George. 'He was pretty bright, and I talked to him quite a bit. That is where I probably got it from. He eventually killed himself because, being a tobacconist, he had just to put his hand out and there was another cigarette.' In later years he remarried, but both he and his new wife remained remote.

George's earliest childhood memories include a series of German air raids over London during the First World War. His home was beneath the Zeppelins' route from Germany, the airships making landfall at Harwich, then flying on to the east of London and the docks. He remembers going out to watch, and stood 'marvelling' at the great airships lit up by searchlights, and ack-ack guns going off. A scrap of metal from a Zeppelin shot down by a Royal Flying Corps pilot landed in his garden, and was retrieved by him, becoming a treasured possession. 'People talk about the barrage in the last war, but it was absolute peanuts to the one I listened to in the First War,' Edwards says.

The Germans also mounted many daylight raids, bomber aircraft sweeping low over the area in large arrowhead formations. On one occasion his aunt dragged George from school to the safety of their home, where he saw them fly right across Highams Park. 'For a small boy of eight years old this was moderately spectacular,' he recalls. But such experience of the new flying machines was not the inspiration for a future career; that came later, as a practical response to his mathematical and logical mind. At that time he and other people thought only about the war and their hatred of the Germans. 'There was no European "let's all be friends together" in those days,' he says.

As a toddler, George had been sent to a small private school which had written on a board outside: 'The Warner College for Ladies – Little Boys accepted'. Young George was one of the little boys accepted. 'It was run by two old ducks who were really brilliant. I could speak French when I was ten, which is more than I could do since,' he says. But money was short, and at 11 years old he was 'shovelled off' to the local elementary school in Selwyn Avenue. The school, which continues to enjoy a high reputation, remains today very much as it did in George's time. He was a bright boy who did well at his lessons, and his name was put down by his father for a scholarship to the local Sir George Monoux's grammar school. Applications were sent off, but to his lasting dismay he was then told his birthday was three days too late for him to sit the exam.

In later years George looked back on this rejection with profound regret. It probably had the greatest impact on his life, though conversely it was to be the spur to his future career and achievements. 'They wrote to me and said they were sorry I was too old, and I went back to the staff and said this is what had come in the post; they don't want me. I remember vividly. I was surrounded by three or four teachers who said "What are we going to do with young George? He's pretty bright." Then somebody said, "There's always the Tech."'

So to the 'Tech' he went, having won a scholarship to what was then the Walthamstow Technical Institute Engineering and Trade School (later called the Junior Technical School and subsequently the South West Essex Technical College). Since then he has often wondered what would have become of him had he gone to grammar school. 'I could have been a barrister, or something like that,' he says.

By some act of providence George Edwards had the 'great good fortune' of having two inspired maths teachers: Harry Brown, with whom he kept in touch for many years, and later an Irishman called Graham, a brilliant mathematician. 'We used to go in for a maths session and old man Graham used to say: "Well now Mister Edwards, what would you like us to do today?" I used to look bright and sparkling and say I enjoyed identities [a mathematical term, defined as 'statements of equality between known or unknown quantities, which hold true for all values of the unknown quantities'], and so identities it was,' he remembers. 'The rest of the lads went on doing their football pools or something while there was I having a private lesson.'

By buttoning on first to Brown and then to Graham, young Edwards emerged as being 'pretty capable' in maths. He also received a good grounding in basic design, physics and chemistry, all the ingredients for an engineering career. 'I was spurred on, as far as I could understand the words, to go into engineering,' he says. 'For most of the chaps I knocked about with, their great ambition was to become a bank clerk or something like that. I could see that had no future. What I had to do in life was manageable because I knew, roughly speaking, how to get the numbers right.' He adds: 'The Lord had given me the right mixture of molecules to start with, and I have seen young chaps who had not got the right mixture flogging their guts out trying to cope with identities and the rest of it. They hadn't got a prayer.'

His technical college reports reflect his progress, and from the autumn of 1922 to the summer of 1926 he finished either top or, at worst, third in his form, excelling in maths and the sciences. The principal of the college, Mr James Edwards, described his overall performance as 'excellent' and in 1925 appointed him school captain. Encouraged by this and by Mr Graham, George Edwards realised the 'smart thing' to do was gain a higher academic qualification. 'There was dangled before me this great mysterious thing of

London University,' he says. 'I was told I could have a go at an external degree if I worked as I never worked before, because the standard was so high. So I put my head down and went nearly mad until the small hours of the morning. I duly got it [a BSc (Eng)], and it opened the door to all sorts of places and people who didn't care what you had got until you said you had a London degree, particularly an external one, which said you had worked.'

Edwards left the technical school in 1926, carrying a glowing and highly perceptive testimonial from Mr Edwards, who wrote: 'His progress in all subjects of the curriculum has been exceedingly good. He is especially good at mathematics and his ability to reason and apply the same to practical problems has placed him far above the average youth in the form. His practical work in science and other subjects has been of a high standard. In fact, I have no hesitation in stating that he is one of the best boys we have ever had in the school.' He added: 'As school captain during his last year he showed tact and ability which was admired by both staff and scholars and showed him capable of organising and carrying out definite plans.' For any boy, however bright, the prospect of finding a good job in 1926, the year of the General Strike, was bleak. As a precautionary measure, young George sat and passed the examination as a probationer inspector in the engineering department of the General Post Office (GPO). Although he was subsequently offered a job, he chose not to take it, preferring to join the clerical staff of the Ocean Accident & Guarantee Corporation in Moorgate in March 1927. Again he was recognised as a bright lad, and within three months he was transferred to their engineering department, with responsibility for 'periodical inspection of all machinery under insurance'. A year later, having seen an advertisement in the *Daily Telegraph*, he applied for and got the job as a junior technical engineer at Hay's Wharf in the London docks. It was his first real step up the ladder.

In those days Dockland was still the commercial heart of the British Empire, teeming with river traffic of all kinds. The Pool of London, administered by the Port of London Authority, covered more than 2,500 acres and employed thousands of people. The new job involved what Edwards described as: 'a pretty clear spread of rough engineering'. This included checking, testing and certificating cranes, elevators and bridges; laying out engines for cold-storage depots or for diesel tugs; and many other things.

George Edwards remembers clearly those early days in the docks.

What I was landed with when I first went there was some new Act of Parliament, which required every piece of lifting tackle, be it a crane or a hoist, to be certificated by somebody to say it was properly stressed. The appropriate tests had to be carried out to ensure it was in good working order and didn't break when you put the stated load on it. I knew enough about strength and structures, and I used to be told to do the certification on a particular crane. That meant I had to collect the drawings and organise a testing programme, which was a fairly hairy operation. This involved climbing to the top of the jib of the crane about 150ft above sea level in the dark, often in the middle of winter with snow on the frame.

Edwards, having shown signs of 'moderate intelligence', soon became 'lumbered' with work of most interest to him: engineering and building cranes. He had been particularly impressed by the clever design and mechanisms of those built by the famous West Country firm of Stothart & Pitt. So when the Docks Authority decided to build their own, he volunteered for the job and was teamed with an experienced colleague. 'Bit by bit I began to find out what he was up to, and bit by bit I began to find out what I was up to; so after a time, I became a pretty hard-arsed engineer,' he says.

To prove it, in July 1930 he took and passed the entrance exam for the Institution of Structural Engineers, and became an associate member. It was his first professional qualification, and it gave him the confidence to progress his career. And so, after seven years in the docks, and encouraged by his friend Watts, Edwards was ready to move. As he put it: 'A strut is a strut and a tie is a tie, whether it is on an aircraft or a crane.' He adds: 'An aeroplane – the vital part of an aeroplane – is its structure. It's no good the engines going along quite happily if the wings fall off!' Armed with such logic, membership of the Structural Engineers, and his continuing studies for his London University degree (for which he was attending classes at the West Ham Municipal College), he applied for and eventually got the job at Vickers.

CHAPTER TWO

A Job at Vickers

Vickers (Aviation) Ltd at Weybridge, to which George Edwards was now destined to be attached for the rest of his working life, was, in 1935, just awakening from a long period of stagnation. The inevitable reduction in military requirements at the end of the 1914–18 war had been followed by an industrial slump and economic recession in the second half of the 1920s. Britain's aircraft builders, although brim-full with new ideas and design concepts, many of which were being proved with successful record-breaking attempts, were short of work. At Weybridge, where wartime output had reached thirty fighters a week, there was now piecemeal production and experimental work, though in time this would reap rich rewards.

For George Edwards, both the mighty Vickers company and the historic Brooklands site had special historic meaning and lasting value. They were synonymous with the advancement of aviation in this country since the earliest pioneering days. Brooklands was still a magical place for the motor racing and the flying fraternities, who encamped there after its opening as the world's first banked motor circuit in 1907. The first flying attempts were made in 1907 and 1908, A.V. Roe making a number of short powered hops in an aeroplane of his own design on a grass strip by the racetrack. Roe was followed by many other early aviators, such as Tom Sopwith, who Edwards was later to get to know well, and the Australian Harry Hawker, who lent his name to the famous aircraft company and died young.

In 1912 Vickers arrived at Brooklands, establishing one of the world's first flying schools in four sheds near the Byfleet banking of the race track. Among its early pupils were Lord Trenchard, founder of the Royal Air Force, Air Chief Marshal Lord Dowding, who directed the fighter squadrons in the Battle of Britain, and the man who was to have such a huge influence on Edwards's career, Rex Pierson. The Vickers school used aircraft of the company's own design, built at their engineering works at Erith in Kent, where they had begun manufacture in 1911.

This was not Vickers's first experience with flying machines. In 1908 they had built Britain's first rigid airship at their famous Barrow shipbuilding works, but this had been wrecked by a sudden gust of wind when it emerged from its shed. Undaunted, three years later, the company began aircraft building at Erith, extending the work to its plants at nearby Crayford and Bexleyheath. It was a natural development for this great company with its roots in Sheffield iron and steel in the 1820s. Vickers and its men were known and respected throughout the world. Its warships, submarines and guns had established it at the heart of the British armaments and heavy engineering industry. The move into aircraft was totally predictable.

With the outbreak of war in 1914 Vickers was subcontracted by the War Office to build a large number of Royal Aircraft Factory-designed aircraft. For this purpose, in 1915, the company acquired the old Itala motor works at Brooklands, situated on the eastern side of the race track, and progressively transferred all the work from the other sites to the new factory, which became, and remained, the centre of its activities. Before long the Vickers aviation company was turning out aircraft such as the B.E.2c reconnaissance biplane, designed by the Royal Aircraft Factory at Farnborough. Later, and more significantly, it began producing its own in-house designed Gunbus, considered to be the world's first real fighter aircraft. Later still, it also built Royal Aircraft Factory S.E.5a fighters.

But the most famous Vickers aircraft of the wartime period to emerge from the Brooklands works at Weybridge came too late to see action. This was the Vimy bomber, designed by Rex Pierson, who had been appointed chief designer at the age of only 26. The Vimy was to gain immortality as the first aircraft to fly the North Atlantic non-stop in the hands of Alcock and Brown in 1919. It also pioneered the Empire routes to Australia and South Africa. But its enduring properties were to be of more value to the peacetime Vickers company, for its commercial and military derivatives provided production continuity in the lean years ahead.

The industrial decline at this time was so serious that, in 1927, it forced Vickers to merge with its rival, Armstrong Whitworth, though that company's aircraft interests were not included in the deal. One year later the renamed Vickers-Armstrongs Ltd acquired the Supermarine company, primarily as an investment in the talents of its brilliant designer, R.J. Mitchell.

Now, in 1935, the threat of a new war was quickening activity again. As Edwards clocked in for the first time as a design draughtsman, he knew things

were changing and he was going to be part of it. A year earlier the Cabinet had
decided to make good the deficiencies in the armed forces. Progressively, but
painfully slowly, Britain's rearmament programme built up, coinciding with
Hitler's remilitarisation of the Rhineland. On the drawing boards and in
development at Weybridge were two new twin-engine bombers incorporating
Barnes Wallis's revolutionary 'geodetic' or 'basket-weave' construction method.
(A geodetic line is defined as the shortest line between two points on a curved
surface, and is known in global navigation as a 'great circle' route. As defined
by Wallis in lattice form applied to aircraft structural design, it resulted in an
ideal form of load-balance and fail-safe construction.)

Across the track in the Hawker sheds, Sydney Camm and his design team
were about to fly the new monoplane Hurricane fighter. In Southampton at
Supermarine, Mitchell was putting the finishing touches to the Spitfire.

On his first day at Weybridge Edwards toured the factory. The first thing he
saw was what he described as: 'an enormous bully-looking man, who was
stripped to the waist, who I later discovered was the works manager, Archie
Knight. He led a gang of men with large sledgehammers, who were breaking
up what looked to me to be an absolutely new aeroplane.' Why they were
doing this Edwards never did discover, but the experience left a lasting
impression. In a paper to the Fellowship of Engineering, many years later, he
reflected: 'That was my first indication that selling aeroplanes was pretty
difficult – although I never had to resort to breaking them up. The second
thing that was dawning upon me was that this was no ordinary industry that
I had strayed into, and I must say that nothing has happened since to make me
change my view.'

It later transpired that the aircraft being scrapped was almost certainly the
first prototype Viastra transport, though some believed it to have been the
Viastra X allocated to the Prince of Wales, which had been little used by him.
This aircraft was broken up at Croydon when it reached the end of its useful life.

During his factory tour Edwards saw a number of older biplanes being
assembled. They included a Vildebeest torpedo-bomber, some Victoria troop
transports, another Viastra, and a line of Hawker Harts being built under a
subcontract to fill a production gap. More significantly, he inspected the Vickers
G.4/31 military general-purpose biplane, which, although old-fashioned
looking, was the first aircraft to use Wallis's geodetic construction, in its rear

fuselage section. It was soon to be the subject of an astonishing decision. Accompanying Edwards on his walk round was George Stannard, a senior section leader in the drawing office who was now George's boss. He remembers him fondly. 'He was a typical old Vickers chap who came from Erith and was a real good-un. He was a plain straight-arsed engineer.' Edwards always appreciated the help and contribution Stannard made to his life and his career: 'He knew I knew damn all about aeroplanes. He had to hold my hand to make sure I really knew the difference between a strut and a tie, or a beam and a continuous beam. I was eternally grateful for that,' he says. In addition to Stannard's job in the drawing office, he had to oversee the many other new recruits who were now arriving in increasing numbers from outside the industry, particularly from other parts of the 'Vickers Empire' such as Newcastle and Barrow. Edwards reckons they had a 'pretty good training' and soon adapted into this 'new line of business'.

So George Edwards took up his job, working in a newly completed but traditional open-plan drawing office, in which he was given a 'pitch' near the front of rows of drawing boards. He describes himself as being a 'very lowly' person engaged in what was 'pretty humble' work alongside more than 100 other people. 'We were in one big room, not dissimilar to being in a big greenhouse. The drawing office itself, I would say, had something like a juvenile air about it; it was as though you were in a large high-powered school classroom.' Sitting above them on a raised platform at the back of the room were the 'hierarchy', such as chief draughtsman Paul Wyand, who had interviewed him, and his assistant Joe Bewsher; and 'tucked away' in the corner were the offices of chief designer Rex Pierson and Barnes Wallis, chief designer (structures).

Initially the work was not up to Edwards's expectations, and much later he recorded his disillusionment. 'My first impressions were almost beyond belief. Whereas before I would take responsibility for a pretty hefty engineering undertaking – design it, stress it, go outside and get it put up, do the tests and sign the test certificate, for the first of God knows how many months at Vickers I was drawing little gusset plates like biscuits. It was like a tin of Peak Frean's [biscuits], only made out of metal. The shapes were almost the same, and this didn't seem to me a very rewarding sort of task. For a time I got pretty brassed off with it.'

Happily, Edwards stuck with it, and by May of that year he was promoted and put in charge of a small sub-section. The first permanent arrivals to his team, who were all to spend the rest of their careers with him, were Ernie

Marshall, who became chief engineer in post-war days, Les Booth, who became a senior design draughtsman, and Norman 'Spud' Boorer, who was to be his closest colleague and friend. Both Marshall and Boorer were graduates of the Kingston Junior Technical College, known in the works as the 'Vickers academy'. They were exact contemporaries, having joined the company in 1931 and worked their way up from the workshops. Boorer says that joining Edwards was 'the luckiest day in my life'.

That Edwards was promoted and shortly afterwards put on the much-prized higher monthly staff grade came as no surprise to his colleagues. Spud Boorer says he was known in the place as 'a bright bloke, and his name was being bandied about'. Both Stannard and Wyand had recognised his talent. His experience as a structural engineer in the docks and his ability to lead men had quickly become an asset.

More important jobs were now to come his way, bringing him into direct contact with both Wallis and Pierson. The influence of these two men was to have a profound effect. Edwards wrote years later: 'It is given to few mortals to have to deal with two men of their calibre at the same time.' Of the two, Edwards was to have more early involvement with the enigmatic Barnes Wallis, particularly over structural matters and the application of the geodetic principle, which was to cause friction between the two for many years.

Wallis had arrived at Weybridge five years earlier, having begun his career with Vickers in 1913, designing airships for the re-established factory at Barrow. By 1917 he was put in total charge of airship development at the age of only 26. With the war's end Vickers temporarily abandoned the work and the lull gave Wallis the opportunity to do what George Edwards did years later: take an external engineering degree at London University. For, surprisingly, he had risen to great heights without any real qualification other than his own instinctive genius and, again like Edwards, an intuitive command of mathematics.

Wallis returned to Vickers in 1923 after the government decided to fund two new airships for long-range passenger services: the Vickers R100 and the rival government-backed R101. He recruited as his chief calculator Neville Shute Norway, later to become famous for his novels, who wrote: 'To my mind Wallis was the greatest engineer in England at that time and for twenty years afterwards. It was an education and a privilege to work under him and I count myself lucky to do so.'

By 1929 his work on the R100, particularly his application of the new lightweight duralumin aluminium alloy, brought Wallis to the attention of Sir Robert McLean, the chairman of Vickers Aviation, and Rex Pierson. They quickly realised its potential for aeroplane structures, and persuaded Wallis to join them at Weybridge. This was even before his R100 had made what was to be a highly successful proving flight to Canada.

Wallis's move proved to be fortuitous, for less than a year later the rival R101 crashed in France on its maiden flight, costing many lives, including the government minister responsible. This ended any further airship development, including the R100. But by now Wallis was already deeply engaged in applying the use of light alloys to geodetic construction. The advantages were greater strength at lighter weights, and unobstructed space to carry more fuel, cargo or passengers inside. The structure would be covered by fabric, which had the advantage of being easily replaced. It was to become the accepted building method for all Vickers aircraft for the next 15 years.

So, in 1935, Edwards, sharing the same structural engineering background and passion for mathematics, came face to face with Wallis himself. 'I was confronted with Wallis, which I must say was a new experience. I got on well with Rex Pierson all right, that was no problem, but Wallis always was a problem, because he was determined that whatever was going to be done was going to be done his way.'

Like other colleagues, he was often disturbed by Wallis's style of working. 'He used to appear and wander round the drawing boards to see what was on them since his last visit. He had the ability to drive chaps mad. Having told a lad how he wanted something done a week or two before, the lad would do his best and burst his boiler to make it look decent. Then Wallis would turn up and say a few words like: "I've never seen such rubbish". The group leader would then be hauled over the coals and told to do a lot better. It went on like that, but we accepted it as a way of life at Vickers.'

Years later, in a television interview, Edwards was able to appreciate the other side of Wallis. 'I used to grizzle about the number of times that I had to do what seemed to me as relatively simple things. But this was the outward and visible sign of Wallis's obsession with quality. I learnt a lot, and I think all those who worked for Wallis learnt a lot about the need to search for quality in this very exacting business. He wasn't easily turned from a course he was on, but he was a chap of great inventive genius and could see things that lesser mortals couldn't see.'

Appropriately, the first aircraft Edwards worked on was the experimental G.4/31 biplane with the geodetic rear fuselage structure, which he had seen on his first-day tour. It had been designed to meet an Air Ministry specification for a general-purpose bombing and torpedo-carrying aircraft. Edwards says his involvement was: 'only negligible – an alteration to the trailing edge of the wing that somebody else thought they had got right!'

Flight trials of the G.4/31 soon showed that the geodetic tail offered huge performance and structural advantage, which resulted in an amazing and courageous decision by Sir Robert McLean. A contract had already been won from the Ministry for 150 of these aircraft. However, the Vickers team, led by Pierson and armed with encouraging flight-test results, believed it to be old fashioned and the specification too pedestrian. They were now sufficiently confident to propose an all-geodetic monoplane with high aerodynamic efficiency and greater range by virtue of its high-aspect-ratio wing, which would enable it to greatly outperform the biplane. (Aspect ratio is the ratio between the wing span and its breadth, or chord. A high-aspect-ratio wing of long span and narrow chord is more efficient and therefore better for long-range operations, while low aspect ratio is required for high-performance, manoeuvrable aircraft such as fighters.) As Edwards explained later, the structural design techniques and materials now employed allowed the wings to be built in a long continuous span, 'without it snapping off at the root, which is inconvenient to everybody!' McLean, a steely Scot who had been a magnate with the Indian State Railways, had been appointed by the Vickers Board in 1927 to oversee the Vickers (and later Supermarine) aircraft operations. Having complete faith in his Weybridge team, he famously wrote to the Air Ministry, rejecting their order for the biplane, which he described as, 'not a modern machine', and stated that the company would start work, as a private initiative, on the monoplane. George Edwards says: 'The state we were in you didn't turn down an order for 150 aircraft without some pretty hefty drinking and thinking.' The decision was soon to be justified, and a new order was forthcoming for what became the Wellesley bomber, which soon made its mark by capturing the world long-distance record, and entered RAF service in 1937.

In addition to the Wellesley, Vickers was working on a new bomber, conceived by Rex Pierson, to meet Air Ministry Specification B.9/32. This was Vickers's second response to the Ministry requirement, the first, proposing an all-metal high-wing monoplane, having been rejected. The new proposal was for an aircraft of mid-wing configuration with a geodetic structure, and a prototype, K4049, was authorised. This would have double the range and carry twice the bomb load of the earlier submission. At first it was called Crecy, but later was named the Wellington.

By now the design office had been reorganised into specialist groups, of which Edwards's was one, tasked to do what he calls 'a big chunk' of the tail unit for the prototype. Edwards was responsible for designing the fin, rudder, tailplane and elevator, while his team detailed it up. His initials, 'GRE', can still be seen on surviving drawings and, as was the custom, it was by his initials that he was ever to be known within the company, and by the aircraft industry at large. For by now, for reasons unknown even to the family, he had dropped his second middle name 'Freeman', his mother's maiden name.

Work on the prototype was not without its problems. Spud Boorer found things were far from easy because they had to keep 're-doing' the tailplane or rudder about once a week as Wallis kept altering it. To help the situation, and to visualise its exact shape, Edwards went to see Rex Pierson, who suggested he talk to Mutt Summers, the much revered chief test pilot who, in six months' time, was to become the first man to fly the Spitfire. Pierson said that Summers had pretty definite views on how fin and rudders should be, and was very keen on the way it was on the Vickers-Supermarine Stranraer flying boat. 'I was instructed to go and get a bit of tracing paper and trace over the Stranraer fin and rudder and put that on our aircraft, which is what I did. It worked; it was quite good.' Edwards says.

Edwards was also able to show his initiative in a rather dramatic way when confronted with a rudder overbalance problem on the prototype, as Spud Boorer remembers. 'He simply cut off some of the ribs, adding a new wooden nose-piece to build up the rear of the fin horn balance. All done and flown the same day.' In June 1936 the prototype made a successful first flight from Brooklands in the hands of Mutt Summers. Edwards and his small team were 'too lowly' to watch it.

In July 1935, after seven years of grindingly hard work, George Edwards eventually received his Bachelor of Science (Engineering) degree from London University. He later recalled just how hard it was. 'I was working in the office until seven o'clock in the evening before going back to my Byfleet lodgings and having my sparse meal, with which I was expected to stay alive. I then worked on until about twelve and got up at five to do some more work before getting back to the office by nine. That was the process by which you had to get external degrees in those days. There were no grants for students. It was just plain straight hard work. It paid off.'

Edwards has always been grateful for the system at London University that allowed him to take his degree in the way he did. It was therefore a matter of great pride to him when the university conferred on him, in 1970, an honorary degree of Doctor of Science, which he received from the Chancellor, The Queen Mother. He took the opportunity to pay tribute to the university, which he said: 'has made more fundamental and far-reaching contributions to the spread and strengthening of higher education than any seat of learning in the world, bar none'. He added: 'Thus it was London University which enabled people (and I was one of them) who were unable to attend full-time university courses, to take external degrees and to acquire the hallmark – and the training and discipline that has to go with it – of a London degree.'

Three months after receiving his degree, in October 1935, there was reason for further celebration when George Edwards married Marjorie Annie 'Dinah' Thurgood at All Saints Church, Highams Park. She had lived close by George's home in Selwyn Avenue, opposite the little school they had both attended. Later, they travelled together by train on the short journey to Walthamstow to go to technical school. He was head boy, and she was head girl of the adjoining commercial college. George says: 'She always maintained that I used to be a very decent fellow and carry her bag. I'm sure I never did, because all the other chaps would have laughed at me.'

His best man was Dinah's brother, George, who shared an interest in engineering, motor cars and cricket. He says his mother and father were pleased about their daughter's marriage: 'he was a decent bloke'. He did not think either had a boy- or girlfriend before.

The occasion was well recorded in the local paper, the *Walthamstow Guardian*, in a story headed 'Well-known newsagent's son married', and describing the event as 'an interesting wedding'. The bride was given away by her father, and 'looked charming in a gown of white cloque and carried a bouquet of crimson roses'. The reception for over seventy guests was held in the Scouts' hut, and afterwards the couple spent their honeymoon in Torquay. 'It was a very proper but working-class occasion,' George says.

The couple came to live in West Byfleet and built a 'little house' in Dartnell Park, where they were to stay until after the Second World War. In 1943 their daughter Angela, forever to be known as 'Dingle', was born.

CHAPTER THREE

Preparing for War

The years leading to the impending war with Nazi Germany were years of ferocious activity in Britain's aircraft industry, as it struggled to keep pace with the massive German military output. In the late summer of 1935 the British government introduced a vast industrial expansion scheme, Scheme F, which required an increase in production from some 3,800 aircraft in two years to over 8,000 in three years. At Weybridge the first and welcome effect was a third order for 80 Wellesleys and, particularly, an order for 150 Wellingtons, to which there would soon be added 227 more.

Since the Wellington's first flight, three months earlier, great efforts had been made to translate the promise of the prototype into a production aircraft. The performance advantages of the geodetic construction had resulted in significant improvements over the specified requirements in range and bomb-carrying capability, which was almost doubled. The production version, with more powerful Bristol Pegasus engines, was much modified and improved, and the Edwards 'traced' rudder had now been revised. Much benefit had also been derived from the parallel design work on the larger and heavier Warwick, which was to follow the Wellington on the assembly lines.

Edwards played only a minor part on Warwick development, but it was not his favourite aeroplane, despite the design contribution it made to the Wellington. 'It wasn't the world's best aeroplane, as it had a flagging rudder. It crashed on the edge of St George's Hill Golf Club,' he says. His lack of enthusiasm for the Warwick as a bomber, which also suffered from engine development problems, proved justified, and only 845 were built, compared with a total of 11,460 Wellingtons. Warwicks were later used for air-sea rescue and general-reconnaissance duties, their long range and spacious cabin suiting them well to these roles.

While design improvements were being incorporated into the Wellington, the works engineers were struggling to produce the bomber. The complexity of its geodetic structure and the complicated curvatures were such that the first aircraft had to be virtually hand built. This was clearly unacceptable, both in man-hour costs and output volume.

The recruitment from Supermarine of Trevor Westbrook as general manager at Weybridge soon helped solve this. According to Spud Boorer, Westbrook said he would get Wallis's geodetics working, provided Wallis did not interfere. So, supported by Jack East, a tool designer whose 'fertile brain' was inspired by Westbrook, and Tony Deedman, a good tool engineer, they set about inventing a remarkable new machine. This could roll a geodetic channel from a flat metal strip and form it automatically to the correct curvatures. 'You would put in a bit of strip in one end, and the right curvature would come out the other; a very clever machine,' says Boorer.

George Edwards maintains that Westbrook and East, who actually designed the machine, have never really been given the credit they deserve for putting geodetics into production. 'I used to be pretty unpopular for saying that the remarkable thing about the Wellington being built was the process by which Westbrook and East got it into production. Had it not been for them being there at the time, nobody would ever have built the Wellington.'

While the production staff were grappling with geodetics, the drawing office was engaged in other new projects, including a high-speed twin-engine fighter of metal construction (in which Edwards was shortly to play a major part), and a long-range four-engine bomber in response to Ministry Specification B.12/36. Both Supermarine and Vickers had tendered for the bomber, but it was a shock to Weybridge that the Supermarine design, the last by R.J. Mitchell, was chosen. The Ministry, however, softened the blow to Weybridge pride by saying they had too much on their plates to do it, anyway.

Although disappointed, Edwards was full of admiration for Mitchell, whom he had met briefly once or twice at Weybridge. 'For the B.12/36, Mitchell produced a design that won hands down, even though he had never done a big aeroplane in his life before. Look at the wing, it was absolutely brilliant. He did a D-shaped box, which was regarded by the blokes who knew as a classic piece of aircraft wing design.' He adds: 'There was gloom and despondency at Weybridge, where it was reckoned that they were the big-aeroplane part of the Vickers aircraft company. They were despondent because these little pipsqueaks who built little fighters down at Southampton had been given the job.'

Nobody would ever know how good the Mitchell bomber was. Both prototypes were destroyed by a German air raid on the Itchen works in September 1940, and that was the end of it. Edwards reckons: 'I don't imagine the Germans had any idea that this was going to be a war-winner, but they took very good care that it wasn't.'

George Edwards rates Mitchell as 'the most versatile' of all the aircraft designers of that time. 'When you look at the range of aeroplanes he did, starting off with stunt planes, to flying boats, to fighters and ending up with B.12/36, it is quite inconceivable. He didn't only have a go, he made them work.' He also felt empathy towards Mitchell. 'The thing that gladdened my heart was that he was just a rough old Midlands engineer, like I was a rough old Southern one. There isn't anybody else on either side of the Atlantic that I know of who could claim the versatility of Mitchell.'

By early 1937, deliveries from Weybridge had fallen behind the demands of the government's Scheme F expansion plan. The arrival in January of Trevor Westbrook, and a large investment in new plant and machinery, were yet to yield any benefit. This was despite an increase in the labour force from around 1,500 in 1934 to over 3,000 by the end of 1936. Unfortunately, a lack of skilled men and a shortage of production capacity, which was soon to lead to the establishment of government-owned 'shadow factories', frustrated progress.

The situation became even more serious during the next few months as British industry slipped further behind the Germans. The true nature of a widening gap was reported back to Vickers by Mutt Summers, who even then retained high-level contact with both the German industry and air force. The Germans recognised his achievements and valued his opinion, while the British valued his intelligence reports. In October 1937 Summers returned from one of his regular trips to Germany in a state of 'complete depression', having seen and flown some of their latest types. He told of their new twin-engine bomber, which was being produced at the rate of two a day, and which, with its new Mercedes engines, could attain speeds in the order of 300mph. He also flew their new dive-bomber and actually tested it in a dive, saying afterwards that he would not want to be on the receiving end (as British troops were soon to find out). His findings were passed on to the Air Ministry, who this time did not appreciate Summers's comments. The Secretary of State wrote to the Vickers chairman: 'Kindly tell your pilots to mind their own bloody business.'

Edwards says that Summers's 'special and privileged' relationship with the German air force was through his long friendship with Gen Milch, the Chief of Staff, who is credited by many as the true creator of Goering's Luftwaffe. But if the Ministry were unimpressed by his latest reports, Edwards says the Vickers chief designer was not. 'Rex Pierson certainly took notice of Mutt, but Wallis, I think, thought he drank and smoked too much.' As for his boss, Sir Robert McLean, it strengthened his view that the Air Ministry had not absorbed the seriousness of the situation.

The Air Ministry's tardy rebuff was also further evidence of a growing strain in relationships with the Vickers aircraft companies. The Ministry had become increasingly irritated by their fiercely guarded independence, and now by their failure to meet the required production rates. This provided the Ministry with the opportunity (and excuse) to exert pressure on Vickers to make top-level organisational changes, which would inevitably bring into question the role of McLean himself.

The background to this situation dated back to the acquisition by Vickers of the Supermarine company in 1927, and the appointment of Sir Robert as chairman of both Vickers Aviation and Supermarine. He was described as 'a man of granite integrity and austere independence of mind' by J.D. Scott in his definitive history of the Vickers company, and, as was his way, McLean exercised almost autonomous (and respected) control. Scott wrote: 'He regarded the Air Ministry in matters of design, development and strategic planning, reactionary and inept,' while the Ministry considered the Vickers aircraft companies, 'or at least with McLean as their head, as, obstinate, over-bold and intrusive'.

McLean was equally uncompromising about the threat of war with Germany and the 'race against time' with the German aircraft industry. Scott wrote that he was not one of the people who ever believed that Hitler was a man you could deal with. 'War with Germany was, in his view, inevitable: and it would be won by the Wellington and the Spitfire was his doctrine, which he preached in and out of season, particularly to the Air Staff. His preaching was like that of John Knox to Mary Queen of Scots, and was received in somewhat the same way.'

Little wonder that McLean and the companies he represented had become unpopular with certain senior members of the Air Staff, a situation that concerned the Vickers Board, which was uncomfortable at being at odds with its largest customer. They decided to restructure their aircraft interests by bringing the two aircraft companies under the main Vickers-Armstrongs armaments 'umbrella'. As a result both Vickers (Aviation) Ltd and Supermarine became Vickers-Armstrongs Ltd, with aviation works at Weybridge and Southampton. Sir Charles Craven was appointed above McLean as chairman of both. Craven, a former Royal Navy officer who had worked in a supervisory capacity at Barrow with Wallis in the early days, was a distinguished 'Vickers man' who had rejuvenated British Steel after the depression. It was hardly surprising that, following his appointment, Sir Robert McLean resigned in October 1938 and left the industry. Later, as chairman of EMI, he was to play an important role in the development of radar.

Although the changes did not affect the day-to-day work of George Edwards and his team, it did remove from them a man of vision and courage who had so publicly supported his 'designers of genius' like Mitchell, Wallis and Pierson. By pushing through both the Wellington and Spitfire as private initiatives before Ministry sanction had been given, and by refusing to be intimidated in doing so, McLean had, in the eyes of many, made the most significant personal contribution to winning the war.

Craven was not of similar character. He was a man of great talent and organisational ability, particularly in achieving production requirements. He was also a man of enterprise, but his inclinations were towards the importance of naval matters at the expense of air power, for which he carried an inherent distrust. Furthermore, he viewed the special position chief designers held in the company as a good deal of nonsense. J.D. Scott wrote: 'Although there was a great deal that could be said for the new arrangement, it also had disadvantages. Perhaps it was as well that, when Craven assumed control of the aircraft companies, the supreme creative effort had already been put forth.'

While the high-level politics were being played out, Weybridge was now responding to fresh government demands with the introduction of another new scheme, Scheme L. This replaced Scheme F, bringing with it a reorder for 120 Wellingtons, production for which, thanks to Westbrook and co., was now beginning to run ahead of schedule. The inevitability of war and the special efforts it would demand of the aircraft industry were now all too apparent to Edwards and his colleagues.

During the few remaining years of peacetime, George and Dinah Edwards had settled into their new home in West Byfleet. With his immediate scholastic work completed, and his star rising at Weybridge, Edwards found time to pursue his many outside interests. He joined Woking Cricket Club, where he met and played with the teenage Bedser twins. Alec Bedser (later Sir Alec) was to become one of England's greatest bowlers, while brother Eric opened the batting, both playing for the Surrey county side. They were to remain close friends with George.

George Edwards also engaged in a rather more serious pursuit: playing the London stock market. By nature he had always been a bit of a gambler. Placing a few bob on a horse was part of his upbringing, but his share dealings then, as throughout his career, remained frequent and in the main successful. He applied a scientific and mathematical approach and confined his activities to the relative safety of gilts. He also had an 'eye for things to come', which could bring further investment opportunity. This did not, however, always pay off. In 1936 he became one of the first to acquire a television set, and with it he bought shares in the company. Unfortunately this was the pioneering but short-lived electro-mechanical system invented by John Logie Baird. It was soon to be outdated by the EMI electronic method, bringing no reward to the Baird company shareholders but much novelty entertainment to its subscribers.

Spud Boorer recalls how he and the other members of the group were invited to watch the new television service at the Edwards's home, where Dinah 'plied' them with sandwiches, pies and sausage rolls. 'Ernie Marshall, Les Booth and I were invited to witness a boxing match on his new TV screen, which was six to eight inches wide. I remember we had spent a good bit of time on the drawing-board working out the geometry of a cinema screen to viewing distance, so we could sit at the proper distance in front of his TV. I don't remember who won the fight,' he says, 'but I know George lost some money on the Baird deal.'

Boorer also remembers another Edwards enterprise: providing second-hand technical books at a discount. Spud never knew from where he obtained them, whether he made anything out of it, or if he did it as a kindness. 'He was obviously a business bloke as well as his drawing. I don't know how he got into it, but I know I bought my *Kempe's Handbook of Aeronautics* at a reduced price from him, which I still have at home.' Many years later George Edwards could not recall any of this, probably because the books were simply those he had acquired for his degree course, which, like many students before and after him, he had sold on after use.

Such private ventures were not always appreciated by his bosses. Boorer recalls how George used to cycle home at lunchtime to 'do a bit of stockbroking and things', which would lead to a clash with Barnes Wallis. 'George used to come back from one of these lunches and Wallis would come round and grumble about something that wasn't what he wanted. He was known to tear sheets he didn't like off the drawing board, and would sometimes write: "Not This – BNW", and you would have to start again. Old George used to say: "If Wally had been home and had a good steak and kidney pie like he had instead of his carrot juice in the office, he would be a lot happier bloke."'

The Nazi invasion of Poland in 1939 dispelled any lingering hopes of peace, as war was declared and the UK was mobilised. George Edwards was not required for military service. His talents were to be put to work of national importance.

CHAPTER FOUR

'Down with 'Itler'

Within weeks of war being declared against Germany on 3 September 1939, George Edwards was pitched into work of the highest priority, to combat the new and deadly threat posed by one of Hitler's 'secret weapons', the anti-shipping magnetic mine. During the first weeks of the war such mines, which were resistant to all known countermeasures, were laid below the surface of the sea across the Thames Estuary and in other strategic places. This included the Firth of Forth, where, in November, the new cruiser HMS *Belfast* was severely damaged. By the end of that month forty-six ships, totalling 180,000 tons, had been lost. The search was on to find an immediate and effective response, and an airborne solution offered a rewarding prospect. Vickers-Armstrongs was entrusted with the task, and George Edwards was put in charge.

The seriousness and severity of the situation was not generally known at the time, and certainly not to Edwards and his team. But Winston Churchill, then First Lord of the Admiralty, was desperately worried. In his history of the Second World War, in which he devoted a whole chapter to the subject, he wrote: 'Presently a new and formidable danger threatened our life.' He described the mounting losses and the failure to find a solution, until an unexploded mine was recovered from the mud near Shoeburyness. Scientists were then able to dissect the firing mechanism and discover how it worked, and thus how it could be counteracted.

Churchill wrote that, from that moment, the position was transformed. 'The whole power and science of the navy was now applied; and it was not long before trial and experiment began to yield practical results.' This took two forms: the first by attacking the mines with new methods of minesweeping and fuze provocation, and the second by passive means, degaussing British ships by girdling them with an electric cable to neutralise the ships' magnetic fields.

While the Admiralty began work on shipborne anti-mine systems, which included the use of specially equipped trawlers known as 'LL sweepers', the possibility of converting aircraft for the task was being explored. The originator of such a scheme was the then Lt Cdr 'Ben' Bolt (later Rear Admiral), who in an article in *Air Pictorial* magazine in 1979 described the sequence of events that finished up at Weybridge, and in the hands of George Edwards.

Bolt, who was commanding a Fleet Air Arm (FAA) squadron specialising in night torpedo attack, had been giving much thought to the problem. At a chance meeting with the Fifth Sea Lord, Admiral Royle, shortly after the mining of the *Belfast*, he explained his idea to him. 'I suggested,' he wrote, 'that an aircraft with a powerful electromagnet should be able to simulate the magnetic field of a ship and be able to explode the mines without itself being damaged by the shock of the explosions, which would be transmitted through the water and hopefully not through the air. The speed of the aircraft should take it clear of the disturbance of gas and water which followed the explosion.'

Shortly afterwards, and following the discovery of the intact German mine, exploratory work by the Admiralty research laboratory and the Royal Aircraft Establishment (RAE) at Farnborough was authorised, resulting in Vickers-Armstrongs at Weybridge being instructed by the Admiralty to design and build an airborne system, modifying a Wellington for the purpose. This would comprise some form of horizontal ring through which an electrical current could be generated, sufficient to detonate the mines. Such a device could be attached around and under the aircraft.

At Weybridge, Barnes Wallis was 'in theory' put in charge, but Edwards says that, in practice, 'he was too busily engaged in other work'. The project was codenamed 'DWI' standing for 'detonation without impact', but called 'directional wireless installation' to put the enemy off the scent. In the works it was ever to be known as 'Down with 'Itler'.

George Edwards, now a section leader in his own right, attended the early meetings with officials from the Ministry and from Farnborough. 'There was a great meeting called in Westbrook's office. There was a hell of a set-to going on about what to do about it. The basic idea came, I think, from Farnborough. I had already been given the job in the drawing office to do all that was necessary, which consisted of designing the ring, putting the coil inside it, putting in the generator and doing the work on the aeroplane. By golly there was some pressure put on the chaps working there,' he says.

The meeting explored both the best method of converting the Wellington safely into a flying magnetic force, and the means by which it could be done quickly. Edwards remembers how the officials decided to abandon the usual procedures and necessary paperwork. They told him: 'You have got to get the thing made as you draw it, there is no other way, and we really must ask you to change the system because of the urgent danger we were in.'

Edwards was, however, mindful that to do this would change the normal working practices in the factory, causing a major upheaval and probably some animosity as well. He was therefore only too aware of the practical difficulties that lay ahead when Westbrook, knowing that he had done all the preparatory work, asked him to take full responsibility for the project. Edwards recalls the conversation: 'He said to me: "Well, what we are now talking about is giving you not only the job to draw the thing, but to take charge of it and get it made. Do you think you can cope with it?" I replied: "As long as you tell the chaps down in production in the works that you are happy with what I am doing when I am shouting the odds, then I will have a go."'

Thus, George Edwards and his section, given almost unfettered authority, set out on a work programme of such intensity and application that it became part of the folklore at Weybridge. It was also one which was, uniquely, overseen by Churchill himself.

Detail work started in late November 1939, and carried on through the Christmas period. The team 'virtually' did not go to bed for weeks, and the speed at which they laboured beggars belief. Edwards says: 'I used to go to work in the drawing office during the morning with Les Booth and the immortal Spud Boorer. Then I would go down in the factory in the afternoon and work down there far into the night. The sense of urgency was extraordinary. But the sugar on the cake was that every day I had to send to Winston Churchill a set of photographs of what had been done, and how much progress I had made since the day before. I learned a few lessons with that one, for it is no good doing a bit of window-dressing, because that just makes the next day look worse than it really is.'

The general idea of the device was to construct a 48ft-diameter aluminium ring encasing an electromagnetic coil, which could be fitted around the Wellington and attached to its nose and tail and under each wing. Weight and aerodynamic efficiency were critical, as was the adverse magnetic effect on the navigational instruments of the aircraft. The ring was to be energised by a motor generator housed in the fuselage. At first a Ford V8 car engine was used, but this was later replaced by a de Havilland Gipsy Queen aero-engine, driving a 90kW generator. This produced current at 500V, powerful enough to create a magnetic field sufficient to detonate the mines.

Apart from working out the aerodynamics for mounting the ring, the team also had to find the best method of constructing it, especially preparing the coil, which consisted of up to 50 turns of insulated aluminium strip. 'The business of winding the strip was an absolute joke,' says Edwards. 'I got hold of scaffold poles, I got a hub with machined holes in it, and then I got a gang of labourers who I had recruited from somewhere. They got on the end of the scaffold poles and walked round and round like being in a medieval prison, or on the deck of an old battleship winding the capstan. I got my leg pulled something awful about that.'

Spud Boorer remembers how George had got the idea of making the winding gear. 'It was like a children's roundabout, with a big pipe in the middle and lots of cable stays supporting a big scaffold pole turntable. It had got to be made of stuff we could find locally. I was sent off to the builder's yard to get a bit of tube 9in or 1ft in diameter. I trundled down and put a chalk mark on a bit of old water piping. George came down and said that would be all right.' Reflecting later on this crude but effective method of construction, those involved are still amused at the contrast that such methods could challenge such a sophisticated foe.

Throughout the project, as authorised, no proper drawings were issued, but up to forty sketches a day were made of the bits that were needed. This method of fast working was not always appreciated, as predicted. 'George got it in the neck from all the under-foremen for getting the OK for bypassing the red tape in the factory,' says Boorer. 'He upset a few of the chaps whose job it was to do the progress chasing, but that is how the job got done.'

On 21 December 1939, less than a month from official go-ahead, the ring was attached to the Wellington like an inverted halo and, after some taxiing trials, Mutt Summers successfully lifted the unseemly-looking device into the air. Barnes Wallis was aboard the aircraft, while Edwards observed from the ground. Its airborne handling proved satisfactory, so the aircraft was flown to the Aeroplane and Armament Experimental Establishment (A&AEE) at Boscombe Down on Salisbury Plain for the installation of the generating equipment. Afterwards, Summers told Lt Cdr Bolt, who witnessed the flight and had now been seconded to the project, that: 'a pretty good pilot would be needed for operational purposes'.

By 3 January 1940 a specially formed RAF flight, No. 1 General Reconnaissance Unit (GRU), under the command of Sqn Ldr John Chaplin, began trials over the Thames Estuary. Five days later, on 8 January, the DWI Wellington took off in marginal weather conditions, flown by Sqn Ldr 'Bruin'

Purvis, who had been specially requested by Bolt, no doubt recalling Summers's words to him. Bolt himself was in the copilot's seat, acting as navigator, and Chaplin was at the generator controls. Several runs were completed, flying at 180mph at only 60ft above the sea in worsening weather conditions, and with the navigation instruments rendered nearly useless by the magnetic force of the coil. The crew had almost abandoned hope when, in the words of Ben Bolt: 'There was a loud bang and the aircraft heaved as in an extra heavy bump, but as we had braced for something more dramatic there was a slight sense of anticlimax.' It was the first successful airborne detonation of a magnetic mine. That evening congratulatory signals were received from Winston Churchill, and later the pilots were decorated. The Vickers Board received a telegram telling them the device had worked.

In all, fifteen Wellingtons were modified for minesweeping, and they successfully exploded some twenty-four mines in the Thames Estuary. By then the navy had developed a highly efficient minesweeping capability of its own and the threat was overcome. No. 1 GRU was subsequently posted to Egypt, where it carried out further operations, primarily protecting the Suez Canal.

Spud Boorer believes the anti-mine Wellington really made George Edwards. 'It started him off, if you like,' he says. Edwards himself is proud of the effort. 'I didn't make a bad fist of that really because it wasn't half an undertaking to give anybody to do. I had enough stamina where ordinary mortals would have fallen by the wayside, and I was able to keep going.' He adds: 'The strength of why I feel good about it was that I really did have the job to do.'

Ben Bolt was fulsome in his praise, describing it as 'an almost unbelievable feat'. He wrote: 'It was a great achievement by Vickers to design and build the ring, attach it to the aircraft, install the motor generator, clear the whole installation for flight and release it to the Service in about one month in mid-winter. . . . It would be very difficult to visualise any other company equalling the performance of the work force at Weybridge led by G.R. (now Sir George) Edwards.'

In his much-admired Wright Brothers lecture to the Royal Aeronautical Society (RAeS), 'Looking Ahead with Hindsight', delivered in 1974, Edwards reflected particularly on this project. 'The reason I make reference to this practical device is to contrast just what could be done under pressure at that time with the complex and bureaucratic processes that we are forced to adopt today,' he said.

A lasting tribute to the effort is the famous painting by the acclaimed artist Terence Cuneo, which depicts the Wellington, 'with its halo attached', flying low over the sea with a great plume of water, caused by the explosion, rising dangerously close to the tailplane. (In a later sortie the aircraft did get too close, and it was only the strength of Wallis's geodetics that saved it.) The painting, which has been reproduced countless times, was presented to Edwards later, and for many years hung in the hallway of his house in Guildford, a reminder of an astonishing achievement.

Within a few months of completing the anti-mine project, Edwards was promoted to the important job of experimental manager.

The experimental department at Weybridge, as elsewhere, played a key role in the development of any new aircraft or system, being the link between the design office and the workshops. The person who ran it therefore needed to have outstanding qualities, and such an appointment required the approval of both Pierson and Wallis. Edwards himself had no idea he was even in line for the job, which became vacant when the incumbent, 'Barny' Duncan, was transferred to run the new Vickers shadow factory at Chester. Duncan's move was precipitated by a general reorganisation when Trevor Westbrook, who had transformed the Weybridge factory, departed. His leaving was somewhat acrimonious. He had fallen out with some senior Vickers directors, which, Edwards says, 'was not difficult to do'. Westbrook was snapped up by Lord Beaverbrook for his wartime Ministry of Aircraft Production (MAP), where he was to play a continuing role in the life of George Edwards.

When the call to run the experimental department came, Edwards was surprised. 'I assumed that it was because I had knocked the skin off my knuckles before I came to Vickers, and knew a bit about putting things together. There was also an attraction that, having worked in the drawing office, I would be able to bring a more sensible relationship with the works that had not previously existed. I think it was also largely influenced by my performance on the magnetic mine job,' he says.

Before taking up the post, Edwards had several meetings with both Wallis and Pierson about his new position. He found they both supported him, but for different reasons. 'Wallis thought I would be more amenable to the things he wanted to do than Westbrook and Duncan had been. Rex Pierson agreed because he and I had always got on well together, and he reckoned it was a good thing for a chap out of the drawing office to be given a decent job in the hierarchy.'

Edwards left the drawing office in the spring of 1940 and moved to the experimental department, then located at one end of the erecting shop. He took with him only Les Booth from his section. Both Spud Boorer and Ernie Marshall applied, but they were not allowed to follow him. Charlie Houghton, who was to become a trusted lifelong colleague and friend, joined as his right-hand man, together with Arthur Jayes, who he inherited from Duncan. Edwards was delighted with his new job, particularly as it gave him a chance personally to strike at the enemy. 'At last I reckoned I had got my hands on winning the war,' he says.

On 4 September 1940 disaster struck Weybridge. A formation of German bombers lost track to their target, probably the Hawker works at Kingston, and by chance picked out the unmistakable outline of the Brooklands circuit, with the Vickers factory located on the eastern side. Despite great efforts to camouflage the site, it was almost impossible to conceal. The official report stated that at 1.12 p.m. six Messerschmitt Bf 110s from the east-north-east and six Junkers Ju 88s from the south-east at 25,000ft to 500ft, attacked, missing the protective balloon barrage. They dropped their bombs on the heavily camouflaged works, afterwards climbing away to the north-east. Approximately twenty aircraft took part.

Because it was lunchtime, George Edwards was in the management mess, to which he had now been promoted. 'There was a squadron of aeroplanes coming over the sandpits, and out of them came bombs which they dropped on the factory. They made a hell of a noise. I was fairly close on the top floor, about 200–300 yards away. About half-a-dozen bombs went down and exploded on the ground floor – that was where the chaps were killed. I was all right.'

In fact the full blast of the first bomb fell on the crowded canteen, where many were killed or seriously injured, while another bomb landed on the machine shop, causing further loss of life. In all, 75 men and 8 women were killed and over 400 injured, many seriously.

Edwards rates it as one of the worst days in his life. He was also particularly concerned because many months before, while still working in the drawing office, he had been tasked with protecting the factory against air raids. He had been chosen because of his experience in the docks and was, as he put it: 'not frightened by the prospect of great big beams holding up the roof'. He devised an ingenious method of installing a 'forest' of huge 30ft-high wooden beams to support the roof trusses of the new erecting shop. The beams were hinged and balanced so they could be swung up into the roof to allow easy passage of airframe movements on the assembly line below. When air raid warnings were sounded they were lowered and secured to the factory floor, giving additional support. Unfortunately, because of the suddenness and surprise of the raid, they were still in the up position, although, happily, damage was not too severe in that area.

An immediate effect of the tragedy was to quicken plans to disperse production to a large number of local sites, while Brooklands remained the hub of the activity. Edwards says this meant 'a hell of an administrative problem', as garages, warehouses, smaller workshops and even the Twickenham film studios and the local Woolworths were commandeered. For Wellington work alone, more than ninety small remote units were established. They even built an erecting shop on Smith's Lawn in Windsor Great Park and flew Wellingtons from a grass strip that is now a polo field. To do so they had to cut down a line of royal oak trees, having gained the full permission of Queen Elizabeth, who told them: 'To defeat that man Hitler – cut them down!'

The dispersals also meant a fast move for George Edwards and his new department away from the vulnerable main erecting shop. He was told to find a new location and move as quickly as possible. He did not have to look far, or for too long, finding a suitable site within the Foxwarren Estate, less than a mile from the main factory. Here he had erected three suitable hangars and outbuildings. One of the original hangars survives today, and is used as a bus museum.

Despite this setback, production was quickly restored, with the new shadow factory at Chester now on stream and a second at Squires Gate, Blackpool, soon to become operational. Edwards and his team got stuck into a range of work, much of it top secret, which included special developments for both the Wellington and Warwick and a new high-speed fighter.

It also brought him into direct contact with the new and powerful Minister of Aircraft Production, Lord Beaverbrook.

CHAPTER FIVE

Working for Beaverbrook

It was Lord Beaverbrook, dynamic proprietor of the *Express* newspaper chain and now appointed by Churchill to galvanise wartime aircraft production, who promoted the next idea. As a morale-boosting gesture of defiance at a grim period of the war (1940), he proposed that some unassailable method be found to bomb the most sensitive German targets, particularly Berlin. To do this he suggested the development of special aircraft which could fly far enough and high enough to avoid enemy fighters and German ground fire. Such a performance would require the aircraft to have a pressurised cabin to allow the aircrew to breath in the rarefied air at high altitude, a concept about which the British knew very little.

The Minister, no doubt aided and abetted by his new recruit Trevor Westbrook, called on Vickers at Weybridge to do the job. Basil Stephenson, who later became chief structural designer, was asked to design the aircraft, and the new experimental manager was asked to build it. A Wellington was put at their disposal for modification.

It was Edwards's first major experimental project, and brought him face-to-face with Beaverbrook. 'The Beaver came up with the idea that, by creeping in at 40,000ft or so, we could put a thumper down the chimney at teatime every day on Berlin. This would do the morale of the man in the street a bit of no good,' he says. 'It was my first big job, and meant we had got to have a pressurised cabin, which nobody else knew anything about. It was one hell of a job because the engines were not too keen on operating at such heights; you see nobody had ever been anywhere near 40,000ft before. It was a new invention.'

It was decided that the best way to tackle the project was to build a pressurised crew capsule which would then be joined to the nose of the aircraft. The work proved difficult, as such an installation entailed marrying a pressure vessel to a geodetic-type airframe, which, according to the author

Dr Norman Barfield, was 'theoretically a contradiction in terms'. This was overcome by attaching the cabin capsule by integral feet anchored to the nodal points of the structure. This, crucially, allowed it to expand and contract independent of the rest of the airframe.

It was dangerous work, too. At the time there was little knowledge outside the USA of the effects of pressurisation on aircraft structures, and there was always a risk of explosion. Edwards says: 'I remember Stephenson coming down, wringing his hands because I couldn't get the thing airtight, it was always leaking. We sealed it in the end with some dark rubber-like glue. Unfortunately, every now and then they would pump in too much air pressure and the cabin would explode. It was like a bomb going off, and there was general consternation around the factory.'

Eventually two prototype aircraft, designated Wellington Mk. V, with extended wings and fitted with more powerful Bristol Hercules engines, were adapted for flight trials. Further development for high-altitude operation was concentrated on a Rolls-Royce Merlin 60-powered Mk. VI version, intended for experiments with the *Oboe* blind-bombing aid. It was in such an aircraft that Edwards had his first experience of flying at very high altitude, with the cabin pressurised down to the equivalent of 8,000ft. 'It was very impressive, flying in my shirtsleeves, going up and down the Welsh coast to see what large lakes looked like from over 30,000ft,' he says.

Adding to the technical problems was a danger to the aircrews, who found it was almost impossible to extricate themselves from their pressurised capsule to the escape hatch in the fuselage. 'It was very difficult to get out of the pressure cabin, which had a sort of cylindrical door that you wound up and back to open,' says Edwards, who then decided to see for himself. 'I remember Bob Handasyde [then a Vickers test pilot, and who later became sales director] and I went on a test flight in the Merlin-engined Wellington in which there hadn't been much testing. Old Bob and I went down to the escape hatch in the fuselage, having successfully got in and out of the pressure cabin. We solemnly shook hands at the emergency exit. There was nothing heroic about it, we just couldn't see how the hell you could get out. The fact remains we did.'

Neither of the projects reached fruition. The idea for bombing Berlin was abandoned because the aircraft could carry only a very limited bomb load at such heights. The blind bombing requirement was transferred to the de Havilland Mosquito, which, with the crew using oxygen, could outperform the Wellington at high altitude. Referring specifically to the bomber version, Edwards says: 'As a bit of engineering – forget old Beaverbrook's quaint ideas about tea-time bombing on Berlin – but as a bit of engineering it wasn't bad, although as a practical means of waging war it was, what you might call a bit limited.' He added later: 'I have got no doubt that the experience we learned helped us when we got into Viscounts and things of that nature.'

In fact, the principles learned with the Wellington high-altitude development were to form the basis for all future British aircraft pressure-cabin installations.

By now Edwards found himself regularly 'loaned out' to the MAP to take on special projects with other companies. One of his first missions for the Ministry took him to the Martin-Baker Aircraft company. Martin-Baker had been contracted to convert the American Douglas DB-7 Boston light bomber into a nightfighter by fitting it with forward-firing guns. Edwards's job was to supervise the work at the behest of Beaverbrook, but at the instigation of Westbrook, with whom he got on 'pretty well'.

At the time there was a desperate need for more nightfighters to combat the nightly pounding German bombers were inflicting on the London docks and the East End. Then 'somebody somewhere' decided there was an aeroplane already available: the American Douglas DB-7, later renamed Havoc, which could be converted for the role. These aircraft would have massive firepower from a group of twelve Browning 0.303in machine guns housed in the nose. Significantly, it was also to be one of the first to be equipped with the new airborne interception (AI) radar.

Edwards was first despatched to the Martin-Baker headquarters at Denham, in Buckinghamshire, where he met for the first time the celebrated leader of the famous firm, Jimmy (later Sir James) Martin. Today Martin-Baker is best known for its ejection seats, which have saved so many lives around the world. Martin himself was another inventor 'of genius', who had developed a range of ideas, from wing-mounted wire cutters to sever the cables of tethered barrage balloons to fighter aircraft, culminating in the single-seat MB.5, which had a top speed of over 450mph. This aircraft, Edwards reckons, could have been a world-beater had it had more Ministry support.

Martin described how they had redesigned the nose-section of the DB-7, into which, 'by an ingenious arrangement', they had fitted the twelve machine guns, alongside and parallel to the Martin-Baker ammunition boxes. Edwards was most impressed, and later wrote in Sir James's autobiography: 'I was asked to go to Denham to see the great man. He was kindness itself, and this visit began a friendship that was to last over all these years. It was immediately obvious to me when I looked at the design of this installation, and the other projects he was doing, which he showed me with great pride, that he was an absolute genius in the art of immaculate detail design.'

The work itself was unusual for its complex contractual arrangements. The DB-7 had originally been ordered by the now disbanded French air force after the fall of France. A number of these aircraft, together with a small batch ordered by the Belgian air force, which were to be supplied through the Fairey company's Belgian factory, were now available to the RAF. Fairey, which was still involved, sent a team to work on the conversion at Burtonwood in Lancashire. Edwards recalls: 'It was a strange experience, coping with a gang of Fairey chaps, mixed up with a large flock of Belgians, putting together an American aeroplane that had been ordered by the French Air Force! I had the interesting experience of trying to explain to the chaps, in my somewhat limited French, the difference between the undercarriage and something else.'

While working on the conversion he met Sqn Ldr Peter Townsend, later to be romantically linked to Princess Margaret. Edwards says Townsend at the time was regarded as 'the ace boy in the air force when it came to nightfighters. He used to be strutting round my ribs when I was trying to put the thing together, offering advice of one sort or the other, which was probably pretty valid.' By the spring of 1941 almost 100 aircraft had been modified for service. Lord Beaverbrook wrote to Martin: 'In designing the twelve-gun nose for the Havoc your firm has achieved an outstanding success.'

Shortly after the Martin-Baker experience Edwards was on the road again, this time to the Gloster Aircraft plant at Hucclecote. He had been called for by Beaverbrook 'to expedite a new fighter', which turned out to be the Hawker Typhoon. 'Beaverbrook reckoned they were lagging behind a bit, and I remember going to see him about this. It was an interesting morning because I was in his office and Beaverbrook was sort of dictating notes to his secretary at one time, answering multi-coloured telephones on his desk at another, and also briefing me about what I had to do. There wasn't any sign of a chap at rest,' he says.

Beaverbrook gave Edwards special authority to do the job. 'He made my position fairly clear, even though it wouldn't make me particularly popular. He gave me a piece of paper saying: "This is to introduce George Edwards, who has my full authority to do whatever he wants. I don't want him interfered with by anybody down there, least of all by any civil servants or other interfering busybodies."'

It was no surprise to Edwards that he received a very mixed reception when he arrived at Hucclecote. 'I was considered an interloper from Vickers – of all places

– to show them where they had got it wrong.' Then one morning he met the boss, Frank Spriggs (later Sir Frank), who he describes as 'a delightful man', but who was not over-impressed with the situation. Spriggs said to Edwards: 'So you're the young bugger that the Beaver has sent down to put us right? Look, boy, I have no doubt what you are up to. I don't want anybody down here telling me it's raining, I can look out of the window and see that for myself. What I need is some bugger who can tell me how to turn it off!' George responded by 'modestly shuffling my feet and saying they were obviously a good outfit, and if there was anything I could do at any time I was on the spot'. But it was something he never forgot. 'That's a bit of advice I have carried about ever since.'

Eventually peaceful relationships were established, and by the time Edwards left Hucclecote, after many months at the plant (on and off) it was reckoned they had done a good job in getting the aircraft into production. The Typhoon went on to prove to be an outstanding ground-attack strike/fighter in operations over Normandy in 1944 and elsewhere.

By this time his Ministry work, in addition to his responsibilities as experimental manager at Vickers, were beginning to take their toll. This was exacerbated by Edwards's having to travel regularly to Vickers's second shadow factory at Squires Gate, Blackpool, where the flight test centre had been moved, away from the easier reaches of enemy action in the south. Looking back, Edwards admits all this was 'a bit of a killer, but I was only a kid then, so I could take it'. It also gave him an insight on the special conditions that applied in developing new aircraft in a wartime situation. In 1981, for an *All Our Working Lives* BBC television broadcast, he gave a detailed account of this:

When you get yourself into a war, one of the basic ingredients is that you have not only got to have something that is a bit better than the other bloke, but you have got to have a lot more of them and quickly. . . . You also had to use labour that previously had very likely never seen an aeroplane at close quarters. They'd come from all sorts of trades, even the furniture trade. The design also had to be done in such a way that you could make use of these little places [the many small dispersed units], the huts and garages and so on . . . You had got to effect a compromise between production, the labour force, the dispersal and the performance of the aircraft, without which you were going to lose. It was very difficult.

He added: 'I think it underlined one of the great British characteristics, for there was not only tremendous spirit on the part of all the people who were doing it, but also the ingenuity and the ability to adapt, find a way through, and take short cuts very quickly.'

Although Beaverbrook work kept Edwards away from Weybridge for long periods, it did not interrupt his work on various new Vickers projects, notably a twin-engine fighter, the first prototype to be built by him at Foxwarren, and the development of the jet engine, using a Wellington as a testbed.

His involvement with the fighter began before he left the drawing office. The design team, led by Rex Pierson, had put forward designs for a high-speed, high-altitude, twin-engine aircraft to incorporate a stressed-skin metal structure devised by Barnes Wallis. It was the third response to the uprated Ministry Specification F.7/41. The specification demanded not only high performance, for which a pressurised cockpit would be necessary, but awesome firepower, which would be provided by a pack of six 20mm Hispano cannon housed in a ventral blister and remotely controlled by the pilot. In theory such capability would have a devastating effect on enemy aircraft formations, as they could be engaged at all angles. The aeroplane, the Vickers Type 432, was best known in the works as the 'Metal Mossie', owing to its superficial resemblance to the Mosquito.

Wallis's stressed-skin solution followed unsatisfactory test results from two wooden airframe proposals, and the ruling-out of a fabric-covered geodetic construction because of the high speeds required. It was the first stressed-skin aircraft to be built by the company. For this, Wallis devised an ingenious method known as 'peapod' or 'lobster-claw' construction, by which the aircraft would be built in two halves, with the wings joined at their leading and trailing edges.

However, this presented potential problems in manufacture like the Wellington, causing an 'altercation' between Edwards (still in the drawing office) and Wallis, as recalled by Spud Boorer. 'They were both at my board, discussing the profile of the F.7/41 wing. Wallis advanced a complicated mathematical solution involving radii of curvature. GRE intervened by saying that the geometrical accuracy given on my drawing was far greater than could be achieved in the workshop, and he saw no point in wasting time on a higher-mathematics lesson. There was a horrible hush, and a menacing look from Wallis as he stormed away.'

Now, as experimental manager, George Edwards 'got lumbered again' with building the prototype. From the start he was concerned about its future prospects. 'I could see by looking back that the thing was going to have a troubled life, (a) because the Mosquito was there, and (b) because of the cost of its complexity.'

Edwards was, however, impressed with the gunnery idea, which had been invented by an Italian named Nannini, an armaments expert who had been taken on by the main Vickers company. 'The aircraft could bore its way into a squadron of Germans,' he says, 'and then produce a high rate of fire which, to their astonishment, would come from points they didn't expect. But it was all too fancy to see the light of day.'

Despite his misgivings, work on the prototype continued apace right up to Christmas 1942, the first flight being arranged to take place at Farnborough on Christmas Eve. But getting the aircraft from Foxwarren to Farnborough proved difficult, because it was such a wide load. Edwards was accompanied by Bill Pledger, the transport manager, and Charlie Houghton, but they ran into trouble at Ash, where they found they could not get the trailer round a corner because of a large holly tree in a man's garden. So Houghton jumped down with a saw that Edwards had thoughtfully provided and cut it down. According to legend, they then 'stuffed it back in place', because they knew holly leaves would take a long time to wither before being noticed. 'Then we marched our way down to Aldershot, breaking all the paving stones in the high street!' says Edwards.

On Christmas Eve the new aircraft made a successful maiden flight in the hands of Vickers test pilot Tommy Lucke, but the evening celebrations at the old Queen's Hotel in Farnborough brought more unforeseen hazards for Edwards and Houghton. 'Mutt Summers succeeded in getting me drunk on gin for the first and only time in my life,' says Edwards. Houghton also fared badly, and it was reported that his wife could not quite understand why she found his overcoat in the cabbage patch at home the next day.

Unfortunately the 'Metal Mossie' suffered from handling difficulties during flight testing and exhibited severe nosewheel shimmy on landing. Edwards and his team quickly found a solution by moving the main undercarriage back by 3in, a task completed in only a few hours, But, as predicted, the project was abandoned six months later in favour of the wooden Mosquito. The aircraft was retained, however, for flight-control evaluations for the new Windsor bomber. Edwards regrets its early demise, and says: 'The Mosquito, of course, wasn't capable of doing the job F.7/41 was designed to do, but then there is nothing new in that, it goes on all the time.'

Edwards's first experience of the jet engine came in 1942. Like almost everybody else he was unaware of its active development. The first successful bench trials of the Whittle engine in 1937, and the subsequent flights in April 1941 in the Gloster E.28/39 experimental aircraft, were a closely guarded secret. The theory of gas-turbine jet propulsion was, however, well known in the scientific world, and Whittle, regarded in England as the inventor and father of the jet, had published papers on the subject. Edwards was now to have first-hand involvement, as it was decided to install a Whittle jet engine in the tail of a Wellington for flight evaluation.

A high-altitude hybrid Wellington with Rolls-Royce Merlin engines, which could reach heights above 36,000ft, was commandeered. At first Edwards found the new engine difficult to comprehend. 'It was a whacking great thing with a centrifugal compressor. But I began to understand that it had three parts to the compressor, which I used to describe as a piece of agricultural machinery, and that hot air used to be fed into these old-fashioned cylindrical combustion chambers, which in turn was squirted into the turbine to produce the power to drive the compressor,' he says. 'I once did a broadcast to Poland in English to make them understand how a jet worked, and that, broadly speaking, is what I told them.'

Although Edwards did not work directly with Whittle, he soon became acquainted with the power and performance of the new engine. 'Much to the surprise of other pilots in the vicinity there was this extraordinary sight of a Wellington, with a bit more streamlining round its tail that usually carried the turret, poodling along very happily with both engines [i.e. propellers] feathered. There was no visible means of propulsion at all. The chaps used to do this as a game they played on other pilots', he says.

The first Wellington to be converted with the Whittle/Power Jets W2/700 engine, which developed 2,500lb thrust, flew in July 1942. It was one of three aircraft to be so converted at Weybridge, and subsequently fifteen types of early jet engines were evaluated this way, although the bulk of the test work was soon transferred to the Rolls-Royce test airfield at Hucknall, Nottinghamshire.

The experience was to be of great and lasting value to Edwards during a fierce and unprecedented battle over the engine choice for the post-war Viscount, destined to become the world's first turbine-powered airliner. But that, in the dark days of 1942, was light years away.

CHAPTER SIX

Bouncing Bombs

The story of the Dambuster raid by the Avro Lancasters of 617 Sqn, RAF, in May 1943 has become an epic of the Second World War. It tells of Dr (later Sir) Barnes Wallis's brilliant concept to destroy the hydroelectric dams in the Ruhr valley; of bombs that bounced, and the unbelievable skill and daring of Guy Gibson's squadron in carrying out the mission. Paul Brickhill's book, and the film that followed, were widely acclaimed. Almost overnight, Barnes Wallis, the 'Prof', became a national hero, admired for his ingenuity and his courageous battle to win support from sceptical senior airmen, scientists, and even his own chairman.

However, an innermost secret of the Dambuster bomb, codenamed *Upkeep*, was not revealed in either the book or the film; it was still on the secret list. Thus was concealed the ingenious method by which the bomb was made to bounce accurately across a long stretch of water, over the dam's defences, and strike its target. The solution, simple and effective, came from George Edwards, and was honed on the cricket fields of England.

It all began in 1941 with a paper by Wallis entitled 'A note on a method of attacking the Axis Powers', which was widely circulated in Whitehall. In it, Wallis proposed a 'revolutionary' new airborne method of hitting Germany's most vulnerable and as yet impenetrable targets, which he identified as the enemy's basic sources of power: coal, underground storage tanks for oil, and water reservoirs for hydroelectric power generation. For this he proposed precision bombing techniques using new types of 'earthquake' bombs of his design. These could generate enormous shock waves on impact, and would have immensely greater destructive power when detonated in denser media such as water or earth, rather than in the air.

Consequently an ad hoc committee was set up by Sir Henry Tizard, scientific adviser to the MAP, to examine the feasible means of putting Wallis's theories into practice. A formal committee was established to which Wallis was co-opted, charged with the single problem of air attacks on the dams. Wallis's solution was recorded by Sir Alfred Pugsley and N.E. Rowe in their 1981 Royal Society biographical memoir. They wrote: 'Wallis's own theoretical work had convinced him that an explosive charge, capable of destroying the dam when detonated in close contact with it, could be airborne. His ingenuity suggested a spherical bomb brought to the target on a ricochet path over the water adjacent to the dam, a method proved feasible by model experiments.'

Wallis had conceived the idea by carrying out crude trials with the help of his children in his garden at his home in Effingham, using a catapult, toy marbles and a tub of water. He was aware of the ricochet technique, which had been employed by naval gunners in Nelson's time. When fired at a depressed muzzle angle, round cannon balls would bounce over the waves, increasing their range and accuracy.

Wallis's experiments were soon elevated to a more sophisticated level. A miniature dam was built at the Road Research Laboratory, and then the large tank at the National Physical Laboratory at Teddington was used. The shock-wave effect, the nub of Wallis's invention, proved shatteringly effective when the bomb was placed against the submerged face of the structure. To do this in a raid the bomb would have to be released from an aircraft at very low level, and at a precise speed and safe distance, in order to bounce towards and strike the dam, after which it would sink to the structure's foundations and be detonated by a hydrostatic pistol. But insufficient bounce and lack of control of the bomb in flight trials were proving critical and obdurate obstacles.

At this point George Edwards entered the picture. As a lifelong lover of the game of cricket, and a good club leg-spin bowler, Edwards knew about the properties of a spinning, bouncing cricket ball. He knew that the application of back-spin by hand movement enabled the ball to skid and bounce higher than normal on contact with the surface in front of the wicket. This, says Edwards, was because the ball propelled in this manner 'carries a bit of air round with it, which will lubricate the bottom of it, and there you are'. If Wallis's bomb could be rotated backwards in the same manner in the aeroplane before release, it should retain the same desired bouncing properties as the cricket ball. This was the theory, later to be so assiduously guarded, that he wished to apply.

By now his experimental department was already engaged in the *Upkeep* project, making the first dummy bombs and building the complicated release-gear mechanism to be housed in the aircraft. Edwards was therefore in a good position to outline his solution to the bouncing problem to Wallis, who at first was far from convinced by such argument. After some prolonged debate between the two it was eventually agreed that the matter could only be resolved by trials. These were to be conducted by Edwards, using model bombs to show the different bounce characteristics created by forward or top-spin, as originally proposed, and induced back-spin when 'fired' across a stretch of water.

Edwards vividly recalls the events surrounding the trials. 'There had been a lot of debate about spinning the bomb, and how we were going to do it. So I went to see Lady Seth Smith, the owner of Silvermere Lake, which was close by, where I wished to do the demonstration. She was a magnificent old lady, and I paddled across in my working clothes and tugged my forelock and said I wanted to borrow the lake for some experiments. She asked me what sort of things I wanted to do, and I said it was very secret, but she could assume it was all to do with beating the Germans. She said: "Anything to do with beating the Germans, me boy, you can have, but don't make much noise while you are doing it."'

So, in February 1943, the demonstration for Wallis began. For the purpose, Edwards had his team make up a catapult that fired a larger billiard-type ball. The catapult had a trigger at the top and another at the bottom, so they could impart top-spin, back-spin or no spin at all. He told his chaps there was to be 'no mucking about. This is the only chance; there will never be another one.' Wallis arrived and told Edwards: 'There is no scientific reason that what you say will happen, will happen, but I will try it, but I don't expect to be bound by it.'

The moment had come, and Edwards can relive the sequence precisely. 'So I said to the blokes, let's have the first one with no spin. It waddled along for four or five bounces, but did nothing spectacular. You didn't want a dirty great bomber to achieve only that! Then I said, let's do one with top spin. All that did was to make it go faster; nothing else was achieved. I then said we had better do the final act with back spin. I can't remember exactly what Wallis said, but it was his usual performance about if I wished to waste my time he couldn't stop me. I then said "Fire!" It was like a Vickers firing range. Out came the bloody ball and hit the water and bounced about fifteen times.'

Spud Boorer remembers the occasion well, and the arguments between the two men. 'They kept digging in at each other, and then they agreed to spin it backwards and it bounced all right, so that is what we did.' He also recalls what he considered to be the most dangerous part of the exercise, when they were running balancing and spinning tests on the rig at Foxwarren: 'Upkeep was a 7ft-diameter ball weighing four-and-a-half tons which was spun up to 500rpm. It was a bit frightening; you stood well away and to the side, especially if you had something to do with the rig design, as I did.'

Years later, Wallis recalled how the back-spin solution had come from 'a county cricketer of my acquaintance'. Edwards, although disappointed that Wallis had not accorded him due credit, was amused by being described as 'a county cricketer', something to which he had never aspired. 'Old Wally wouldn't have had such advice from anybody less than a county cricketer,' he says. Asked if the problem would have ever been solved if he hadn't been a bowler, Edwards adds: 'Wallis would have solved it by some other means. He would have invented another way, because most things can be solved, but it would have been more complicated.'

The application of back-spin was not the only solution that had to be found. With less than three months to go before the projected raid, early trials revealed that every time the early bombs hit the water their casing disintegrated. In the movie, original film footage of the trials at Reculver, on the south bank of the Thames Estuary, showed the bombs bursting on impact. A distraught Wallis, played by Sir Michael Redgrave, is seen recovering the bits. The problem was the spherical shape of the bombs, for which the steelmakers could not manufacture a round casing in such a short time. A compromise was found whereby the cylindrical core, which contained the explosive, was covered with wooden segments, like orange slices, and held together with steel bands to form the correct rounded shape.

Edwards remembers there was 'much grief' when the structure failed on impact with the water, and how this problem was also solved in a simple way. 'The steel rods burst and the bits of wood flashed all over the place, but left just the cylinder containing the gunpowder cavorting on. To our astonishment it kept going straight. But since it had kept on going straight, what was the matter with that? And that is what happened. The covering was removed and we ended up with a cylinder. It was just a bit of luck really.'

The chosen vehicle for the raid was the Avro Lancaster, which brought Edwards into personal contact for the first time with its designer, Roy Chadwick. The Lancaster, powered by four Rolls-Royce Merlins, had the range and carrying capability to reach and strike its target. Unlike the Wellington, it was built in sections of stressed-skin components that could be moved around easily, and were more amenable to modification. This was particularly necessary because the cylindrical bomb, weighing 9,000lb, would not fit inside the aircraft, so it was suspended half in and half outside the fuselage in a special jig. In turn this was connected to winding gear and a motor capable of rotating the bomb counter-clockwise up to the necessary 500rpm.

Edwards believes that Chadwick was never given the credit he deserved for adapting the Lancaster with such great speed to carry the bomb. 'He was the hero of the piece. The way old Chaddy let everybody carve his Lancasters about, and the way he stood up to Wallis, I thought, was quite heroic.' Edwards also admired (and noted) the stressed-skin method of construction, which allowed the bomber to be built in sections. 'This gave them a chance of making a lot more Lancasters by being chopped up in jigs, whereas Wallis would have insisted on the fuselage being made in one continuous piece. Perhaps by being made in little pieces you wouldn't quite get the total number of bombs in, but you would have a lot more aircraft to drop them from,' he says.

On the night of Sunday 16 May 1943, Lancasters of 617 Sqn took off from RAF Scampton, watched by Wallis, who had briefed the aircrews beforehand, and Mutt Summers, who had done most of the trial test flying. The story of the raid and the breaching of both the Mohne and Eder dams, and its effect on the outcome of the war, is still a matter of debate, but to Wallis, Edwards, Summers, Gibson and all those involved, its success was viewed as a moral and timely victory.

While Vickers and the RAF were planning and executing the Dambuster raid, others had set their sights on an equally dramatic venture, one that also would strike a devastating blow against German resources: the sinking of the German battleship *Tirpitz*. For this the use of a bouncing bomb as a lethal naval weapon, as originally advocated by Wallis to the Whitehall Committee of 1941, presented a serious possibility.

With a displacement of 50,000 tons, *Tirpitz* was then the largest battleship ever built in Europe. It carried a formidable array of armament, including eight 15in main guns and more than 100 anti-aircraft guns. The battleship presented a constant threat as it lay in safety in various Norwegian fjords, poised to break out and pounce on the vital shipping convoys of the North Atlantic. Its very presence bottled up a disproportionate amount of precious Allied manpower and machinery to monitor and, hopefully, restrict its movements.

In February 1943 *Tirpitz* was moved to the northernmost fjord at Kaafjord, where it was protected by mountainous terrain and a series of boom defences. In many ways it presented a similar target to the dams. An air attack, if it were to be successful, needed bombs with the same characteristics. They would have to hurdle the booms and then roll down the ship's side to explode against its soft underbelly, where the shock waves would have the same breaching effect.

At Weybridge, Wallis and his men had a solution codenamed *Highball*. This was a much smaller (36in-diameter) spherical version of *Upkeep*, which was being developed in parallel as an anti-shipping device. Its very existence has been shrouded in mystery and secrecy, and those concerned with it, including George Edwards, were reluctant to talk about it until comparatively recently. Designed to be operated in pairs from lighter, faster aircraft such as the Mosquito, *Highball* could be deployed up to a mile from the target, back-spin being applied before release. It was reckoned it would be a devastating weapon against the most heavily armed warships.

By the spring of 1943 Wallis was concentrating almost exclusively on the raid against the dams, which had to be executed by 26 May to take advantage of high water and a full moon. As a result, the *Highball* project was for the time being effectively handed over to Edwards. 'What everybody forgets about is *Highball*,' Edwards says. 'I had the job on two counts; one because Wallis was so occupied doing the Dambuster end of it, and the other because that was really what he was after. So I got it shoved on to me.'

The *Highball* project brought George Edwards into early contact with the secret RAF squadron formed to attack the *Tirpitz*. Similar in purpose to 617 'Dambuster' Sqn, and numbered consecutively, 618 Sqn was equipped with Mosquitoes and based at RAF Skitten in the north of Scotland. Here, amid the mountainous terrain and away from prying eyes, its crews could practise the low-level flying techniques, for which a target ship, the retired French battleship *l'Amiral Courbet*, was moored on Loch Striven. Edwards was a frequent visitor, and flew on trial bombing runs in the Mosquitoes. 'I must say it was pretty exciting, tearing down the sides of these Scottish mountains firing these great balls into the ribs of the ship,' he says.

Then on 17 May 1943, as news was filtering through of the successful Dambuster raid the night before, near-disaster struck, which could easily have cost George Edwards his life. He tells the story:

I had scheduled myself to be flown up [to Skitten] from Weybridge. We were tight on getting chaps up there, and I was given a seat in the bomb aimer's seat, where there is nothing between you and fresh air but a bit of Perspex. At the last minute the chap who was going up as an extra pilot in another aeroplane didn't go for some reason. This meant I could move and sit in his copilot's seat.

Operating Mosquitoes out of Brooklands was a fairly precarious undertaking anyway, and the thing about the Mosquito was the way it swung on take-off. The pilot who was flying the aircraft I had just left didn't seem to know how to keep it straight – a lot of people were the same. The bloody thing swung on him on take-off. There were two Warwicks standing alongside the banking, and he knocked the fin off one and impaled the bomb-aimer's seat into the banking itself, which would have had George in it. I was sitting in the aeroplane behind, and could see it all from where I was. So that would have been an untimely end.

Miraculously the pilot, who was also the unit's commanding officer, Wg Cdr G.H.B. Hutchinson, and the occupant of the navigator's seat, escaped without injury.

The Brooklands accident was not the only *Highball* near miss to worry Edwards. For some time they had been experiencing the premature airborne release of the bombs, caused by a recurring problem with the release mechanism when high g (gravity) forces were applied while manoeuvring. 'We had one or two mishaps when the bomb dropped off on the way into Wisley [the grass airfield 3 miles from Weybridge recently commandeered by Summers for test flying],' he recalls. 'Fortunately they were without any gunpowder, but dropped on the house at the end of the runway.'

Edwards adds: 'In fact, we knocked the same house over twice. I remember going round the second time with Shorty Longbottom, who had flown the aircraft on both occasions. The lady who lived there came round the corner and looked at old Shorty and said: "not you again!" Talk about British phlegm. I mean, here was this dear old soul, sitting in her own house, which had just been repaired, all peace and quiet, when a bloody bomb comes and knocks it over once again. And then the same little chap turns up to say he's sorry.'

By now, time was running out for the *Tirpitz* raid. Try as they might, the RAF could not find a way to overcome the problem of extreme distance, which was well beyond the Mosquito's range. They considered launching the aircraft from carriers at sea, the use of drop tanks with extra fuel, and even operating from a Russian base. All proved too difficult, and in the end the raid was called off. The subsequent daring attack by naval miniature submarines, an epic in which two VCs were won, crippled the *Tirpitz*, which was unable to move from its berth. It was finally, and ironically, destroyed in 1944 by high-altitude precision bombing using one of Wallis's special 'Tallboy' 12,000lb bombs.

Development of *Highball* continued, however. By now Wallis had resumed design command, while Edwards took on his familiar role of trying to make it work. The long, frustrating and ultimately abandoned attempts to do so, and the continued unsuccessful search for likely targets, is well told in Stephen Flower's book *Barnes Wallis' Bombs*. Flower believes that much of this was due to 'the question of security which was to act as a restraint throughout the remainder of the war'. He also tells of the dangers faced by Edwards and his men testing the device at Foxwarren.

George Roake, a Vickers tinsmith, described how they were spin-testing at high speed on a rig both smooth-faced and dimpled miniature bombs, a technology now well exploited by golf ball manufacturers. 'They released it and it was going to go along the workshop floor and into these sandbags, but it didn't. It went through them and finished in the lake which is [now] part of Silvermere golf course.' Since they were also experimenting with forward-spinning bombs which could penetrate deep into railway tunnels, it must have been a very frightening moment for Roake and his chums.

An even more alarming incident at Foxwarren is described in Flower's book by Ted Petty, who told what happened when they were testing an air turbine to provide the necessary power to spin the bomb on the Mosquito (the aircraft was too small to house a motor generator, as in the Lancaster). 'It disintegrated and went through the roof of the hangar,' Petty says. 'We phoned up Mr Edwards at about midnight and told him what had happened. His first words were: "Are you blokes all right?" That was the measure of this sort of family and friendship that you always got from the management. He didn't worry about the job. His first thoughts were – are you chaps all right? It was a marvellous illustration of the attitude that has pertained all through the years.'

In early 1944, after various experiments with *Highball*, it was decided they could effectively be used against the Japanese fleet in the Pacific. Number 618 Sqn was deployed to the region to carry out carrier-based missions. Top priority was given to conversion training for deck-borne operation, and the squadron eventually reached Melbourne, Australia, in December 1944. But as this was an American theatre, permission had to be sought from the US naval authorities. The Americans were already aware of *Highball* and its potential, having received technical briefings. Unfortunately their interest and intervention was to add a final twist to the tale.

Edwards explains: 'I remember somebody, not me, being sent to the United States to explain what *Highball* was all about. There was a considerable wave of excitement, to the extent that a squadron of American carrier-based aircraft were fitted with them. We did the prototype over here, just to get the whirling machinery tucked in. The squadron was put together with Avengers, I think, and put on to one of their big carriers. It could have knocked the living daylights out of the Japanese ships; it was lethal. Then, to the general astonishment of all parties, the aircraft were taken off the carriers, and never used again.'

(According to Stephen Flower there were two *Highball* initiatives involving American aircraft. The first was the modification of a Grumman Avenger, initially known in Britain as the Tarpon, which had been supplied to the FAA under lend-lease arrangements. This was flown to Brooklands, suitably modified, and test flown by Shorty Longbottom, but was never used in anger. The second involved the Douglas A-26 Invader, which Edwards particularly remembers being adapted at Foxwarren before trials by the US Army Air Force (USAAF). This sadly ended in a fatal accident, and is believed to have been a contributing factor in the Americans' not pursuing the project.)

There is still controversy as to what happened. Des Curtis in his book *The Most Secret Squadron*, which covers the whole of the *Highball* saga, refers to reports in which the US Navy left the trials in the hands of the USAAF. These trials had been 'moderately successful', but the USAAF was not prepared to set aside airfield space in the Pacific for specialist squadrons. Meanwhile, the Navy, it appears, had opposed the use of *Highball* on the grounds of 'disclosure'.

Commenting on these decisions by the Americans, Curtis writes: 'There was a general feeling that this is our war and we are winning it our way. We do not need your help.' Edwards still finds it difficult to believe that the US Navy 'got the wind up', and withdrew the weapon because they were worried that the Japanese, who were great copiers, would then use the weapon against them. Spud Boorer says: 'The more likely story is that because the Americans had got in mind to drop the Atom bomb they decided to make one big job of it.'

So *Highball* was never used in anger. Having been sent to Australia to await developments, 618 Sqn was returned to Britain and assigned other duties, in which it distinguished itself. The *Highball* equipment was taken out to sea in Australia and jettisoned overboard, while the weapon itself was statically destroyed at a base near Sydney.

The final major project to engage Edwards and his experimental department during the war was the four-engined Windsor bomber. The history of the Windsor went back to Air Ministry Specification B.12/36 for a long-range heavy bomber, which Weybridge had lost to Mitchell's ill-fated last design. In

1942 a new requirement was issued, B.3/42, to which Vickers responded with the Windsor, designed to the most advanced geodetic principles. Three prototypes were built by Edwards at Foxwarren, and the first was flown by Mutt Summers in October 1943. They were the last wartime aircraft built at Weybridge, and the last to be built using geodetic construction.

George Edwards has mixed memories of the aircraft. 'The Windsor was such a funny aeroplane. It had four undercarriages and drooping wings, so that as soon as you got airborne the wings came up and went level. It was a freak aeroplane, but flew like a bird, that was the maddening part about it.' Spud Boorer remembers the problems of construction, for it had a highly complicated geodetic structure and a lightweight wing. 'It was a dog's dinner to build,' he says, 'and they had the devil of a job doing it. Three were built, and how George and his people built them I do not know.'

The end of the war in Europe in 1945 brought a swift termination to further development of the Windsor, and no more were built. But the argument about the future use of geodetic structures, which had been applied only at Weybridge, was to rumble on, and soon became the cause of a bitter and decisive row between Wallis and Edwards.

CHAPTER SEVEN

Mission to Germany

Within just two months of Germany's formal unconditional surrender on 7 May 1945, George Edwards became one of the first British civilians to set foot in that shattered and defeated country. He did so as a member of the Farren Mission, comprising some of the country's leading scientists and engineers, led by William (later Sir William) Farren, Director of the RAE. The Mission was part of an Anglo-American initiative to retrieve as quickly as possible Germany's most guarded technological secrets. In their excellent history of the RAE, Reginald Turnill and Arthur Reed described Farnborough's involvement as 'the systematic and legalised looting of German brains and technology'.

There were, of course, very good reasons for doing this. The Allies were determined that German military technology should neither spark a Nazi revival nor fall into the hands of the advancing Russians or be acquired by the Japanese, with whom war was still raging. As a result of various incursions by various groups, attempts were made by the British and US Joint Staff Commission in Washington to share the information that had been gathered. But in practice the division eventually split more naturally between the Americans, who wanted the rocket science, and the British, who were looking for high-speed and supersonic flight advancement.

Farren's remit was 'to survey a cross-section of German aircraft, engine and armaments industries', and to find out how 'they developed, introduced, and manufactured military types of aircraft'. Other members of the Mission were B.B. Henderson, chief designer of Parnall Aircraft Ltd; Capt A.J. Nannini, the armaments expert from Vickers who had worked with Edwards on the 'Metal Mossie'; and Arthur Sheffield, who ran English Electric's aircraft works at Preston, and with whom Edwards was to have, many years later, a somewhat stormy relationship. Escorting the mission and representing the Ministry was Dr (later Sir) Alec Cairncross, who described its findings in his book *Planning in Wartime*.

Also attached to the Mission were several other senior Farnborough men, including Morien Morgan (later Sir Morien), then head of the Aero Flight section, who was to become the Director of the RAE, and test pilot Capt 'Winkle' Brown. They were given a roving commission, and 'Winkle' Brown says they were provided with special passes from Churchill's office to do so. 'We were given carte blanche to lay hands on German aircraft and German scientists, and we were given a list of ten people to be interrogated,' he says.

Farren split the Mission into small specialist groups, and Edwards was asked to study German progress on wing design and rocket propulsion methods. Appropriately, for the first and only time in his life, he kept a daily diary of the visit, which was to be for him a disturbing but enlightening experience. The diary, written in hand on scraps of lined paper, gives an interesting contemporary impression of Germany and its people within weeks of defeat, together with much technical detail, although the more sensitive observations were confined to the secret dossier and questionnaire provided to each member. These findings are not divulged in the diary, but were passed to Farnborough for evaluation. They are referred to later.

The journey began on George Edwards's birthday, 9 July, with a flight from RAF Northolt to Schleswig Holstein and then continuing by road to the nearby naval base of Kiel on the Baltic. The route took them over the Dutch coast near Haarlem. Edwards noted: 'Passed over an aerodrome pitted with craters, some flooding visible but not extensive. Emden was badly bombed in centre of town . . . landed at 5.30pm.' The party was driven the 35 miles to Kiel. At first, things seemed quite ordinary. 'All people well dressed and very healthy appearance – no signs of bombing. Saw stork's nest with two storks near Schleswig.' But on reaching Kiel things were different. 'The bombing in Kiel is terrific. Heaps of rubble line both sides of all the streets in almost uninterrupted rows. There are still many bodies left beneath it.'

The following day the Mission made its first visit to a secret rocket establishment at Plon, east of Kiel, known as the Walter Werke, after its founder, Prof Hellmuth Walter, a chemical engineer and rocket propulsion expert who originally had concentrated his work on naval propulsion methods. Walter had been tracked down by British intelligence officers during the last days of the war. His arrest was considered to be 'the jewel in the crown' by the British. What the intelligence officers found was described as 'astonishing', and concerned his development of rocket power for naval application and the sensational Messerschmitt Me 163 rocket-powered interceptor. Later the rocket aircraft was test flown by 'Winkle' Brown, who reached 32,000ft in an incredible 2.7min. It could attain speeds in excess of 600mph.

Prof Walter, who was at first unco-operative with the British, had by then relented and was still at the works, which was under the control of a British naval officer, when Farren's men arrived. Edwards noted in his diary that the Walter Werke had been established in 1935 to explore the most advanced applications of rocket propulsion for aircraft, flying bombs and naval vessels. During the tour he witnessed six demonstrations, which he enumerated and described in detail thus:

1. A demonstration run of the unit used in the Me 163. This I have described elsewhere [in the questionnaire]. Of particular novelty was the supersonic patterns produced in the flame jet at high power.

2. An inspection of a U-boat hull equipped with a rocket drive to give a boost of 1,750hp to enable a submerged speed of 22kt (or 26?) to be maintained for 6hr. Normal engine power 250hp. Three of the vessels have been out to sea. The exhaust is absorbed by the sea water and thus leaves no track.

3. H_2O_2 (hydrogen peroxide) turbine unit for driving sea and air torpedoes – with propellers. Speed – 50kt range – 10 miles.

4. H_2O_2 storage tanks – high alloy lined with wax mounted in deep troughs in case of overflow. Lashings of water will neutralise it readily.

5. Demonstrations of violent action between various fuels and catalysts demonstrated in laboratory by Dr Von Duran.

6. New type of schnorkel for subs, containing a valve pneumatically shut by an electrically controlled switch-valve when dipped below. A 2ft-diameter cover with anti-radar material in it and is impossible to detect.

In the afternoon they met and interrogated Hellmuth Walter himself, together with a Dr Schmitt, but no details were recorded in the diary, being confined to the questionnaire. Later Walter was taken to Britain for further interrogation and then returned to Germany.

Back in Kiel the party was taken on a launch around the harbour and the dockyards. Edwards saw the sad remains of two of Germany's largest ships, the heavy cruiser *Admiral Hipper* in dry dock, which he describes as being 'well filled with holes – completely busted up', and the battleship *Admiral Scheer*, which was 'in a wet dock upside down'. He also saw the 'massive concrete U-boat pens which looked undamaged although hit'. Damage in the town he attributed to an RAF raid probably using the Wallis *Tallboy* bombs.

The Mission returned to the Walter Werke the following day, but were taken to a test range on a lake at Bosau, which was used for V1 flying bomb launch trials. Edwards, like most people in the south of England, had often been forced to dive for cover when the dreaded drone of the 'doodlebugs' was heard overhead. Now he had a chance to see one close-up and observe the complicated mechanics of the launch process, which he described: 'Here the latest form of launching gear was developed. H_2O_2 drives a piston along a very long cylinder carrying the V1 by a hook poked down through a slot, afterwards sealed by a tube hung by clips. Replacing these clips, I should think, determined the time taken between launching. In operations, 24 per day was good and 30 the maximum.'

Later, a dummy V1 was launched into the lake 'accompanied by clouds of steam and violet smoke (from the catalyst calc. permangante)'. After an incongruous swim in the lake they returned to the Walter Werke for further questioning of Professors Walter and Gersch (*sic*), which again was separately noted.

It was later established by the Mission that the Walter Werke employed 5,000 people at five separate sites. Although it was a private company 'on the fringes of the industry', it had received huge subsidy on a 'lavish scale' from the German government. This not only paid for all its capital expenditure, but also for its running costs, which amounted to around £20 million per annum. The Mission contrasted such support for research and development with what it regarded as 'the parsimony of the British government in financing R&D in aviation'. No doubt all those from the aircraft industry, such as George Edwards, enthusiastically supported that assertion.

On 12 July the party left Kiel and drove to Hamburg to visit the famous Blohm und Voss seaplane works. Edwards was not overly impressed by the quality and quantity of work they found. 'The general design,' he remarked, 'is very ordinary, but they have a control system which I think looks possible for large aircraft. Their test pilot was very enthusiastic.' He added: 'The buildings embracing the design office and shops, entirely devoted to experimental work, are very fine. Over 300,000sq ft privately owned.'

The Mission remained in Hamburg overnight, where bomb damage in the centre of the town was not as great as he expected. Edwards wrote: 'Stayed at the Atlantic, the finest hotel in the town, very luxurious but no hot water due to no coal. A walk in the evening showed what a wonderful city this was before being damaged.' Later he went to the docks, which presented a very different picture. 'For the outer areas near the docks very large areas of working class houses are laid waste.' He noted the damaged railway station, which had been hit by day and night bombing. 'It really is fantastic, a vast area of mangled coaches, lines, roofs and platforms.' He estimated that Hamburg was 'now 50 per cent out and Kiel 90 per cent, the latter of course being much smaller,' and added 'repairs to all bomb damage are not going on anywhere – the organisation of the labour is a colossal job.'

On the following day they left Hamburg for Unterloss, where the Rheinmetall-Borsig works were located. On the way they were driven through Luneberg Heath, where, only two months before, Montgomery had accepted the surrender from the German commanders. Edwards observed: 'No real signs of war except occasional shot-up vehicles by the road and two or three burnt-out tanks. It is very pleasant country similar to Bagshot Heath and the pine woods at Haslemere . . . but on a much greater scale.'

At the Rheinmetall-Borsig factory Edwards was dismayed by what he saw. 'Found the works was blown to hell by one day and one night raid. As this was done near the end and it is purely a research and development site, it seems a bit unnecessary.' He added: 'Left the questioning to the arms kings – Henderson and Nannini'. Clearly he had some sympathy with the local workforce when he stated that the 'head man' was respected by the staff, and that they were all 'good-class scientists, functioning over self-contained research units, divorced from the main production'.

The party was lodged at the nearby town of Celle, where they stayed at a former Luftwaffe base. Edwards was most impressed: 'Built in 1935, the hangars and messes are in very fine style and taste, far better than anything I have seen in England. It has a high panelled dining hall, an underground crypt-like bar and beautiful appointments. All windows double glassed [sic] to exclude noise, but practically no baths and no hot water system.' But there was 'a fine swimming pool into which I go tomorrow'.

The next day (14 July), the party split up. 'The arms kings left for Unterloss again, while we aircraft types stayed at the aerodrome to examine the German aircraft spread about.' Among them he noted several Italian Savoia-Marchetti transports and 'a new and good-looking version of the Junkers Ju 88, complete with SBAC wiring system'. Then, by way of the autobahn, which Edwards described as 'a very fast road, almost deserted except for military vehicles and the inevitable refugees on cycles or pulling their belongings by hand cart', the Mission headed for the major German research centre at Brunswick.

Brunswick was, and is, the German equivalent of the RAE at Farnborough. It was therefore a considerable coup when it fell into British hands following the apportionment of occupied areas to the Allies after the surrender. Within two days of the agreement, British Ministry and RAE officials arrived. What they found at the former Hermann Goering Institute, located nearby at Volkenrode, 'made the Farnborough men gasp', wrote Turnill and Reed. In the words of Jack Henson, a senior armaments research and development officer who had been ordered to take charge, it was 'a unique establishment, with facilities beyond the dreams of Farnborough's scientists'. These included the most advanced windtunnels, which had been buried below a forest for camouflage, and which later were remarkably shipped back to Britain to form the basis for the new RAE research centre at Bedford and the newly forming Cranfield College of Aeronautics.

Edwards visited Volkenrode with his colleagues on 15 July. Although his findings were mostly restricted to his dossier, he did record that the whole establishment had formed about one-fifth of Germany's basic fundamental research capability. It had been organised and split into four separate sections: aerodynamics, engines, armament and structures, and he was asked to examine first the engines section and then the armament area.

He wrote: 'The former [engine section] was notable for a camera taking 200,000 [sic] frames per second, used for filming flame growth in cylinders. The armaments section was notable for two tunnels, one for blowing sideways on a projectile at 100mph by an evacuated chamber underneath and exploding valves, and secondly, a 400-metre tunnel which has the wind blowing up it and could be evacuated down to 0.02 atmospheres. They cost two million, I should think.'

He then recorded a 'lively argument' with Farren about the 'real use of such a place on which no money has been spared'. The outcome resulted in a compromise, when they agreed that a joint committee from both industry and research should be formed 'to guide their footsteps'.

For the Brunswick visit the party had been billeted in the historic and 'picturesque' town of Goslar. It had been occupied by the crown kings of Prussia, and Edwards was able to catch up with its history when he visited the headquarters of the local British commander, Lt Col Wreford-Brown. This was located on top of one of the surrounding hills, where he describes 'a fine view, including a mineral mine and one of Hitler's baby farms. The Russian boundary is only 10 miles away.'

Here they were shown an amazing and 'marvellous assortment' of royal treasure that had been rescued by Wreford-Brown from the Russians. Edwards writes: 'In two large cases were the seven great seals of the Princes of Prussia and a document lavishly bound and attached by silk cord, containing the signatures of the said Princes.' He was also shown a collection of eastern swords and German and foreign orders belonging to the Princes. Edwards reckoned that they were 'altogether a pretty priceless packet'.

The final destination was Munich, to see the BMW works, which, after a frustrating day's delay due to the 'complete unreliability of air travel', they reached in a Douglas Dakota at tea-time on 17 July. Edwards observed during the flight that 'all the bridges over the larger rivers are blown with monotonous regularity'. They passed over Nuremberg, the scene of the Nazi pre-war rallies. 'The damage is very considerable but mainly confined to the railway and factory area. If this was done by night bombing it was very good indeed . . . picked out the sports stadium, which looked all right.'

Arriving at the old Munich civil airfield, the party was met by the Americans and treated to 'an American high tea', before being taken by Third Army transport to Freising, where it was lodged at US Intelligence Headquarters. Here Edwards had his first taste of American hospitality. 'We met real extremes of comfort. Washing and bathing arrangements as crude as hell, beds reasonably good and food like I haven't seen for five years. A large thick tender grilled steak, preceded by soup, followed by a colossal sweet, fine coffee (the first we've had), more cake, iced tea to drink – it's crazy.'

Afterwards, in the officers' mess, which originally served the Wehrmacht, they played table tennis and drank Coca-Cola 'in unlimited supplies'. 'The standard of living that these Americans set for themselves is incredible. I've seen more food in the last two hours than most people in England see in two days.'

At the BMW engine works the following day, after inspecting the high-altitude test bed and development shops, they met up with Sir Roy Fedden. As special adviser to the MAP, Fedden had responsibility for co-ordinating the various missions now roaming Germany. According to Edwards, 'Fedden had snaffled the bloke we wanted to see, but agreed to cough him up in the afternoon.' This was achieved after lunch. 'We tackled the leading Huns available [names not divulged] for four hours solid. Thought we did rather well . . . Farren did his stuff extremely well,' he wrote.

Next morning the party drove through Munich centre. It confirmed Edwards's impression of being heavily bombed. 'It is of the same intensity as at Kiel, and I should say it is definitely worse than Hamburg.' That evening, back at Freising, Fedden told him that the high-altitude chamber they had seen had been financed by the German government, who financially controlled BMW. This was 'at complete variance' with the information given by the Germans. Fedden said it was due to be blown up, but he hoped to save it and keep it running for their own use, which he subsequently did.

Edwards was now suffering from 'a violent cold in the head', and also complained of being 'slightly off song'. This he attributed to the 'wallop those injections gave me at the start', but added that it was 'not enough to interfere with the job in hand'. There were also irritating deficiencies in the organisation of visits, which were being managed by the Americans. The reaction of his friend Nannini cheered him. 'Nannini is very funny,' he wrote. 'He keeps writing wisecracks on bits of paper, which I've christened depth charges, aimed at the organisation, or lack of it, with which we are inflicted. Today's effort is really chaos.'

There is further delay the next day. 'All ready to go to another BMW plant and find that all Third Army transport is frozen. So again we are suspended in mid-air. Henderson, who weighs nearly 20 stone, thinks we should each have a cycle.' By the evening, however, 'we became unfrozen – tomorrow we go to Kolbermoor. Also we gather that the French will not play with Jenbach (in Austria now under French control).'

They were driven along the autobahn to Kolbermoor to see the Heinkel-Hirth aircraft works, and Edwards observed that the road 'showed definite signs of having been used as landing strips for fighters – centre verge concreted over, trees cleared on either side, and small dispersal points'. They found 'nothing much going on' at the factory, and returned to Freising, then moving on into the Bavarian Alps, to the mountain resort of Garmisch. From here they made their last visit, to see Messerschmitt's main research and development flying centre at Lager Lechfield near Oberammergau.

Edwards enjoyed the drive to Garmisch, which he described as: 'fantastic, with its pretty little houses with flat roofs, balconies at all windows and religious paintings on the outside walls'. They ate at the Post House Hotel, where they were served by 'plump Prussian girls – the food is not so good as at Freising'. He added: 'We sleep at the other end of town on really good beds but with cold water. It seems impossible to get all the creature comforts in one joint.'

Their planned visit the next day, Sunday, to Oberammergau, was delayed. 'No joy at Messerschmitt today, they don't work on Sundays – only the occupying armies and associate dog's bodies (us),' he wrote. Instead they travelled up the mountain by 'railways, funicular, and shanks'. On his return Edwards managed to strike up some rapport with a German guard. 'Sat with guard in his cubby hole, and with a few cigarettes got him talking (in pigeon German). We discussed cameras, rations, Hitler, Stalin (they don't like him), harvests, manpower – everything under the sun, largely with the aid of my small (phrase) book.'

On Monday, 23 July, they finally reached the Messerschmitt plant, where they had: 'the best day of the whole trip. Hope to get going with some more tomorrow . . . Fedden let me do the questioning today, which I enjoyed greatly.'

The next day they returned to Oberammergau. 'We talked to Voigt [chief designer] and Von Fabel. The former is a good type. This has been the best visit of the lot.' The contents of the talk were not, however, divulged, but an account by Morien Morgan is quoted in the Turnill/Reed book. Morgan described how his luck changed at Lechfield when they successfully tracked down and interviewed a number of key Messerschmitt test pilots, including the chief pilot, who were able to give them invaluable information regarding the Me 262 twin-jet fighter.

The Mission flew back to Britain from Munich three days later, on 26 July, and its members subsequently filed their individual reports. Much of the technical data was retained by the RAE, along with a 'captured German Air Force' of some of its most advanced aircraft, largely thanks to the efforts of 'Winkle' Brown and colleagues. They also successfully recruited many prominent German scientists and engineers. Among them was Dr Dietrich Kuchemann, who remained in this country following a distinguished career at Farnborough and became a Fellow of the Royal Society. According to Brown it was Kuchemann who was instrumental in the choosing of a slender delta shape for the supersonic transport, later to become Concorde, based on his work at Volkerode.

In his book Sir Alec Cairncross refers to the comparisons the Farren Mission made between the British and German research and development methods. He observes three important differences. These include the greater number of prototypes the Germans built to reduce test flying (the interval between the last prototype and series production of the Me 262 was less than a year), and, most particularly, the far greater amount of investment both in manpower – the Mission found there was a 'higher calibre' of staff available – and facilities, on which huge sums had been spent. As examples, it quoted the high-altitude plant at BMW, which was 'without equal of any engine factory in Britain' and cost half a million pounds, and the Walter Werke.

Many years later Edwards recalled his experience with the Farren Mission. 'I was sent to Germany with others to try and pick up as much as we could about the German technique in wing design. There was a great kerfuffle then about the virtues of sweeping wings. There was another lot there at the same time, the Americans, and they were pretty ruthless in the way they scooped up German technicians. They scooped up Von Braun, who did the rocket design over there. They took him to America and turned him into an American.'

He says: 'The general impression one got [about the Germans] was the way they really stuck their necks out. Hitler obviously encouraged them to do way-out things, and way-out things were done. Anything that looked a bit flashy, like V1s and V2s, got plenty of support and were manned by the best chaps who were knocking about.'

In other areas, work that had been ordered by Hitler was carried out 'regardless of what it did and how many test pilots got killed in the process,' he says. 'I have a clear recollection of a thing called the Natter [a piloted rocket produced by Bachem that was launched vertically]. The story was that the initial trials were done with a chap in the pilot's seat who came from a concentration camp and was then killed on the first flight. He was about to be knocked off anyway, so they were giving him a free ride for a little while.'

Edwards also believes that the Germans missed out on reaping advantage from several advanced aircraft, particularly the Me 262 fighter, which was the subject of special interest during the visit to Oberammergau. Edwards says this was because the Me 262 did not get the necessary support from Hitler, who had insisted it be turned into a high-speed bomber. 'I got to know Willy Messerschmitt, and the fact was they had got an aeroplane that would have murdered the Americans on their daylight raids. They wouldn't have stood a cat in hell's chance if there had been a fair smattering of 262s about . . . which was just as well for the Americans.'

But of enduring value resulting from the work of the Farren Mission and initiatives to Germany in 1945/46 was the acquisition of added knowledge about high-speed and supersonic flight and the contribution made by Kuchemann and Dr Karl Doetsch, also recruited to Farnborough, who was an expert on aircraft handling characteristics. Ten years later, in November 1956, these assets were instrumental in the design approach of the newly formed Supersonic Transport Aircraft Committee (STAC), the recommendations of which eventually led to the development of Concorde, in which both the committee's chairman Morien Morgan and George Edwards were to play pivotal roles.

CHAPTER EIGHT

Chief Designer

Victory celebrations at the Vickers-Armstrongs aircraft company were short-lived. Peace brought with it the inevitable threat of large-scale redundancy in the industry, which had been geared to meet huge military demand. As at the end of the First World War, production was severely reduced, probably to about the same one-tenth of peak wartime output, with a corresponding costly rise in overheads. Furthermore, in Britain alone there were no fewer than twenty-seven airframe companies and eight engine suppliers, all bidding for what little work remained. Not all could survive, so it was a profoundly worrying time for George Edwards and his colleagues at Weybridge.

The government, however, was nevertheless committed to retaining a strong but reduced aircraft industry, mainly because of the increasing threat from the Soviet Union. There was also going to be greater demand for peacetime air travel, which would probably be the salvation of many aircraft companies. Well before the end of the war the Brabazon Committee had been established to recommend future requirements and specify the types of transport aircraft that would be needed. The government was to exercise control of the civil sector, as with the military, by providing the necessary development funding for new aircraft, and by ownership of the principal British operators, British Overseas Airways Corporation (BOAC) and British European Airways (BEA).

Vickers Ltd, with its diversity of industrial interests, was in a relatively strong position to respond. Public acclaim for the Supermarine Spitfire, the Wellington ('Wimpy'), and for the recognised contribution made by men such as Mitchell, Wallis and Pierson, had greatly enhanced the company's reputation in Whitehall. At the highest level, Vickers was confident that it could retain its position as a leading aircraft builder and, despite the risks, could successfully develop the new generation of commercial and military aircraft that were going to be needed in the dawning jet age. An investment of £750,000, a huge figure in those days, was authorised by the main Vickers Board for the outright purchase of the old, and now irreparably damaged, Brooklands race circuit, within which new drawing offices and research, test and production plant would be built.

The Weybridge team, led by Pierson, had already anticipated the impending slump in military production and the need to replace it with new transport aircraft. Before the war's end, design work had already begun on the VC1 (Vickers Commercial One), a derivative of the Wellington, which was to become Britain's first post-war airliner. With Ministry authorisation, the first prototype was now under construction in Edwards's experimental shops at Foxwarren. Although considered only an interim aircraft, it had already been ordered by the newly formed state airline, BEA. On 22 June 1945, just six weeks after Germany's capitulation, the first prototype, soon to be called the Viking, made its maiden flight under the command (as usual) of Mutt Summers.

Important as the Viking was for the immediate survival of Weybridge, the company placed more significance on proposals now on the drawing board for a brand new purpose-built and jet-propelled airliner, designated VC2. This had been designed in response to a Brabazon Committee specification for which there would be fierce competition from within the British industry. If the committee had the confidence to take a risk, the VC2 could be the first airliner in the world to be powered by gas-turbine engines.

With the immediate emphasis at Weybridge now on new transport aircraft, there also came swift and major changes in the hierarchy. In the autumn of 1945 George Edwards was summoned to a meeting with managing director, Hew Kilner (later Sir Hew), to 'talk about things'. It was to be a momentous meeting for Edwards, who recalls: 'He said there was going to be a reorganisation in which Wallis, then 58, would go off to head up a research outfit, and Pierson was going to be appointed overall chief engineer. On that basis I was going to be appointed chief designer, working under Pierson.'

At first, Edwards says, he did not respond to the offer. 'I remember Kilner blinking through his glasses and saying: "You haven't said anything and have just sat there. Does this job appeal to you, and are you prepared to take it?" I said what did Rex Pierson think about this? He said he was quite pleased to have me as his right-hand man.'

Thus George Edwards returned to the drawing office, which, since the bombings of 1940, had been dispersed to the nearby Brooklands House, once the home of Hugh Locke-King, who had built the motor course. Barnes Wallis, who had spent most of the war at Burhill Golf Club, moved into offices in the old Brooklands clubhouse, where he established his new research and development department. Edwards says: 'The changes were designed to get Barnes Wallis where he really wanted to be, which was in research and work on specialised jobs like supersonic bombs and aeroplanes with sweeping wings and all that. This cleared away any differences there might have been between Wallis and Pierson, and meant that Wallis was not involved in the day-to-day business of building aeroplanes.'

To Edwards and his family his promotion was the most significant step in his career. Along with it came the news that he had been appointed an MBE in recognition of his wartime work, an honour not generously bestowed on engineers at that time. But within only months of taking up his new job, further responsibility landed on his shoulders. Rex Pierson became ill, and his prolonged absence left Edwards, at the age of 39, prematurely in charge of the design capability of the great Vickers-Armstrongs aircraft company at Weybridge.

Very sadly, in January 1948, Rex Pierson died of cancer. His passing was a great blow to everybody, especially Edwards, whose protégé he had been. 'He was one of the greatest pioneer designers, and it was a privilege to work under him,' he says. Pierson's achievements were often underrated by some, but not by those who knew or worked with him.

Pierson is still remembered at Weybridge to this day. His achievements are commemorated by the annual prestigious Rex Pierson Memorial lecture, organised by the local branch of the RAeS, which is traditionally delivered by a prominent aviation personality, in time including Edwards himself.

George Edwards's first job on becoming chief designer was to push through and develop the Viking, which he described as 'a sort of British version' of the immensely successful American Douglas DC-3/C-47 Dakota. Although it was only considered a stop-gap aeroplane, it would hopefully keep the factory going until the new VC2, for which he was now entirely responsible, came on stream. Although the Viking was essentially a derivative of the Wellington, it was to be the first Weybridge aircraft to have a stressed-skin semi-monocoque fuselage, though it was to retain a geodetic wing for a time. Edwards described it more simplistically as 'a metal body on Wellington wings'.

For some time Edwards had been convinced that the geodetic era had passed, and that stressed-skin construction was the way forward for a variety of reasons. This belief had been reinforced by his experience with Roy Chadwick in building the Lancaster. He was very much at odds with Barnes Wallis, who, although distanced from day-to-day operations, was nevertheless a potent and respected voice at Weybridge. However, stressed-skin construction had been adopted by everyone else as early as the mid-1930s, and only Vickers had persisted with other techniques. Now, with the prospect of turbine powered, pressurised aircraft flying faster and higher, the notion of covering the wings and fuselage with billowing fabric was unrealistic. Even Sir Alfred Pugsley and N.E. Rowe, in their biographical appreciation of Wallis, found it 'strange' that he persisted with geodetic rather than metal-skinned construction after his experience with the Lancaster and the bouncing bombs.

Since the Weybridge factory was, at that time, entirely geared to the geodetic methods and tooled up accordingly, the main problem facing Edwards was to convert the factory to stressed-skin production. He remembers: 'We spent quite a lot of time with Basil Stephenson on how we were going to do the fuselage, how we were going to make it, and what sort of jigs we should use. The trouble was there was no experience in the factory for manufacturing stressed-skin components. But together we cooked up a pretty reasonable design, and I could sit down now and draw the fuselage jigs on which I made the first prototype.'

What they designed became the basic form of tooling for both fuselage and wing assembly that was to be used at Weybridge for many years to come. Edwards adds: 'I suppose, having blasted our way through the geodetic area, doing tin fuselages was rather straightforward.'

Despite the transformation of the Weybridge factory, Wallis persisted with his geodetic arguments. Edwards says: 'He was unhappy about having a tin fuselage, and for quite a time he pressed on, trying to convince people that a geodetic fuselage with a bit of fabric on it would be all right.' But the matter rumbled on, and eventually it required some decisive action from the new chief designer.

Spud Boorer, who was now working with Wallis in the R&D department, recalls George Edwards coming over and having an 'up and downer' with Wallis, after which all geodetic work came to an abrupt end. Boorer says: 'Sir George told me afterwards that he had to be blunt in the end and tell Wally that geodetics were going nowhere and we should have nothing more to do with them. This is where he was right, because everybody else in the industry said geodetics were far too complicated and man-power expensive, which they were . . . everybody else can't be wrong and only Wallis right.'

In retrospect, Boorer was able to weigh up the arguments. He believes that geodetic construction had distinct advantages for the wartime requirements of the Wellington, providing extra unobstructed interior space and performance improvements which outweighed the additional cost in man-hours to manufacture. He also dismissed the belief that it was devised to be virtually indestructible from enemy fire, although, thankfully, it saved the lives of many airmen. 'I don't think that had anything to do with it,' he says. 'I am sure Wallis didn't think of that when he was designing it.'

Far more conclusive was the rapid development of aircraft with increased performance. 'Civil aircraft were going to fly faster than a Wellington, and you could never put passengers in a pressurised cabin encased in only a fabric skin that was going to billow up while they were flying,' says Spud, adding: 'There were so many reasons why geodetics had to go, but they may be of use in other structures, such as domes.'

Despite the change of production methods at Weybridge, the first Viking was delivered to BEA in the summer of 1946, and entered service on 1 September. Powered by two Bristol Hercules radial engines and seating twenty-one passengers, it was Britain's first airliner to see service after the war. It was also the first to offer an alternative to the challenge of the Americans, who had produced a phenomenal number of transport aircraft for troop carrying that were easily converted for commercial use.

As with most new aircraft, Viking operation in the early days with BEA was not without difficulty. Shortly after entering service, in December 1946, severe icing problems were encountered on higher-altitude routes, presenting Edwards and his design team with their first major crisis. It was found that ice build-up on the tailplane leading edge was causing overbalanced elevator control, with obvious critical safety implications. BEA was so worried that it decided to ground the whole fleet until a satisfactory fix could be found. All of the Vickers technical departments, including flight test, together with the airline's own engineers, were engaged in an intensive programme of investigation.

By early 1947, having had the Christmas holidays interrupted, Edwards and the combined team solved both ice-build up and elevator overbalance by increasing the flow rate of the deicing fluids to the tailplane and altering the asymmetric horn-balance areas of both elevators. Modifications were made to a test aircraft, which was then flown in the worst icing conditions possible to prove the modifications. A series of flights were made that attracted national newspaper attention and brought George Edwards to public prominence for the first time.

Under the flamboyant heading 'Three Men Stake Their Lives Against Ice' the *Empire News* reported: 'In the face of a thick blizzard three men had made repeated flights from Northolt in a Viking, looking for the worst weather to test a cure for the icing problems which had grounded the BEA fleet.' The three men were Capt Jimmy James, BEA's chief pilot, Mutt Summers and George Edwards, 'one of the most brilliant technicians in Britain's air industry. He has a three-year-old daughter and his other baby is the Viking', the report added.

A Vickers official stated: 'Mr Edwards was really the leading spirit in the adventure. There was no need for him to go, flying is not part of his job, but he refused to be left behind. It was his idea that the pilots were trying out and he was determined to share the risk with them.' In all, twelve flights were made in what the paper described (with some journalistic exaggeration) as, 'the most severe test to which any plane has ever been subjected to in Europe'.

The report concluded: 'Mr Edwards's theories were triumphantly proved in every possible kind of icing condition.' One month later all the Vikings were returned to duty. When interviewed, Edwards, was more circumspect. 'We collected a great deal of information which has never been obtained before and produced evidence which will be invaluable to aircraft designers in the future,' he stated. 'Much of the time we were flying in ten-tenths cloud, and I was deeply impressed by the importance of radio aids to air navigation. I came out of the flight very radio-minded.'

It is not recorded how George Edwards reacted to this burst of publicity. As a modest man he might well have been embarrassed by the dramatic portrayal of events, but he would also have been inwardly pleased that the often-unsung efforts of the British aircraft industry to develop safe passenger aircraft had been recognised.

Although the Viking was not considered a glamorous aircraft, it became a solid performer for BEA, which eventually operated eighty-three in ever-improved versions. This included the later production Vikings, which were entirely of stressed-skin construction (including the wings), effectively marking an end to geodetic construction. In all, 163 were produced, including (pleasingly) those supplied to the newly re-formed King's Flight.

Although the Viking kept Weybridge alive at a critical period, it was not a financial success, as Edwards revealed in a lecture to the Fellowship of Engineering in 1982. He estimated the loss at £1 million (in the value of the time). 'Considering we sold them at £34,000 each all in, including the radio, seats and lavatories,' he stated, 'it is not surprising – you would be lucky to get a lavatory for £34,000 now.'

The financial disappointment of the Viking brought pressure on him from the main Vickers Board. Edwards responded in what was to become typical fashion, by 'ringing the drips out of the aircraft'. He looked particularly at other applications, especially with the military. As a true disciple of Pierson he had always believed in his mentor's dictum to keep close with the RAF at all times and anticipate its needs, sometimes before the Service itself realised them. 'Poking around and finding out what requirements were going to be is half the battle, which I suspect the chaps today haven't quite got the art of doing,' Edwards says. So he 'poked around' his wartime RAF contacts and discovered they needed a larger transport aircraft for general duties and troop carrying. 'Having developed the Viking by civilianising the Wellington, I then set about turning the thing backwards, and de-civilianised it into the Valetta, designed to carry 30–40 chaps with strengthened wartime seat arrangements.'

But that was not the end of it. 'I then sniffed around and found out about this big trainer they wanted, which led to the Varsity. It was a logical sequence that I have tried to carry on all my life,' says Edwards. 'If you have an aeroplane that was already doing a decent job, and if there was a variant possible like the Varsity, then you are a bloody sight better off than anybody else who is trying to beat you with a brand new aeroplane.'

He now believes that the Varsity was one of his more successful aeroplanes. The most notable feature of its design was its conversion to a tricycle undercarriage. It was considered at Weybridge to be the ultimate development of the Viking family, and was put to many uses in addition to training, including research work. The Varsity remained flying until as late as 1991, and was frequently seen at Weybridge and Wisley for routine 'return to works' programmes.

In all, 163 Vikings, 263 Valettas and 163 Varsitys were built, turning a loss-making airliner into a very profitable venture. Edwards says: 'The Viking was alleged to be an interim aeroplane that wouldn't last long. There were still one or two around, which proves the old adage that there is nothing so permanent as a temporary job.'

Years later, in a BBC television programme entitled *Swords into Ploughshares*, George Edwards was asked how Vickers coped after the war. He replied: 'Instead of inventing something brand new, we spent a lot of effort adapting something we already had got that worked and was in production. It was a much easier job for the chaps and the staff to do a major conversion without bringing the whole place to a grinding halt.' He added: 'Although unexciting, it was a means of providing blokes with work and the users with a pretty genuine practical old aeroplane.'

The Viking was to achieve one further distinction. As a portent of the coming jet age it became the world's first airliner to be powered exclusively by jet propulsion. Sponsored by the Ministry of Supply (MoS), a demonstration aircraft fitted with two Rolls-Royce Nene turbojets was built to assess the advantages of speed and comfort that jet propulsion could bring. To demonstrate this it was decided to make a record attempt on the London-to-Paris route to commemorate the thirty-ninth anniversary of Louis Blériot's cross-Channel flight, the first by an aeroplane. Thus, on 6 April 1948, the Nene Viking, piloted by Mutt Summers and with George Edwards 'spending a little time' in the copilot's seat, took off from London Heathrow and arrived at Paris Villacoublay in a record time of just over 34min. Its average speed was 384mph, a performance that would be admired even today.

Although proud of the record, Edwards considers the flight, 'a bit of balony but a lot of fun'. He remembers being met by Blériot's widow at Paris, and a passenger window blowing in during the flight, but without damage as the cabin was not pressurised. He also recalls upsetting the commandant at Heathrow when the aircraft wrecked his flower beds with its jet efflux, which was too low to the ground. But he was not over-impressed with the flight as a serious exercise. 'In those days a lot of people used to run around with fanciful ideas, particularly test pilots who had become salesmen. They used to get carried away with it all, but I never thought it would cut much ice.' On his return to London, however, he put on a much more positive face when interviewed with Mutt Summers on the popular BBC programme *In Town Tonight*. 'We both went suitably over the edge,' he recalls.

Nevertheless, the record stands, and, as Edwards says: 'A couple of Nenes were two pretty big engines in a relatively light aeroplane. It was bound to scoot along. I suppose the value was the exposure of what happens when you put a jet in an airframe previously powered by two old thumpers.'

George Edwards made two important personal decisions soon after becoming chief designer. The first was to move house, and the second was to learn to fly. Both were to have their own 'dramas', but neither left him with any regret.

His flying career began as a result of his need to interpret correctly the advice he was getting from the test pilots, who, in those days before computerisation, played an essential part in developing the design of an aircraft. Ever since he had entered the aircraft industry Edwards had established a close rapport with the pilots, and he felt strongly that it was incumbent on him to understand better what they were saying. So, 'under no pressure from anybody', he took the unusual step of learning to fly. 'I could sense there was always a touch of attitude with test pilots, who believed that when they complained nobody understood or took any notice. I therefore decided that I was going to be the first chief designer who actually learned to fly – which is probably untrue, but is what I did.'

The task of teaching him fell to an ex-RAF pilot named Wenham, using a de Havilland Tiger Moth at the nearby airfield at Fairoaks at Chobham. Edwards says: 'Wenham was a pretty good bloke, as well as being a pretty good trainer,' but admits that things did not always run smoothly. On one occasion, after a heavy arrival, Wenham told him he did not know the difference between 'a dangerous landing and one that was all right'.

Edwards's progress was watched anxiously by both his wife and the Vickers Board, who were not much enamoured at the prospect of the new chief designer risking his life in a Tiger Moth. They sent Mutt Summers down to keep an eye on things. According to Edwards: 'Mutt read Wenham quite a lecture, and told him how he had got to take great care of me, because I was very important to the firm.'

On 14 May, to the relief of the watchers, Edwards made his first successful solo flight from Fairoaks in a Tiger Moth. From then on he was to fly every aircraft for which he had design responsibility, and many other types besides.

His second decision, taken in 1946, was to move home. 'The house in Dartnell Park was quite a nice little place, but it was right on the doorstep of the factory. We decided there was something to be said for getting further away; we were a bit on call when things didn't go right,' he says. The couple searched the area, and eventually settled on a substantial grey-brick house called Durleston in Great Bookham, Surrey, some 8 miles from Weybridge. The house was occupied by the widow of the man who built Putney Bridge, and much of the unwanted stonework found its way into his house, giving it an imposing and pleasing frontage. The only problem was that the asking price was judged to be too expensive.

George Edwards tells how, after some soul searching, he made the decision to make an offer while playing cricket for Guildford, leaving Dinah to pursue the purchase. 'I was getting ready to bat, and the chap who was in looked pretty shaky, and I reckoned it wouldn't be long before I was batting. Then the groundsman came up and said: "Your wife wants you on the telephone, sir." I said: "Didn't you tell her I was next in, and I can't stand here talking to her on the telephone?" But the groundsman said she seemed worried. So I went to the 'phone and asked Dinah what was going on. She said: "You know the offer you made on the house in Bookham? If you want it, you have got to say during the course of this conversation that we will buy it." I said: "You know we are a bit short of money," but she said it was a nice place, let's buy it. I went in to bat, I can't remember how many runs I made, but with the house in my pocket.'

The family were to remain happily at Durleston for over 20 years, before moving to their final home, Albury Heights in Guildford, in 1967.

CHAPTER NINE

'The Heat and Burden of the Viscount'

Design work on the new VC2 airliner, upon which the future of Weybridge much depended, was well advanced when George Edwards took up his duties as chief designer in September 1945. The aircraft was a radical departure from anything that had been done before. With its four turboprop engines and pressurised and air-conditioned cabin it would fly over the weather, faster, higher and more smoothly than any of its predecessors. Although the overall parameters had already been decided, critical decisions on its exact size, shape and weight lay ahead. Most important of all was the choice of engines. These decisions would determine the success or failure of the project on which Edwards's reputation would be made.

The origins of the VC2 are somewhat blurred. The specification for such an aeroplane arose from a requirement drawn up by the Second Brabazon Committee in November 1944. This foresaw a regional carrier of twenty-four seats, suitable for European routes, to supersede the Viking and replace the DC-3. Two alternatives were to emerge from the committee, one to be powered by conventional piston engines, the other to be a turbo jet.

At Weybridge, Rex Pierson liked neither proposal. In December of that year he appeared before the committee to convince them that the second specification should be for propeller turbines (a jet engine driving propellers), which he believed offered a smoother, quieter ride and better fuel economy on short-haul routes than straight jets. After some deliberation the Brabazon Committee agreed with him, being much influenced by their technical adviser, N.E. Rowe, or 'Nero', as he was known throughout the industry, who was to play a continuing part in the aircraft's evolution. The specification was accordingly changed and designated Type IIB (to differentiate from the original proposal) to require 'gas-turbine engines driving airscrews'.

In March 1946 Pierson submitted a firm proposal for an aircraft with a 'double-bubble' fuselage to accommodate passengers with freight underneath, a slightly swept wing and four as yet unspecified propeller-turbines. Importantly, after much internal discussion, the VC2 was given a pressurised passenger cabin to enable it to cruise at heights between 20,000ft and 30,000ft. The MAP (shortly to become the MoS), which had closely monitored the design's progress, stated that, as a result, Vickers-Armstrongs would 'probably be given the contract', a view shared by BEA.

Such was the state of play when George Edwards became chief designer. Concerning the design origins and Pierson's influence on the type of engine, Edwards says: 'There has always been a hell of an argument as to whether or not the Viscount was a direct descendant of the Brabazon Committee. We at Vickers, by which I mean Rex Pierson and me, had decided it wasn't just a Viking replacement, which is what it was called at the time, but needed a pressure cabin. We took a poor view of it being labelled a committee sponsored aeroplane, which it wasn't.'

There has also been debate about its exact design parentage. Edwards is quite clear on the matter. He says: 'There is a plinth at Brooklands to the memory of Rex Pierson which describes him as the designer of the Viscount. His son Michael rang me up very embarrassed about it. I said to him: "You forget at the time the Viscount started off, your old boy was chief designer. You leave the inscription they are putting on it with your father's name – I am quite relaxed about it."'

Although George Edwards has always been self-deprecating about this, there is no doubt that it was he who supervised the design changes and spurred on all the later developments. And it was he who selected the Rolls-Royce engine in the face of overwhelming evidence against it. But above all, it was he who had unshakeable faith in the aircraft when most around him had deserted it. Edwards himself says simply: 'It so worked out that I had the donkey work to do. In particular I had to cope with the powerplant which, in fact, was the hard part, because nobody had ever got near to doing it before. I carried the heat and burden of the Viscount.'

The then Mr Peter (later Sir Peter) Masefield, who became so important in the successful development of the aircraft, described its early evolution in *Flight* magazine in 1955. He wrote: 'From this time [September 1945] George Edwards played an increasingly important part in the VC2 project. Pierson's influence was paramount in pushing the VC2 through from first proposals to prototype contract, but Edwards took charge of the actual design work from the autumn of 1945 onwards.'

By the end of that year, design modifications had been made. The 'double-bubble' fuselage had been replaced by one having a circular cross section, and the wing shape had been altered to have equal taper on its leading and trailing edges. The length had been increased, and was further stretched to accommodate thirty-two passengers, though the nose and tail design, together with the distinctive oval windows, were retained. Cruising speed was to be 240kt (276mph) over a still-air range of 900 nautical miles. But the choice of engines had still not been decided, and when the MoS approved the revised design and ordered two prototypes, it at first specified Armstrong Siddeley Mamba engines. A third prototype would also be built, but as a private venture funded by Vickers-Armstrongs.

The MoS predictably favoured the Mamba, which it had funded and for which it had great hopes. It was therefore a courageous decision by Edwards to ignore the recommendations of the MoS, his customer, and choose the rival Rolls-Royce Dart.

There were, in fact, three engines from which to choose. The third was the Napier Naiad, which was more powerful than the others. It had been developed by the company's chief engineer and managing director, Herbert Sammons, and although both he and his engine greatly impressed Edwards, the Naiad would require costly design changes to the aircraft to accommodate its increased weight and size. In reality the choice came down to the other two, of which the Mamba was showing the best results in test-bed running. The performance of the Dart was, conversely, 'little short of disastrous', and had little to offer except the 'magic' of the Rolls-Royce name.

So why did George Edwards opt for an engine he himself described as 'a rugged piece of agricultural machinery'? Years later he recalled the events leading up to his controversial decision. 'By this time I was pretty clued up and was spending a lot of time at Derby with Lovesey [development engineer] and the rest of them. I formed some pretty clear ideas that getting the first jet engine to work on a civil aeroplane was going to be a hell of a job in which safety and reliability were the main factors. I could see that without being a great scientist. The size of the blades in the axial-flow compressor of the Mamba were so thin that you had only to get a paper clip coming off the intake to turn what had been a row of [ten] blades into a broom handle!'

On the other hand, the Dart had a centrifugal compressor, which Edwards judged would be more robust than the Mamba and give the engine the 'rugged reliability' he was looking for. 'You cannot take chances with engines when you are doing something fairly special with the aeroplane,' he says. 'If you were embarking on a stressed-skin pressurised fuselage which you have never done before, you couldn't take a risk on the engine. I backed the lot up at Rolls that they were more capable of putting it together, and the judgement proved right.'

Predictably, his engine preference brought him into conflict with the MoS, with whom he was engaged in 'heated arguments', particularly with Air Chief Marshal Sir Alec Coryton, the Controller of Research and Development, and a man he very much admired. Edwards was not surprised at such a response, recognising that the Ministry had already 'burned its boats' on the Mamba and expected to see some return from the investment. He could imagine Coryton's consternation, and reckoned he would be thinking: 'Here was this bloody man George from Weybridge running round saying that the Mamba was fragile and would fall to bits if it got hailstones going down it – all he wants is a thing that looks like a lawnmower!'

Adding to Edwards's difficulties was lack of progress at Rolls on their engine, despite the confidence that he had shown in it. 'The Dart's performance made everyone who had anything to do with it burst into tears,' he says. 'It was about 50 per cent overweight and 50 per cent below design performance, while the Mamba was meeting its design objectives.' He described the two engines as: 'One was a gleaming star and the other a load of old iron.' As a consequence, Ernest Hives, later Lord Hives, a huge and highly respected figure in the industry, who ran the Rolls-Royce aero-engine company in Derby, visited Weybridge. Edwards says he pulled no punches and told Hives: 'The way things are going, you had better chuck the Dart in the river and the name would be right! We need a major effort from you.'

By now, further pressure was mounting from his own managing director, Hew Kilner, who, although very supportive, told Edwards the time had come for him to make a 'Napoleonic decision'. A timely 'crisis meeting' called by Hives in Derby gave Edwards the opportunity to make his final judgements. Unfortunately he found 'no real enthusiasm' from those present. 'Lombard [chief designer] only wanted to build a big straight jet, regardless of the fact that there was no aeroplane to put it in,' he says. So he made 'an impassioned plea' to everybody to put some effort in to make the engine succeed. 'It was pretty plain the time had come for the performance, the weight and all the rest of it to get back to something near right.'

His remarks appear to have had an impact on Hives, who told him later that he had been 'very touched' by his appeal at the meeting. Hives ordered that renewed efforts be made and, most significantly, decided to give the Viscount exclusive rights on the engine for 'a year or two'. He told Edwards that he had been fully aware of the pressure he was under, and had told his chaps: 'If George has stuck his neck out for you, you should stick your neck out for him.' He promised that the Dart would not be put into any other civil airliner for the time being, and forbade any canvassing for the engine with other customers, so that it would receive their undivided attention. 'So that is what he did, and it worked,' says Edwards.

George Edwards never forgot Hives's personal support at a crucial time. Of Hives himself he said in a BBC television interview many years later: 'He was a great man, a tremendous person, I absolutely loved him, I sat at his feet and really listened to what he said.'

Before long, a promised development programme for the Dart was also activated to increase its 1,000shp (shaft horsepower) to 1,400shp, which Edwards now sought for larger, uprated versions of the aircraft, which now had a new name. It had originally been called Viceroy, but in deference to sensitivities to the end of colonial power in India a new name was required. That name, soon to be enshrined with the most successful post-war British airliner, was Viscount.

The controversy over the Viscount engine was closely followed by BEA, for whom the Brabazon Committee specification had largely been written. Relationships between the airline and Weybridge were cordial, reflecting the mutual benefit that could be gained. BEA's own engineers had worked closely with the company from the beginning, and several of their proposals were incorporated into the design, especially concerning passenger comfort. It was therefore a body blow to Vickers when, in December 1947, they announced an order for the rival, and less-ambitious, piston-engined Ambassador.

The Ambassador, built by the Airspeed company set up by A. Hessell Tiltman and Neville Shute Norway in 1931 after Shute left Vickers, was larger than the Viscount, with a 40-seat capacity. It had been a response to the alternative Brabazon Committee specification for a piston-engine aircraft in the same class as the Viscount. But it would not be able to match the speed or comfort that the more advanced technology could bring.

George Edwards and his team knew of the challenge the Ambassador posed. They were aware that Airspeed was lobbying BEA hard, both on safety grounds and on the aircraft's increased payload, which should have made it economically more viable. At this point, disturbed by the BEA decision, the Vickers company ordered Edwards to take what he later described as 'hysterical defensive measures'. It called for further studies to be carried out to look at a range of different configurations for the Viscount, including alternative engines, both piston and turbine.

At a stroke, the Ambassador decision threatened the very survival of the Viscount. George Edwards remembers those dark days. 'When BEA placed the order it was, in the eyes of most people close to it, the end of the old Viscount. They said: "George has done his best. It was a brave try, but that's the end of it."' As far as the Vickers Board were concerned, Edwards says they were relieved and did not really understand what it was all about. 'They were mostly accountants, and to them it looked as though the Viscount was going to cost them a lot of money.'

Looking back, Edwards says he can understand the reasoning of the BEA Board. 'The Ambassador was quite a nice aeroplane, but it was a step backwards.' He believes their decision was much influenced by N.E. Rowe, who, having been a staunch proponent of the turboprop on the Brabazon Committee, was now being asked to give judgement as a board member of BEA. Edwards says: 'Nero felt unhappy about it because, although he wanted to see me and my propeller-turbine go on, he was genuinely worried about the powerplant I had got. Let's face it, Rolls had a hell of a start, and the Mamba wasn't all that much better. He could make out a pretty good case that we were landing passengers in these aeroplanes with an engine about which we had no experience.'

Since Rowe acted as a technical adviser to BEA, his opinion carried much weight. Edwards says: 'BEA reckoned that, if there was anybody who really knew where the margin of gain and excitement lay against unreliability, it was Nero.' He adds: 'Sholto Douglas [Lord Douglas of Kirtleside, chairman of BEA], and many of the great and good who were plonked on him in BEA, were frightened to death of the possibility of this brand-new aeroplane suddenly coming apart and grounding the whole fleet.'

Despite this setback, Edwards retained his 'unshakeable faith' in the Viscount, as did Hew Kilner. Edwards's determination to succeed is described by J.D. Scott in his Vickers history as 'missionary enthusiasm', which was infectious to such an extent that he persuaded his customer, the MoS, to continue funding the two prototypes. For this he was indebted to two men: Sir Alec Coryton, with whom he had earlier argued over his choice of the Dart engine, and his civil service colleague, Cyril (later Sir Cyril) Musgrave. Edwards later described Sir Alec as a 'great man' and one of the few he had known who were 'pretty special'.

As far as their influence in the MoS is concerned, George Edwards says: 'I think Musgrave had his hands on the money bags rather than Alec, who was, I suspect, being an airman, whereas Musgrave, being a classical civil servant, would be regarded as a proper guardian of national funds. Between them, they saved the Viscount.'

With the prolonged absence of Rex Pierson, and then his untimely death, Edwards was now exclusively responsible for the design effort for all Weybridge projects. In December 1948 he was invited to make his first major contribution to the RAeS. In a lecture entitled 'Problems in the development of a new aeroplane' he not only spelled out the difficulties facing the industry, but gave a full account of the design process for the new Viscount.

Many of his observations are worth repeating, especially as they have more of a touch of déjà vu about them. Edwards said that chief among the present-day problems was the high development cost of a new aircraft. 'It is one which causes grave concern in the aircraft industry and among all concerned with aviation. Modern aircraft have now become so complicated that the stage between the inception of a new design and the final acceptance trials has become both lengthy and expensive.' Among many solutions, he advocated less complexity and 'concentration on a good basic aeroplane and less reliance on complications that just get by'.

More controversially, he suggested an end to the existing disparity between military and civil requirements. 'The cure is that civil aircraft should be derived from basic military types, the original specification being laid down by the Director of Requirements, Air Ministry, advised by civil operators,' he stated, adding: 'It is an indisputable fact civil aircraft so far employed on the world's airlines have always been preceded by long service in the air forces by a comparable type.' As far as this affected the Viscount, which had no direct military pedigree, he said: 'One of the chief difficulties confronting the civil operation of propeller turbines is the absence of previous military operation.'

His views were not wholly shared by some distinguished members of the RAeS, but George Edwards was never afraid to speak his mind. Nevertheless, his explanation of the technical considerations which dictated the design and shape of the Viscount were well received and worth recording.

On the general design philosophy he stated: 'The wing area, aspect ratio and planform, together with the type of flaps used, were dictated by a compromise between the aerodrome size and the optimum performance in cruising flight. . . . The relationship between the wing, body and tail was decided by consideration of the centre of gravity position and the required longitudinal stability. Because of the long overhung (and distinctive) nacelles and the large fuselage, the aerodynamic centre of gravity had succeeded in moving forward, which had necessitated a large tail.'

He spoke also of the 'universal difficulties' in obtaining satisfactory stability and elevator control in the slipstream. This made the design team 'very cautious in the vertical disposition of the tail'. The outcome, he said, was to raise the tailplane 'by sweeping up the fuselage and employing dihedral until the tailplane was clear of the slipstream and high in the downwash'.

In describing other essential features, Edwards said that the safety aspect was allowed to influence the whole design. 'In addition to a low wing loading and four engines, high-lift, double-slotted flaps to give low landing speeds were installed. The tricycle undercarriage was fitted with twin wheels and duplicate brakes, the paraffin was housed in crash-proof tanks and all the windows were emergency exits. The elliptical shape of doors and windows required the minimum reinforcing in a pressure cabin.'

Lastly, Edwards referred to the adoption of a single-spar wing, a device introduced by Barnes Wallis, and one which was to cause concern with future American operators. He stated: 'The main structure was basically that employed on a previous aeroplane. There is no point in change for change's sake, and the well tried single-spar, chordwise-former type of structure was considered to be the most efficient.'

For the record, on 16 July 1948 the first prototype Viscount 630, registration G-AHRF, which had been built in the experimental department, made its first flight from the grass runway at Wisley in the hands of Mutt Summers and G.R. 'Jock' Bryce, who had recently been recruited from the King's Flight. It was a defining moment for all concerned, and pointed the way to the coming revolution in civil aircraft design.

On the eve of the flight, George Edwards and Mutt Summers might have been expected to have a 'touch of nervousness'. Actually they were less than anxious, even sanguine. Edwards tells the pre-flight story, which takes on almost comical proportions. 'My chief recollection was of old Mutt, with whom I used to play golf, saying to me the day before: "Georgy, your swing has got too flat. Let's take some balls up to Wisley and do something to sort it out."'

So the two men most responsible for the proceedings the following day made their way to Wisley to practise their golf. While doing so they were interrupted by a request from a film crew who had turned up at the airfield. 'I didn't realise it but, someone had laid on a film crew to interview Mutt on a day in the life of a test pilot. They had presented themselves to Doris Wagstaff in the control tower and asked to see the chief pilot. She said he was busy with the chief designer, and couldn't possibly be interrupted. They said it was essential that, on the day before the first flight, they spoke to us. But Doris said they hadn't got a hope; they were down there sorting out the chief designer's golf swing!'

The short flight next day was a complete success. It was monitored by Edwards on the radio link in the tower. He says: 'It was fun. I talked to Mutt, who said they were having a bad dose of "swithering". As soon as I heard that, I knew there was nothing the matter with the aeroplane. "Swithering" was a stock joke between us after a pilot, who didn't know too much, described his aircraft as having it, but nobody knew what he was talking about. So we adopted "swithering", meaning that nothing was wrong.'

Jock Bryce, in an article in the *Sunday Express* in 1978, recalled that first flight and another eccentricity of the chief pilot. 'Before we took off, Mutt Summers did something that I'm told was a ritual for test pilots of that era: he marred the aircraft's polished exterior by urinating on the wheel. . . . Mutt explained afterwards that it was not mere flamboyance, not even superstition. Many pilots, he said, had survived crashes but had died because they burst their bladders.'

Of the flight, Bryce said, it consisted of a quick circuit of Wisley and landing again. 'That was the way Mutt Summers always played it on a first flight. It proved very little in a way, yet it proved an enormous amount; it proved that the plane could fly. That was a tremendous psychological victory.'

Afterwards Summers congratulated both Edwards and Elfyn 'Sam' Richards, the chief aerodynamicist, something Bryce says he had never done before. The aircraft, Summers said, was 'one of the smoothest and best I have ever flown'. To Edwards he paid his highest compliment, using the same comment he used after the first flight of the Spitfire. When asked then if there was anything that needed to be done with the aeroplane, he replied emphatically: 'No, don't touch it.'

There now lay ahead a long period of development and a constant struggle to gain the acceptance Edwards and the team knew the Viscount rightly deserved. The continued progress of the flight test programme and the increasing confidence in the much improved Dart engine were soon to ensure this would happen. But not without a little difficulty on the way.

CHAPTER TEN

'Falling in Love with the Viscount'

If three men, Coryton, Musgrave and Kilner, had been largely responsible for backing George Edwards and saving the Viscount, two others, Masefield and McGregor, ensured its commercial success. To Masefield of BEA goes much of the credit for persuading his reluctant airline to buy the aircraft, while McGregor of Trans-Canada Airlines (TCA) introduced it to the massive and lucrative North American market.

According to Edwards, both were visionary in their outlook, both had practical and technical knowledge as qualified pilots, and both were invited to fly the prototype themselves. After his flight, Gordon McGregor, who was president of his airline, said he had come a long way towards 'falling in love with the Viscount'. Masefield wrote: 'It was to lead to greater things in my later life.'

First to fly in 1948 was Peter Masefield, while still a senior official at the Ministry of Civil Aviation and before he joined BEA. A former aviation writer with the magazine *Aeroplane*, and a wartime protégé of Lord Beaverbrook, he was now the Director General of Long Term Planning. He was already well disposed to both Vickers-Armstrongs and its chief designer. In his autobiography, *Flight Path*, he describes Vickers as: 'the only British company other than de Havilland which could be relied upon to produce aircraft that were world class and developed on time'. Of George Edwards he writes: 'He is one of the most impressive people in the entire British plane-making industry.'

George Edwards, recalling Masefield's first flight says: 'I remember Peter Masefield, who was a bit of a pilot, taking it round Wisley and seeing what this great device was that I was going on about. I think we did enough on the [Series] 630 to convince people that this was something pretty different. We did all the tricks, like standing coins on edge and all that. He started to reckon that this was a pretty good aeroplane.'

But Masefield had by now made his own assessment of the Viscount and its new engine. In his Ministry evaluation he had decided that Pierson and Edwards had been right to have faith in the Dart, even though it was 'somewhat crude and retrograde' in comparison with the more advanced Armstrong Siddeley Mamba and the Napier Naiad. He also compared the Ambassador with the Viscount: 'There was, however, a significant difference. Like other airliners of the day the Ambassador had piston engines and vibrated through the sky at 240mph. The Viscount had turboprops and promised to give its passengers a ride almost 100mph faster and so smooth that they could stand coins on their edges on the seat-back tables.'

Furthermore, Rolls-Royce had begun testing even more powerful versions of the Dart, which would allow Edwards to stretch the production Viscount to at least forty-seven seats, the same capacity as the Ambassador. So when Masefield joined BEA in early 1949 as assistant to the chairman, and soon to become chief executive, his enthusiasm for the Viscount gave great hope to the Weybridge team, who were becoming discouraged by the lack of orders, despite the almost trouble-free flight testing.

By this time BEA was awaiting delivery of its new fleet of Ambassadors, an aeroplane for which Masefield has some regard. In his Ministry days he had 'concurred' with the decision to order the aircraft, 'as an insurance measure' against probable development delays with the new turboprops. But, conversely, it was the Ambassador that ran into problems, and its entry into service had to be postponed to March 1952. 'I simply had to accept the fact that there were never going to be more than twenty Ambassadors, and no airline likes to be the only operator of a complex modern aeroplane. Moreover, I was convinced that the future lay with jets and turboprops,' Masefield wrote.

Even so, George Edwards says: 'It was a fearsome battle getting it in, and there is no doubt that Masefield's move to BEA with Sholto Douglas was pretty important then. It was at a point when the whole Viscount programme was very shaky and jolly nearly came undone. It was hard work because, although Masefield was there and was full of it, they could see it costing the airline a lot putting in a brand new aeroplane.' He adds: 'If they could have paddled along with standard thumpers, it was going to cost a lot less than the Viscount. Masefield had a hell of a job convincing the BEA Board that it was a good venture. The amount of time I spent in defeating Isaac Newton was nothing to what I spent defeating the doubters in BEA.'

The key factor in convincing the airline was the arrival (on paper at the time) of the promised stretched Viscount 700 with its uprated engines. This became 'a device which they were prepared to operate', says Edwards. The 700 would now offer a passenger capacity up to fifty-three seats, and Rolls-Royce was promising even more power increases of up to 50 per cent, with still more to come.

Edwards was 'flat out' to do the 700 because he knew the 630 was too small. 'I had no illusions about it. It was very nice, very quiet, but too small.' He compared it with the rival US Convair 340, powered by two conventional Pratt & Whitney radial piston engines. 'The operating costs of having four engines against two are a lot higher if you are only carting around thirty-two passengers. The seat-mile costs were not in the same street. So it was essential we put the body size up, because, if you did it properly, you wouldn't put up the operating costs of the total aeroplane by the same amount as you put up the body size; you will always produce a cheaper seat-mile cost.'

So Edwards and Masefield 'really got at it together', and led a new collaboration in the design detail of the intended production aircraft, with engineers from the company and the airline working closely together. It also brought about contractual changes with the MoS. It agreed to fund a 700 prototype and alter the role of the original second 630 prototype into a research vehicle for pure jet propulsion, to be fitted with two Rolls-Royce Tay turbojets.

In August 1949 the first orders for the Viscount were announced. BEA stated its intention to buy twenty 700 Series aircraft (although the order was not placed officially until August 1950), while BOAC, which had been following the BEA situation closely, decided to place orders for a similar number for its subsidiary, British West Indian Airways, although this order was not ratified until June 1953.

One month later the Viscount became the first turboprop airliner in the world to be granted a Certificate of Airworthiness (C of A). Both Sir Hew Kilner and George Edwards attended a press conference to make the announcement. Sir Hew said that, as a result of the orders for forty aircraft received from BEA and BOAC, they were now going to lay down a production line for 100 aircraft, and were proposing to 'have a crack at the American market'. Edwards, who had recently returned from the USA, said there was not much danger of an American aircraft of the type of the Viscount appearing for some time because they were not developing the propeller turbine to the same extent.

He was talking from detailed knowledge, having been a speaker at a prestigious Anglo-American aeronautical conference in New York to discuss the future shape of civil aviation. At the time the Americans were convinced that their transport aircraft would continue to be powered by piston engines until the advent of reliable pure jets. Edwards, in the very heartland of American aviation, refuted this on the evidence of the progress in Britain of the development of gas-turbine engines, and his own experience with the propeller turbines in the Viscount, which had now successfully completed its flight trials.

He told his audience, which contained many of the USA's leading designers and airline executives, that technical troubles had been encountered, but that phase had now passed and the development stage was now approaching completion. 'These engines have now arrived as reliable efficient powerplants,' he said. His experience on the installation of turbine engines with and without propellers in civil aircraft had convinced him that 'there was no engineering problem which is not capable of satisfactory resolution'.

In conclusion, he stated: 'Although a great (technical) case can be made for the airscrew turbine aircraft on the basis of direct operating cost, safety and improved maintenance, the most important factor is one which cannot be assessed by sheer numbers. It is the prospective passenger's reaction to being transported in an aeroplane of this type. If he chooses to travel in a turbine aircraft to the exclusion of all other types so long as he has the choice, then that factor must outweigh all others.'

Many years later, while on the campaign trail for both the BAC One-Eleven and Concorde, George Edwards was to refer frequently to his contribution at the New York conference as an illustration of the far-sighted ability of the British industry to pioneer and develop new concepts in air travel.

In August 1950 the first Viscount 700 was ready to make its maiden flight. This was successfully accomplished from Brooklands in the hands, for the first time, of Jock Bryce. The aircraft then embarked on a series of flight and climatic trials, together with airline demonstrations around the world. By now BEA was so optimistic about passenger acceptance of its new fast and smooth airliner that it commandeered the Ministry-owned prototype 630 for a month's service trial. Thus, on 29 July 1950, the Viscount became the world's first gas-turbine-powered airliner to operate scheduled fare-paying passenger services. The first flight was made to Paris, and later the service was extended to Edinburgh. During this period 838 passengers were carried in 88 flights. Masefield wrote: 'Passenger reaction was all we had hoped it would be.'

One month later BEA became the first official customer by confirming its order for twenty Viscount 700s. It was the first of a series of orders and reorders as the aircraft was developed and stretched again as 'astonishing' increases in power from the Dart engine became available. By February 1953 BEA had placed further orders for the first batch of twelve new enlarged 800 Series aircraft with a seating capacity of sixty-six passengers. More was to come. Masefield wrote: 'In the event George Edwards and I did even better.' By stretching the fuselage by a mere 46in and moving the aft bulkhead back they were able to increase cabin capacity by 9ft 3in. This allowed the maximum payload to be carried at 365mph over ranges up to 1,725 miles, approximately double that of the original 700.

By 1958 BEA had increased its total Viscount fleet to seventy-seven aircraft.

Surprisingly, the initial BEA and BOAC commitments of 1950 did not stimulate the expected rush of new orders. There followed a worrying period for Edwards and his team, especially as the company had, as promised by Kilner, laid down a new production and assembly plant at Hurn Airport, near Bournemouth. In November 1951 Air France (twelve) and Aer Lingus (four) placed orders for the 700 Series aircraft, which helped the production loading situation but did not open the way to greater international acceptance, particularly in North America. At this point enter Gordon McGregor of TCA.

McGregor, who had a distinguished war record as an RAF fighter pilot (George Edwards says he was the oldest pilot to fly in the Battle of Britain), had his first Viscount experience in September 1949. He had visited the Farnborough Air Show (an annual event in those days), where he was invited to fly the prototype 630. Accompanied by Sir Hew Kilner he was taken to Wisley, where he met for the first time Mr G.R. Edwards, chief designer, who was waiting for him. It was the beginning of a close friendship that was to last for over 30 years, until McGregor's death.

In his book *Adolescence of an Airline*, McGregor wrote a detailed account of the flight and his reaction to the Viscount, together with a very personal description of George Edwards. He wrote of him: 'Naturally I had met a great many Englishmen during the war, but George proved to be unique in my experience. He was slightly built with aquiline features and a pair of eyes that radiated intelligence, for which there was ample room in a massive Kipling-esque cranium.'

Of his manner and style he said: 'To a newly met Canadian his speech was an astonishing conglomerate of cleverly imitated dialects, possibly described as a mixture of New York Madison Avenue and cockney, heavily interlarded with the slang of both countries. His idiom, most of which I suspect was original, was a constant source of amusement to his listeners, although he was talking sound and serious aerodynamics and economics; how sound was to be proved to the hilt over the next two decades.'

During his first Viscount flight, which he described as 'quite memorable', McGregor was invited to take the controls. It was his first experience of a non-piston-engine aircraft. 'I was exposed to the delights of flying an aircraft which, for its time, was quite fast, yet so delightfully designed as to its control surfaces that it felt like one of the later marks of Spitfires. . . . I was tremendously impressed by the smoothness of the four Dart turboprops.' Having been given the 'full treatment' of coin and pencil balancing in the cabin, he added: 'As a demonstration of the freedom of vibration of this aircraft, nothing could have been more convincing.'

While flying the aircraft, McGregor was subjected to one other demonstration when he was 'surprisingly' disturbed by George Edwards, who 'reached between the other pilot, Jock Bryce and me, and pulled back the throttles on both starboard engines simultaneously. Under this treatment one would expect any aircraft to yaw violently to starboard; not so, the Viscount was easily kept on track by a small amount of aileron and rudder pressure.'

At the end of the demonstration McGregor found it difficult to conceal his enthusiasm, as would have been prudent for a prospective purchaser. 'Any reasonably intelligent airline executive does not over-enthuse to a manufacturer about his product,' he wrote.

He returned to Canada 'singing her praises', but was surprised to find his own management team were 'not a little sceptical'. This was because Canada had always traditionally bought from its 'big brother' next door. To step out of line and buy a non-US aircraft was considered by many as a risk. But McGregor's enthusiasm, like Masefield's, was unflagging. He sent his senior engineer Jim Bain with a specialist team to Weybridge to make a full technical evaluation, and particularly to assess its suitability for the very different conditions it would encounter in Canada, especially in ultra-cold weather.

Bain's team produced a massive document recommending many design modifications, which was instrumental in producing a modified aircraft that would now attract the attention of all the regional carriers throughout North America. But for the moment the many changes required by TCA were a matter of negotiation, both technical and fiscal, with the manufacturers. Edwards was accordingly invited to Montreal to discuss these matters.

He remembers well the meeting, which was with the full TCA Board. Edwards says: 'Bain explained how he had put together a whole list of things TCA wanted done, changes that would be needed in the Canadian cold-weather environment and the rest of it. Jim told them he didn't think we could face the things they had asked to be done. What do you think happened? We gave them a statement that showed that every one of their points that really mattered we were prepared to do.' This response was 'quite unexpected' from us, says Edwards. It included a promise to fly a Viscount to Canada to undergo cold-weather trials and, rather surprisingly, an agreement to 'tidy up' the Weybridge factory, which had not impressed the Canadians, who were used to the more sophisticated clean-air environment of Burbank or Seattle.

Later, McGregor told him that his offer had 'completely taken the wind out of their sails'. But Edwards was certain it was necessary in his company's long-term interests, even though it would incur considerable extra cost. 'From that moment on we were in business, because TCA was an accredited airline and I knew it was going to be a murderous job getting it down into America. Now we had at least a doorway into America and into their style of flying,' he says.

In late 1952 McGregor was able to confirm an order for fifteen modified Viscount 700s at a cost of $15 million, which he said later would 'make a present-day purchaser green with envy'. The following February, as promised, a Viscount 700 became the first turboprop airliner to cross the Atlantic, to conduct its cold-weather trials. These proved to be 'reasonably successful', and sufficient to persuade the airline to negotiate for more aircraft. In the end Air Canada, as TCA had now become, acquired fifty-one Viscounts, whose operations opened the door to the US market, beginning, as we shall see, with an unprecedented order for up to sixty aircraft from Capital Airlines of Washington, DC.

While things were beginning to move on the sales front, the Weybridge team were confronted with their first major technical problem with the Viscount 700, which they had to conceal from their potential customers. While the little 630 prototype flew as 'smooth as silk', the unthinkable was now happening. The bigger 700 had developed severe vibrations.

'It was worrying, all right,' says Edwards. 'The whole job was worrying, for suddenly we discovered that this aeroplane that everybody was raving about as a revelation in smoothness had now collected a bit of vibration. It started bubbling and bouncing like you couldn't imagine. So we had to go back to the drawing board and change it.' He acknowledges that it was one of the best-kept secrets at that time. 'I am not surprised people didn't know about it – it wasn't the sort of thing we bandied about,' he says.

It later emerged that the problem was caused by the addition of strengthening struts under the flooring, necessary for carrying the longer cabin. Edwards says this caused a 'strange connection' between the wing structure and the circular fuselage. 'I think it was pulses coming off the propellers beating the sides of the fuselage.' Matters were soon put right by strengthening and stiffening the floor beams. 'We made them stiffer still by good old brute force and ignorance,' he says.

While Weybridge was fully engaged in the development and introduction of the Viscount, more threatening and pressing demands were being placed upon the country and the company. Relationships with Stalin's Soviet Union had deteriorated rapidly since the end of the war. With the raising of what Churchill graphically described as the 'iron curtain' in 1946, matters had reached a point where hostilities seemed almost inevitable. Britain needed a deterrent, and the RAF needed new bombers to carry it.

George Edwards and the design team were about to embark on a project that, for speed of execution and technical capability, is without equal even today.

CHAPTER ELEVEN

Britain's First V-Bomber

Soon after becoming chief designer, George Edwards, in the utmost secrecy, was required to take responsibility for designing a new state-of-the-art jet bomber for the RAF. Britain needed a new bomber, and needed it quickly. The devastating effect of the wartime atomic bomb attacks on Japan, and increasingly hostile relationships with Russia, necessitated an immediate rethink on future war strategy and military requirements. The British government, as a nuclear power, had to have the means to defend itself and, if necessary, retaliate. The prospect of developing derivatives of the Wellington or Lancaster, as originally planned, was now as outmoded as the biplane in the Second World War.

In January 1947 the Air Ministry issued a specification based on an operational requirement drawn up in 1946 for an aircraft that could fly fast enough, high enough and far enough to deliver an 'A' bomb or conventional weapons on Moscow. The frightening age of the nuclear deterrent and Britain's V-bomber force had dawned.

Within a ten-year span Britain produced five new bombers with four different engines to meet the requirement. Today it is quite inconceivable to imagine this country producing just one new military aircraft within the same period. Even more remarkably, the first, the Valiant, designed at Weybridge by George Edwards and the Vickers team, made its maiden flight right on schedule just twenty-seven months from authorisation, and the first production aircraft was delivered to the RAF right on time, less than four years after receiving a contract. It is not surprising that Edwards considers the Valiant his hardest but 'favourite aeroplane'.

Looking back, he remembers the original Air Ministry Specification B.35/46 that triggered everything off. It had been 'dreamed up by Geoffrey Tuttle and the boys in OR [Operational Requirements]'. Tuttle, then an air vice-marshal, was

Assistant Chief of Air Staff (ACAS OR). The specification called for a bomber of medium range, 3,500 nautical miles, capable of operating at a speed of 500kt (575mph), at an over-the-target height of 50,000ft by day or night, from any air base in the world. This included, particularly, the many short-field and grass strips in the UK. It had to accommodate internally a 10,000lb weapon load consisting of either a special (nuclear) bomb or a range of conventional weapons. In addition, it was to take on a reconnaissance role. Significantly, it was decided that no defensive armament would be needed. Finally, it would have a pressure cabin in the nose, accommodating a crew of five, and was to be equipped with the new H_2S radar for navigation and bomb aiming.

Tuttle, later Air Marshal Sir Geoffrey Tuttle, in a lecture given in the early 1980s, quantified the specification for which he had been largely responsible. 'It was dictated by two major factors – the size of the bomb and the geographic position of Moscow. This led to many problems, and one of the main ones was survival; either to use performance or armaments. It was decided to use performance. The Americans chose the other course and armed their jet bombers.'

Tuttle also talked of the reason for having so many types of aircraft. 'It is not easy to see why such a plethora of machinery was produced. I believe the real effect of the atom bomb on war did not get through to the Ministry of Supply, who wanted a big aircraft industry to fight a long big war – maybe they wanted a big staff. Korea kept the ball rolling, and Mr Attlee had a defence budget of £4,700 million for three years, so all the projects went ahead.' He added: 'The A bomb was a complete discontinuity in that it entirely altered war and the equipment needed for it. I do not personally believe it was necessary to produce five different V-bombers with four different engines. One would have been sufficient, and I said so.'

Given that the jet age was still in its infancy, the V-bomber specification presented an unprecedented technical challenge to the British industry. Two responses, from Handley Page with its crescent-wing Victor and Avro with the delta-wing Vulcan, were the most advanced. In addition English Electric proposed its twin-engine Canberra, which later became a world-beater but in a different role; while Shorts of Belfast was later asked to produce a 'stop-gap' aircraft of a more conventional design, which emerged as the Sperrin.

Weybridge took a very practical approach with its submission, designated Vickers Type 660. For this, Edwards had the experience of both jet propulsion and pressurisation (essential for operation at the required altitudes) with trials on the Wellington during the war. He had also gathered much valuable information on swept-wing design during his tour of German research establishments in 1945. He therefore decided to go for an aircraft with slightly lesser performance, but one which he felt confident could do the job and be delivered within the very short timescale required.

Although his proposals were initially turned down in favour of the more ambitious but risky alternatives, the Air Ministry urgently needed the new equipment, for which they gave the highest priority. As a 'banker' they decided to re-examine the Vickers proposal (the name Valiant was not adopted until 1951).

In arriving at their design concept, Edwards and his team had to reconcile the conflicting aerodynamic requirements for high-speed weapons delivery and lower-speed cruise capability for extra range and airfield performance. This had to be achieved within their boundaries of knowledge to be certain of meeting the specification within the severe time and budget constraints. Edwards consulted Weybridge's chief aerodynamicist, Elfyn 'Sam' Richards, who had made a notable contribution to the Viscount. The conversation focused on the wing design, constrained by the necessity of burying the engines in the wing-root area.

'I remember talking to Elfyn at Weybridge,' says Edwards. 'He was a Welshman, but everybody called him Sam. I got into a deep huddle with him about how difficult it was going to be to meet the performance required, coupled with airfield conditions. There were all sorts of things to do with the handling characteristics. The amount of sweepback you have got to put on to do the 500kt, the amount of aspect ratio to meet your airfield performance and enable you to cruise at subsonic speeds, together with producing a wing planform in which the aspect ratio was high enough to get the range.'

Edwards and Richards were most concerned, however, about the dangers of wingtip stall that can occur with high sweepback and long, thin, high-aspect ratio-wings, as used for the USA's Boeing B-47 Stratojet. 'That was a bugger for stalling, and everybody was always twitchy about it,' Edwards says. 'When you are coming in to an airfield on a dark and dirty night, the one thing you don't want as you are making your approach down the glidepath is to find that one of your wingtips has given up producing any lift quite suddenly. Everybody had a hell of a barney to get over this wingtip stalling.'

It was Richards who had a solution, the cranked wing, which Edwards says 'was definitely his invention'. He explains: 'We increased the sweepback against the body of the aircraft on the basis that the vices of high sweepback against the body were not that serious because it was away from the centre of gravity, which is where you don't want a stalling lift. Then we decreased the sweepback over the outer part of the wing because that is where you don't want a sudden drop-off in lift.' Eventually the aircraft emerged with a high, clean shoulder wing, a high-set cruciform tailplane to avoid the jet efflux, and a cranked wing with a mean sweep of 20°.

The use of the cranked wing, which was later patented, caused a row with Handley Page, which was promoting what it called the 'crescent wing' on the Victor, but which had similar characteristics to the Valiant's wing. Edwards says: 'Reg Stafford, who was chief engineer, claimed that the crescent wing was a great invention by them. I remember on one occasion I went into a meeting somewhere and I stoutly asserted that the original crescent wing was in fact the one we had on the Valiant.'

Although the wing design gave assurance against wingtip stall, it compromised maximum speed and height requirements, causing the slight reduction in performance guarantees. Edwards says the revised numbers 'were engraved on my chest'. To meet the specification in full they had to achieve 500kt at 50,000ft. 'We offered them 460kt at 46,000ft, so we got 90 per cent of the original requirement.'

According to Tuttle, the Air Ministry's view of the Weybridge proposal was that the Valiant was 'an insurance' against the Victor and the Vulcan, which were regarded by the Ministry as rather a technical gamble. Furthermore, both required piloted flying scale models to be flown to prove performance claims. This would inevitably delay their development.

Soon after submitting the final Weybridge proposal, Edwards met with the Chief of the Air Staff (CAS), Sir Arthur Tedder, and other senior RAF officers. He remembers the meeting, and being given a virtual ultimatum requiring him to commit to the tightest of tight timescales, with the first prototype flying by mid-1951, the first production flights by the end of 1953, and quantity deliveries by early 1955. He was told that he had 'got the legs' over his rivals because they had to build one-third-scale models to prove their designs. If they gave him the order he would have to have 'the nerve' to give them assurances that flying scale models were not necessary. The CAS told him: 'When we say commit yourself we mean it. We won't take delivery of anything that is outside those dates.'

Edwards says: 'It wasn't half a bloody decision to make, because nobody else in the outfit really knew what I was talking about by committing ourselves to that programme. I mean, there was the manufacturing ability to do it in the factory, and all the rest of it.' He didn't even discuss the matter with the Vickers Board. 'I don't think talking to the main Vickers Board would have worked,' he says. 'They would have left it to me to take a momentous decision like that. They knew pretty well that was all they could do – that is what you are paid for.'

If Edwards was supremely confident that Weybridge could deliver the aircraft as specified, he was less certain of his customer, especially as the Short Sperrin had been added to the bid list with a revised and lesser specification. This, like the Valiant, was also viewed as an insurance aircraft of less performance capability than the Victor or Vulcan. 'There was a touch of wind-up in the various ministries,' he says, 'so they set up an interim aeroplane, out of which came the Sperrin. Three bits of wood nailed together, I always called it. As far as I remember there was no sweepback on it anywhere. They probably had the range, but they certainly didn't get the performance, or anything like it. It was sort of hovering in the background. . . . We could not ignore this because of the political thing about work for Shorts, Northern Ireland, and all that jazz.'

Even so, Edwards admits to being put 'in a fix' by the Shorts aircraft. He now had two competitors of higher performance plus the lower-rated Sperrin, if all went wrong. 'So I couldn't fiddle about too much with the Valiant's performance, but I had to keep in reach of the Vulcan and Victor,' he says. He had to make one of his 'Napoleonic decisions'. He told the RAF that he would claim no more than the performance figures put into the brochure. If they were accepted he would commit to them and the dates, because he thought they knew how to do it, especially as this was the condition for getting the job.

Although Edwards was technically 'only' chief designer, he carried overriding authority, as was the tradition for chief designers at Weybridge. His position was further strengthened by being appointed a special director of the aircraft company, a duty which had become more onerous because of the failing health of his managing director, Sir Hew Kilner. Nevertheless, in accepting the Ministry and RAF conditions he took a considered risk. This was further tested by a tightening of the delivery timescale because of heightened tension with the Russians over the Berlin blockade, and the Korean War.

'The biggest single element that worked in my favour was that I wasn't overcalling the odds,' says Edwards. 'I had settled at 46,000ft at 460kt although I was pushed by the blokes in the design team to stick my neck out for the extra bit so that I got it into the same ballpark as the Victor and Vulcan. But I just wouldn't do it, because I could see the troubles that lay in wait for getting that extra bit of height and speed.' Pressure came also from RAF officers in Operational Requirements. 'I remember I got quite bloody-minded. I said: 'Look, I am being crucified on timescales, there is no scope for keeping them if your wing commanders keep twitching around changing the equipment and all that.'

Geoffrey Tuttle told Edwards later that he thought he had submitted 'a pretty shrewd set of figures', because most in the Air Ministry were still apprehensive about the Vulcan and the Victor. Tuttle also told him that the Valiant was 'a damn sight better than anything they had got already', and that their proposal was a pretty good balance between the performance the Air Staff wanted and what in all honesty they could expect. Edwards says: 'The crux of the thing was the performance was good enough to stand a decent chance of getting through the Russian defences. Everything I have seen ever since would lead me to believe that it was good enough to get where we wanted, which was over the Kremlin at that time.'

In April 1948 the Ministry issued Vickers-Armstrongs with an Instruction To Proceed (ITP) for a revised specification, B.9/48, accommodating the Valiant's performance. This was followed by a contract in February 1949, requiring the company to produce two prototypes, the first to be flying by mid-1951. In anybody's language this was a very tall order indeed.

Edwards and the team set about turning a paper aeroplane into reality and 'put our heads down and got at it'. Sam Richards was appointed chief designer (aerodynamics), Basil Stephenson was put in charge of structures and Henry Gardner headed the stress office. 'There was a pretty clear, hard-arsed realistic approach to what we were taking on,' says Edwards. 'What we were building up, as far as Vickers was concerned, was a pretty high powered bit of machinery. There was no fancy pants about it.' One of the first things Edwards did to speed the programme was to design and have built the jigs to put the wings in before the design had been finalised. 'We were actually building the aeroplane in tin while we were still doing the windtunnel testing to see if we had got the right shape. There are not many people who are bloody fool enough to do that.'

His decision to forge ahead in this way had its critics. 'People used to grizzle about me sorting out the shape of the wing as the windtunnel models were still being tested. But there wasn't any other way round it. We had committed ourselves sufficiently on the basic concepts, but there was scope for relatively minor fiddling about. Obviously, if we had found something in the windtunnel tests that indicated what we were doing wasn't going to work, then we would have changed it. Fortunately, to Sam Richards's credit, most of the work that was done on the general basic aerodynamics, particularly the wing, turned out to be all right.'

Because the V-bombers were very much political aircraft, the choice of engine was also politically charged, particularly to ensure and preserve Britain's leading engine design and manufacturing capability. When the first official

Ministry contract was issued, in February 1949, it specified that the first prototype would be powered by the Rolls-Royce Avon turbojet, and the second by its rival, the Armstrong Siddeley Sapphire of similar rating. Edwards was only too familiar with the situation from his Viscount experience, and once again all his instincts (against the odds) were in favour of Rolls-Royce.

He decided to set up trial runs at Weybridge. 'I put together in a hangar a stand on which we mounted the part of the wing which had the engine installation, and ran the engines in the stump. The compressor design was different between the two engines; there were a lot more blades in the Sapphire, and the blade loading was accordingly lower, while the Avon was pretty high. When we ran the engines we couldn't get the Avons to work properly because the compressors were stalling.'

The facts were stacking against Edwards' instincts. 'There was a great deal of grief and woe,' he says. 'Rolls, in its usual style, produced a string of theories as to why this was happening, none of which had anything to do with its engine.' Edwards decided to lay on a demonstration, and invited Cyril Lovesey, the Rolls-Royce development engineer, to witness the trials. 'We ran the Avon, but when we increased the thrust the compressor stalled. But with the Sapphire, when we increased the thrust it just picked up and went on like a bird. That produced a state of crisis at Rolls that was almost unbelievable.' Once again it was Ernest Hives who had the answer. 'He was a big-enough man to paddle over to Armstrong Siddeley to see who had designed the compressor. Then he more or less copied it. This was basically putting more blades in, which cut down the stalling speed.'

By now Edwards also had a special insight into Armstrong Siddeley, having been sent to look at the company by Vickers, which was contemplating acquiring it. 'I had the opportunity to poke around quite a bit. They really had not got the clout that Rolls had got. So, as I could see it, despite the fact we had got problems with coping with the compressor surging on the Avon, I was prepared to bet that Rolls would fix it; which they did.'

For the record, Vickers did not acquire Armstrong Siddeley. The Sapphire, which had originally been specified for the second Valiant prototype, was dropped, but was later installed in the Victor.

These early days of the Valiant (and Viscount) were described by George Edwards in his Hinton lecture to the Fellowship of Engineering in 1981 as: 'great days, and life was the most tremendous fun. The designers of the British aircraft industry were made much of then; we really were like the goodies in an old Western film. It seemed a long way off before we became profligate baddies.' No doubt the comradeship of his enthusiastic team, together with the most testing intellectual design challenge, prompted those remarks.

As chief designer, Edwards had now moved from Brooklands House and was installed in a 'fancy new office' in a brand new custom-built design building, part of the development of the Brooklands factory funded by the Vickers Board at the end of the war. The new office was located alongside the works and close to the windtunnels. From here he organised and controlled a massive and complex work programme. Describing his role later in a television interview, Edwards said: 'A chief designer takes all the decisions and is responsible for everything that is done. He has therefore got to know enough about it, so he is more likely to be right than wrong.'

The most difficult part of the job, Edwards says, was reconciling the different demands of the specialists from the various sub-groups such as aerodynamics, structures, stress and undercarriage. 'They were all conflicting with one another because their bit of design could adversely affect the other. So there was an on-going competition. I wouldn't call it conflict, but the various blokes wanted their pound of flesh.'

Edwards had a novel way of dealing with this. 'I used to say to my then secretary: "I need a meeting and it is not going to go on after lunch, so you had better tell them that". I would then read out to her the list of the ones that I was prepared to take on at one go, all of them fighting their corner. I used to get a bit tired by lunchtime, but the fact remains that at the end of it all – and this is where I suppose I earned my money – I would say: "I have listened to you all stating your case, but this is what we are going to do."' He adds: 'It was a balance between the conflicting requirements of the group leaders and the threat they weren't going to get any lunch until they had finished!'

But there were 'the most fearful rows', and Edwards recalls particularly the difficulties accommodating the bicycle undercarriage, which retracted sideways into the wing, for which his 'old mate' Ernie Marshall was responsible. 'It was a cow, because you had to manoeuvre the thing so that it turned round without wringing the neck off the two wheels fore and aft. This made life very difficult for the other blokes who had to accommodate it, like the chaps designing the wing. The structure of the wing to a large extent was dictated by getting this big undercarriage in it.' Another problem was fitting the H2S ground-mapping radar, which had such a big scanner that it determined the shape of the nose section.

In the main, however, relationships were good and Edwards enjoyed the confidence of his team. 'Everybody was so bloody chuffed at having got the job in the first instance, that the ones that counted knew that the only way I had got them the job was by nailing my colours to the mast. They knew there were a set of dates and performance figures without which the thing didn't run. That was a fair old spur both for prestige and financial reasons to get it done as I had offered,' he says.

The manufacturing effort was equally intense. The factory had to be geared up to do it, and Edwards says: 'The reason we were given the job was because we had got the chaps already there deployed in an organisation that worked really well. There was a fair amount of short-cutting, and we only got away with it because our basic knowledge and basic understanding of designing and building aeroplanes was right. That sounds pretty pompous, but that was the way we did it.' In his history of the Valiant, published in *Air International* magazine in 1992, Dr Norman Barfield described it as 'an outstanding example of excellence and achievement in programme management'.

In early 1951 the first prototype was moved from the secure surroundings of George Edwards's old experimental sheds at Foxwarren and transported under shrouds to Wisley airfield, a couple of miles away. The move and the transition from a prototype under construction to a flying machine in less than six months was 'little short of a miracle', says Edwards, who was a great believer in building prototypes.

Such was the progress that had been made on the prototype and on the gearing-up for production at Weybridge that the Ministry was suitably encouraged to place an initial production order for twenty-five aircraft, which was signed in April 1951. One month later, on 18 May 1951, right on schedule, the first prototype Valiant made its maiden flight from the grass strip at Wisley.

The decision by George Edwards to fly from the grass was controversial, and had caused some anxiety among the test pilots, especially as the airfield was prone to flooding. Brian Trubshaw, who had recently joined Vickers from the RAF as a test pilot, tells in his autobiography, *Test Pilot*, how Mutt Summers's suggestion that they could use Boscombe Down instead gained short shrift from Edwards. Trubshaw writes: 'I thought George Edwards was going to explode, as the aircraft would have had to be transported by road, when he replied: "If I had thought that, I would have built it differently." Not a popular observation from Mutt, and fortunately the airfield dried out in time, but I saw it as the first demise of Mutt.'

In deciding to have the prototype fly from Wisley, Edwards was also conscious of the need to demonstrate immediately to the RAF its capability to operate from short and, if necessary, grass strips. He says: 'It was a fairly brave thing to do, but we designed the undercarriage in accordance with the requirement. This meant the footprint of the tyres was pretty big because we had to operate off existing Bomber Command runways, so doing it out of Wisley on grass wasn't as barmy as it looked.'

The flight itself, in the hands of Mutt Summers (his last as chief test pilot in a prototype), accompanied by Jock Bryce, was typically short – about 20min, with the undercarriage down and at low altitude. It also caused some consternation between the two pilots. For the first time in Mutt Summers's experience, the Valiant had powered controls with manual reversion, which in itself was considered to be 'pretty breakthrough stuff'. Unfortunately Mutt, described by Bryce as 'one of the greatest pilots I ever flew with', was not fully conversant with its operation. It was only by Bryce's 'flicking the switch to power control' before take-off that the flight was made, as set up, in power mode – though Summers always reckoned it was done manually.

'It looked fairly horrible from the ground, seeing this great monster making its first flight at less than 500ft,' writes Trubshaw. Afterwards, Edwards says, Summers told him: 'The one thing about you, Georgie, is when you have done an aeroplane, the thing we know is that it is going to be well balanced. So when we get to the end of the runway and start pushing tabs and all the rest of it, we assume that there is no one feature that would make life very difficult for us.' Edwards was pleased with that reaction: 'That was a nice thing for a test pilot to say.'

The worries over the sodden ground at Wisley were, however, soon realised when the Valiant's undercarriage cut deep ruts in the grass when turning. It was decided to move the aircraft and the flight-test team to Hurn, near Bournemouth, which had a tarmac runway and less air traffic in the area to worry about. This allowed a new paved runway to be laid down at Wisley.

The almost superhuman efforts of Edwards and his team in getting the Valiant in the air so quickly, and his earlier work with both the Viking and the Viscount, had not gone unnoticed by the RAF, which was later to honour him, or the Vickers management, who were soon to promote him. Within a year the entire responsibility of all the aircraft interests of the great Vickers company were to rest on George Edwards's shoulders.

CHAPTER TWELVE

Managing Director

By the early 1950s George Edwards, at 45, was at the height of his powers. He had successfully launched a family of Vickers commercial aircraft, with the Viscount now gaining a foothold in the international market, and he had kept the Valiant on its highly ambitious delivery schedule despite a severe setback. Production capacity had been increased with the transfer of Viscount assembly to the recently established Hurn factory, and a new erecting hall extension had been built at Weybridge for the Valiant. In 1952, to his great delight, he was appointed CBE, and in the same year he received the RAeS's Gold Medal, its highest honour.

It was no surprise, therefore, that in 1953 Edwards was appointed managing director of Vickers-Armstrongs (Aircraft) Ltd. His promotion came about when his boss, Sir Hew Kilner, who had so solidly backed him as chief designer, finally became too ill to carry out his full duties. What would have been a surprise (had it been widely known) was the fact that he had previously turned the job down.

George Edwards takes up the story:

The idea was first mooted by Weeks [Lord Weeks, chairman of Vickers] because Kilner was too ill to perform. One way out was to push me up, but I wouldn't do it. Weeks went back to London to see the moguls, and said he had just been told by me to stuff the job! I didn't want to be weaned off my design responsibilities. It didn't make sense, because the state we were in at that time needed undiluted concentration on making sure we got the aeroplanes right that weren't right.

I was conceited enough to think that I wasn't bad as chief designer, but I didn't put much money on my ability to perform as an accountant. I settled for general manager and chief engineer instead, which roped in Supermarine as well. But this arrangement didn't last long. One day I had a phone call from Weeks to say they must talk seriously to me. I was wheeled up to London and told to take it. I can remember Weeks saying we had been messing about with this long enough and I had got my way so far, but the time had come to straighten it out. They were going to announce that I was going to be managing director, and that was that.

When Edwards returned to Weybridge in his new position there was little outward change. The only visible sign of his appointment came when he moved his office from the design office into the main administration block on Brooklands Road. In fact, he had been de facto boss since the death of Rex Pierson. As was the tradition at Weybridge, the chief designer 'ruled' by directing all aircraft-related matters. Sir Hew Kilner, who had been a career army officer, was content with the arrangement when he became managing director, seeing himself in a supportive role, especially on financial and political matters. Kilner favoured a hands-off approach, and based himself much of the time at Vickers's headquarters in London, where he could keep close to the main Board.

So Edwards really took up where he left off, although he was very aware of his added financial responsibilities. 'It all got difficult, for I had to take responsibility for running the outfit, including whether we were making profits or not, which was something I had not previously done. Except if you didn't design it right you didn't make profits or anything else.' 'But,' he adds, 'I found being managing director a good thing insofar as the power put at your elbow; all round the clock, both with the government and everybody else. Nevertheless, I had to spend a lot of time at Board meetings instead of shuffling my slide rule up and down.'

Since Edwards had already appointed most of his senior positions, it was not necessary to carry out any immediate large-scale reorganisation. As far as his new charge, the Supermarine company, was concerned, he decided to leave it very much alone. Its chief engineer was Joe Smith, who had taken over from Mitchell. Smith had proved to be a worthy successor to the great man, and was responsible for successfully developing the Spitfire into the finest fighter of the war. Edwards believed they should work better at arm's length. 'I worked out a deal whereby he didn't expect to see any more of me than he had previously seen of Rex Pierson.' Even so, he was shortly to be embroiled with Supermarine in the development of the Swift fighter for the RAF and, later, the Scimitar naval jet fighter.

Edwards did have one newcomer to his team: Joyce Brixey. She had joined his outer-office staff as a secretary, and was to become his personal assistant. Mrs Brixey had previously worked for Sir Hew Kilner in London, but when he became ill he asked Edwards if he would, in her words 'take on my gal'. She was to remain his secretary and personal assistant for the rest of his career and throughout his retirement, a period of fifty years.

Mrs Brixey recalls those early days with George Edwards: 'I can remember thinking that I would never get as close to this man as I had been to Sir Hew. Sir Hew was a very warm sort of man, and at that time Sir George was, I would say, ambitious. He says he wasn't.' But before long she gained 'enormous respect and admiration' for him. 'I think it was his total dedication to the job, and the fact that he had clawed his way up from being an East End little boy, a dock worker, self educated, and had got, with a little bit of luck, to the pinnacle of industry. Yet he never lost that touch with people, bringing out the best in them, making the most of what they could offer, and using it because it reflected glory on to them,' she says.

Edwards himself employed a strict but humanitarian style of leadership. 'You have the responsibility of putting chaps in the jobs they are capable of doing, and you also have the responsibility to people who work under them,' he says. 'Too often you get chaps put in charge of some particular job, and the blokes under them can knock spots off the chap who has been put in charge. You have got to see that as far as humanly possible (short of murder) you have got the right chaps in the right jobs with the right experience, and that is very difficult to do.'

He adds: 'I used to kick their backsides when they got it wrong; they used to know they were not being patted on the back. If it were too difficult for them to do the job, appropriate allowance ought to be made. Then somebody else got a kick in the backside for giving him the job in the first place. It's the old basic law of the jungle. If you do a decent job you get a pat on the back; if you make a mess of it you get a kick in the pants.'

An observer of this uncomplicated approach was Jack Thorne, who joined the company in 1925. In a letter to the house newspaper many years later, he remembered George Edwards as 'a hard-working' colleague in the design office at Weybridge. He wrote: 'Later, as chief designer and my boss, I knew great respect for him and his ability to lead. I acknowledge him as a man of character, whom I have never failed to admire, particularly in his dealings with people as human beings.'

He also threw some light on Edwards's approach to decision-making. Thorne recalled how Edwards had developed three slogans that he applied when considering a matter, which were always referred to by acronyms. They were: 1 Singleness of purpose (SOP); 2 Take it or leave it (TIOLI); and 3 I couldn't care less (ICCL).

By the autumn of 1953 Edwards found himself dividing his attention between the Valiant programme, which continued to occupy him in long hours in the design office, and promoting and marketing the Viscount. For this purpose he was spending much time abroad with customers and potential customers, especially in North America.

The Viscount was now attracting the sort of passenger appeal that had always been hoped for. Its smooth, fast ride was setting new standards of air travel that no airline could ignore. The BEA order in February 1953 for the stretched 800 Series aircraft, with the promise of a further-developed 810 Series, had established a continuity of purpose which encouraged confidence in the product in the world market.

Now an even greater prize beckoned in the form of a huge order from the first US customer, Capital Airlines of Washington, DC. Capital's interest had been aroused by the TCA order and by the 'Americanisation' of the aircraft. The same developed 700 Series (700D) appealed to Capital mostly for the airline's many regional routes in the eastern half of the USA. Edwards soon found himself in direct contact with the airline, an experience he describes as: 'the most extraordinary affair because of the Capital chaps themselves. They really were very different from anything that I had ever come across anywhere.'

Edwards valued personal contact and friendship with his customers, both civil and military, and sometimes he was forced to 'put his liver at the disposal of the company'. He says: 'People, of course, are the vital part of the thing. If you got on well you stood a chance. The Capital chaps were the nearest approach to the classic wild westerners that I have ever come across in the airline business. They were tremendous fun if you had strong nerves, a strong stomach and a stronger head. It was really pretty different from the prim and proper British airline chiefs.'

Again Edwards struck up a good relationship with the airline's president, J.H. 'Slim' Carmichael, and his general manager, Jim Franklin. 'They took some getting used to. If you took them out on a normal social occasion, like you did with customers, if you went to bed conscious, let alone with a headache, you had done pretty well!'

His efforts, and no doubt his headaches, were handsomely rewarded. In the summer of 1954 Capital signed the largest single dollar order ever placed in Britain, for forty Viscount 700D Series aircraft valued at $45 million. This was soon increased to sixty, worth $68 million. The aircraft were again modified to

North American passenger standards, and featured other improvements such as integral passenger stairs for quick turn-round.

The first Capital Viscounts were delivered a year later, and were an immediate success with the passengers, providing the airline with all the advantages they hoped for in challenging their bigger rivals. The pilots also loved the aircraft, which they dubbed, 'fast, forgiving and fun to fly'. So successful were the operations that Capital placed a further order for fifteen aircraft, with the ultimate intention of bringing its fleet to seventy-five.

Unfortunately, although the airline always affirmed that the Viscount's economy had more than fulfilled expectations, it soon became apparent that Capital had overreached itself. Its financial situation was later described by Edwards as 'terrible'. He recalls how the Vickers commercial director, Ronnie Yapp, tried to save the carrier by putting together deals with numerous banks. 'It used to drive him absolutely out of his mind, the twists and twirls he had to go through with the various banks it was already up to its ears with.' Eventually, in 1960, Capital staved off bankruptcy by a forced merger with its larger competitor United Airlines, which absorbed the bulk of the Viscount fleet (forty-one aircraft). Much to the airline's surprise, its Viscounts proved sufficiently effective to add a further six aircraft to its fleet, which it continued to operate successfully for another ten years.

But if the lifespan of Capital Airlines' Viscounts was shorter than expected, the operator's pioneering efforts with a British airliner certainly helped open the door to the American market, which was to be well populated with new British types for the next fifty years and more. Within months of the Capital contract in 1954, the Vickers team were in sight of another breakthrough order, this time from Continental Airlines of Denver, Colorado. This was followed by interest from the then mighty TWA, leading to a prolonged and extraordinary negotiation with reclusive aviation pioneer and business mogul Howard Hughes, who owned the airline, which was soon to embroil George Edwards personally.

Viscount appeal was by no means confined to North America. In almost every corner of the world Viscounts were being ordered and entering service. They became particularly popular in what was then known as old British colonial countries. In Australia, South Africa, India, Pakistan, the Middle East, Central Africa, Malaya, Burma, Hong Kong, the West Indies and New Zealand, Viscounts of both the 700 and 800 Series were now operating. Many other airlines of international repute became customers too, such as KLM, Lufthansa, All Nippon, Alitalia, several other British operators and CAAC in China. Around the world, passengers were appreciating the difference between what was described at the time as the 'thump and rattle of the piston engine and the smooth and quiet comfort of the turboprops'.

But two of the earliest customers, Air France and Aer Lingus, had personal significance for George Edwards. The Air France order brought him into contact for the first time with its boss, Henri Ziegler, who was later to become his opposite number during critical days of the Concorde programme, while the pursuit of the Aer Lingus contract nearly cost him his life.

Jock Bryce told the Aer Lingus story in an article in the *Sunday Express* in 1978. He described a demonstration flight for the Board of the Irish airline from Dublin in December 1949, when he found his elevator, aileron and rudder controls were jamming as he reached 19,000ft. After the usual checks, which were negative, he became seriously worried that there was something fundamentally wrong with the aircraft. Having told the passengers to strap themselves in because of 'bad weather', he summoned George Edwards, who was aboard as a passenger, to the flight deck.

'Quiet and unshakeable, he was the last man in the world to panic,' wrote Bryce. '"What's the trouble, brother?" he asked. "Mr Edwards, we have a problem. I can't move the elevator on this 'plane and I can't move the rudder."' Edwards tried himself to move the control column, but could not move it. Moreover, neither he nor the other Vickers technical staff aboard could offer an explanation.

By reducing engine power, and thereby causing a change in trim, Bryce, with great skill, was able to keep the Viscount in a nose-down attitude. Then, by using his ailerons, which were not completely jammed, he was able slowly to reduce height and steer towards the airfield. But as he descended the controls began to free themselves, and he was able to make a good landing. During the descent Edwards told his important passengers that bad weather was the cause of the premature return. Neither he nor the pilots gave them any indication of the real cause of the trouble, nor was it mentioned to air traffic control, as it might have jeopardised the sale.

The Viscount was quickly towed into the hangar, and behind locked doors the examination began. 'I was discussing the symptoms with George Edwards when we noticed a long, thin puddle appearing on the concrete floor of the hangar. It had exactly the same span as the tailplane and was about six inches wide, except under the rudder, where it bulged into a circle. A steady leak of something that looked like water was dripping from the leading edge of the elevator and from the base of the rudder. We began to understand what had gone wrong,' wrote Bryce.

The leak betrayed a problem that might have taken months of flight testing, and possibly lives, to resolve. Jock Bryce explained that in every aircraft there is a small clearance between the main structure and the control surfaces to allow them to move up and down or, in the case of the rudder, from side to side. For aerodynamic efficiency this gap had been bridged by a thin fabric screen, and this had frozen in the cold air at higher altitudes, preventing the controls from moving. The fault had not been discovered earlier because the aircraft was always hangared at Wisley after flight. In Dublin it had been left out on the tarmac overnight, and during a rainstorm the fabric screens had absorbed moisture which had subsequently frozen at altitude, locking the controls solid until the descent into warmer air thawed them out.

The incident, whether known or not to Aer Lingus, did not dampen the airline's enthusiasm for the Viscount, and it eventually acquired a fleet of twelve aircraft.

While the Viscount was breaking into new markets, Valiant production was recovering from a near-disastrous total loss of the first prototype. In January 1952, some seven months after the test programme had been transferred to Hurn, the aircraft crashed a few miles from its base when fire broke out in the starboard wing. The crew of five, including Jock Bryce, who was in command, were forced to eject, but tragically the RAF liaison pilot, Sqn Ldr Brian Foster, was lost in the process. It was a setback that could have threatened the aircraft's future.

Edwards recalls: 'It was a fire in the engine bay due to re-lights. Somehow the fuel it burned got splashed about. The secondary effects of that sort of thing are always most worrying, because the aileron controls were burnt away and he lost lateral control.' Fortunately the second prototype was nearing completion. After suitable modification it was flying three months later, regaining much of the lost ground, much to the relief of everybody, particularly Edwards, who was all too aware of the potential delay to the delivery guarantees and the financial penalties that would accrue.

By this time Weybridge was working on a developed version of the Valiant designed for low-level operations. This aircraft, the Valiant B.2 Pathfinder, for ever to be known as the 'Black Bomber' because of its overall black night finish, was nearing completion as a prototype at Foxwarren. It was the last to be built there, and flew in time to make its first public appearance at the Society of British Aircraft Constructors' (SBAC) annual flying display at Farnborough in September 1953.

Edwards explains the reason for the development: 'There was a fair amount of interest in being able to drop a big-enough bomb from low level [to avoid enemy radar defences]. This meant you had got to have the performance to get in and out of Moscow and live. The aeroplane had to be pretty different, and the structure was totally different, although it looked the same.' In essence, the main load-bearing wing structure was considerably strengthened for the more demanding denser air encountered at low level. The undercarriage was rearranged to retract rearwards into pods on the wing, and the forward fuselage was extended to house the extra role equipment.

Unfortunately, soon after its first appearance, the Air Ministry changed its mind about the desirability of low-level penetration. 'I don't really know why it didn't go on,' says Edwards. 'There was somebody somewhere who originally had an idea that attacking Moscow at low level was a good idea, and that was the only device you could do it with.' The irony of this became all too apparent in the early 1960s, when the same low-level requirement was reinstated and the V-bomber force was re-tasked accordingly. High-altitude subsonic missions, for which the Valiant had been designed, were now deemed 'too dangerous' by the Ministry. By then the Black Bomber, which would have filled the bill, had been scrapped.

The role change in 1963 was a major disaster for the RAF Valiant squadrons, as the aircraft were now forced to undertake low-level flying, for which they were not suited. So when fatigue cracks were found in the wings it was decided to withdraw the entire fleet, as they were too expensive to repair. Edwards says: 'We didn't know about fatigue. . . . It was a bit of the march of progress, because nobody worried about fatigue, particularly cracks, in those days. They weren't expected to last long enough to show any cracks.'

At the time of the withdrawal, in 1964, Valiants equipped nine bomber squadrons, one tanker squadron, one photo-reconnaissance squadron, an operational conversion unit and a Bomber Command development unit.

It later transpired that the decision to remove Valiants from service, taken by the then Minister of Aviation, Roy Jenkins, was not communicated to the company or to George Edwards, who admonished the Minister in a personal letter for not having the courtesy to advise him of the withdrawal.

In all, 104 Valiants were produced in four basic versions, sometimes at a rate of as many as four a month. From the sixth production aircraft onwards every one was delivered on or ahead of schedule to the RAF, the last being flown out of the short 3,600ft Brooklands runway in 1957. Much of the credit for this was due to the introduction of advanced design and manufacturing technology in the works. In the production shops a new process was introduced whereby large components were milled from solid alloy planks, replacing the fabrication of such parts by riveting or bonding. Large-scale power-stretching and forming tools were installed, complemented by synthetic bonding equipment, and a special glassfibre plastic bonding shop was opened.

Such methods not only ensured that Valiant production kept to schedule, but were developed to form the basis for efficient manufacture of all Weybridge aircraft for the next thirty years. In his history of Vickers, J.D. Scott wrote: 'The Valiant production programme was an engineering achievement as remarkable as any recorded in these pages.'

While in service from 1955 the Valiant distinguished itself in many ways. It pioneered in-flight refuelling of large jet aircraft, bringing a completely new approach to range endurance for all RAF aircraft. In various bombing competitions it achieved outstanding success against United States Air Force (USAF) units. In 1956 it was used for the first and only time in anger, when it became the first post-war bomber to see action during the Suez campaign.

But for many the Valiant will always be remembered as the first British aircraft to carry the nuclear weapon. In 1956 it was used to drop Britain's first atomic bomb, during tests in Australia, and a year later a Valiant dropped the first hydrogen bomb in trials at Christmas Island in the Pacific. The Weybridge team's involvement in the incorporation of the 'special' weapon was kept to a minimum. Edwards recalls that they were simply given outline drawings. 'All we really wanted to know was shape, size and weight, where the centre of gravity was, and all the physical dimensions. We weren't given a short course on how to make the bomb, and we didn't want to.'

Asked years later if the nuclear role for the Valiant worried him, Edwards says: 'Not really. We had tottered our way through a war where the quality of the mechanism the troops were given to win it with was an essential ingredient. If we were going to have to take on the Russians, which of course was the concept of the thing, then it would have to be lined up with what the Russians could do.' He adds: 'It was a professional job we had been given to do, and we had to get our heads down and do it.'

Assessing the performance of the Valiant during its Service life, Air Chief Marshal Sir Kenneth Cross, who commanded Bomber Command from 1959 to 1963, stated that it had been the backbone of Bomber Command, and for two years was the only aircraft in the Command capable of carrying nuclear weapons. 'In bombing competitions,' he stated, 'Valiant squadrons covered themselves in glory and convincingly demonstrated the technical proficiency and strike potential of the Royal Air Force. To all those who designed, built and tested it, and to those who operated the aircraft, great credit is due.'

As a postscript, for a time the Valiant attracted serious attention from the USA, the ramifications of which were to have lasting value for that nation's own new bomber fleet. George Edwards recalls a visit in the early 1950s of 'a collection of brass' from the USAF. They included the redoubtable Gen Curtis Le May, then Head of Strategic Air Command (SAC), and Gen Vandenburg, Chief of the American Air Staff. Edwards says: 'The Americans alleged they had interest in the Valiant, and one of the ideas they had was to put it on one of their big aircraft carriers.'

The party was flown to Hurn for a demonstration. 'Jock Bryce was flying the Valiant,' says Edwards. 'We did a really spectacular performance because the thing could handle like their various devices couldn't. We took them in a Viscount, which also made their eyes come out. It impressed everybody, and Curtis Le May was quite interested.'

But the visit came to nothing, with one exception, which resulted in a major modification to the Boeing B-52 strategic bomber. Edwards, with a twinkle in his eye, remembers how it came about. 'I was pretty friendly with Boeing at that time. Their chief designer, Wellwood Beall, got hold of me after the visit and told me he had been at his wit's end to persuade the USAF that they couldn't do side-by-side seating in the B-52. "What I told them they should go for," he said, "was a tandem arrangement, as in the B-47. Then you turn up with an aeroplane that has a performance if anything better than the one we are offering, with side-by-side seating. Le May was so impressed with your aeroplane that I have had to go back to square one and re-cast the whole thing with side-by-side seating."'

From the third aircraft onwards, all B-52s were modified to have side-by-side seating like the Valiant. Edwards believes to this day that all USAF B-52 pilots should be grateful to him for that.

CHAPTER THIRTEEN

Ethel Merman, Bob Six, but Mostly Howard Hughes

The burgeoning airline industry in post-war North America produced its own brand of tough, ambitious and sometimes outrageous entrepreneurs and businessmen. George Edwards was to meet many of them. For his part he usually enjoyed their company, and they liked him, recognising the same free spirit of the self-made man. His encounter with Capital's 'wild westerners' was a foretaste of the rough-and-tumble of 'doing business in the States'. Now, in pursuit of Viscount sales, he was to meet two Hollywood legends and the toughest of tough negotiators.

Edwards's introduction to American glitz and glamour came with the hastening but vital negotiations with the important Midwest carrier Continental Airlines, based in Denver, Colorado. Its president was Robert B. Six, a larger-than-life character with a luxurious but public lifestyle befitting the husband of Ethel Merman, one of Broadway's biggest stars.

Six had closely followed the Capital Airlines experience, but decided that Viscount 700s were too small for his purposes. The advent of the new 800/810 Series quickly changed matters. In his book *Maverick Airliners*, Robert Serling wrote that the airline estimated that, with the larger 52-seat Viscount, its break-even passenger load factor on its key route, between Los Angeles and Denver, was only twenty passengers, compared with thirty-five and thirty-seven respectively for the slower piston-engined Lockheed Electra and Douglas DC-6.

Serious talks with Vickers began in 1953, and the 810 Series, with more powerful engines and extra weight-carrying capability, was offered. Accordingly, Edwards became a regular visitor to the airline, and took an instant liking to Bob Six, whom he describes as 'all right and a good bloke', his highest accolade. This was just as well, as their friendship was to undergo a severe test.

Meetings often took place in New York, where Edwards first encountered Ethel Merman. 'The first time I set eyes on her at close quarters was in Bob's New York apartment, doing a deal with Bob when she wasn't aware that I was in the room,' he says. 'But that wouldn't have worried her much. The door swung open, and through it came this extraordinary vision of Ethel in a pale blue dressing gown that was ballooning like a parachute as she swept into the room. Talk about born to the stage and making an entry! We giggled about this quite a lot later. I had an open invitation to see her shows in London and New York, and I would send my card round to her dressing room and go in. She really was a good 'un.'

Preliminary contract discussions went well, and Six and the Continental team visited the UK to see the aircraft in the making. But the talks took an unexpected turn when Six raised what was to prove a 'major sticking point'. He did not like the single-spar wing and tailplane construction, which had been successfully applied to previous Weybridge-built aircraft, and which Edwards had described in detail in his 1948 RAeS lecture.

'Six flatly refused to accept the Viscount unless its major structural components were designed to American standards,' wrote Serling. 'He particularly and sharply questioned George Edwards on the Viscount's single-spar construction; US planes effectively had three main spars; one for each wing, plus a massive centre spar. Edwards defended the Viscount's design rigorously, pointing out it wasn't really a single spar but in reality two box structures welded into one, relatively light but strong.'

Serling says that Edwards eventually agreed to beef up the Viscount to the structural standards demanded by Six, but not before further argument between the two. Edwards was quoted as saying: 'The bloke just kept talking and talking, and I went back to England convinced he was right and we were wrong.'

But that was far from the end of it. Bob Six had a further unwanted surprise for George Edwards. According to Serling, once the specifications and selling price had been agreed, Edwards asked Six how much down payment he could expect. Six responded by holding out his hand and making a circle with his thumb and forefinger, indicating zero. He then added that his airline might have to ask Vickers to loan it money to help pay the import duty (12.5 per cent) on all the aircraft. A long discussion followed, the upshot being an agreement to loan the airline enough money for the duty. Serling wrote: 'Others in the Continental group marvelled at Six's cool audacity and his sense of timing.'

In agreeing to the loan Edwards took a risk, for he had to answer to the Vickers Board, but he had faith in Six and his airline, and most of all supreme confidence in his aircraft. He was sure that, once it was in service, passenger appeal would generate the revenues and profits from which Vickers would be paid in full. That was to say nothing of the stimulating effect of having another prestige operator on the customer list.

So, in December 1955, Continental announced an order for fifteen of the uprated Viscount 810s that Brian Trubshaw describes in his autobiography as 'the best of all Viscounts because it was very solid with a feeling of great power'. It was nearly 100mph faster than the original prototype and carried twice the payload.

Continental was to justify Edwards's faith in the airline and the aeroplane. Serling wrote: 'The appeal of the new 'plane, plus good merchandising and what was to be Continental's trademark – excellent in-flight service – had some almost immediate results that surprised a lot of industry doubters. In the first four months of Viscount operations Continental had grabbed more than 43 per cent of the Chicago–Denver and Los Angeles–Denver first-class markets, and nearly 30 per cent of the Kansas City–Los Angeles market.'

If the Continental experience was an eye-opener, the brush with Howard Hughes was even more remarkable, but less rewarding. For five years, from 1951–7, Edwards was in regular contact with Hughes by telephone, but he never actually met the legendary billionaire. His abiding memory through those years was of 3 a.m. phone calls at home from Hughes. 'Dinah used to say: "If that's that man Hughes again, tell him you're in bed asleep." I would say: "I can't do that, there could be a whacking great order at the end of this."'

Interest from Hughes and his airline, TWA, began in 1951, when Hughes flew in the Viscount while on a visit to Britain. He was accompanied by Robert Rummel, a highly experienced senior engineer with the airline, who subsequently wrote a book, *Howard Hughes and TWA*, in which he gives a full account of the extraordinary events that were to unfold.

Following the flight in England, which impressed both men, Rummel was told to follow developments and report back. He writes: 'The contrast between the Viscount and the piston engines was striking. The high-altitude, over-the-weather ride passengers would enjoy in relaxed comfort was such, that in my opinion, they would never fly in pistons if turbines were standing by.'

In the spring of 1952 TWA began 'serious negotiations' with Vickers. However, despite his genuine enthusiasm for the Viscount, Rummel 'agonisingly recommended against procurement' when asked his opinion. He did so, he says, for several reasons, but primarily because he felt the airline was fully committed in absorbing a new fleet of other aircraft, and because he had concern over the US certification process. Like Bob Six, he did not like the single-spar wings and tail surfaces, though he admitted later that the Viscount's history 'showed this concern to be unjustified'.

Consequently TWA's interest lapsed, and it was not until four years later, in 1956 and at Hughes's instigation, that the airline took a fresh look at the aircraft. This followed the good reports the Viscount was getting in service around the world. Substantive talks were reopened with George Edwards and Christopher Clarkson, the Vickers US representative, who had continued to send TWA detailed technical information and route analyses.

Again TWA's preoccupation with the procurement of long-haul jets led to further delay. However, matters had progressed far enough, and interest was great enough, to enable Edwards and Clarkson to deliver what was effectively an ultimatum to the airline. They set a deadline beyond which prices and delivery positions could no longer be held to. 'Howard usually did not react well to pressure tactics,' wrote Rummel. But on this occasion, although delivery positions were lost, Hughes retained his interest and resumed direct contact with Edwards.

This time Hughes had a great idea, for which he demanded total secrecy. He had long wanted to manufacture aircraft himself in the USA, and the Viscount presented an ideal opportunity for him to do so. He would then sell them on to TWA, and presumably to other North American carriers. To do this he would set up his own plant, using management personnel and engineers from the Hughes Aircraft Division of Toolco, the Hughes Tool Company established by his father for drilling operations, from which he derived his wealth.

'Howard directed that no one was to get even a hint of this activity except those who were directly and unavoidably involved, whom he identified,' Rummel wrote. He was told to discuss production details with George Edwards on a 'super secret' basis, but not before he had 'laid the ground work'.

The plan was for a progressive transfer of work to the USA. This required a completely new approach from the Weybridge production and manufacturing staff, who were tasked with working out the feasibility and costs for such a complex scheme. It is hardly surprising that difficulties arose, especially in supplying initial major assemblies so that a small number of aircraft could be delivered quickly to TWA for rapid introduction into service.

To add to the complications, Hughes refused to divulge his manufacturing scheme to the newly appointed president of the airline, Carter Burgess. Burgess, however, had already instigated his own review of fleet needs, which envisaged the 'possible acquisition' of twenty-two Viscount 700Ds. However, a detailed route analysis suggested they would be unprofitable, and it was Rummel himself (who still opposed the sale for much the same reasons as before) who intervened to show that the figures were flawed, and the reverse was true.

By now matters were somewhat confused between Hughes's manufacturing aspirations and the debatable fleet needs of TWA. Direct airline interest was activated again by a special offer from Vickers for the early delivery of fifteen aircraft at a price of £400,000 each. These were the 700Ds originally ordered by Capital to increase its fleet to seventy-five, but which it could no longer afford. Their production positions were, however, still available.

Hughes showed immediate interest in the offer, but the saga continued. He called Edwards, who by now was used to his opening greeting of 'Now see here, mister!', said he liked the deal and even agreed to make a firm decision by the following Wednesday, but did not do so. There followed 'an intense flurry of activity' in TWA, and senior management visited England and contractual negotiations were 'expedited'. On request, Vickers sent a demonstration aircraft to New York for Hughes to see (and, if necessary, fly).

But when it arrived in New York 'Hughes had it placed under armed guard, even though he had no right to do so,' says Rummel. 'No one was allowed to approach it or even to remove food from the galley. Howard provided the crew, who remained on standby status in a top accommodation in a New York hotel at his expense. Despite Vickers' pleadings and protestations, the 'plane remained under guard for months, presumably awaiting for Howard to fly it. He never did.'

Hughes's flight crew were not the only people stranded in New York, awaiting the great man's arrival. The Vickers flight crew who had delivered the aircraft to New York, led by Jock Bryce, were also stranded and placed in the equally luxurious surroundings of the exclusive Waldorf Towers. Bryce says they were prevented from leaving their rooms and banned from their aeroplane. 'I never got into the aeroplane again because it could only be opened up by Mr Hughes himself.' When a Vickers team did get back inside the airliner, eleven months later, they found that everything in the interior had been eaten up by rats, which had got in through the undercarriage bays.

Bryce and his crew were 'trapped' in the Waldorf Towers for nearly three weeks, though Howard Hughes rang him several times to apologise for the delay. Jock says that, on the first occasion, Hughes told him that the American government was carrying out atomic bomb explosions in the Middle West, and he did not want them flying over there in case they were infected by radiation. On another occasion Hughes rang to apologise for the delay again and told Bryce not to eat pork, because there was a glut on the market and he would appreciate it if they helped to slow the market down. 'I was taken by surprise, but he might be buying sixty Viscounts; it definitely wasn't a leg-pull, he was just a funny sort of guy,' he says.

After the Vickers crew had spent a 'thoroughly boring time' in New York, Hughes telephoned Bryce again to say that things had changed and he wanted them up in Montreal, where he had arranged to use a TCA Viscount for the demonstration. Why he ignored the aircraft awaiting him in New York is unknown. Bryce rang Edwards to tell him about the change of plan and express his concerns, especially that they had been refused permission to fly their own aircraft up there. 'GRE told me to leave the aircraft in New York and do what Mr Hughes wanted,' he said.

In Montreal the five-man Vickers crew was treated to the utmost luxury in the Ritz Carlton hotel, where Hughes had taken the whole of the ninth floor. Again they were told not to leave, but because they suspected that all their telephone calls were being monitored, Jock decided to try to 'escape' so that he could telephone George Edwards from the safety of the Vickers office, which was nearby. He arranged with the local Vickers representative, Norman Wadsworth, to meet at 2 a.m. so they could call Edwards early in the morning (UK time) at home in Bookham. Bryce crept down the back stairs of the hotel and let himself out of the emergency exit. But he had only gone 25 yards before he was confronted by 'a guy who looked like an FBI agent', who apologised but told him Mr Hughes would not like it if he left the hotel. 'I have never been so depressed and frightened in my life,' says Bryce.

Eventually, in the middle of the night, a demonstration flight was laid on. The Vickers crew was sworn to secrecy, and even today Jock Bryce will not talk in detail about the arrangements that had been made. He was, however, able to describe how Hughes handled the aircraft. 'He took off and then went back four or five miles, way down, and did what you would have called a precautionary landing. He got the nose cocked up, the flaps down and dragged it at 200ft for miles and miles, and did a very nice landing. When I asked him why he did that, he said he flew many aeroplanes, and if he did it the same way he would get a better comparison. . . . There was some justification in that – he was a good pilot,' he says.

After more delay, Bryce eventually got through to Edwards. 'I don't think he knew Hughes had flown the aircraft, because I was too frightened to mention that. I told him we were getting nowhere, and he told me to come home with his approval, and we were put on a flight back to London.' However, Jock still feels he might have been 'letting the side down' by returning, even though he was assured this was not the case.

Meanwhile, talks with TWA rumbled on, and in the summer of 1957 the airline made up its mind. After another review, which took into account the revised study instigated by Rummel, it decided that the aircraft could make a profitable contribution if Viscount services were restricted to east of Kansas City, and that twenty-two aircraft should be ordered. They also thought that the Viscounts would have enough passenger appeal to attract traffic to the rest of their fleet.

On being informed of the TWA decision, Hughes immediately rang George Edwards and personally committed to the purchase of the fifteen Viscount 700s that had originally been offered. Edwards for his part 'accepted Howard's word as his bond' and authorised work to continue on the aircraft, which were to be transferred to the USA in stages.

But once again there came a final twist. 'At the most critical time of my negotiation with Vickers, when final resolution of numbers of items required clearance from Hughes, he suddenly left the country without comment,' wrote Rummel. 'To make an awkward situation worse,' he added, 'no one knew where he was or when he would return.'

In the interregnum, Rummel urged Vickers to draw up a new draft of the procurement specifications and, in his boss's absence, took a short camping holiday with his 8-year-old son in Colorado. Within days he was interrupted by a telephone call from Hughes, who was in Nassau in the Bahamas. He wanted to know 'where the hell have you been', and said that Edwards was 'putting the heat on him to execute the deal'.

The starting gun had been fired again, and a Weybridge team led by Derek Lambert, the senior sales executive, and including Bert Dymott, who was a manufacturing cost expert, were despatched immediately. At Hughes's insistence, 'because they couldn't afford to lose a day', Rummel fixed the meeting close to where he was staying on holiday, at an hotel near the Rocky Mountain National Park. Hughes also believed that, because he was being pressed for a quick resolve, there was a good chance they could 'make hay' and negotiate a good deal.

The contractual work was completed 'fairly rapidly' in Colorado, but no final agreement could be reached, mainly because there had been what Rummel described as a 'misunderstanding' between Hughes and Edwards on purchase price. Talks dragged on without resolve until George Edwards brought matters to a head some time later. He telephoned Rummel and told him they had extended themselves 'beyond reasonable measure', and he now required a duly executed contract with 'overdue progress payments'. He suggested they now make an offer, 'any offer', which would be considered.

The scene was set for the final act. But, as Hughes and Edwards found agreement elusive, TWA effectively and irrevocably pulled the plug, changing its mind and deciding it no longer wanted the Viscounts. Hughes, who had committed himself to acquiring the fifteen aircraft, responded with some anger. 'My reputation in Europe is worth a damn sight more than the price of fifteen 'planes,' he told Rummel. Perhaps surprisingly, he called Edwards and told him that, despite TWA's decision, he would personally honour his pledge and see that every one of the fifteen aircraft were disposed of to Edwards's complete satisfaction.

This he duly did. Rummel tells of a telephone call he received some time later, when Hughes told him 'with some pride' that he had spoken to Edwards to say he had discharged every obligation, and that George was happy about it. In fact he had arranged for the bulk of the aircraft (ten) to be supplied to another US operator, Northeast Airlines. Furthermore, Hughes was to acquire his own Viscount for the tool company. Unfortunately, although it was paid for, it was never delivered. It stood on the Weybridge assembly line for months, guarded by Hughes's own men, who would not even let the Vickers staff on the aircraft for essential maintenance.

The final say is left to George Edwards. Many years later he met Rummel in New York and confirmed that Howard Hughes had properly disposed of the fifteen aircraft. He described Hughes as 'a truly good friend and a great gentleman'. But, on later reflection, he might possibly have preferred to take his wife's advice when called in the middle of the night, and gone back to sleep.

CHAPTER FOURTEEN

'The Biggest Blunder of All'

At a press conference on 12 November 1955 a spokesman for the MoS announced what George Edwards later described as 'the biggest blunder of all'. The Ministry had decided to cancel the Vickers V1000 long-range military jet transport in favour of the turboprop Bristol Britannia. Furthermore, it would discontinue funding the civil version of the V1000, the VC7, since BOAC, the prime customer, had now stated that it had no requirement for such a transatlantic jet. 'BOAC is satisfied that it can hold its own commercially on the North Atlantic route until well into the 1960s with the Comet IV and the long-range Britannia,' the Parliamentary Secretary to the Minister stated later.

But by October the following year Harold Watkinson, Minister of Transport and Civil Aviation, was announcing to the House of Commons that permission had been given for BOAC to purchase from America fifteen Boeing 707 long-range jets at a cost of £44 million. 'This was in order that the Corporation may hold their competitive position on the North Atlantic route from 1959 to the 1960s. At that time no suitable new British aircraft can be made available for that purpose – the purchase is an exceptional measure to bridge the gap,' he stated.

So ended, with a complete government *volte-face*, the hopes and aspiration that lay with the V1000/VC7, a prototype of which had been within six months of completion. It had promised to be the first jet airliner in the world to be capable of flying the North Atlantic non-stop, and would have flown two years ahead of its American rivals. 'I think it was the most serious cancellation that has taken place in a whole string of cancellations,' Edwards said later.

The story of the V1000 began in 1951, as the Valiant started its test-flying programme. Even in these early days a transport derivative had been outlined on the drawing boards at Weybridge. Edwards was a past master of developing basic types and, by keeping close to Whitehall, quickly identified new opportunities. The conversion of the Viking for military roles was a good example. The result was a formal request from the MoS in 1951 for

Vickers to submit designs for a dual-purpose long-range jet transport based on the Valiant.

The specification was complicated and difficult, for the new aircraft would have to meet an RAF requirement for fast troop-carrying, and also provide BOAC with a new jet airliner that was larger than the Comet IV and capable of flying the North Atlantic without a refuelling stop. In addition, it needed to be of the same basic dimensions as the Valiant so as to have a similar radar signature, to act as an effective decoy on bombing missions.

Although there were obvious economic advantages in designing the V1000 as a derivative of the Valiant, Edwards has always stressed the importance of the decoy role. 'Some parts of the Air Staff had this great idea of having electronic countermeasures buried in the aeroplane so you could put a few of them in with a squadron of bombers to confuse enemy radar. For the RAF it did a couple of jobs, of which one was of confusion as to which was the Valiant with an A-bomb, and which one wasn't.'

Under Edwards's direct supervision as chief designer, the Weybridge team proposed an aircraft of similar size and wing shape to the Valiant, but with a fully pressurised fuselage capable of carrying up to 100 passengers or 150 troops. To enable it to carry its full payload across the Atlantic, and also meet the short-field performance for the RAF, a more powerful engine was required. The new Rolls-Royce Conway, rated at 15,000lb thrust, was selected.

The Conway was the world's first bypass or fan engine to enter service, offering greater propulsive and fuel efficiency. This was achieved by ducting or 'bypassing' cold intake air around the hot parts of the engine and mixing it with the hot exhaust gas at the rear. This reaction lowered the jet velocity, giving better thrust levels for less fuel burn than in normal pure jets.

The aircraft itself was also advanced and complex in design, manufacture and in its systems. Mindful of the Comet I disaster two years before, new stronger construction methods were applied, such as the milling-out of solid metal billets for the main wing spars, a technique pioneered and developed at Weybridge. Full power-operated flying controls were introduced, and for the first time the fuselage was to be wide enough for six-abreast seating. In addition, extra fuel for added range could be provided in wing-mounted 'slipper' tanks.

For the civil version, the VC7, which was almost identical to the V1000, BOAC was involved in the studies from the start. If successful, it could give the airline a clear lead over its rivals. Edwards was delighted that at last it seemed possible to develop both military and civil versions together, thus allowing the full force of military support, especially RAF test-flying facilities, to come into play. He had championed such a prospect as far back as his RAeS lecture in 1948, when he had strongly advocated such an approach to reduce costs and enhance development.

Construction work began in October 1952, with an order from the MoS for a prototype and a structural test specimen. By January 1953 the Ministry had increased its order to six aircraft. But the joint requirement to meet both the tight military specification, particularly for short take-off and landing, and the airline's need for maximum efficiency, were incompatible and hard to reconcile. Edwards said afterwards: 'The V1000 had a difficult airfield performance to meet and really all the aeroplanes we've designed in this country have been bedevilled by having to have a short-field performance, which is something the Americans never seem to be unduly bothered about.'

Faced with this huge technical challenge, which took Vickers into uncharted waters, it was hardly surprising that the programme became delayed. Furthermore, as with most new aeroplanes, the all-up weight increased (but not by a disastrous amount), a point latched on to by the aircraft's rivals and critics. The solution was relatively simple: to ask for an increase in engine thrust from 15,000lb to 17,500lb, well within the development potential envisaged by Rolls-Royce and, in fact, already promised for the Victor B.2 bomber. Nevertheless, rumours began to circulate, often exaggerating the true situation.

During the spring and summer of 1955, coincident with the teething problems of the V1000, the RAF was put under extreme pressure by the Treasury to reduce spending. The V1000 was the most expensive item in its inventory, and quickly came under severe scrutiny. As a result, the Air Ministry decided, crucially for the V1000, to abandon the high-speed requirement, together with the decoy role, in favour of a cheaper and quicker solution.

At this point politics took over. The turboprop Bristol Britannia, which first flew in 1952, had already been ordered by BOAC for its long-haul routes. Despite delays, the airline stuck with it, especially as a faster, more economic development was promised for which it announced an order for sixty aircraft. Both the airline and the MoS had invested heavily in the programme, to the extent of some £20 million. The Britannia could now meet the reduced RAF air transport specification and, to suit a political dimension, it could be built at the Shorts factory in Belfast, which was in desperate need of work.

The prospect was both expedient and compelling to a Conservative government struggling with the economy and concern over Northern Ireland. Nevertheless, the Minister of Supply, Reginald Maudling, had regard for the V1000 and its potential. He hoped BOAC would keep faith with it. But the airline's chairman, Sir Miles Thomas, refused point blank. His airline had already suffered with the Comet I disaster and delays with the Britannia. This meant he had to seek government approval to buy American DC-7 piston-engine aircraft as an interim measure before Britannia deliveries could begin.

Although he was bitter about BOAC's attitude, George Edwards could see its point of view about American products. 'The real thing that is so easy to forget is that up to that time there weren't any British jet aeroplanes capable of doing a job after the Comet disaster. We were trundling around with conventional piston-engine aircraft like the [Avro] York and the [Handley Page] Hermes, which were either converted bombers or troop carriers, whereas the Americans had gone on building civil aircraft like the DC-6 and DC-7.'

He also acknowledged that BOAC felt safer buying aeroplanes that other people were operating. 'If an airline like BOAC reckoned it was having to wet-nurse the growing British aircraft industry, it was going to be held back because it wasn't allowed to use the equipment that its competing airlines were using. There was a strong body of opinion within BOAC that was absolutely bloody-minded about the government using the airline for the sole purpose of bringing the British aircraft industry into civil aeroplane manufacturing.' He adds: 'That is possibly a fairly generous statement of why BOAC was strong on American aeroplanes, because it wanted to be in a position where it could compete with airlines like KLM, who were not being held up and were free to buy American if they wanted to.'

But Edwards also says: 'There were individual elements within BOAC that we all knew were well and truly in the American camp. Quite a few of them, who had got quite decent jobs, got away with their support of the American aircraft industry because part of the British government responsible for British aircraft didn't really know what they were talking about. I think their intentions were all right, but they hadn't got a clue as to how to handle it.' He adds: 'It is so easy to forget that the Americans were by then in full production building transport aeroplanes, and had a big civil business on the go when the war ended. The government was trying to get our industry going, so we needed all the help we could get, and, roughly speaking, as far as BOAC was concerned, we didn't get any.'

However, behind the BOAC decision lurked Treasury influence, as Edwards knew only too well. 'To give BOAC the opportunity to fly a British aeroplane of the same standard that could be bought off the shelf meant the Treasury had to face a new development programme of a sort that British industry had no experience of at all,' he says. 'The only reason we got as far as we did was the military requirement that we had got on a military budget. That was the irony of the whole thing, because the Americans had been doing it for years. If BOAC was not going to play ball with it, then it was not going to get anywhere.'

From the political point of view, Edwards says; 'They could see that developing a new range of jet aeroplanes was going to be bloody expensive and a lot of domestic needs like the National Health Service, and that sort of thing, were going to be deprived of vote-winning cash. And, in some ways more important than that, it was putting pressure on BOAC to buy the products of the British aircraft industry which its competitors didn't have to.'

There was, however, one last chance of saving the V1000. Edwards's old friend Gordon McGregor of TCA, having been well served by the Viscount, was so enthusiastic about the VC7 that he travelled to London to meet Mr Maudling and urge him to continue with the programme. Maudling again consulted Sir Miles Thomas, who, having called for the latest VC7 specifications, still would not change his mind.

According to Derek Wood in his book *Project Cancelled*: 'Thomas was quite adamant he was not going to buy the VC7. The reason given that weight increases had penalised the aircraft's performance to such an extent that it would not be suitable for the North Atlantic as a non-stopper.' But he adds: 'All that was required was extra thrust from the Conway, but BOAC could not see it being made available. In fact this was a complete smoke screen to cover the Corporation having to support another British aircraft in addition to the Comet IV and the Britannia.'

Thus, in November 1955, the axe fell on the V1000, costing the taxpayer some £4 million. Edwards regarded the cancellation as finite, and quickly ordered that the prototype be destroyed and the jigs torn up. 'It's no good leaving a corpse about for the chaps to mourn over,' he said in a television interview later. 'You have got to kick them in the backside and excite them with enthusiasm about the next one you are going to do. It's not a great incentive for them to do something else if they are constantly reminded that the one they had just been doing was now lying around covered in dust, with a shroud over it. So I got the jigs up and the thing out of the way.'

The cancellation came just six months before the V1000 was due to fly, and one month after Pan American had placed a launch order for the Boeing 707. In the same month United Airlines ordered its rival, the Douglas DC-8.

That these similar four-engined jet airliners would soon be coming into service on the North Atlantic might well have alerted BOAC against buying the slower turboprop Britannia. For just ten months later the story of disappointment and destruction become one of pure farce. George Edwards was summoned to the office of the Minister, Harold Watkinson, who was also a local MP. He was well aware of the V1000, its lost potential and the threat to the jobs of many of his constituents. It was no surprise to Edwards when he asked a 'dreadful question': could the V1000 be reactivated?

Remembering the meeting, Edwards says: 'He [Watkinson] was one of the best Ministers ever, as honest as they come. He said to me that he had to go through the motions and ask me the question. I said: "You jolly well know I can't, because what was going to be the prototype within six months, and the jigs, have all been uprooted. The whole thing is finished."'

Watkinson then explained that he had to ask the question because the government was now being asked by BOAC to buy Boeing 707s from America. He asked Edwards how 'difficult' was he going to be about it. 'I swallowed hard,' says Edwards, 'and said I didn't see much point in being difficult. I reckoned I was always going to be difficult when it was going to do some good.' He adds: 'I can truthfully say it wasn't what I would describe as the most rewarding hour's conversation I had in my life.'

On 24 October 1956 Watkinson duly announced that the government had approved the purchase by BOAC of fifteen Boeing 707s at a cost of £44 million, of which, it was later divulged, £35 million would have to be paid for in precious dollars that Britain could ill afford at the time.

The decision presented the American manufacturers with an advantage of up to two years. The V1000 was scheduled to fly in 1956, while the long-range 707 did not fly until 1959, and the DC-8 one year later. The Britannia, which was 'so urgently needed', did not enter service until 1959. Edwards is quoted by Scott in his Vickers history as saying: 'We therefore have the galling position that a British non-stop jet could be flying the Atlantic next year alongside the 707 and DC-8, the former of which is only operating on a stopping frequency, and the latter not operating at all. This is coupled with the fact that Transport Command have not yet received any long-range transport aircraft.'

Derek Wood wrote: 'Even more ironical was the fact that these airliners [707s] were powered by four Rolls-Royce Conway engines, each rated at 17,500lb thrust. Apparently the Conway could deliver the power for the 707, but not the VC7. The V1000/VC7 affair marked the point at which airliner development [in Britain] really began to go wrong and there has never been a full recovery.'

It was no consolation to Edwards to collect on wagers he had made long ago that, when the 707 came into service, its all-up weight would be greater than that of the VC7 and, furthermore, it would still be unable to fly the Atlantic non-stop. 'It merely confirmed me in the belief that the truth always comes out, but often it comes out too late,' he says.

CHAPTER FIFTEEN

Accolades, Worries and the Vanguard

In June 1956 George Edwards made his first visit to Russia. He did so as a member of a British delegation led by the Secretary of State for Air, Nigel Birch, and containing high-ranking RAF officers, government officials and other senior colleagues in the aircraft industry. Theirs was one of twenty delegations, including the North Americans, who had been invited to attend the Soviet Air Force flying display at Tushino military airfield near Moscow. Afterwards, arrangements had been made for them to tour a selected number of academies, factories and air bases, where Edwards was to meet many Russian aircraft designers and engineers, and the Soviet leaders, Mr Bulganin and Mr Khrushchev. He was also to receive an astonishing job offer.

The party was flown to Moscow in an RAF Comet II, which was to be shown off to the Russians and compared with their twin-engine Tupolev Tu-104, which had been flying for less than a year. Not to be outdone, Edwards had arranged for a Viscount 700, awaiting delivery to Central African Airways, to be flown to Moscow for similar demonstrations and to return some of the delegation to Britain. The Viscount was the first British civil airliner and the first turboprop of British manufacture to land in Moscow.

The proceedings were widely reported in the British media, for it gave Western observers a rare insight into Soviet capability (and threat), which was demonstrated by the flying display of their latest military and civil types. The invitation to the British delegation followed the first visit to Britain by Bulganin and Khrushchev the year before. During their UK tour the Russians had been taken to RAF Marham, where they had seen Valiants in operation. George Edwards was conspicuous among the British delegation and unsurprisingly was soon introduced to the great designer Andrei Tupolev.

Tupolev was the eponymous head of the most prolific design bureau in the Soviet Union, responsible for a string of bombers with chilling NATO call-signs, such as *Badger, Bear* and *Blinder*, and the civil Tu-104, which was comparable with the Comet. He and Edwards spent more than an hour together when he came to look round the Viscount as a member of the invited Russian party. Although their conversation would have suffered from the usual translation difficulties, Tupolev was able to make it quite clear to Edwards, then and later, that he would like him to come to Russia and join his company. How serious his offer was is unknown.

For his part, Edwards says: 'Tupolev offered me the job in charge of part of his design team; this was the old man Andrei Tupolev, whose wife told me they were the first of the new aristocracy. I didn't argue about that. He had got a big design team there, and there were plenty of jobs I could have done. I came home and said to Dinah: "What do you think?" "Oh, that's interesting," she says, cool as a cucumber, "when are you going?" That rather put an end to it, although I had no serious thoughts about it. I wouldn't have been allowed to go anyway.'

If the Russians appreciated the talents of George Edwards, so did his country when he was created Knight Bachelor in the 1957 New Year Honours, for 'outstanding services to aviation'. Messages of congratulations came from throughout the industry and from abroad. The new Sir George was modest about it, although he must have been conscious that it was a signal achievement for somebody who, without privilege or advantage, had attained the highest recognition the nation could then bestow. 'The Air Force was largely responsible for it. I think they reckoned I did a pretty fair job for them one way or another and I deserved a pat on the back,' was all he would say.

His good news was all the more welcome as the outlook for the company was 'gloomy' following the cancellation of the V1000, which had left a void that was to have lasting repercussions. Sir George now found 'a lack of sympathy' from some of his Vickers colleagues at main Board level (he had been appointed to the Board in 1955). They believed that the future lay in the military field and not in the civil market, as exemplified by BOAC's rejection of the VC7.

'There was a great spate of bloody-mindedness about BOAC because it really was their decision that clobbered the RAF transport at the same time,' says

Sir George. 'There was an attitude among the chaps that the thing for us to do was to build aeroplanes for the RAF, and not be messed about by BOAC, who were wedded to the Americans anyway.'

'As far as the Board of Directors was concerned, you have to remember that a lot of them had been generals and had a military approach to the whole game. So it was not difficult for them to say: "This is what happens if you go and get tangled up with the civil business. The best thing you can do is concentrate on building aeroplanes for the air force, because we do at least know where we are when we do that."'

His critics must have ignored the continuing Viscount success and the unpalatable fact that, after the Valiant, the production of which would soon end, there were no military orders in sight. The only significant military contracts were held by Supermarine for its high-performance jet fighters: the Swift for the RAF and the Scimitar for the Royal Navy. By mutual agreement with chief designer Joe Smith, Sir George had kept 'at arm's length', but technical problems with the Scimitar and the political ramifications of the Swift brought him into the picture.

The Swift had emerged in prototype form in 1948 as Britain's first swept-wing jet fighter. Its progress had been slow until 1950, when war broke out in Korea. The RAF had no swept-wing fighters, and as a matter of urgency ordered the rival Hawker Hunter 'off the drawing board'. In addition, as 'an insurance measure', it placed orders for the developed version of the Swift. Unlike the Hunter, the Swift was fitted with a reheated Rolls-Royce Avon engine for enhanced performance. This was excitingly demonstrated by its appearance in the contemporary award-winning British film *Sound Barrier*.

For some time the two aircraft had been engaged in a very public 'fly-off' at air shows and displays. Their rivalry became headline news, and in Coronation Year, 1953, the Swift (with a little help from Weybridge) gained the headlines by capturing the world absolute airspeed record. This was set in the heat of the North African desert near Tripoli, when, on 25 September, piloted by Mike 'Lucky' Lithgow, the aircraft achieved a straight-and-level speed of 735.7mph.

Although this was great encouragement for all concerned, the aircraft suffered from over-hasty development (as did the early Hunters), and it was not a success in RAF service. The Swift was eventually switched from its principal interceptor role to photo-reconnaissance and other duties, which it performed well.

Sir George recalls the situation and the rivalry. 'The Hunter was showing signs of being a better aeroplane, among other things because it didn't need reheat. I got thrust into my usual role of persuading everybody that the Swift was a better aeroplane, even though I knew it was really living on the back of a bit of brute force and ignorance, and the fact that it had the legacy of the Spitfire to it. The RAF was not very keen on it.' Nevertheless, in the end the not-inconsiderable total of 193 Swifts was built, and its somewhat overstated reputation as 'the aircraft that cracked the sound barrier' still lives on in the memories of many of those who saw the film.

The twin-engine Scimitar, the first swept-wing naval fighter, proved to be a more challenging technical task. It incorporated an ingenious method of 'flap blowing', using high-pressure air bled from the engine and directed over the flaps to give extra lift to reduce speed for deck landings. Its prototype predecessor was unusual in having a butterfly tail designed to avoid the jet efflux, and had conventional tail surfaces with the tailplane set at a dihedral angle. It was this that was causing handling and structural problems.

Sir George says: 'The only contribution I remember making was I suggested they turn the tailplane upside down [i.e. giving it anhedral], which got rid of the stalling characteristics. The hard part was getting the tailplane in the right place. The machined fitting that attached the tailplane to the fin was capable of being re-machined. So, without rebuilding the back of the aeroplane, you could take these two big fittings and screw them on upside down. This was really what the stalling characteristics wanted, and the change of position took the wake from the wing, so it was really a more sedate arrangement when you came in to land than before. That was really my only claim to fame; making the Scimitar a flyable aeroplane.'

But neither the Swift nor the later Scimitar offered any substantial work to plug the gap at the Weybridge factory after the Valiant. The only continuing production programme was for the new Viscount 800. Hopes, therefore, rested on the aircraft devised as a Viscount successor, the big turboprop Vanguard. But this was still on the drawing boards and, worryingly, there were now serious questions regarding its suitability in the fashionable new age of jet travel.

The Vanguard was conceived as a private venture in 1953 to a very precise BEA specification. It was in many ways a logical successor to the Viscount, being larger, faster and, most importantly, more economical, with a considerably reduced seat-mile cost. BEA was soon to order twenty for service by the late 1950s on its high-density medium-range routes. One insider, John Motum, says: 'It was an immaculate conception for a short/middle-distance turbine-powered airliner, set against a well-framed requirement from BEA, the best airline operating within the area of its title.'

In his autobiography, Sir Peter Masefield wrote that turboprops could provide any power that was needed for a larger aeroplane, and he could see that the Viscount, which at the time was BEA's heaviest and most powerful aircraft, 'would appear a mere tiddler'. In 1953 he began talks with George Edwards about something much bigger. This led to the Viscount Major, later to be known as the Vanguard. 'Had it been produced more quickly,' he wrote, 'it should have repeated the success of the Viscount.'

Sir George recalls those meetings. 'Peter Masefield wanted the new design to be such that the seat-mile costs had to be, I think, 10 per cent lower than those of the Viscount 800. That could only be achieved by making the body a bit bigger. There was also the need to carry freight as well. So the thing burst out with a double-bubble fuselage so we had the capacity under the passenger floor to put a fair amount of freight in.'

In general terms, the Vanguard design concept was described at the time by Sir George as 'pretty orthodox', though the ideal layout was not so obvious. The design staff had tried, he said, 'everything but a biplane'. Nearly sixty different studies were produced by the Weybridge project office, being referred to by Sir George as the proverbial '57 Varieties'. These included pure-jet alternatives, which would have more passenger appeal by the time it came into service. But pure jets did not have the required low operating costs demanded by BEA, and were abandoned.

The final version of the Vanguard owed much to the experience gained from the Viscount. When it was formally announced by both Vickers and BEA (along with the airline's order for twenty) in 1955, it was promoted as 'the first second-generation turboprop with all the desirable attributes associated with the Viscount of smooth quiet comfort'. It would, it was claimed, 'be ahead of all known competition' in speed, comfort, economy and maintenance.

From the beginning Edwards favoured the new Rolls-Royce Tyne propeller-turbine engine, which had sufficient power and performance for the larger and heavier aircraft. Of very advanced design, the Tyne was also far more fuel-efficient than the Dart, burning about half as much fuel for the equivalent power. In its original form the Vanguard would cruise at speeds greater than 400mph, carrying 100 passengers up to 1,000 miles. But by 1957 Vickers was offering the aircraft with a cruising speed of 412mph, seating up to 139 passengers in six-abreast accommodation, and with a maximum range of 2,000 miles.

Structurally, the Vanguard was ruggedly built to the latest 'fail-safe' standards, and it was the first Weybridge-built aircraft to incorporate a triple-spar wing, which the Americans had demanded of the Viscount. This, however, was not the reason for the change. It had more to do with providing more fuel in integral wing tanks, which could not have been accommodated otherwise.

The Vanguard benefited also from all the advanced Weybridge manufacturing techniques, such as the sculptured milling process that provided lighter, stronger components. Moreover, as part of the original BEA specification, great emphasis was put on passenger comfort. The Viscount's popular oval windows were retained, the cabin was designed to provide extra space, and the insulation was improved to provide a more comfortable environment.

For the pilots, the cockpit was spacious, with a large wrap-around windscreen for excellent visibility, which helped make the Vanguard a favourite with flight crews throughout its service life. For ground handling, low-level cargo doors and forward and aft integral stairs were designed to enable a quick turn-round.

Expectations for a bright sales future were raised when TCA, led by Gordon McGregor, decided the Vanguard would offer the lowest fares in North America and, with its large hold, meet their important freight business requirement. In January 1957 he placed an initial order for twenty aircraft, with options on another four (three of which were later to be taken up), valued at $67.1 million. At the time this was the 'largest single dollar order ever placed with the British aircraft industry'. Sir George was delighted, and said so, especially as the order had been placed 'off the drawing board'. But there the order book stopped.

For although the Vanguard could offer fares 'lower than a Greyhound Bus' on some routes, airlines were now being convinced that only pure-jet travel would attract the necessary passenger acceptance. Edwards and the Weybridge team, having designed for a specific low-cost requirement for their own home-grown airline, were only too aware that jet appeal was easily outweighing economic logic in the minds of the operators.

On top of this, stories of engine development difficulties were beginning to emerge from Rolls-Royce, although at first they were dismissed as 'teething problems'. More critically, the aircraft was coming under the close scrutiny of the Vickers Board, who had funded the project and were now extremely worried about its financial viability. But by then it was too late. The Vanguard was well into production. To cancel would incur not only huge penalty payments, but would endanger the whole future of the aircraft company. Charles Gardner, in his history of BAC, was more succinct. He wrote: 'Vickers had little choice but to accept the Vanguard or contemplate closing the site.'

Sir George remembers the period well, and how BEA was now seriously worried, especially about the choice of engine. The airline even interrupted his family holiday in Ireland by sending a special envoy, a senior engineer, to discuss matters with him. 'He was sent over on a special mission to work out how we could get what BEA wanted with a jet instead of the Tyne. There was a lot of wishful thinking that you could build an aeroplane of that size and still arrive at the operating economy you were looking for, and get the bonus of the extra speed a jet would bring.' He adds; 'The great clarion cry from BEA was that operating costs had got to be down on what they were achieving on the Viscount. You couldn't do that with a jet at the state of the art then.'

He also received a call from the Vickers chairman, Lord Weeks. 'Ronnie Weeks was very interested in turning it into a jet. He rang me up in Ireland to make quite sure I knew what I was up to. Of course, the thing I didn't know was that the Tyne was going to turn out to be a pretty difficult engine to put with anything.'

The full extent of the Tyne problems was now becoming more apparent. They centred on a series of high-pressure-compressor failures. 'There was a stage when I got stuck with a whole clutch of Vanguards in the erecting sheds and no engines to put in them,' says Sir George. 'I think the Tyne has been abused unnecessarily, but it did the Vanguard no good. It made the aeroplane shake and vibrate. Of course, the thing we had sold it on was it would be like the Viscount, smooth and quiet, whereas the damn great propellers needed to be a lot further away from where they were. The tip speed as well produced its own private version of noise.'

Eventually, on 20 January 1959, the prototype Vanguard, in BEA colours, made its maiden flight in front of cheering Weybridge workers, flying from the short strip at Brooklands to Wisley, which now had a tarmac runway. It was flown by Jock Bryce, with Brian Trubshaw as copilot. At the end of the 18-min flight Bryce described its performance as 'quite sprightly'.

As was traditional at Vickers, all those concerned gathered at the nearby Wisley Hut pub after the flight, to celebrate. Jock Bryce says that when he got there the place was already packed, and that George Edwards and his old colleague Charlie Houghton, who was now production director of the company, had arranged the guest list to fill the place. At about 9 p.m. he popped out for some fresh air, and found Edwards and Houghton outside doing the same thing. A car arrived and two locals, an elderly man and his wife, got out. 'They looked at the Hut and wondered why they couldn't get in. They asked Sir George what was happening, and he said they had just flown the Vanguard from Brooklands to Wisley. The woman replied: "But that's not very far!" GRE and Charlie were speechless.'

A few months later, at TCA's request, the prototype was dispatched across the Atlantic to be shown off to its Canadian customer. But for a miracle, the Vanguard, with all on board, including Sir George, would have been lost.

Jock Bryce, who was flying the aircraft, tells how a leaking underfloor heating duct brought them near to disaster while they were cruising at some 28,000ft halfway across the Atlantic. 'A call came from one of our flight test observers to say: "Why are you putting in the flying control locks?" I said I wasn't, he had to be kidding! [The flying control locks are only engaged on the ground for safety reasons, to prevent any inadvertent movement of the aircraft's control surfaces by wind gusts.] George Edwards then came up to see what was wrong. We took out the autopilot. I was still able to move the controls all right, but I was fairly gentle in doing it. But still the observer, who was monitoring the control systems, said the locks were still moving.'

Bryce says he immediately thought of the Aer Lingus Viscount incident, and could not believe it was happening again. 'It is most unusual for there to be two major hiccups when we could have lost the aeroplane with GRE on board both times. It might have changed the whole history of Vickers,' he says.

This time, however, they had a ground crew travelling as passengers, and by great good fortune some had their toolkits with them. They were able to lift the floor panels, and on inspection found that a heating duct had cracked, leaking red-hot air on to the push-pull control locking rod, which had expanded, and in doing so begun to move towards the locking position. The offending rod was quickly dismantled, watched by Edwards in shirtsleeves, and danger was averted.

'If we hadn't had a ground crew on board', says Bryce, 'and if they hadn't had the appropriate toolkit and if the flight observer had not decided to retain an indicator that monitored the flying-control locks, we would have finished in the oggin. Like the Viscount incident, I don't think you would have ever found the cause.' The aircraft arrived safely in Montreal.

Although the sight of the new aeroplane in the air brought fresh hope for additional sales, it was in direct competition with the Lockheed Electra. By now the Electra was already in service and had become the preferred choice of American carriers, though it was not without its own serious technical difficulties. With the delays caused by the Tyne engine, and by the design diversions at Weybridge into jet alternatives, the Americans had captured the available, but shrinking, market. Pure jets were rapidly replacing propeller-driven aircraft in most key carriers, and Vanguard orders, which in the early 1950s had been estimated at around 250, remained static.

When asked to explain the lack of sales in a BBC television interview eight months after the first flight, Sir George said: 'This sort of hysterical situation about using jets . . . you don't have propellers on, and everyone gets emotional about getting there a bit quicker. Whether it costs any more to go quicker seems to be rather secondary. The Vanguard is designed to have maximum economy. By international agreements [standardisation of fares, etc.] and one thing and another, it doesn't get a chance to use it. It's just the same as building a fast aeroplane and putting a speed limit on it.'

In the end BEA and TCA were the only 'from-new' customers operating Vanguards for some ten years, during which time they received a mixed reception. Passengers did not like them as much as Viscounts, and in any case they now preferred the advantages pure jet travel could bring. Even so, the low seat-mile costs and the heavy freight carriage earned both airlines a good return over the years. But by the late 1960s the development of more efficient high-bypass-ratio jets was making them highly economic on short journeys as well, and the Vanguards were phased out. A good number were converted into cargo carriers, in which role they operated successfully for many years.

While the manufacturer lost heavily, the operators did not. This point was made by Sir George when he assessed the Vanguard in a paper to the RAeS in 1973. He said: 'The Vanguard is full of morals. It came into head-to-head conflict with the American Electra, whereas it ought to have been a further extension of the Viscount and not a new aeroplane – and we lost our shirt on it. The chief moral of the Vanguard is that it is never any good doing something that is either level with, or behind the state of the art, merely because the operating costs are low. It is very true that the seat-mile costs on the Vanguard were attractively low. However, the only people who were not rewarded were those of us who made it – it lost us £16 million.'

During this period Sir George decided to take his flying proficiency to the next level by seeking to gain a Private Pilot's Licence (PPL) for multi-engined aircraft. Since first going solo in a Tiger Moth in 1948, he had flown regularly as second pilot in the Viscount (many times), Viking, Valetta and Valiant, and often in the company's Dove and Heron communications aircraft. Most of his flying was with Jock Bryce, but his formal training for his licence was put in the hands of Peter Marsh, formerly with BEA and now on the Vickers staff as a training captain.

Peter was selected for the duty by his colleagues, and approached the task with some trepidation. On their first flight together, Marsh asked Sir George how he wanted to play it. Edwards replied: 'Peter, inside the aeroplane you are in charge; outside, I am.'

Bryce has the highest regard for Edwards as a pilot. 'I think I must have been the only chief test pilot in Britain or America who had as their managing director an ex-chief designer who had a pilot's licence and was quite capable of flying the latest project under supervision. As for flying a serviceable aeroplane with an engine out or making a flapless landing, he was bloody good.'

But it was Edwards's contribution to and understanding of the flight development programme that impressed Bryce most. 'I think we have had the wrong idea over the years about GRE when he went flying, that it got him away from the trials and tribulations of the design office and gave him a bit of relief. It was nothing of the kind. He seriously wanted to understand how the aeroplane operated, just as much as how the fuel systems were designed and working. He took up flying seriously because of that. It was an extension of the design office, but it was the finished product, and he wanted to understand it.'

Duly, in August 1957, after being checked out by a Ministry examiner on a cross-country flight in the company's twin-engined Dove, Edwards was granted PPL number 46977, clearing him to command single- and multi-engined types including, and particularly, the Viscount and Heron. His licence was to remain valid throughout his career and up to 1976, after he had retired.

CHAPTER SIXTEEN

The VC10 – 'A Sorry Story'

In 1957, while the Vickers Board were debating the future of the Vanguard they were presented with a new and more ambitious proposal for another civil project. This was for a long-range, high-performance jet airliner for BOAC. It came just over a year after the airline's rejection of the V1000, and must have been viewed with a high degree of scepticism and concern. As a private venture it would carry a huge financial risk for the company. To compound the problem, BOAC required a specialist aircraft that could operate in the difficult 'hot-and-high' airfield conditions in the Far East and the southern hemisphere, which prohibited the use of its 707s, which needed longer runways than were available. Consequently only a limited number of aircraft was needed. The opportunity had already been rejected by de Havilland as uneconomic when asked to develop a Comet V for the purpose.

Once again Vickers faced the dilemma of building an aircraft to a tailor-made and limiting specification from a national airline which had already proved unreliable, or face the possibility of a serious work shortage. By now Valiant production at Weybridge had less than a year to run, and there were no further orders in the pipeline. Sir George was quoted at the time as saying: 'It looks as if we will have to keep Weybridge going without a single piece of government paper in the place. Nobody has ever tried it before, and it's going to be a highly interesting experience.'

The details of the BOAC requirement were spelt out at a meeting between the two parties in April 1957. Although the government could offer no financial aid, it did show sufficient interest by sending senior officials to the meeting. BOAC confirmed its need for twenty-five aircraft, with options on a further ten. Vickers, which had rather optimistically put the break-even figure at forty-five aircraft, insisted that the first order must be at least for the full thirty-five aircraft at a higher price than was being offered. Sir George reminded the meeting of the heavy losses that could be incurred on the Vanguard, another aircraft designed specifically to meet the needs of a national carrier.

Vickers, however, was aware of a BOAC forecast for sixty-two aircraft of this type, and believed that further orders must come. Encouraged by this, and by a much more favourable relationship with the airline's current chairman, Sir Gerard 'Pops' d'Erlanger, the gamble was taken and the VC10 was born. In January 1958 BOAC signed a contact for thirty-five Standard VC10s seating 147 passengers, plus options on twenty more, valued at £77.5 million. By this time the airline was even talking about 'an all-VC10 fleet', encouraged by the development proposal for a stretched, longer-range version, the Super VC10, seating up to 191 passengers. Such an aircraft would be suitable for the North Atlantic services and other routes being served by the 707. For the time being the prospect looked good.

Sir George remembers how the design evolved, working with his senior team headed by Hugh Hemsley, chief engineer. 'BOAC wanted an aeroplane that could fly from Singapore to Karachi and get in and out of Kano [Nigeria] and Nairobi. It was that sort of hop, with difficult airfields at both ends and difficult temperatures. It was obvious that we had to do something pretty special in the way of overall lift-curve coefficient to get it out of an airfield at one end (Singapore was then a pocket handkerchief) and get it in the other end. We poked about at some length to see what we could do about it.'

But it was Edwards himself who sketched out the first drawings at home one weekend. His contribution came to light only when Princess Margaret, before visiting Weybridge, asked if she could see how an aeroplane was designed. Sir George recalled later that he 'turned pale', but suggested they put out as many drawings as they could get. 'We found these original bits I'd done at home, and put them end to end on the bench for her to see,' he says.

The final design was 'all very straightforward', says Sir George. 'In the Valiant we buried the engines in the wing roots. It was pretty obvious that the sort of power we were now going to need to carry the fuel and do the range meant that there was no practical way of stuffing the engines of the right size in the wing roots. They had to be put somewhere else. There was the usual argy-bargy about hanging the engines under the wing like a Christmas tree, for which you needed to break the landing flaps into small sections, with a loss of lift. To get the performance we needed you had to have unbroken flaps and slats, and there was nowhere else to put the engines except at the back.'

Sir George recalls that everybody told him he could not do that, but he reminded them that the French had done it successfully with the Caravelle. 'So we took a brave decision and did some projects with the engines stuck on the back. We optimistically worked out the lift coefficient we were going to get, and then built in a bit of drag into the engine installation in the back that we hadn't reckoned with.'

The result was an aircraft that could land and take off around 20kt slower than the 707 and had enough power and performance to meet the very demanding airfield requirements. Placing the engines in the rear with 'the noise at the back' gave an added and unexpected advantage: the passenger cabin was exceptionally quiet. Sir George says: 'This was sheer accident.'

With the basic configuration settled, the VC10 emerged as the first aircraft to have four engines grouped in the rear. These were to be the Rolls-Royce Conway bypass turbojets originally selected for the V1000, but now uprated to over 20,000lb thrust, a level disputed by BOAC for the V1000, and as used in its 707s. The aircraft could carry a maximum of 150 passengers in six-abreast seating over distances up to 4,000 miles. It was destined to become the most powerful airliner in the world when it entered service, having 10,000lb more thrust on take-off than any other jet transport at that time.

Like its predecessors, the VC10 benefited from the Weybridge manufacturing techniques, with massive integrally machined members in a multi-spar wing and in the supporting fuselage hoop frames. It was estimated that more than half of its structural weight was made up of parts machined from solid aluminium alloy.

In 1957 BOAC described the aircraft as 'The most promising conception of which we have details and as attractive an aeroplane as we can hope to obtain for our eastern-hemisphere operations for service 1963–64'. Sir Gerard d'Erlanger wrote to the Minister: 'The VC10 fulfils technically and operationally all the requirements of the Corporation on these routes.'

Sir George says he had a deal with the chairman 'that, despite all the bad feeling that had gone on over the years, this was one in which they were really going to support it and us. They expected me to turn out a good aeroplane that they were ready to use and make some money on. There was a period when there was some agreement. But it didn't last.'

What happened next, and why Vickers had gambled on the VC10, was recounted by Sir George for the television programme *All Our Working Lives*, broadcast by the BBC in 1981. He said: 'There certainly was a programme in which a large fleet of VC10s was going to be the backbone of the BOAC operation, and there was certainly a number of people in important positions in the airline who at that time saw the elimination of the 707 fleet and BOAC becoming a total VC10 fleet. This was because we had already invented a larger version of the aeroplane in which its good airfield performance enabled us to put on a bigger body and carry a much bigger payload within the bigger airfields that were now beginning to appear. So it looked a good bet.'

But the BOAC position was soon to change, as Sir George explained. 'As time went by the pressure within the Corporation to unify the fleet went through 180° to unify the fleet on the 707 instead of the VC10s. The compromise that came out at the end was that they had a mixed fleet.'

The shift in BOAC policy coincided with financial troubles at Vickers, when it was discovered that the cost estimates for the aircraft had been underestimated by what George Edwards described to a Parliamentary Select Committee as 'quite a lot'. It was essential for the continuation of the programme that ten of the outstanding option aircraft be converted into orders. Despite opposition to the contract from the new BOAC chairman, Sir Mathew Slattery, the Minister, Duncan Sandys, supported the proposal. This was mainly because it fitted into government merger plans for the aircraft industry, of which a healthy Vickers would be a major part.

Accordingly, in June 1960, BOAC signed contracts for ten of the twenty aircraft on option, but specified that they be the enlarged Super VC10, bringing the order to forty-five aircraft in all.

Within the next year further alterations were made by BOAC, both to the mix between the two VC10 types and the size of the Super VC10, which was cut down from 193 to 163 seats because the airline thought it was too big for the North Atlantic and other routes. The contract was altered to fifteen Standard (later reduced to twelve, for which compensation was paid) and thirty Super VC10s.

So, with the known lack of enthusiasm in the highest ranks of the airline, it was a huge relief to Vickers that the RAF was now showing interest in the aircraft for its renewed high-speed, long-range transport requirement, for which the Ministry had issued Specification C.239. An initial order for six military versions was placed, though Vickers had to apply twice for launching aid, which totalled £10.2 million and eventually reached £50 million. But, as Charles Gardner pointed out: 'Nonetheless, there was a military need for the RAF VC10 which was for so many years to give splendid service to the nation.'

The RAF aircraft had a standard VC10 fuselage matched to uprated engines and the wings of the Super VC10. Capacity had been slightly reduced to provide outstanding performance suitable for flexible military operations on many of the same routes as BOAC. It proved to be highly effective in service, primarily as a fast long-range transport and later as an aerial tanker, and was still operating at the time of writing.

In his book *Test Pilot*, Brian Trubshaw recalls how, much later, the RAF adopted the Super VC10 for the tanker role. He had been talking to Air Marshal Sir Peter Terry at Sir George Edwards's annual cricket match against the Operational Requirements Branch (ORB) at Weybridge. Trubshaw told him that they were repossessing four Super VC10s that had been supplied to East African Airways. 'That is just what I may be looking for,' the Air Marshal replied. That evening an ad hoc detailed discussion took place between Sir Peter Terry, Sir George Edwards and Ernie Marshall, who was now VC10 project designer. 'Calculations for conversion of nine VC10/Super VC10s were done on a scrap of paper. I remember a figure of about £35 million being spoken of and a serious project begun,' wrote Trubshaw.

Sir George says: 'I had a good relationship with the OR blokes and the Air Ministry. They knew that if I said we would do something there would have to be a pretty sound reason why not.'

On 29 June 1962 the first VC10 made its first flight with Jock Bryce and Brian Trubshaw at the controls. It was made from the Brooklands runway, which was only 1,300yd long. Not for the first time the choice of a short runway for a maiden flight surprised many. But not those who knew that Sir George wanted to demonstrate its short-field performance from the outset, in the same way that he had insisted on the Valiant flying from the grass strip at Wisley. 'Everybody thought I was bonkers to make a first flight with a big new-style aeroplane like that out of a little saucer of an aerodrome like Brooklands,' he says.

A large crowd gathered at Weybridge to witness the event, including the media and the Minister of Aviation, Julian Amery. Sir George remembers waiting for the flight with the Minister, sitting in the Dove communications aircraft that would follow the VC10 to Wisley. 'Amery asked me how I felt. I said I thought a country bank manager would be a highly attractive job at the moment. When we got to Wisley he asked how I now felt about the country bank manager's job. I said I think I had better stick with this one.'

Although the first flight was a success, the aircraft was soon found to have serious drag and stalling problems. 'It was what you might call an interesting programme right from the start, and when we got on to the stalling it became more interesting,' says Sir George. 'We couldn't get it right for a long time. We had to put fences along the wing to stop the flow outwards. Stalls on a high-aspect-ratio, high-sweep-back aircraft are the devil to put right. But we did, and got there in the end.'

It was 'typical Sir George Edwards' that he insisted on experiencing the dangerous stalling problem himself, as an observer on a test flight. He recalls: 'It wasn't a very light-hearted occupation, going on a VC10 and stalling the thing, knowing that the right-hand wing was going to go down like a ton of bricks. I had to see at first hand what a wing-drop was like. You couldn't really get any idea from the words somebody was telling you. You had to go and measure the rate at which we were taking the speed off and sit there, all composed, and say to yourself: "What are they all worried about? I can't see it." Then suddenly, whoosh – oh boy! You stopped arguing about it after that; but I enjoyed it.'

Did the pilots enjoy having the boss on board for such critical tests? 'No, they welcomed it,' says Sir George. 'I was the sort of bloke they had been looking for for years. Somebody to whom they could say – "You do that, and see what happens".'

The VC10 entered service with BOAC in 1963, and soon began to win favour with the passengers, who liked the quiet, smooth ride. It was attracting higher payloads than the 707, but BOAC's new chairman, Sir Giles Guthrie, was unimpressed, as he wished to convert to an all-American fleet. He decided to cut the order for thirty Super VC10s to seven, and then to cancel them all.

By now, according to Charles Gardner, the airline 'orchestrated a campaign against the VC10 in certain parts of the media'. The government, however, refused to let BOAC cancel all its VC10s, although it did allow a further reduction to 12 Standard and 17 Super VC10s, a total of 29 aircraft out of a projected 62 at the time of the first contracts. The damage to any other prospective sales was insurmountable, and only British United Airways (BUA) (3), Ghana Airways (3) and East African Airways (5) placed orders.

Sir George says: 'I suppose the conditions BOAC laid down, range, aerodrome performance and all that, made it more expensive per seat-mile cost to operate than Boeing got into the 707. So there must have been some justification for BOAC going for the 707, but there wasn't much. Roughly speaking, if you couldn't sell to your own airline the chance of selling it outside wasn't very great.' He adds: 'It was a sorry story. The whole relationship between BOAC and the industry at that time was bloody awful and did the industry a power of no good. It has never been repaired. If I were given the job all over again to produce a BOAC jet that was a bit special, I would be looking over my shoulder all the time to see what was following up behind. It seems childish, but the atmosphere has never really been repaired.'

The VC10's effectiveness in service has long been the subject of debate. There is evidence that, on introduction into service, they were achieving load factors nearly 20 per cent higher than the average of fourteen other airlines, and were soon attracting average payloads of 70 per cent, which, according to Charles Gardner, made them a bigger profit earner than the optimum 707. These high numbers were sustained by BOAC as the aircraft became ever more popular, becoming the preferred choice of regular passengers despite extensive choice.

Gardner concluded: 'So the Super VC10, denigrated in advance by BOAC as too expensive to operate economically – and for which they obtained some £30 million in subsidy as recompense – turned out to be actually cheaper to fly than the 707 and also attract more passengers.'

And it did not impress Sir George to read in the BOAC annual report that, after ten years in service, its Super VC10s returned higher utilisation and lower costs than the contemporary Boeing 707. He commented at the time: 'Whatever the arguments, we gave the VC10 the fundamental advantage of superior passenger attraction, which no amount of comparative cost formulae take any account of, and which has sustained it to this day.'

CHAPTER SEVENTEEN

Rationalisation

In 1959 steps were taken by the government to rationalise the British aircraft industry. As a prelude to describing this process, it is necessary to return to the beginning of the decade. At that time the industry, reactivated by the demands of the Korean War and the continuing Russian threat, had survived virtually intact despite earlier attempts to reduce it. Of the twenty-seven airframe and eight engine manufacturers that existed at the end of the Second World War, all but two airframe manufacturers and one engine manufacturer (nearly all of whom were involved in mergers) were still operating. There were now more airframe companies in the UK than in the USA, which was patently absurd.

Despite a series of crippling and wasteful cancellations the industry had built up a formidable technical capability. British brains and talent were in abundance, as demonstrated by the technology employed in designing and building the world's first jet and turboprop airliners, three V-bombers (however unnecessary), and a series of high-performance jet fighters. It was now turning its attention to a supersonic transport, vertical take-off and landing (VTOL), and advanced projects of all kinds. No wonder Sir George referred to the period as 'great days' for the designers in Britain's aircraft industry.

By general consensus, however, the industry was too big for the national requirement, especially as development times and costs were increasing pro rata at a significant and ever quickening rate. It had survived in its present form only because of the dogged resistance of the companies themselves and their indomitable leaders, which had been sustained by a government procurement system that allowed contracts to be awarded on a 'Buggins's turn' basis. Although this encouraged competition and stimulated technological advancement, it had also led to misjudgement and miscalculation, causing the abandonment or modification of so many projects that could have been true world-beaters.

In 1954 the distinguished civil servant Denis Haviland, then Under Secretary at the MoS, produced a carefully constructed paper in which he said the industry could no longer rely on 'Buggins's turn', which had spread even more thinly the work affordable by the nation. Haviland said the industry should reorganise itself into fewer, stronger units, and that new contracts should be placed only with firms or groups of firms with the resources to handle them.

'But there was great unwillingness to do so,' says Sir George. 'It was fairly obvious there were a lot of companies for the amount of work that was spread around. And of course nobody was keen to give up their patch and present it to somebody else. A minister, Aubrey Jones, was given the job of persuading the companies, who were a pretty rugged lot, to accept the inevitable and join with other people. But the thing that governed the government's hopes was that the industry would do it themselves. Nobody had great faith in Aubrey Jones doing it. I remember Handley Page discussing Aubrey Jones's antics in very unfavourable terms and, of course, he hung out to the bitter end when everybody else had done some sort of merger.'

Another reason why the companies were 'not mad keen to do it' was the loss of competitiveness among them, says Sir George. 'You see, it was pretty necessary to give blokes who were working for you the general feeling that their aim in life was to knock the hell out of everybody else who was in the way. So there was no great enthusiasm on the part of the individuals in the old companies, a number of which had a tremendous history, to merge.'

Did he have sympathy for the government in trying to reduce numbers? 'Not seriously,' he says. 'I think it needed the sort of pressure that said: "Here is a job of work for you to do if you are willing to join up with somebody else. If you are not, that's too bad, there aren't any jobs." The chap who would know, who was in the middle of it, was Denis Haviland.'

Another problem that frustrated the development of projects and a sensible reshaping of the industry was the destructive role played by the Treasury. Denis Haviland later confirmed what Sir George and others believed: that there was nothing less than civil war raging in Whitehall between the Treasury, often supported by the Board of Trade, and the RAF, supported by other aviation interests.

Haviland wrote: 'From 1954 to the time I left the civil service in 1964, and indeed after, the Treasury never missed the opportunity presented by a proposed new programme, or by a variation or extension of an existing one, or even by the due provisioning of the next slice of funding for a cabinet authorised project, to mount a major attack. Its continual objective was to reverse government aviation policy and decisions on the grounds that the military programme of the day was too large and that the civil programme was uneconomic.'

In his 1981 television broadcast, Sir George referred to this situation, and how the industry was denied direct formal contact with the Treasury. 'You never got officially into the Treasury. Rough chaps from industry weren't allowed in.' He added: 'You got to know chaps from the Treasury, and, as you got to know them, you talked to them and understood their process of thinking. One of their first processes, when somebody wants some money for something, is to say "No". That is process number one, and that goes on for as long as they can sustain it.'

But it was not directly the Treasury that delivered the knock-out blow to the self interests of British aviation and brought about the shotgun marriages that redefined the industry. That came in 1957, with the controversial Sandys White Paper on Defence, which effectively advocated the scrapping of almost all of the RAF's manned aircraft in favour of unmanned missiles. It precipitated another round of cancellations. These included the Avro Mach 2-plus bomber, the Fairey Delta world airspeed record holder (later 'highjacked' by the French and turned into the fabulously successful Dassault Mirage family), the Saunders-Roe mixed-powerplant rocket-plus-jet fighter (which had already attracted interest from Germany and Japan) and, perhaps most significantly, the nearly complete Hawker P.1121 supersonic fighter. Sir Sydney Camm, Hawker's most celebrated designer and a good friend of George Edwards, described it as 'the greatest miss in British aviation'. The only surviving major project was OR.339, the Canberra replacement, which was to become TSR.2 (Tactical Strike and Reconnaissance Mach 2), and the catalyst for merger.

In his history of BAC, Charles Gardner wrote: 'The brutal fact remained that at a stroke Sandys killed all the advanced projects together with some of the engines to power them which were in the 1957 pipeline. He demoralised the Royal Air Force and the industry and set British military aviation back by at least several years – some say by a decade. Looking back on the period 1946–58, it still challenges comprehension that such a mess could be made of such a favourable initial situation.'

Sir George Edwards was at first 'shattered' by the Sandys Report, but was more sanguine about its purpose. 'It was essentially pointing the way towards a new technique of waging war in which you didn't need a man. It would all get done with the aid of electronics and, taking a long view, it was pretty far-seeing as to what eventually happened. Geoffrey Tuttle got in the doghouse in the Air Ministry because he was seen to be, if not in favour, then prepared to listen to what Sandys was saying. They became quite friendly. All those who had become Air Marshals by virtue of flying aeroplanes could see it was possible that nobody was going to fly any more. They were all going to sit at desks and press buttons, and they could see that would be the beginning of the end of pilots in the RAF.'

Some years later, after the Sandys proposals had been much modified, Sir George told an audience in London that he believed the document had been 'misinterpreted', particularly as it had the 'great merit of pulling together the confused and sprawling situation' following the Korean War, and set out a recognisable defence policy. 'Although some of us disagreed with much of its detail (and a good deal of this has been straightened out since) we must recognise that it was a courageous and necessary step.'

Although the Sandys Report was to bring about the destruction of many of Britain's most advanced and promising new aircraft of the period, in 1959 it did achieve, perhaps inadvertently, the government objective of rationalisation. The carrot of TSR.2 successfully forced the industry into mergers, reducing it from some twenty-five airframe companies to two major groups. It was a process Sir George described as 'golden welding flux'.

While the ramifications over Sandys were being digested by an industry which depended on 70 per cent military work, the civil sector was still struggling with the vacillating and precise demands of the country's two major airlines. Their limited but understandably tailor-made requirements had already frustrated hopes of international market penetration. Sir George had repeatedly warned of the dangers of such narrow definition, which could confine a new airliner's prospects to meeting only a national need, possibly at the expense of the wider international acceptance necessary for large-scale orders which would reduce the unit price to competitive levels. He described the situation as 'trying to sell off the thick end of the learning curve', while the USA could export from the 'thin end' of the large production numbers required for its own home market alone.

Such was the case in 1957, when BEA laid down a specification for a new airliner. The airline, already equipped with Viscounts and awaiting delivery of the Vanguard, now required a short/medium-haul jet for service in 1964. It wanted an 80-seat aircraft with a range of 1,000 miles, preferably with three engines. De Havilland, Bristol and Vickers (by necessity of the shortage of work) all entered the contest. Weybridge proposed the VC11, a smaller version of the VC10 powered by four Rolls-Royce RB.163 engines, later to become the Spey.

In meeting such a specific requirement, for which the prospect of some government launching aid offered the most compelling inducement, Edwards and the team decided to design an aircraft that was not totally compliant. To be a viable proposition it had to have a broader appeal to attract essential overseas airline customers.

'For a time we took the VC11 quite seriously,' says Sir George. 'The government viewed it with some favour, because it wasn't going to demand a lot of money out of them to build it. The basic design we had already got in the VC10, and I don't think there is any doubt it would have been a good aeroplane.' However, by now the Sandys Report and the efforts of Aubrey Jones and Denis Haviland to achieve rationalisation were being brought to bear in the civil market. They decided that the BEA contract would only be placed with a new merged company or group of companies. Although they had stated a preference for the de Havilland design, the whole procurement process was held up while the contestants vied for partners.

However, before partnerships could be settled, BEA effectively sealed the VC11's fate. It deemed it to be too big. In Sir George's view a scaled-down version would have been too small for worldwide appeal. He withdrew from the BEA competition, but continued development, as a private venture, for the international market.

The BEA order was finally placed with a consortium led by de Havilland for the three-engine DH.121, later to become the Trident, to be powered by the new Rolls-Royce RB.141 bypass engine, the Medway. In this form it was almost identical to the rival Boeing 727. Unfortunately, a reduction in BEA passenger numbers convinced the airline that the DH.121 was too big. It decided to cut it down, both in capacity and range, thus severely limiting overseas appeal and robbing the British industry once again of huge export potential. This was lapped up by the Boeing 727, which went on to become the world's largest-selling airliner in its era. In his book *Project Cancelled*, Derek Wood writes that Britain was on the verge of building the right aeroplane for the market: 'But with a dip in traffic growth BEA panicked and decided the 121 was too large and had to be cut down. . . . At one blow the 121 was emasculated.'

BEA's 'panic' measure had the most profound implications, not only for the Trident, but for Britain and for Sir George personally. Not only did it give the Boeing 727 free rein in the market, but the 'emasculated' Trident relinquished the very promising Rolls-Royce Medway engine in favour of the less-powerful RB.163 Spey. Eventually the Medway, lacking a firm foundation, was scrapped, depriving both the TSR.2 and, later, the BAC One-Eleven, of a powerplant that could have materially enhanced the progress of both. Sir George later described the cancellation of the Medway as one of the key bad decisions of all time, ranking with the V1000. 'If the Medway had been chosen for the TSR.2, then the TSR.2 might well never have been cancelled,' he said.

For a time the VC11 retained a high priority at Weybridge. Many airlines showed interest, among them TCA, through Sir George's old friend Gordon McGregor, who confirmed options on fourteen aircraft. In doing so he overruled some of his senior colleagues, who again favoured US aircraft. 'It is true to say Gordon McGregor placed the importance of his own personal judgement of the outfit he was buying from, and most importantly the chaps who were in charge of it, above [the judgement of] those in his airline, who were wedded to Douglas and all that,' says Sir George. Continental Airlines, too, was 'quite firm' that the VC11 was the best medium jet for its purpose.

Hopes for the VC11 were further boosted when, as a sop to encourage Vickers to merge to form what was to become BAC, the government offered to pay 50 per cent of the launching costs, subject to go-ahead. However, by now some market resistance to a four-engine short/medium-haul jet was being experienced. Sir George was aware of this. 'You are always between the devil and the deep blue sea. You have got to have enough power to do the things it has to do. That was the argument for the [six-engine Convair] B-36 [American bomber]. But when you are working out the operating costs, it is pretty pricey having four engines,' he says.

But, most worryingly, at a time when both the Vanguard and VC10 were running into trouble, the financial break-even figure for the VC11 was put at seventy-two aircraft in order to qualify for launching aid, and that figure still looked a long way off. By now a new prospect had emerged from within the company, the Hunting H.107, acquired when Hunting was absorbed into BAC. It was to lead to the BAC One-Eleven, the full story of which will be told later.

An early photograph of the young George Edwards, together with his 'beloved' auntie Sal (Medlock), who, with her husband, brought him up. The picture was taken in the garden of their house in Handsworth Avenue, Highams Park, date unknown, but probably 1919, when George was 11. Even at such an early age George is unmistakable, dressed in his Eton collar and Sunday-best suit. *(Edwards family)*

Below: George Edwards was born above his father's toyshop, now a solicitor's office (as here) but then 12 The Parade, Hale End Road, Highams Park, on 9 July 1908. His twin sister died in childbirth, and his mother of childbirth fever shortly afterwards. *(Author)*

Waltham Forest Heritage has erected a plaque to mark Edwards's birthplace and acknowledge his achievements. *(Author)*

A rare photograph of George's father, Edwin, with characteristic and almost permanently attached cigarette. His son said his father eventually killed himself by smoking. 'Being a tobacconist, he had just to put his hand out and there was another cigarette,' he said. After the death of George's mother in childbirth, Edwin became a somewhat remote figure to his son, but retained a keen interest in his education. *(Edwards family)*

George married Marjorie Thurgood, forever known as 'Dinah', at All Saints' Church, Highams Park in October 1935. Dinah lived close by and was his only known girlfriend, having met him on the train taking them to technical college. Six months earlier he had left his job in London's docks to join the Vickers Aviation Company at Weybridge, and shortly afterwards the couple moved into their first home in Dartnell Park, West Byfleet. *(Ada Marshall/Edwards family)*

The Weybridge drawing office in 1935, at the time of George Edwards's arrival as a design-draughtsman at the Vickers Aviation Company. 'It was pretty humble, working alongside 300 other people. We were in one big room, not dissimilar to being in a greenhouse,' he said later. Edwards had a 'pitch' near the front, and he can just be identified immediately to the right of the second window frame from the left. In the front row on the extreme left, working on a temporary trestle table, is a youthful Norman 'Spud' Boorer, who became a member of Edwards's first group and remained with him, on and off, throughout his career. (Fox Photos)

The Vickers aircraft factory at Brooklands, Weybridge, 1936. On the east side of the racing circuit, the factory was originally started in 1915, in the former Itala motor works, before being expanded for wartime aircraft production. (Vickers (Aviation) Ltd)

The G.4/31 general-purpose military biplane (top) was the first aircraft George Edwards worked on, and the first Weybridge aircraft to incorporate Barnes Wallis's geodetic structure, in its rear fuselage. Its success led to the technically advanced all-geodetic Wellesley monoplane (above) and, later, the Wellington. (Norman Barfield)

Rex Pierson, Vickers's revered chief designer for twenty-eight years, from 1917 to 1945. *(Vickers (Aviation) Ltd)*

The prototype Wellington, K4049, with the George Edwards-designed tail section, for which the fin shape was copied from the Supermarine Stranraer flying boat on the advice of chief designer Rex Pierson and chief test pilot Mutt Summers. *(Vickers (Aircraft) Ltd)*

The famous Terence Cuneo painting of the specially adapted anti-magnetic-mine Wellington detonating its first German mine over the Thames Estuary. George Edwards and his group had project responsibility, and completed the task, from drawings to delivery, in just over two months. This was later described as 'an almost unbelievable feat', and the device's success led to his promotion to experimental manager during the war. Much later the painting was presented to Sir George Edwards, and hung in the hallway of his home in Guildford. *(British Aerospace Aircraft Group)*

The high-performance 'Metal Mossie' under construction in George Edwards's experimental shops at Foxwarren, Cobham. The aircraft was flown in December 1942 at Farnborough, but did not go into production as the wooden de Havilland Mosquito was adopted for its intended role. (*Vickers-Armstrongs Ltd*)

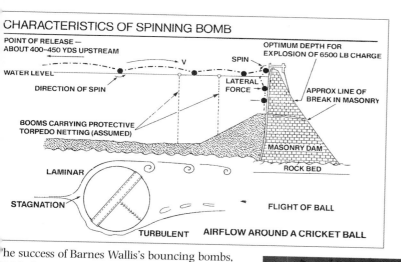

CHARACTERISTICS OF SPINNING BOMB

POINT OF RELEASE —
ABOUT 400–450 YDS UPSTREAM

OPTIMUM DEPTH FOR
EXPLOSION OF 6500 LB CHARGE

V   SPIN

WATER LEVEL

DIRECTION OF SPIN

LATERAL
FORCE

APPROX LINE OF
BREAK IN MASONRY

BOOMS CARRYING PROTECTIVE
TORPEDO NETTING (ASSUMED)

MASONRY DAM

ROCK BED

LAMINAR

STAGNATION

TURBULENT

FLIGHT OF BALL

AIRFLOW AROUND A CRICKET BALL

The success of Barnes Wallis's bouncing bombs, which destroyed the dams on the Ruhr, has become an epic of the Second World War. Applying back-spin to the bomb before release, as proposed by George Edwards based on his experience as a leg-spin bowler, allowed it to bounce regularly and accurately. (*Norman Barfield*)

Barnes Wallis, the legendary designer with whom George Edwards had a respectful but uneasy relationship. (*Vickers Aircraft Ltd*)

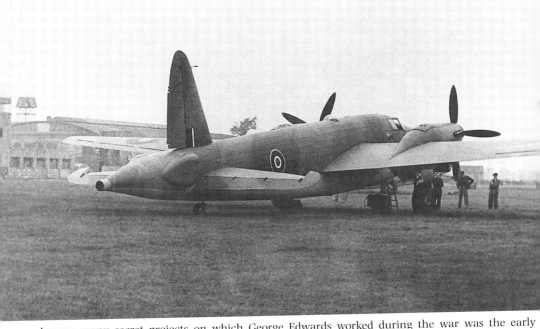

Among many secret projects on which George Edwards worked during the war was the early development of the jet engine. He was responsible for installing the experimental Frank Whittle-designed Power Jets engine in the tail of a Wellington. (*Vickers-Armstrongs Ltd*)

The prototype Viking, built in ten months by George Edwards in his experimental department, is rolled out for flight in June 1945. The Viking was Britain's first post-war airliner. On becoming chief designer that year, Edwards was responsible for developing the aircraft and expanding the family to include the Valetta military transport and the Varsity trainer. Nearly 600 aircraft were built. Seen walking in front of the new Viking are two stalwarts of the experimental department: Bill Vincent on the left and Bob Simpson on the right. (*Norman Barfield*)

In July 1945 George Edwards became one of the first civilians to enter Germany within weeks of the capitulation. Dressed in obligatory RAF observer's uniform, he toured Germany's secret research and production facilities as a member of the Farren Mission. He is seen here near the Messerschmitt flight development centre near Oberammergau with two colleagues, J.E. Serby (left), who represented the governmental director of technical development, and F.H. Lloyd (centre), manager of the Hawker Aircraft drawing office. *(RAE/Edwards family)*

Mutt Summers, Vickers's renowned chief test pilot (right) with George Edwards, chief designer, in 1948 after successfully capturing the speed record between London and Paris in a jet-powered Nene Viking in a time of just over 34min. *(Keystone Press Agency)*

George and Dinah Edwards moved into their new home Durleston, in Lower Road, Bookham, Surrey, in 1946, soon after he was appointed chief designer. The family were to remain there for more than twenty happy years. *(Edwards family)*

The prototype Viscount, on which George Edwards made his name. The original design concept came from Rex Pierson, but when Edwards became chief designer in 1945 he developed the aircraft, made several important design changes and, against the odds, chose the Rolls-Royce Dart engine. (*British European Airways*)

Lord Brabazon (left) with George Edwards in the mid-1950s. The original Viscount design was produced in response to a general requirement laid down by the Brabazon Committee of 1944, but was much altered to allow for a propeller-turbine aircraft, at the insistence of Vickers. (*Unknown/Edwards family*)

George Edwards and Peter Masefield (right) about to board the new BEA Vickers Viscount in 1955. Edwards credits Masefield with being responsible for getting the new airliner into service with BEA from 1950. Masefield wrote that George Edwards was 'one of the most impressive people in the entire plane-making industry'. (*BEA/Edwards family*)

Gordon McGregor, president of TCA (left), first flew the Viscount in 1949, and returned to Canada 'singing its praises'. His airline became the first North American operator to choose the Viscount, and eventually bought fifty-one aircraft. McGregor much admired Edwards (right), and the two became close personal friends. *(Ed Bermingham/Edwards family)*

J.H. 'Slim' Carmachael (right), president of Capital Airlines of Washington, DC, with George Edwards shortly after Capital had ordered forty Viscounts in 1954. It was the largest single dollar order ever placed in Britain, valued at $45 million. This was quickly increased to sixty aircraft. *(Vickers-Armstrongs (Aircraft) Ltd)*

Throughout his working life George Edwards was never happier than when he was at the drawing board, mapping out his ideas. He is seen here (centre) in characteristic pose in the late 1940s with his senior design office colleagues. Left to right: Hugh Hemsley (aerodynamics and flight test), Ernie Marshall (projects) and Basil Stephenson (structures). *(Norman Barfield)*

Away from the office, George Edwards always enjoyed competitive sport. His love of cricket was well known, but he was also a keen golfer. He played regularly at the RAC Club in Epsom, and later usually turned out for the annual golf match for the industry against the RAF. (*Edwards family*)

George Edwards and his secretary, Joyce Brixey, hand out the presents at the annual children's Christmas party at Weybridge in 1953. Mrs Brixey remained his secretary/personal assistant for more than fifty years. (*Vickers-Armstrongs (Aircraft) Ltd*)

Sir Hew Kilner, managing director at Weybridge (third from the left), with his wife and George and Dinah Edwards shortly before Kilner retired owing to ill health in 1953. He was succeeded by Edwards, whom he had appointed chief designer in 1945. Kilner had always provided solid support for Edwards and the Viscount, even through its difficult early days. (*A.V. Swaebe W.1./Edwards family*)

The classic photograph by Charles E. Brown of the Vickers Valiant, Britain's first V-bomber, designed by George Edwards. It first flew in 1951, having been developed and built in record time. (*Charles E. Brown/Vickers Ltd*)

The Valiant was George Edwards's favourite aeroplane, and to mark its introduction into service a painting by the then promising artist David Shepherd was commissioned and proudly shown off by George Edwards. It now hangs in the RAF Club in London. (*Vickers-Armstrongs (Aircraft) Ltd*)

For a time the USA took a keen interest in the Valiant, and senior USAF officers visited the new flight test centre at Hurn, near Bournemouth, to inspect the aircraft. They included the famed Gen Curtis Le May (second from left, next to George Edwards), head of Strategic Air Command. Also in the photograph are Air Chief Marshal Sir Ralph Cochrane (extreme left) and, next to Edwards from left to right: Sir John Slessor, formerly CAS, Sir Hew Kilner, managing director at Weybridge, Gen Vandenburg, Chief of the American Air Staff, and Gen Griswold, who commanded the USAF in Britain. (*Vickers-Armstrongs (Aircraft) Ltd*)

The cancellation of the George Edwards-designed V1000 jet transport, seen nearing completion at Wisley, was later described by Edwards as 'the biggest blunder of all'. It could have been the first non-stop jet airliner in service across the key North Atlantic route, but was abandoned within a few months of first flight, leaving the field open to the American Boeing 707 and the Douglas DC-8. (BAESYSTEMS)

Ernie Bass (second from right) with George, Dinah and Dingle (right) aboard the *Queen Elizabeth* in 1956. Ernie Bass was chief engineer with the Shell Aviation Petroleum Company, and worked closely with both Vickers and Rolls-Royce on the development of the fuel required for the new age of turbine-powered aircraft. Ernie and George and their families became the closest friends. (Edwards family)

The Vanguard was designed as a logical successor to the Viscount, but technical problems with the engines, and other matters, delayed its entry into service, by which time airlines were abandoning turboprop aircraft to meet public demand for jets. (BAESYSTEMS)

In the hot seat. The now Sir George Edwards came under increasing pressure over the failure of the Vanguard to win substantial sales, and in 1959 was interviewed for BBC television by Raymond Baxter. Sir George said the Vanguard had been conceived to be the most economic airliner in the world, which it was, but had been overtaken by the swift development of jet airliners, which were less efficient but faster. *(Frandor (Frank Rice) of Byfleet)*

The prototype TSR.2 nears completion at Weybridge in 1964. TSR.2 was the most ambitious, technically demanding, and controversial military aircraft of its time, but it was also the catalyst for the formation of BAC in 1960. *(BAC)*

Lord Mountbatten, Chief of the Defence Staff, arrives at Weybridge for a TSR.2 briefing. He is met by Sir George, who was in charge of the project, and Lord Portal, chairman of BAC (to his right). Sir Geoffrey Tuttle is just alighting from the company's Dove communications aircraft. Mountbatten strongly opposed TSR.2, preferring the Royal Navy's Buccaneer, but his methods were criticised by his biographer, Philip Ziegler, who wrote: 'He pushed his campaign against TSR.2 to the limit of the scrupulous, some would say beyond it.' *(BAESYSTEMS)*

The first prototype TSR.2 takes off from Boscombe Down on Sunday 27 September 1964 on its maiden flight. Six months later it was cancelled. *(BAESYSTEMS)*

Prime Minister Harold Wilson is greeted by Sir George on arriving at BAC Warton. Freddie Page, then managing director of the Military Aircraft Division, is making the introductions. In the 1964 election campaign, which was won by Labour, Wilson was reported to have given assurances on the future of TSR.2 at a meeting at Preston. But in March 1965 he presided over a cabinet meeting which voted to cancel it in preference to the American TFX (F-111), which was also later abandoned. *(BAESYSTEMS)*

The Anglo-French Jaguar was one of two new collaborative aircraft projects negotiated with the French by Defence Minister Denis Healey after the cancellation of TSR.2. Jaguar became a highly successful and long-serving fighter in both Britain and France and with overseas customers, notably India, where it was built under licence. *(Image in Industry)*

The aircraft that replaced the abandoned TSR.2 in the essential strike roles was the Tornado multi-role combat aircraft, built by Britain, Germany and Italy. Here, a model of the new aircraft is shown to Prince Charles at the 1970 Farnborough Air Show by chief designer Ollie Heath (far right), while Sir Reginald Verdon-Smith, chairman of BAC, and Sir George look on. The Tornado became the most successful military collaborative programme in Europe, just under 1,000 being built. *(BAC)*

The VC10, which first flew in 1962, was built to meet a specific BOAC requirement for an aircraft able to operate from difficult 'hot-and-high' airfields on its long-distance Empire routes. But the airline's continual changes of specification and policy reduced the order to thirty-five, which greatly damaged its sales prospects. *(Vickers-Armstrongs (Aircraft) Ltd)*

Princes Margaret and Lord Snowdon visited Weybridge in 1962 to see VC10 production, accompanied by Sir George. Earlier the Princess had asked to see how an aircraft was designed, and Sir George was asked to lay out his original sketches for the aircraft for her to see. *(Central Press Photos/Edwards family)*

The Edwards family celebrate daughter Dingle's 21st birthday in 1964. To the right of Dinah is Dr John Morgan, who was not only the family physician but also a personal friend. *(Edwards family)*

The first customer for the new BAC One-Eleven was Freddie Laker's British United Airways. Laker's launch order in 1961 set the sales ball rolling, and shortly afterwards the aircraft was introduced to the lucrative US regional market. *(Brooklands Museum)*

In 1967 Sir Anthony Milward, chairman of BEA (right), signed contracts with Sir George for eighteen of the new, enlarged BAC One-Eleven Series 500. The contract was described as a 'turning point' in the affairs of BAC. *(Vickers Ltd/Edwards family)*

The first United States customer for the One-Eleven was Texas-based airline Braniff, whose president, 'Chuck' Beard (left), is seen with Sir George in 1961, at the time the airline signed for six aircraft plus another six on option, later increased to twelve. Beard and Edwards became good personal friends. *(BAESYSTEMS)*

On the Concorde campaign trail. Sir George and Dr (later Sir) Archibald Russell, chief designer, outside 10 Downing Street after briefing Prime Minister Edward Heath on the Concorde programme. *(Unknown/Edwards family)*

The Queen and the Duke of Edinburgh visited BAC Filton, Bristol, to see progress on the Concorde programme shortly after the signing of the Anglo-French treaty in 1962 to proceed with the project.
Sir George is showing the Queen a model of the massive Concorde assembly hangar. Standing to the Queen's right is Gen André Puget, head of the French Concorde team, with whom Sir George enjoyed a fruitful and productive relationship. Between them is Louis Guista, the French deputy director of production. *(Airbus UK)*

John Stonehouse (left), the wayward Labour Minister of Aviation, who 'drowned' after swimming in the sea and was later found alive in Australia. Sir George, who reckoned he was an energetic and capable minister, first met him during a high-level government mission to Russia in 1967. *(Central Press Photos)*

Sir George met President Nixon at the White House in 1969. The Americans were then pursuing their own Mach 3 supersonic airliner, despite fierce criticism that eventually killed it. Nixon told Sir George that he personally thought it was a pity they were not doing something like Concorde. *(The White House)*

The first Concorde prototype, 001, is rolled out with great ceremony at the Sud-Aviation plant in Toulouse in December 1967. Tony Benn, Minister of Technology and a great supporter of the programme, announced that, formally, the 'e' had been reinstated on the name. 'The "e" is for excellence, for England and entente Concordiale,' he said. The logos of the sixteen airlines that had taken out options are displayed above the aircraft. *(Airbus UK/Author)*

Sir George (to the right), fully kitted out in a flying suit, became the first non-flight-test member to pilot Concorde in a test flight from Fairford, Gloucestershire, the British prototype's home base, on 7 August 1969. He is seen with chief test pilot Brian Trubshaw (left) and Trubshaw's French opposite number, André Turcat. Edwards recorded a flight of 1hr 41min, during which he took the controls for a time as second pilot. *(BAC)*

Tony Benn (right) with Sir George at the Farnborough Air Show, September 1974. Earlier that year Benn had 'saved Concorde' but his plans for nationalising the aircraft industry brought him into conflict with Sir George, although both men shared the same ambition of seeing the industry prosper. *(SBAC/Norman Barfield)*

Concorde 002, the British prototype, photographed over Singapore by the outstanding aerial photographer Arthur Gibson during its 1972 sales tour. *(Image in Industry/Author)*

Dr Andrei Tupolev, chief designer of the USSR's rival supersonic airliner, the Tu-144, and son of Alexi, the famous founder of the Tupolev design bureau, visited the BAC chalet at the Paris Air Show in 1971. To his right is Dr Archibald Russell, chief designer at Filton, and to his left are Sir George and Charles Gardner, BAC's publicity manager. Edwards told the younger Tupolev that he had got the Tu-144's engines in the wrong place when he visited Russia in 1967. *(BAESYSTEMS)*

The most expensive piece of paper ever written' was how Sir George described the C of A for Concorde, which he received from Lord Boyd-Carpenter, chairman of the CAA, in December 1975. Looking on and clapping is Lord Beswick, Minister of State for Industry, who became a consultant to the company and, later, first chairman of the nationalised British Aerospace. *(BAESYSTEMS)*

Albury Heights, near Guildford, became the Edwards family's new home in 1967, after more than twenty years at Durleston in Bookham. The new house was larger than Durleston, with spectacular views over the Surrey Downs. *(Edwards family)*

The move to Albury Heights enabled Sir George to provide accommodation for his long-time driver, Archie Shields (left), together with his mother and wife Rene. At Weybridge everybody looked out for Archie, for wherever he was, Sir George was sure to be close behind. *(Edwards family)*

Sir George's Bentley, the 'giant racer', was lovingly maintained by Archie Shields and was only brought out on 'high days and holidays' or to fetch the grandchildren, who loved being picked up by Archie to visit their grandparents. *(Edwards family)*

From the early 1960s until his retirement, Sir George challenged the Air Staff to an annual game of cricket at the company's ground in Byfleet. Many of his colleagues were good club cricketers, and were warned to 'go easy on the air marshals', who were their most important customers. Among those in this early 1970s team are, seated left to right: Jeffrey Quill, the famous Spitfire pilot and later BAC marketing director; Charles Gardner, broadcaster and BAC publicity manager; Brian Trubshaw, Concorde chief test pilot; Harold Smith, commercial director; and a young Sid Gillibrand, a county-class player who was 'drafted in' from Warton and later became vice-chairman of British Aerospace. Standing fourth from the left is Frank Denning, executive director at Weybridge, who later presented Sir George with the ball with which he claimed a hat-trick on his last appearance in 1975. (*BAESYSTEMS*)

The local Byfleet Parish Day was an annual event to which Sir George (right) gave his wholehearted support. He also provided the celebrities to open the event, as here in the early 1970s, when television personality and friend Cliff Michelmore (left) was the guest of honour. Next to him is the young-looking author, who was 'commanded' to see that the company put up a good show with an aviation film theatre, and Maj Wieland of the organising committee. (*BAESYSTEMS*)

From 1966 Sir George was devoted to the new University of Surrey, where he was appointed first Pro-Chancellor. In 1970 he presided over the first degree ceremony to take place in Guildford Cathedral. He is seen with Dr Peter Leggett the university's Vice-Chancellor. (*University of Surrey/Edwards family*)

In 1972 Sir George was granted his own coat of arms with the motto '*Fermeté et Ténacité*', the nearest translation to his whole outlook on life: 'never give up, press on'. The arms displays five representations of Concorde and, at the base, the propeller of a Viscount. (*BAESYSTEMS/The White Lion Society*)

One of Sir George's last battles with Whitehall was to secure funding for the projected new BAC Three-Eleven wide-body airliner. Hopes of support were dashed in 1971 when Rolls-Royce became bankrupt and its resurrection absorbed all potential government funding. *(Image in Industry)*

During Sir George's stewardship of BAC the guided weapons business rose from being 'the Cinderella of the industry to the Prince Charming' under the able leadership of managing director George (later Sir George) Jefferson. Although GRE, by his own admission, was less familiar with the new technology employed, he recognised GW's increasing value to the company. 'He's been a good supporter of ours, but a supporter, not an involver.' was Jefferson's description. Seen here are the principal guided-missile programmes for land, sea and air, which performed so effectively during the Falklands conflict. *(BAC)*

Sir George's last overseas mission was to Saudi Arabia in 1975, where he met King Faisal. BAC had secured Britain's largest-ever export contract in that country, to provide, at their request, defence support services. The contract, which has involved over 3,000 expatriate employees, is still extant. (*The Royal Saudi household/Edwards family*)

In 1975 Sir George attended a special farewell retirement party in his honour at Weybridge. Many of his 'old mates' were gathered for the occasion, including George Stannard (seated), who had been such a help to the young Edwards when he joined the company in 1935. Surrounding George are many long-standing colleagues who served their whole careers at Vickers/BAC. They are, from left to right: Bob Handasyde, former test pilot and later sales director; Henry Gardner, who headed the TSR.2 design team; Ernie Marshall and 'Spud' Boorer, who worked for Sir George in his first group in 1935 and went on to have distinguished careers at Weybridge. Seated is Yvonne Trubshaw, Brian Trubshaw's wife. (*BAC*)

On his retirement Sir George received many accolades and gifts from the company and from many other colleagues and friends. Allen Greenwood (left), who succeeded Sir George as chairman of BAC, presented him with a Jubilee Plate produced to commemorate the diamond jubilee of the Order of the British Empire, of which Sir George had been a member since 1945. Later, Sir George and his wife, Dinah, were guests at a glittering farewell dinner at Claridge's in London. (*BAC*)

During his retirement years Sir George became a prolific speaker to schools, universities and colleges. He is seen here at St John's School, Leatherhead, where in 1977 he was guest of honour and handed out the prizes. He and the headmaster, Ted Hartwell, are admiring an unseen racing tricycle that the boys had built for a charity 24hr race. *(Author)*

Sir George took up painting in 1963, and over the years became an accomplished artist. His tutor from the earliest days was Roger Steel (left), who is admiring Sir George's painting of a VC10 at an exhibition by the Guild of Aviation Artists, of which Roger was the founder and Sir George the patron. *(BAESYSTEMS)*

Following a visit by the Duke of Edinburgh to Weybridge, Sir George was asked if he could provide lightweight carriage wheels for the Duke's racing buggy. Later Sir George produced a painting of it, which many think was one of his best works. *(British Aerospace/Roger Steel)*

In retirement Sir George became actively engaged with Surrey County Cricket Club, where he became president 1979–80. In that role he conducted Prince Charles on a visit to the Oval in 1979. He is seen here with Ian Scott-Brown, the secretary (extreme left), and Derek Newton, chairman (right). *(Surrey County Cricket Club)*

In 1981 the University of Surrey honoured Sir George by naming its new library after him. He is seen with the Duke of Kent, a personal friend, who became Chancellor in 1977. *(University of Surrey)*

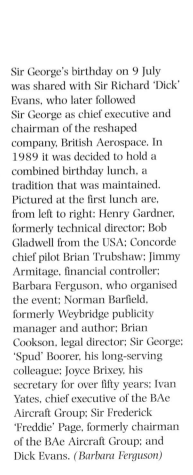

Since Viscount days Sir George enjoyed a mutual admiration with the Americans, from whom he received many honours, including the Guggenheim Medal. In 1989 he was further honoured when he was elected to their International Aerospace Hall of Fame. Unfortunately Sir George was not well enough to travel, and the award was received on his behalf by his old colleague, Bob Gladwell, seen on the left with his wife, Valerie. *(International Aerospace Hall of Fame/Bob Gladwell)*

Sir George's birthday on 9 July was shared with Sir Richard 'Dick' Evans, who later followed Sir George as chief executive and chairman of the reshaped company, British Aerospace. In 1989 it was decided to hold a combined birthday lunch, a tradition that was maintained. Pictured at the first lunch are, from left to right: Henry Gardner, formerly technical director; Bob Gladwell from the USA; Concorde chief pilot Brian Trubshaw; Jimmy Armitage, financial controller; Barbara Ferguson, who organised the event; Norman Barfield, formerly Weybridge publicity manager and author; Brian Cookson, legal director; Sir George; 'Spud' Boorer, his long-serving colleague; Joyce Brixey, his secretary for over fifty years; Ivan Yates, chief executive of the BAe Aircraft Group; Sir Frederick 'Freddie' Page, formerly chairman of the BAe Aircraft Group; and Dick Evans. *(Barbara Ferguson)*

Shortly after becoming prime minister in 1990, John Major invited members of his favourite Surrey County Cricket Club to a reception at 10 Downing Street. He is seen in deep discussion with Sir George, unusually wearing glasses, while former England and Surrey batsman Raman Subba Row looks on. *(UPPA)*

Sir George's last public appearance before the aircraft industry was in 1994 at the Farnborough Air Show dinner, when he received the John Curtis Sword of Honour, sponsored by the influential American aviation publication *Aviation Week and Space Technology*. Later the sword was displayed at the RAF Museum at Hendon, with his Valiant bomber. Michael Fopp, director of the museum, is seen here with Sir George. *(Geoffrey Lee)*

In the year 2000, at 93 years of age, Sir George achieved his greatest remaining ambition, to have a painting hung in the Royal Academy Summer Exhibition. He is seen here during his visit to the academy to see the picture, entitled *Ben the Log Carrier* (top centre). *(Edwards family)*

To his grandchildren Sir George was a revered figure who could become 'a mad grandad', as here, celebrating on the dance floor at his granddaughter Clair's wedding (left). *(Edwards family)*

For more than sixty-five years since they first played cricket together for Woking in 1935, Sir George remained friends with the great cricketing Bedser twins. He is seen here in 2001 with Sir Alec (left) and Eric holding the mounted cricket ball with which he took a hat-trick on his last appearance captaining his BAC side against the Air Ministry. *(Author)*

A happy family photograph, taken in 1988 to celebrate Sir George's eightieth birthday, for which he produced his first one-man exhibition of paintings, shown at the University of Surrey. Lady Edwards is sitting next to her daughter, Angela 'Dingle' Jeffreys, while her children, Clair and Richard, are at the back. *(BAESYSTEMS/Edwards family)*

CHAPTER EIGHTEEN

TSR.2 and a New Partner

The political furore that was soon to break over 'Britain's Wonder Jet', as certain sections of the press described TSR.2, was yet to burden the men from two rival companies who sat down at Weybridge early in 1959 to plan its development and construction. At the head of the table was Sir George Edwards. He had been appointed leader of the newly established consortium of Vickers-Armstrongs (Aircraft) Ltd and English Electric Aviation Ltd, which had been chosen to build the new aircraft. Before them lay a task so daunting that it would have taxed the most experienced and talented team, let alone a new and uneasy combination, forged together by government decree.

The selection of the two companies had marked the end of a ferocious competition to meet General Operational Requirement 339 (usually referred to colloquially as OR.339), the Canberra replacement, which had involved no fewer than eleven British design teams. Its origins can be traced back to what has been described as an 'historic' meeting in Shell-Mex House in London in September 1957. The heads of the British aircraft industry, including Sir George Edwards, had been summoned by the MoS to be told of a new government policy following the Sandys Report.

In the absence of the Minister (Aubrey Jones), the meeting was chaired by Sir Cyril Musgrave, the Permanent Secretary, who stated that, with the full authority of the Minister, there was now no certainty of any further military contracts being awarded other than OR.339. Furthermore, this would only be placed with a group of firms with one acting as leader. The government hoped this would encourage eventual amalgamation. As a consequence, the Controller (Air), Air Chief Marshal Sir Claude Pelly, had invited eight companies, plus the Hawker Siddeley Group, to submit ideas before January 1958.

The predictable response of the industry, faced with such an ultimatum, was one of deep concern as the companies considered the prospect of forced mergers and only one new major military contract in the offing. And that was to say nothing of the effect on their civil business. Sir George said it was 'unrealistic' to think the industry could survive on civil orders alone.

Sir George recalls particularly the role played at the meeting by Sir Claude Pelly. 'He was significant as being the air force representative, who had got to see that they were not going to be fobbed off with half-baked aeroplanes and a half-baked industry to do it.' He also remembers the reaction of Sir Frederick Handley Page, who said there was no way he was going to join up with anybody. 'As far as he was concerned, it was Handley Page's for ever, and it was always going to be like that.'

But effectively the die was cast, and according to Derek Wood the watchword was 'amalgamate or die'.

In May 1958 the new policy was formalised by Aubrey Jones. He believed that the UK industry could compete with America only by forming smaller, more powerful groups. He told parliament that his idea of an ideal company was one engaged in both military and civil work, and also in non-aircraft activities, so it could raise its capital on the basis of its entire diversified structure. This would mean it would be expected to finance the development of new civil projects on its own, without government assistance. Although the government would not say how the industry should reorganise, there were only three groups which fitted Aubrey Jones's description: the Hawker Siddeley Group, Vickers and English Electric.

If the business of reforming was not hard enough for the British aircraft industry, the OR and technical specification of the new aircraft was as demanding and difficult as anything it had experienced before. The specification for TSR.2 was, in the words of Derek Wood, 'An exceptionally complex requirement by any yardstick. The Air Staff had put literally everything in the pot.' This was hardly surprising with the Sandys threat of no more new military aircraft hanging over them.

The requirement (which was progressively uprated), specified that the aircraft was to fly at ultra-low level to avoid radar detection, and operate day and night in all weather conditions, over a radius of action in excess of 1,000 nautical miles. It would carry both conventional and nuclear weapons, the delivery of which would require TSR.2 to have outstanding performance, with a supersonic target dash speed of Mach 1 (the speed of sound, around 750mph at sea level) at low level, rising to Mach 2 (twice the speed of sound) at medium and high altitude. The latter was even beyond the capabilities of the RAF's most advanced interceptor of the time, the English Electric Lightning. At the other end of the scale, the aircraft was to have the usual, and in Sir George's view 'unnecessary', complication of short-field and rough runway take-off and landing capability.

To achieve all this, TSR.2 would have to be equipped with the most advanced avionic systems. This would include, critically, an automatic terrain-following flight control system so sensitive that it could avoid all obstacles (natural and man-made) in pitch darkness, even down to the height of high-tension cables. For this, an array of sophisticated and linked sensors was required, with a forward-looking radar, an inertial navigation platform, sideways-looking radar, a Doppler radar (for measuring speed and drift very accurately), active optical Linescan (for day/night vision) and enough computer power to handle the data. For accurate weapons delivery and minimum crew fatigue in the bumpy air encountered at low level, it was also essential that the airframe had low gust response and, of course, a long fatigue life.

Worryingly for Sir George, this specification was beyond the experience of the current Weybridge design team. In the absence of any new military work following the delivery of the last Valiant, they were now mostly engaged in the civil programmes: the Viscount, Vanguard, VC10 and the short-lived VC11. Of these, only the Viscount was in production and earning money; the others were still in the design and development stage. Since he believed, and had already stated to the Ministry, that no aircraft company could survive on civil work alone, it was essential for the company to re-establish itself in the military business and produce a design capable of winning the competition.

Sir George turned to Supermarine, which had the necessary background and expertise in fast jets. He recruited their key designers, headed by George Henson, and embedded them as a team in a special TSR.2 unit at Weybridge. Their move was fortuitous, for at the time the future of Supermarine was equally insecure, design work on the Scimitar being virtually completed.

'The climate in the company that brought it about was the realisation that, if we were going to tackle OR.339, we at Weybridge had got to get used to something that was pretty fast, and faster than anything we had dealt with before,' says Sir George. 'We realised that at Supermarine there was the nucleus of a team that had done high-speed aeroplanes. I got to see George Henson, who had been doing the Scimitar, and there was Alan Clifton; he knew all about the aerodynamics. I suppose I must have persuaded George Henson out and put him on the OR.339 job on the basis that, of all of us, he was the one most likely to get right the aerodynamics of an aeroplane for that performance.'

Henson and his team set to work in what was now an inner cell at Weybridge. They came up with two proposals that Derek Wood described as 'surprise designs'. The first was for a twin-seat, single-engine aircraft using blown flaps for greater lift at slow speeds, as pioneered on the Scimitar. The second was for a twin-engine version with an integrated terrain-following navigation and attack system. This, significantly, turned out to be the only proposal to offer a far-sighted, fully-integrated weapons systems concept, which is now adopted on every modern fighter aircraft. Derek Wood wrote: 'The revolutionary nature of the design cut across RAF and Royal Aircraft Establishment thinking.' He added: 'In order to keep up the momentum, Vickers literally bombarded Whitehall and Farnborough with technical papers to back up their theories.'

To George Edwards, such a technique followed his long-held belief of 'keeping close to the customer'. But while the design competition was absorbing the new team at Weybridge, the 'politics of pairing', with the TSR.2 contract as the prize, was being played out at the highest levels of industry and government. A detailed account is contained in Charles Gardner's book. It tells of the de Havilland company being considered a more likely partner for Vickers, while English Electric at first favoured Shorts in Belfast, with whom it had a contractual agreement. Within the Hawker Siddeley Group, 'internal warfare' had broken out among its constituent parts, with rival submissions being produced by Avro, Gloster and Hawker Siddeley itself.

After the final submission of all the designs had been lodged with the Air Staff, smoke signals from the Ministry indicated a preference for a combination of Vickers-Armstrongs and English Electric. The Vickers integrated systems approach and proven management ability could be matched with the English Electric P.17 proposal, which was the most favoured airframe design. The P.17, with variations, was for a delta-wing configuration with two seats in tandem, powered by twin Rolls-Royce RB.142/3 engines with reheat. One variation of the aircraft had full VTOL capability, using Short's revolutionary VTO platform. For this, the two companies had agreed to work together if either was awarded the contract. This was a binding agreement, and it was only after the RAF reissued OR.339 as the definitive requirement OR.343, based on the Vickers/ English Electric submission, that the contractual impasse could be broken.

Finally, on 1 January 1959, the Ministry announced the award of a contract for TSR.2 to Vickers-Armstrongs and English Electric Aviation on a fifty-fifty work basis, with Vickers to lead and act as main contractor. This was unexpected, as the selected airframe design was based on the P.17, although it was to be stretched and developed, while the Vickers integrated weapons systems concept would be incorporated. Sir George was 'tickled pink' to win the contract, but was fully aware that it would be 'a hell of a job to be landed with'.

He recalls how he learned of the decision after the Vickers senior directors met with Duncan Sandys. Edwards was not invited. 'This was top, top brass,' he says. 'I think they were made aware that the government regarded a joint activity between Vickers and English Electric as likely to produce the best aeroplane. There was some attraction for the design team at English Electric, because we hadn't got into supersonics as they had through the Lightning. Duncan Sandys, I assume, said they would like to give us the aeroplane, but only on the basis that we were able to get the expertise at English Electric. In other words, what they were saying was: "If you want TSR.2, you are going to have to merge with English Electric to get it."' Sir George adds: 'The Vickers directors emerged with the job of convincing blokes like me that it was a fate worse than death on one hand, but sooner or later we would have to get on with English Electric on the other.'

The appointment of Vickers to lead the consortium severely disappointed English Electric. Sir George says: 'This will sound pompous, but I think there was a fair degree of confidence in OR in us. They reckoned they would generate a more robust bit of fighting machinery out of Vickers leading it.'

Contemporary evidence suggests that the RAF, impressed by his authority and leadership of the Valiant programme, wished to see George Edwards at the helm of its most ambitious project. Handel Davies, then Director General Scientific Research (Air), confirmed this view. 'Although English Electric had produced the best design,' he said, 'the project demanded a leader of the stature of George Edwards. . . . the decision had been made for reasons of exploiting Sir George's very special capabilities.'

So what of Vickers's new partners? The English Electric Aviation company of 1959 was still a relative newcomer in the industry. It had not seriously entered the business as a designer and builder of its own aircraft until after the war, although it had been involved in large-scale wartime production, notably of the Handley Page Hampden and Halifax bombers (over 3,000 aircraft produced). Its first jet aircraft was the legendary Canberra, for which it recruited from Westland the brilliant designer W.E.W. 'Teddy' Petter, who in turn built up a design organisation made up of some of the best brains in the country. The

Canberra, which is still in service with the RAF, was followed by the Lightning, the first and only truly supersonic aircraft to be fully developed in Britain.

Such experience in supersonics enabled the English Electric design team, now led by Freddie (later Sir Frederick) Page, was able to submit what was considered the best airframe design. Page, a Cambridge engineering graduate, had worked for Hawker at Kingston, before being poached by Petter for the Canberra, on which he won his spurs. Sir George had the highest regard for him, and credited Page with the success of the Lightning. With such background, it was not surprising that there was some resentment within the English Electric team at not being given the lead. 'It was going to be difficult, and it was,' says Sir George, adding: 'Merging two outfits with their varying strengths, and building an aeroplane with the complication of TSR.2, had got to be difficult.'

Nevertheless, the outfits shared many similarities. Both were offshoots of huge industrial enterprises. While Vickers was known mainly as an armaments company, English Electric was involved in all things electrical, in telecommunications, and in marine engineering, while its enormous Strand Road factories in Preston were famous for their railway engines and tramcars – not aeroplanes. At the head of the company was the revered first Lord Nelson of Stafford. Sir George admired and liked him, and quickly came to regard him as 'one of his own'. Both were engineers, both had been educated through the technical college system, and both had worked through the ranks to the top. With Lord Nelson was his talented son, the Hon. H.G. Nelson, who was soon to succeed him, and Lord Robin Caldecote, the company's aviation administrator. They formed a powerful and influential trio.

But there was and remained a cultural difference between the two companies, which was never fully reconciled. Whereas Vickers had traditionally been led by its chief designers – Pierson, Wallis and now Edwards – English Electric Aviation was ruled by those at its manufacturing power base at Preston, presided over by the dominating figure of Arthur Sheffield. Designers such as Petter and Page were given short shrift by Sheffield, who reported directly to Lord Nelson. The aviation company was merely a subsidiary, and was treated as such.

As an example, prototype work on the Canberra, which became one of the great success stories in British aviation, had to be carried out in a garage in the centre of Preston. Only the later Hawk advanced jet trainer was to be so widely chosen by most of the world's air forces including those of the USA and Australia. Even the sceptical Sheffield was forced to admire the progress on the Canberra and the work of the 'boffins'. Only then was it decided to move the aircraft operation to the nearby former USAAF aircraft maintenance base at Warton, on the Fylde coast. With its long runway and large hangar capacity it became, and remains, the centre of all military aircraft activity in the UK to this day.

Back in 1959, however, Sir George was tasked with pulling together the two companies, for which a good relationship with the all-powerful Arthur Sheffield was essential. He knew Sheffield well (they had both served on the Farren Mission to Germany at the end of the war), and he regarded him, as himself, as 'a hard-arsed engineer'. But although there was mutual respect, he had no illusions about Sheffield or the way he operated. 'He dominated the English Electric scene at Preston because he was in charge of production. He ruled Preston like a tsar, and it was no good anybody from Warton talking about what production rates should be if Sheffield hadn't agreed it,' he says.

Sir George recalls how Sheffield resented any interference from outside, even from somebody as eminent as Lord Caldecote. 'I was in Sheffield's office one day, and I had Robin Caldecote with me. I had got to the stage where Robin was something of a lesser light [his deputy]. Robin was twittering away about something to do with the factory, and Sheffield got incensed because he reckoned Caldecote should not be allowed in the factory in Strand Road in the first place. Sheffield then ordered Robin out . . . he slid up out of his chair like a snake from a hole, and shouted at Robin: "Get out of my office. You are not going to stand there saying things like that!" And Robin went.'

'I confess it made me very angry,' says Sir George. 'I turned round to Sheffield and said something like: "You are an old mate of mine, but don't you ever, ever do that again." How I had the nerve to say that to him I don't know, but I did, and he understood what I was saying. I must have been managing director by then.'

Sir Richard 'Dick' Evans, until recently the chairman of BAE Systems, which has become the inheritor of all the major aerospace companies in Britain, began his career at Warton in the late 1960s. He was brought up in the folklore and history of the English Electric company, and was not surprised by the Caldecote episode. 'Sheffield was a tyrant,' he says. 'The design company was totally separate from the manufacturing company run by Sheffield. Sheffield had run the whole of the Hampden programme during the war and built up expertise in building aircraft. He treated Petter and his guys as a bunch of complete amateurs. . . . They were treated with utter and complete contempt, and they were certainly never taken seriously. . . . So there was a very unusual coexistence between the two organisations.'

Such occurrences did not happen at Vickers-Armstrongs. As Charles Gardner noted: 'Sir George's writ ran to every corner of the Weybridge factory.' It was not only by writ that Edwards dominated the Weybridge scene, but by the respect and confidence that all those who worked for him had in him. And it was not only in the higher echelons of the company. Edwards would often walk alone through the production shops, where he would meet and be greeted by many old colleagues who remembered him from pre-war days.

Sir George was, therefore, unused to the situation he now faced at Preston. 'I had got to face up to designing a pretty difficult aeroplane and coping with a very difficult production problem in one ball of wax. The timescale really didn't allow for a lot of farting about between two big companies that had got themselves into one. As far as I remember, I was bloody anxious as to how I was to overcome the law of the jungle between the two, and at the same time design and make an aeroplane of the performance and general quality of TSR.2.'

He adds, 'I realised in the days of running Weybridge, and getting things done the way I wanted (although it might look very attractive from the outside) that this was only done because I had got an organisation who knew that when I told them to do something, they went off to do it. I knew this wouldn't work out at English Electric because I had enough insight into Robin Caldecote's difficulties with Sheffield and the rest of them to know. But somebody had to get hold of it and turn it into one.'

On a personal level, at this critical time in his career, Sir George received reassurance, if reassurance was needed, as to his true status in the world of aviation, when the USA awarded him the 1959 Daniel Guggenheim Medal, its most prestigious award. Edwards was thus placed within an exclusive body of pioneers and aircraft designers and engineers, of whom the first member was Orville Wright. In his acceptance speech in 1960, just four months before the formation of BAC, Sir George chose to talk about another great prospect of the day: supersonic air travel. He was able to do so with confidence, following agreement the year before between the British and French governments to proceed with design studies for the aircraft that was to become Concorde. In the years to come it was to present him with his greatest challenge.

CHAPTER NINETEEN

British Aircraft Corporation

George Edwards's recollections of the foundation of the British Aircraft Corporation (BAC) in 1960, and the politics surrounding its early years, are less vivid than those of the technical challenge of the aircraft it produced. Whereas he was less precise about the process of formation, he was, even at the age of 93, able to describe and sketch a wing or tailplane of every aircraft for which he was responsible.

This was not because he was uninterested in the mechanics of establishment of a vast new enterprise; far from it. Rather it was because his initial role as the executive director for aircraft meant he had overall authority for all the current programmes, of which the most pressing and burdensome was TSR.2. Preliminary matchmaking and organisational arrangements (financial and administrative) were made at the highest levels within the constituent partner companies. This was led by Lord Knollys (chairman) and Sir Charles Dunphie (managing director) of Vickers, the Nelsons (father and son) from English Electric and Sir Reginald Verdon-Smith from the Bristol Aeroplane Company, which was a late addition to the partnership.

As those who witnessed the events at BAC in the early 1960s can testify, Sir George was seldom seen at the corporation's brand new headquarters at 100 Pall Mall, except to attend meetings. He preferred to stay near the Weybridge design teams, who were fully occupied with TSR.2, the VC10 and the emerging BAC One-Eleven twin-jet airliner. A favourite phrase of his at the time was: 'a headquarters never built anything'.

History records that BAC was formed on 1 July 1960, based on the aircraft and guided weapons interests of the TSR.2 partners, Vickers and English Electric, as prescribed by the government. Each would hold a 40 per cent share, to which was added a 20 per cent stake from the Bristol Aeroplane Company, whose subsidiary, Bristol Aircraft, had now joined the group. A fourth company,

Hunting Aircraft, was acquired for £1.3 million during the formation process, bringing with it the embryo design that was to become the One-Eleven.

Underpinning the new corporation was the avowed support of the government, sufficient to persuade the partner companies to go along with it. This was spelt out in a policy document drawn up in late 1959 by Duncan Sandys, now Minister of Aviation, following the re-election of the Conservatives that year. The contents were disclosed by Sir Reginald Verdon-Smith many years later, in a lecture at Bristol. It stated that the government believed that 'in the general interest' the aircraft industry should concentrate the bulk of its technical and financial resources into four strong groups, two making airframes and guided weapons, and two making aero-engines. 'In that event, the government intended to concentrate their orders, as far as practicable, on these four groups, except where specialised requirements or social policy made it necessary to do otherwise.'

There followed other statements of intent, designed to encourage acceptance from the industry. These included an 'endeavour' to harmonise civil and military requirements for new types of aircraft, provide support to develop markets at home and abroad, and provide, at public expense, a continued research and development programme 'of about the present size'. But, most crucially for the shareholders, the government recognised it would have to contribute towards the cost of the development of promising new types of civil aircraft, which would, as normal, be recouped from earnings from sales.

Sir Reginald commented that this was as positive a statement of government policy as industry had ever received. The caveat about concentrating orders on the four new groups 'except where specialised requirements or social policy make it necessary to do otherwise', had not, however, gone unnoticed. But it was sufficient to reassure the parent companies. Accordingly, agreement to form a new combined company was reached in January 1960, and structural and administrative details were worked out. In July BAC came into being with capital of £20 million, nine manufacturing sites in the UK, and over 30,000 people employed on some twenty major and identifiable aircraft and guided weapons programmes.

The addition of Bristol to the enterprise was not only late, but a surprise. With the Vickers–English Electric alliance established for TSR.2, and the Hawker Siddeley Aviation Group already in being, de Havilland and Bristol had been left outside the two major partnerships. It had originally been generally accepted that de Havilland and Vickers would make good bedfellows, and discussions along these lines had been progressed. But late in the day, the de Havilland board, led by Sir Aubrey Burke, decided to throw in their lot with

Hawker, and accepted an offer in which the Hawker Siddeley Group would acquired all their shares.

There has been much conjecture about this move, especially as Vickers and de Havilland were the only ones seriously engaged in the civil-aircraft business. Charles Gardner, in his BAC history, suggests that 'Sir Aubrey foresaw the possibility that in such a merger he might well find himself playing second fiddle to Sir George, who was clearly likely to head up the aircraft side of the group, and whose financial mainstay would be TSR.2 rather than the Trident.'

Sir George says: 'Roughly speaking, I think that is about right. He [Sir Aubrey] wasn't an engineer. He was very high up in political manoeuvring in ministerial circles and was much better at it than I was.' The inevitable consequence was for Bristol, who had hoped to join the Hawker Siddeley Group itself, to join BAC instead.

Again Charles Gardner tells of the suddenness of these events, and how Willie Masterton and Tom Pritchard, who were negotiating on behalf of the Bristol company, were 'ushered unceremoniously' out of talks they were having with Hawker as soon as the deal with de Havilland was struck. It was agreed to reapproach Vickers and English Electric immediately. Sir George remembers his first warning of the shift when he received an urgent call from Lord Knollys, telling him the talks with de Havilland were off and that 'he must forthwith have a look at Bristols'.

It should be noted that both Masterton, as BAC's first financial director, and Pritchard, as treasurer, were to earn the highest respect from Sir George and make an enormous and lasting contribution to the new company.

In November of that year, with the die now cast and customers anxious about the prospects for the new corporation, Sir George Edwards made his first official public comment on the reorganisation in a speech to the Air League at the Mansion House in London. He believed it was now a good thing for the industry. 'We are much stronger by reason of the flexibility and mobilisation of resources it brings,' he said. But, he warned.

The one thing we must not be asked to endure is the starting and stopping of jobs when there is no reason. I have seen too many cases of an order being placed for an excessive number of aircraft because the political mood at the time made it possible, with the break clause as a comfort factor against the day when the mood changed, and the axe fell. And just in case anyone here thinks the break clause in government contracts is a defensive measure seldom used, let me tell you that one big aircraft company with which I am acquainted has not completed a single contract since the war without the break clause being invoked – sometimes weeks after it has been placed and sometimes at the tail of a production run.

How prophetic those words were to become just four years later.

At the beginning of BAC, two crucial decisions were made that did much to ease the early relationships between four different companies with many rival products. The first was the appointment of Lord Portal as chairman, and the second was the agreement to operate as a joint company, with the four partners continuing to work under their own names as subsidiaries of BAC. A further consideration was the choice of the company name.

The new chairman, Marshal of the RAF Lord Portal of Hungerford, was acclaimed both in industry and the RAF for his leadership as CAS during the war. Churchill described him as 'The accepted star of the Royal Air Force'. After the war Portal had taken up (reluctantly) the appointment of Controller of Production Atomic Energy, for which he assumed responsibility for Britain's atom bomb. From 1951 he had entered commerce and industry as chairman and a director of public companies, through which he became known to, and friendly with, Lord Knollys. His appointment as the non-executive chairman of BAC was widely welcomed, although in attracting him to a job that would be full of difficulty, Portal's biographer, Denis Richards, stated that the trump card was its appeal 'in the national interest'.

George Edwards was delighted with the appointment, and quickly formed a close friendship and working association with Portal, which did much to steer the company safely through its formative years. 'He was one of my three heroes – Nelson, Isambard Kingdom Brunel and Lord Portal – you can't get much better than that', says Sir George. 'When you ask what they have in common, I say they were capable of making chaps that worked for them do things they wouldn't have accepted they were capable of doing. Portal certainly did that. He was a leader of men.'

Denis Richards wrote of the association: 'That he [Portal] was able to enjoy the work despite his dislike of controversy and of having to battle against the government, was largely due to the ability and personality of Edwards, with whom he was quickly on terms of warm friendship and absolute trust.'

The second decision that 'oiled the wheels' was to allow the four companies to continue to operate under their own names, retaining their local management, financial responsibilities and identity with their previous parent. Thus they preserved their individual traditions and, reassuringly, their own employment rights and conditions of service. Corporately, the power and overall strength of the new company was widely promoted to impress its customers and backers. Portal believed it would take at least eight years before BAC would represent the unifying banner under which they all marched.

The constitution of the first Corporate Board reflected this policy, with the appointment of two deputy chairmen under Lord Portal: Sir Charles Dunphie from Vickers and the Hon. George Nelson from English Electric. Sir Reginald Verdon-Smith and Willie Masterton represented the Bristol company, with G.A 'Sandy' Riddell and R.P.H. 'Ronnie' Yapp from English Electric and Vickers respectively.

But the two key executive appointments, the two men who would effectively run the company, were Sir George Edwards as executive director (aircraft) and Lord Caldecote as executive director (guided weapons).

Sir George's early comments on the structure were recorded on what Charles Gardner described as 'scribbled home-written weekend notes'. Edwards was mostly concerned about the authority of the executive directors. 'This could be made to work provided it was made absolutely clear to the subsidiary company MDs that the executive director in charge was in effect the boss, and what he said, went.' He also referred to the proposed name, expressing a 'strong preference for British Aircraft Corporation'.

There had been much discussion and argument over this. A working party had been established for the purpose, and after considering more than six serious proposals it came up with 'Consolidated British Aviation Ltd'. According to Sir George, it was Portal who resolved the matter. 'It needed a fairly Napoleonic decision from the chairman. I said: "They are all running around in circles, what do you think?" He didn't have any trouble with British Aircraft Corporation, and you wouldn't expect it. If he was going to run a big aircraft company, as far as he was concerned it was going to be British.'

Fifteen months after the formation of BAC, Sir George Edwards was elevated to the top job: managing director with executive authority for all company affairs. Lord Caldecote became his deputy, but retained responsibility for the guided weapons divisions. 'We started off with a triumvirate running the shop, with a financial director, an aircraft director and a guided weapons director. Then I was seduced into taking on the managing director's job,' was how Sir George describes it. 'But the most important appointment was Lord Portal as chairman, because we needed a great figure, a man of humanity and understanding, who we could all look up to, and before whom the internecine strife that had existed before was puny,' he says.

His new appointment was predictable. Sir George's growing relationship with Portal, his firm but even-handed treatment of the aircraft divisions, together with his responsibility for the king-pin TSR.2 contract, all pointed that way. 'It was a job-and-a-half, and I needed to learn about other things so as not to have my leg pulled,' was all he would say on reflection. His more immediate and much-quoted response was: 'I am now the wearer of the labelled pants which the Minister of Aviation can kick!'

Although the groups 'settled down' after the merger, George Edwards, as day-to-day boss, inherited all the residual 'internecine strife', as he called it. To the rumbling but 'manageable' problems between Weybridge, Warton and Preston, was added growing resentment of the guided weapons divisions, as expressed by Lord Caldecote. Although Sir George rated Robin Caldecote 'a decent bloke', he soon became aware that Caldecote was becoming increasingly frustrated about his (Sir George's) influence on the chairman and the importance of the guided weapons programmes. 'Portal seemed to have no interest in the guided weapons. He was very interested in the aircraft,' Caldecote stated, adding: 'George Edwards had regular conversations with him, and I felt Portal was getting a wrong picture of the balance.'

Lord Caldecote also offered an explanation for Portal's apparent ambivalence. 'It must have been a function of age: difficult to embrace entirely new concepts. I was rather sad and disappointed. My chaps were doing a terrific job, and their efforts then were not properly appreciated. There were no outward signs, but he was not really interested . . .' Furthermore, he did not feel Portal put as much effort into defending guided weapons programmes as he put into defending TSR.2. In his book, in which Caldecote's remarks are quoted, Denis Richards suggests that Portal himself 'felt that he had for some time underestimated the potentialities of guided weapons'.

Portal was not alone. For although Edwards had established a small but very effective guided weapons group at Weybridge some years before, he, by his own admission, 'knew nothing about the techniques you needed . . . electronics hadn't been heard of at that time. People knew about electrics but they didn't know about electronics.' That was not to say he was dismissive of their contribution or potential, but just that 'as a hard-arsed structural engineer', his most significant technical contributions would be towards aircraft. His fairness in approach, however, was noted later by the brilliant managing director of the Guided Weapons Division (GW), George Jefferson, who wrote of him: 'He's been a good supporter of ours, but a supporter, not an involver.'

Lord Caldecote's reaction is understandable, although there may have been a touch of resentment over Portal's habit of working almost exclusively through the managing director. His reaction prompted Portal to write to Edwards: 'He [Caldecote] said that what he really wanted was an assurance that if we wanted to change anything we would consult him first, and that he should get from me the same degree of support that I give you. I said that if I was as equally convinced by him that he was right as I am by you that you are right, he could count on it.'

But more pressing and more dangerous to the newly constituted BAC was the inherited situation at the Bristol factory at Filton. Sir George was 'horrified' at what he found. 'They had virtually nothing. There was some Britannia work, and they were building the first of the little Type 188 all-steel Mach 2-plus experimental aircraft, and that was it. The design team was working on the supersonic transport [SST] study, which was a long way from being a contract, and on a Silver City freighter that came to nothing.' He adds: 'The last thing I wanted to do was start BAC off with a closure or even serious unemployment, so I had to shift some work down to Filton from other sites and do it right away.' This eventually entailed moving the work on the two-seat Lightning and VC10 to Bristol, by which means he was able to keep them afloat, but 'only just'.

The full and detailed history of BAC from its foundation is told in Charles Gardner's book. It tells of a continuing row with the government over their defaulting on proper payment on ministry contracts, including TSR.2, which placed a crippling and unfair burden on the parent companies, together with their failure to award any significant new contract to either group, despite their declared intention to do so. A series of all-industry protest meetings with ministers and officials, led by Edwards and the Hawker Siddeley team, came to nothing, putting the whole industry in some peril.

There was also growing concern for Sir George on the financial prospects of the Vanguard and VC10. These had been deemed as 'old account' aircraft. This was the accounting method by which all BAC programmes were categorised as either 'old account' or 'new account', to identify whether they were the responsibility of the original companies or the new BAC. In this case, financial return on the investment made by Vickers looked increasingly uncertain.

In many ways it must be considered a miracle that BAC survived these early days at all. Within only a year Sir George had to advise the Minister of

Aviation, Peter Thorneycroft, who had taken over from Duncan Sandys, that 42 per cent of the labour force was employed on work that had begun as private ventures. On that basis alone, he told the Minister that employment would be reduced to 21,500 (from 30,000) by 1964, and that they would be out of business by 1966.

In truth, there had been several abortive government attempts to start new projects, such as 'a nonsensical stately dance' around a so-called NATO aeroplane that was never going to reach fruition because NATO had no funds of its own. There was also the 'affair Shorts', in which the government tried to sell off its 69.5 per cent shareholding in Shorts to either BAC or Hawker Siddeley Aviation (HSA) using a requirement for a new short take-off and landing (STOL) transport for the RAF (OR.351) as bait. BAC, through Bristol, had submitted a design, guaranteeing that it would place 40 per cent of the work in Belfast if successful. But BAC, like HSA, rejected the government proposal.

At a meeting with Peter Thorneycroft in November 1961 Sir George told the Minister that they could not 'seriously discuss such a course [to buy Shorts] until we are in possession of a forward programme of government work coming to BAC'. He added: 'It did not seem to us wise to increase our labour force and capital employed; indeed it was difficult to see how the necessary capital, whatever it may be, required to purchase and operate Shorts could be raised until we reached a point of profitability on the capital already in our business, and an assurance of extra profit to service the capital in Shorts itself.'

The Minister was unable to give BAC a forward programme at that time as to the government's intentions for the future of the industry. After many twists and turns, the RAF's new aircraft eventually turned out to be the American Lockheed C-130 Hercules, already a veteran design, of which sixty-six were procured in a straight dollar deal.

Now an even greater threat loomed. TSR.2, the very foundation of the company, was the subject of mounting rumours of cancellation. Costs were mounting rapidly, and calls for its abandonment were regularly appearing in the national media, fuelled by the Treasury and others in positions of influence, including the Chief of the Defence Staff, Admiral Lord Louis Mountbatten. Such speculation did not surprise Sir George, who was quoted later as saying: 'Right from the start I heard the hoofbeats of this united opposition to TSR.2. I knew it would be a struggle to survive.'

One small jet airliner, the BAC One-Eleven, derived from the inherited Hunting 107 project, together with the bravery of one British independent airline boss, did much to keep the company alive.

CHAPTER TWENTY

TSR.2 – the Beginning of the End

Although George Edwards knew from the outset that TSR.2 was going to be difficult, he could not have guessed just how difficult it would prove. Had he been aware that, as prime contractor, he was to be responsible for no more than 40 per cent of the project, that effective control lay with a proliferation of Whitehall committees, and that production disharmony between the factories in the north and south would seriously delay the programme, he might have had serious doubts about proceeding. Had he known that its champions, the RAF Air Staff and the CAS, would eventually turn against it in favour of an American rival, he might not have started at all.

As early as September 1960, in answer to a congratulatory letter from George Nelson on the award (after prolonged wrangling) of a contract from the Ministry for the first nine development aircraft, Sir George wrote: 'I have no doubt as the years go by we shall have to fight a series of rearguard actions on TSR.2.' By August 1962, following production setbacks mainly associated with the Preston factory, he was writing a personal note to Lord Portal, warning of the danger of cancellation. He stated: 'TSR.2 has proved to be a bigger and more difficult job than we (and the Ministry of Aviation) thought. . . . There is no doubt that splitting a job of this complexity between English Electric and Vickers has cost the earth on development.'

Edwards was also deeply concerned about the viability of the whole company. Not only was TSR.2 under threat, so was the flagship *Blue Water* missile programme and another project, the PT.428 anti-aircraft system, both essential for the well-being of the guided weapons divisions. In the same note to Portal, evidently written in moments of anguish, Sir George stated: 'All the foregoing convinces me that BAC cannot leave itself at the mercy of government policy. There must be sufficient of a hard core of non-government work to ensure employment of the BAC-owned assets, and absorption of overheads in the works we own and must operate, to stay in business.'

He added, bitterly: 'The government are already prepared to rat on the spirit of the merger. The departure of most of the ministers responsible [Jones, Mills and Watkinson] makes this easier. I am convinced we can place little reliance on what they may say, and we must work out our own salvation, Spartan though it may be, on the lines I have indicated.' These 'lines' proposed the sharing of One-Eleven and VC10 work around the sites, and contemplated the closure of various factories.

With such frustration mounting within BAC, and the continual wrangling in Whitehall, the TSR.2 project soon became the focus of sceptical press and public attention. Roy Jenkins, the Labour Minister of Aviation, wrote in his autobiography: 'I have never known an argument about military aircraft so engage lay attention.' A learned debate in 1997, 'TSR.2 with Hindsight', involving many of those most deeply engaged in the programme, illustrated the degree of difficulty that was encountered from both sides of the house. The senior civil servant, Sir Frank Cooper, who was Assistant Under Secretary (Air) from 1962, said he was drawn to the conclusion that TSR.2 was 'an extraordinary and complex story. Cancellation was inevitable.'

The fact that the aircraft was actually built and flown, and flew very well, might now be considered miraculous, and a great tribute to the designers, engineers and pilots who brought it about.

The first signs of prolonged trouble ahead came within months of securing the contract, when Sir George realised that the choice of engine was not going to be made by the prime contractor, as was usual, but by the Ministry. They favoured the government-backed Bristol Siddeley Olympus 22R turbojet. He preferred the lighter and 'more potential' Rolls-Royce Medway. 'This is the first time I have ever been told what engines I must have for an aeroplane, and I have taken the precaution of getting the Minister [Aubrey Jones] to give me the order in writing,' he said at the time.

Of more critical concern was the fact that, because the engine was supplied under the MoS embodiment loan procedure, Sir George and the team had no control over its progress and were unaware of its true costs. 'The civil servants – the government – wanted their own influence on the engines so they were in line with government policy as to which engine companies to keep going and which ones were not,' he says. 'So any bloke who was responsible for the aeroplane had, in fact, to accept the engine that was being dished out to him. There were occasions when I wanted to raise hell with the engine chaps, but I was promptly kicked off on the basis that they were doing what the government told them to do.' He adds: 'You wouldn't normally start designing an aeroplane until you knew what you would get from the engine.'

The same conditions were applied to the aircraft's main avionics, which were likewise procured by direct contract to the Ministry. This included the inertial navigation system, the forward-looking radar and the reconnaissance system. Other items, the automatic flying control, the sideways-looking radar and the associated computers, could only be acquired by the prime contractor with Ministry permission. Again, BAC had little understanding of the costs involved or the progress being made.

To administer and control all this, a multitude of committees appeared in Whitehall. Derek Wood wrote: 'Committees examined every aspect of the project and disagreed on most of them. No single man could or did take an instant decision based on experience. . . . It became commonplace for as many as sixty to sit down without a result.'

Henry Gardner, who had been appointed overall project director by Edwards, is quoted as saying he could do nothing of significance without Whitehall approval, 'assuming we could discover who in Whitehall was the proper person to ask!'

Gardner also pointed out the cost implications of all of this, especially the increasing difficulty in getting support from their own equipment suppliers. They were 'convinced by the voracious anti-TSR.2 lobby that the project would never survive. . . . As a result all prices quoted were extremely high and extremely late,' he said.

But most damaging to the programme's financial situation was the introduction of a new Ministry accounting procedure, from which most of the cost arguments were to arise. For the first time, all the research and development costs for the aircraft's equipment, normally amortised by the suppliers against other usages, were lumped into one basket and set against TSR.2.

Sir George remembers having several serious arguments about this with Sir Henry Hardman, Permanent Secretary at the Ministry of Defence, who 'insisted' that the cost of all the equipment had to be stuck on to the TSR.2 bill. Edwards says: 'I raised hell because in the past, when there had been a pretty funny bit of electronics called for in a new aeroplane, it was priced and put on the budget as a separate piece of equipment in the sort of trade it belonged in;

electronics or whatever it might be. You then procured through the government agency and stuck it on the aeroplane as an add-on that the government was supplying and paying for.'

But Whitehall was immutable. Sir George could not 'shift them', and this was, in his words, 'an enormous factor in showing up the extravagance of the Air Staff and me and the rest of them in making it all cost so much. . . . It had to be an important instrument in getting its throat cut.' He adds: 'My battle was that every aeroplane that had been built down through the ages was through the previously established procurement system. If you had always isolated the cost of equipment on one particular aeroplane, then more of them would not have stood the test of time.'

On top of this were numerous costly performance enhancements demanded by the customer. Sir Frederick Page, in the 'TSR.2 with Hindsight' debate, which was sponsored by the RAF Historical Society, noted: 'The prolonged and competitive gestation period of TSR.2 provided ample scope for costly embellishment by enthusiastic OR officers in MoD [Ministry of Defence] and equipment specialists in MoS and their suppliers.'

He illustrated the growth in size, complication and therefore cost, by comparing the first submissions in 1957 with the project as it stood in 1965. This showed an increase in weight from less than 70,000lb for a single-engine aircraft to 110,000lb for a twin; enhanced performance in speed from no specific figure to Mach 2.25; a drop in the low-level penetration height from a minimum of 1,000ft to not more than 200ft; and a drop in the runway load classification number (so that lesser airfields could be used) from 40 to 22. In addition, he said, the new equipment specified had increased greatly. The initial interim fits of mostly existing items, as proposed for the English Electric P.17A, were ruled out; twin Olympus 22R engines became mandatory, and at a late stage the main computer installation was doubled.

While extra performance demands were driving up costs, Sir George was much occupied by the slippage in production of the development aircraft, and particularly by delays at Preston, where Arthur Sheffield still exercised almost total autonomous control. 'I had a hell of a job with production of TSR.2 because of that, and I moved the assembly of a development aircraft away from them because they just weren't doing it. I could see they had got it round their necks, and it was no good pretending they hadn't. But it really caused a revolution; compared with that, the French Revolution was a tea party!' He adds: 'Sheffield and his lads were good "nailers-together" of aeroplanes, but they had never done any real production of an aeroplane at the same time as it was being designed and worked out, whereas the Weybridge lot were pretty used to tackling things that were only half-baked.'

Sir George was reluctant to make the move, not only because of the political sensitivities that would be aroused, but because he had promised at the beginning of the project to allocate the assembly of one development aircraft to Warton, instead of to Weybridge, where all the others were to be completed. This offer had been made to Lord Caldecote to resolve a contractual row between the two parent companies. By now, however, Edwards was under great pressure from the Ministry regarding the slippages in the programme. 'I had the most fearful time. Henry Hardman was constantly attacking me because I had been giving him programme dates that couldn't be kept. I used to go along with plausible reasons as to why they weren't. But in fact the whole thing was really losing the place,' he says.

His deep concern can be judged from a memorandum to Lord Caldecote dated 2 January 1963, about delays in delivering to Weybridge the rear fuselage section, which was being built at Preston. Referring to the heavy pressure he was being put under by both the Minister and Ministry, Sir George wrote: 'I have spent many hours this week going through the position, and am disturbed to find yet another slippage in the Preston programme of a further six to seven weeks. You will recall that, based on the delivery of the complete rear fuselage at the end of December, I promised Julian Amery [Minister of Aviation] when he was at Weybridge in September, in the presence of the chairman and Freddie Page, that we could achieve first flight in August, although this was a pretty unpopular statement. We have not given the Ministry any official intimation that we are changing the August date, although I was, of course, told by Shorrock [the works director] shortly after the meeting with Amery, the end of December was in fact becoming mid-March [1964].'

Since so much depended on getting the aircraft airborne, it was not surprising that Sir George concluded his memo to Lord Caldecote with the terse comment: 'I need hardly say how desperate I think the position has now become,' and ended it by demanding that he receive the latest programme from Preston 'within two days'.

Freddie Page, in the TSR.2 debate, recalled a meeting with Sir George and Lord Caldecote in late 1962 about the problem. 'I promised that, if the whole aircraft manufacturing and associated financial, administrative and commercial departments were brought into English Electric Aviation (as distinct from the parent company, English Electric), no Preston units would delay assembly. . . . Things moved quickly, and by early April 1963 the amalgamation had been completed formally, and all Preston units arrived at or before the time Weybridge needed them,' he stated.

While production delays were causing concern at BAC, internal differences in Whitehall and the country's worsening economic position were adding to the problems. Sir Frank Cooper, in his paper presented at the TSR.2 debate, gave an insight into this. He recalled the period after the Sandys White Paper, resulting in heavy defence cancellations, the reorganising of the principal ministries involved and the introduction of a new functional costing system adapted from a system used in the USA. 'But perhaps above all the country was financially in dire straits for much of the time and financial crises were a recurrent theme. Systems of budgetary control were crude, and for complex projects the arrangements for forecasting, monitoring and controlling expenditure were inadequate,' he said.

Sir Frank also recalled the intense inter-service rivalry between the RAF and the Royal Navy, which wanted the RAF to take its Hawker Siddeley Buccaneer as 'an interim solution', together with the growing lack of confidence 'by those concerned with research, development and production of the aircraft'. He stated: 'From the start, the overall management of the project was regarded as suspect – to put it at its highest. In some ways this was not surprising, given the shotgun nature of the industrial consortium, coupled with the fact that Whitehall itself spawned committees, the consequences of which was to make matters worse. At no time was the project management system well regarded. To add to the confusion, the operational requirement was upped on several occasions.'

According to Sir Frank, relationships between the MoS/Aviation and the Air Ministry went from bad to worse, and these poor relations spread to the MoD. The continual slippage of the forecast in-service date, delays to the first flight and the engine problems – 'not least the blowing up of three engines' – together with 'horrific' rising costs, all added to growing disenchantment. He said: 'There is no doubt that during the first half of 1964 there was a change in attitude in the Air Ministry among some senior people (including CAS, the Director of Plans (Air) and the Secretariat), and the Air Ministry began to question seriously whether the RAF programme could bear the cost of the TSR.2 and about its effectiveness in terms of performance.'

But to many, and particularly to Sir George, the decisive blow leading to the ultimate destruction of TSR.2 was delivered a year before, in October 1963, by the Australian government. Prime Minister Robert Menzies announced they would purchase from the USA two squadrons (twenty-four aircraft) of General

Dynamics swing-wing F-111 fighter/ bombers. As an interim measure they had also been offered the free loan of two squadrons of Boeing B-47 Stratojets pending delivery. The order was at the expense of the TSR.2, and followed a long and sometimes bitter sales campaign. Thus ended any hope of securing the project in Britain by contract obligation to a second party.

George Edwards says: 'The chap who got the credit for Australia cancelling it was Mountbatten.' Mountbatten, then Chief of the Defence Staff, had visited Australia and repeatedly told them that TSR.2 would never be built. He suggested that the navy's Buccaneer, which could be adapted for the role, was a better option. Press reports, quoted by Derek Wood, claim he had the habit of slapping down five card-size photos of the Buccaneer and one of TSR.2 and saying: 'Five of one or one of the other at the same cost.'

Sir George felt particularly bitter about Mountbatten's interjection, especially as it followed his own encouraging visit to Australia in 1962, from which he derived reasonable confidence of winning the order. He also believed that Mountbatten, as Chief of Defence Staff, should not have been engaged in such activity. His concern was shared by Mountbatten's biographer, Philip Ziegler, who wrote: 'He pushed his campaign against TSR.2 to the limit of the scrupulous, some would say beyond it'.

The Royal Australian Air Force (RAAF) had expressed interest in TSR.2 from the very beginning of the project. In 1960 a BAC TSR.2 marketing team, led by Jeffrey Quill, who had been the principal test pilot for the Spitfire, had been active in the country. Australia, like the/ UK, operated the Canberra (and inspired its name), which TSR.2 was designed to replace, and unsurprisingly took especial note of its successor. Furthermore, a growing Australian requirement for a strike/reconnaissance aircraft, as a deterrent to an increasingly volatile situation in Indonesia and South East Asia, almost precisely matched the TSR.2 specification.

The British proposals were virtually unopposed until the Americans, worried about Vietnam and its repercussions in the region, entered the competition with a variety of solutions, of which the new TFX (Tactical Fighter Experimental, which led to the F-111) became the linchpin. To this were added a number of benefits in trade and price, and the offer to provide the B-47s as an interim measure. This was done at a time when Australia was loosening its ties with Britain and looking more towards the USA as a trading partner.

Prime Minister Menzies, although an anglophile, recognised that an American deal might give him an advantage politically, and indeed called a snap election (which he won) a month after the decision.

By early 1962 Sir George had become acutely aware of the importance of Australia to lend credibility at home, where the 'anti brigade' was now mounting a sustained attack. 'It was only a tiddly little order [originally twelve and rising to twenty-four aircraft],' he says, 'but if we had managed to get the Australians in the net the British government would not have been able to do away with it, which Mountbatten knew.'

So, in March 1962, Sir George visited Australia and met the Prime Minister, the Defence Minister and all the service chiefs, led by Air Chief Marshal Sir Frederick Scherger, who was Chairman of the Joint Chiefs, and Chief of the Air Staff, Air Marshal Valston Hancock. 'At the end of my visit I was fairly confident that they had abandoned the idea of purchasing an American bomber [then the North American Vigilante and the Convair B-58 Hustler], and are likely to order a batch of TSR.2s, possibly twelve, for delivery in 1967,' he wrote to the Aviation Minister, Peter Thorneycroft, on 17 April 1962.

But the main thrust of his letter to the Minister was to ask for help to combat the expected worries the Australians had expressed about the long-term viability of the aircraft and the current lack of production orders. He continued: 'I would therefore recommend, if you feel able to do so, you should write to the Australian government telling them in the firmest terms possible that a production quantity of no less than seventy-five TSR.2s will be ordered for the RAF and that you hope this will enable them to make the decision now to purchase some TSR.2s for the RAAF.'

As far as the technical evaluation was concerned, Edwards wrote: 'In the course of my discussions it became apparent that the technical presentations that had been carried out had convinced the RAAF that TSR.2 provided the best technical solution to their problem.' But he also warned of an emerging challenge coming from the USA: 'I am slightly apprehensive that the American TFX, which is forecast to commence production in 1967, may become a new threat as time passes, and we should try to get the Australians to make a commitment as soon as possible.'

. Thorneycroft's response was supportive but not conclusive. 'I fully share your views on the importance of persuading the Australians to join with us in buying TSR.2,' he replied. He added that the High Commissioner had been fully briefed earlier in the month and a telegram had been sent to Canberra, 'setting out our present TSR.2 programme and intentions for ordering the aircraft'. He concluded: 'I shall certainly try to follow up your suggestion [to place orders] as soon as I am in a position to do so.'

But, according to Australian military historian Phil Strickland, in his contribution to the TSR.2 debate, stated that in April 1963 'Lord Mountbatten expressed his doubts about the TSR.2 ever going into production to Air Chief Marshal Scherger. Scherger had previously been the TSR.2's most important proponent in Australia – according to Alan Stephens [the Australian defence writer] his confidence in the project was shaken by Mountbatten's comments.'

Mountbatten's opinion certainly put 'a large wobble' into Australian interest in TSR.2. In June 1963 a high-level Australian evaluation mission, led by CAS Valston Hancock, visited the UK before inspecting the TFX in the USA. Their conclusion, however, was that: 'TFX would meet their requirements better than any other aircraft they had investigated.'

But Phil Strickland stated that the process employed to select the TFX/F-111 'was extremely flawed'. It was, in some respects, he said: 'a surprising judgement because the report noted that the TSR.2 had progressed rather more than they thought and there was no great evidence of TFX manufacture'. He added: 'By mid-1963 TSR.2's development had advanced to the point where precise data could be supplied to the evaluation team on key items such as the aircraft cost – A\$122 million for twenty-four aircraft, and its availability for entry into squadron service mid-1969. By contrast, the team was unable to obtain a satisfactory estimate of the TFX price and was advised by the US Department of Defense to ignore the figures supplied by General Dynamics.'

Had Sir George been able to attend the TSR.2 debate as planned (ill health prevented him doing so), he would have found little consolation in Strickland's belief that 'TSR.2 was denied a fair day in court.' Nor would he have been surprised by his conclusion that Mountbatten's meeting with Scherger 'predisposed the RAAF against TSR.2'. Strickland added: 'It is quite clear from Hancock's comments that by August 1963 at the latest, the RAAF's early interest in the TSR.2 had evaporated as a result of its doubts about the TSR.2 entering production.'

In determining Mountbatten's anti-TSR.2 motives, Sir George refers back to the origins of the project. 'What happened,' he says, 'was that there was a shortage of defence money and, as always, there was a competition between the various services. The navy were blowing their cheeks out about money that was being poured into TSR.2 and being poured out of battleships.' As to Mountbatten's influence in Australia, he adds: 'Here was I beating the Australians over the head on the basis that no government would dare to do away with it because it had got so far established, and here was Mountbatten, Chief of Defence Staff, cheerfully saying there was not a cat in hell's chance of it going on. . . . The Australian interest just faded away.'

It should be noted that, during the next few years, the F-111, with swing-wing variable geometry, a technology ironically 'borrowed' from Barnes Wallis, underwent as many technical delays and cost increases as TSR.2. Eventually the RAAF's F-111s were delivered six years late and at a cost of A$344 million, a rise of A$232 million. The promised B-47s, at the RAAF request, never materialised.

CHAPTER TWENTY-ONE

TSR.2 – the End

Without an overseas order, and with the TSR.2 programme running late and considerably over budget, it was almost inevitable that the new Labour Government of 1964 would do away with it, and with much else of importance in the industry. Had it not been for a binding treaty with France, the Concorde SST programme too would have been cancelled. Sir George was, of course, aware of Labour's inherent dislike and distrust of TSR.2, and particularly its nuclear capability. 'There was a political thing about the aeroplane in that it did carry an atom bomb, and that, I think, didn't endear it to the government in power,' he said later.

But in truth, TSR.2 was, as described, in dire trouble before Labour came to power. Before the general election in October 1964, CAS Sir Charles Elworthy (later Lord Elworthy) had written a note to the Aviation Minister, Hugh Fraser, recommending cancellation in favour of the American TFX/F-111, as costs were out of control. No doubt the Air Chief Marshal was worried that TSR.2 was increasingly absorbing the RAF budget. Fraser showed the note to Defence Secretary Peter Thorneycroft, who told him not to discuss it before the election. Effectively the last bastion of TSR.2 support was crumbling, and crumbling fast.

That the RAF at the highest level had undergone such a change of heart was little known outside what Sir Frank Cooper described as 'a very limited circle'. It was certainly not apparent to many senior RAF officers, both serving and retired. Although Sir George was aware of the enthusiasm for the F-111 within certain sections of the RAF, and later was made aware of MoD opposition to TSR.2, it is unlikely he knew precisely the part Elworthy and other senior officers had played.

Lord Elworthy's two immediate predecessors, Sir Dermot Boyle and Sir Thomas Pike, who had advocated the aircraft from the beginning, remained enthusiastically loyal to the project. Indeed, Sir Dermot, who had now joined the BAC Board, did not know about the CAS's true position. According to Air Cdre Henry Probert, the RAF's historian in the TSR.2 debate, Sir Dermot had originally written in his draft memoirs that he was sure that Lord Elworthy had done all he possibly could to defend TSR.2. He later retracted the reference when advised by Probert that this was not the case.

All that BAC could do now, and their only realistic chance of saving TSR.2, was to take every conceivable step to get the aircraft airborne as soon as possible to demonstrate its capability, which was clearly ahead of any known rival at the time. With the 1964 election in the offing, and predictions as to the outcome on a knife edge, such a demonstration to the likes of Aviation Minister Julian Amery might swing the balance if the Conservatives were to win. Sir George liked Amery, who was also a local Preston constituency MP. Despite Amery's irritation at the delays in flying the aircraft, he had always tried to support TSR.2 on its technical and industrial merit. But he badly needed some evidence to support his view.

So it was with relief that, on Sunday 27 September 1964, the first TSR.2 development aircraft, XR219, flew for the first time in the hands of chief test pilot Roland 'Bee' Beamont, with Don Bowen as navigator/observer. The flight was made from the government test airfield at Boscombe Down on Salisbury Plain. As with many things associated with TSR.2, the choice of airfield caused some internal strife between Warton, which was in charge of the flight-test programme, and Weybridge, which was responsible for final assembly. Each would have preferred to use its own airfield, where its own staff and facilities were on hand, to avoid having to dismantle and reassemble the aircraft, which caused extra complication and cost (a point Freddie Page made in the TSR.2 debate). In the end Sir George agreed to a neutral venue.

The flight itself, which comprised two lengthy circuits with the wheels down, successfully proved the basic flying qualities and handling of the aircraft. It suffered one major technical fault, however, when, on landing, a violent undercarriage-induced oscillation temporarily blurred the vision of the pilot. It would, according to Beamont's notes, 'need investigation', which was duly carried out, and the problem was later rectified.

That Beamont flew at all was a brave decision. Aware of the huge pressure on the programme to fly, he accepted limitations on engine power caused by a prolonged shaft-resonance problem with the Olympus engine. It must have been an enormous relief to the whole team when Beamont reported that the flight had met all its planned test points. In his book *The Years Flew Past* he wrote: 'From take-off onwards throughout the flight I could not fault the control and stability in any aspect. . . . This untried prototype might just as well have been an already developed and proved aeroplane.'

In his 1981 television broadcast Sir George conveyed some of his enthusiasm for the aeroplane. 'I think the design of TSR.2 was tremendous,' he said. 'I think the performance we achieved in the test flights proved it. There were features in that aeroplane that have not been excelled since. For example, we got a take-off and landing performance with a fixed wing that you can now only get with a variable-geometry aircraft like the Tornado. We had all sorts of revolutionary features that brought that about. The aeroplane had tailerons, the whole of the trailing edge of the wing was flaps, and we rolled it by differential movement of the tailplane.'

But the celebrations over the first flight and the aircraft's performance were short-lived. Within just over two weeks Labour came to power, but with an overall majority of only four. Denis Healey was appointed Defence Secretary, which was unwelcome but not unexpected. Healey had been a vociferous opponent of TSR.2 and was known to have a liking for US products and a huge respect for their Defense Secretary, Robert McNamara. Despite reported 'assurances' by Harold Wilson that a Labour administration would retain TSR.2, given on an electioneering visit to Preston, Sir George had no doubt about their intentions and the role Healey would play. 'I used to get on all right with Wilson, but it wasn't the same with Healey. He certainly was not on our side,' he says.

On taking up office, Healey was given and accepted a financial threshold of total defence expenditure by the Chancellor, Jim Callaghan, of £2,000 million by the end of the decade. Healey commissioned an interim report before his first Defence Review, which concluded that if all three major aircraft projects then on the go, the P.1154 supersonic vertical/short take-off and landing (V/STOL) aircraft, the HS.681 STOL tactical transport and TSR.2, were continued, forecast expenditure would be at least £2,400 million. Healey himself, according to Edward Pearce's biography *A Life in our Times*, concluded that this forecast 'might well have been an underestimate'. If all three were replaced by purchases of US aircraft, and a couple of other adjustments were made, between £600 and £800 million could be saved in the next decade.

The interim report made it 'very plain', however, that the continuation of TSR.2 would also automatically rule out any prospect of containing defence expenditure within the budget. Edward Pearce wrote: 'This was quotable authority for what Healey already knew he had to do – cancel TSR.2.'

George Edwards was fully aware that, behind Healey, there were many other like-minded TSR.2 opponents such as Mountbatten, his scientific adviser

Sir Solly Zuckerman (whose credentials as a professor of zoology could hardly be described as relevant), the Treasury, and a host of 'advisers', academics and journalists. Edwards turned his attention to government departments where he might expect some support, such as Technology, Employment and, most of all, Aviation. He backed this up with a robust public-relations campaign which attracted much public support.

In December 1964 Sir George fired the first shots. In a letter dated 21 December to Roy Jenkins, the newly appointed Minister of Aviation, he emphasised the 'dominant part which TSR.2 plays in the affairs of the Corporation'. In it, he gave a complete breakdown of BAC's financial position, showing that on predicted low profits over the next four years TSR.2 was expected to contribute £1.75 million out of a total of £3.45 million.

He wrote: 'Cancellation of the TSR.2 contract will not only delete 50 per cent of our forecast profitability, it will also make it impossible to recover our fixed overheads, which would result in an incalculable increase in the cost of all other projects, especially civil aircraft, for which prices are fixed by world competition.' Having reminded the Minister that they had received no major military work since the TSR.2 contract had been awarded, he concluded: 'You will understand therefore why I say that the removal of the TSR.2 will through inability to earn any return on capital, put us out of business.'

After a brief pause for Christmas, Sir George wrote again to the Minister, this time on the impact on their employment situation. He estimated that without TSR.2 this would fall from the present 41,000 to at worst 15,000 over the next four years, which would include 'the virtual collapse of the Preston Division'. He also amplified the damaging effect on the very promising BAC One-Eleven, of which seventy-four had already been sold, the bulk to US customers.

On 11 January a high-level BAC delegation, including Sir George and headed by Lord Portal, met Roy Jenkins. Sir George recalled Lord Portal having an opening exchange with Jenkins in which he told him that it would pay the USA to give the UK TFX free of charge to achieve the closure of our aircraft industry. To this the Minister replied that this was no part of the bargain, and the UK would pay the commercial price. Portal retorted: 'The effect would be the same, except HMG would be paying to close down the British aircraft industry instead!'

Sir George referred to his two letters to the Minister, and Jenkins assured him he had 'studied them carefully'. Edwards reiterated the effect it would have on employment and the damage it would inflict on future sales prospects, including lack of prestige overseas, where 'it still had powerful meaning'. He added: 'To put it mildly, it was maddening that dollars so hard-earned in the One-Eleven might be gifted back to the USA on TFX.' On the technical situation, he asked the Minister to keep in mind that TSR.2 had been evolved as the first 'weapons system' aircraft. 'It was the first time the job had been tackled, and if the team was sacrificed after six years of endeavour and achievement it could not be brought together again. TSR.2 was superior to alternatives being considered, and the Air Staff had had good military reason for requesting it,' he stated.

Roy Jenkins replied that TSR.2 looked like costing £800 million for 158 aircraft, or £5 million per copy. He said TFX was much cheaper, even though it might be thought to be less good and would cost £2 million per copy. He also confirmed that the MoD was of the opinion that the project should be cancelled. Sir George responded by saying that, because TFX had variable-sweep wings, of which BAC had particular knowledge, it would require special training for aircrews, and that the cost of £2 million each did not include the special systems that would be needed.

Four days later, at BAC's request, Jenkins set up a meeting with the Prime Minister at Chequers. Sir George and Sir Reginald Verdon-Smith met privately with Harold Wilson before a more extensive dinner meeting that included the other leaders of the industry. According to Edwards's own notes, Wilson asked if he agreed to a figure of £750 million that was currently being quoted for TSR.2. Sir George replied that he could not, because he was unaware of how it had been made up, as only about one third of that figure was attributable to BAC. The Prime Minister, he said, 'appeared surprised that this was the case'.

Wilson's main concern was over establishing a fixed price for the project. Sir George told him that, following a meeting with the Ministry of Aviation, they had already agreed to a provisional figure for the eleven pre-production aircraft and were prepared, 'at great risk to BAC', to discuss a basis of fixing prices on a large part of the airframe production. Although this 'seemed to meet with the PM's approval', Edwards was subsequently 'put under pressure' on the question of development costs. Wilson left him in no doubt that a fixed price on production aircraft without a maximum price on development 'did not meet the case'.

Responding to the Prime Minister, Sir George said that, because of the success of the flight development programme, and their confidence in the aircraft, they were now in a position to talk about fixing prices on development costs. 'Normally speaking, one would never reckon to do that at this stage of a project, but if this was the only means of ensuring its continuation we would be prepared to commence serious discussions.' The PM reiterated that cost was the whole problem and that TFX was 'a known quantity – we know what we shall have to pay for it,' he said.

Wilson also gave Sir George the impression that the government would have settled for a reduced number of fifty TSR.2s (a proposal made by Roy Jenkins), but the Air Staff had insisted on a minimum of 110. Edwards knew that fifty on their own would not have been enough, but, as he said later, if the RAF had taken the gamble on getting another fifty, 'I could have invented a Mark 1 and a Mark 2 and had twenty-five off each, and Bob's your uncle!'

But in Sir George's contemporaneous report he held out no hope of such a solution. 'Where we are in real trouble,' he wrote, 'is there seems to be no worthwhile compromise with the Air Staff on numbers.' He added gloomily: 'I am convinced the present mood is to cancel 681, 1154 and TSR.2. The latter can only be saved by our agreeing to fix prices for the bulk of the cost of 100 aircraft.'

There followed a hectic round of internal meetings within BAC to see if a satisfactory fixed-price formula could be found. At a meeting of the Board on 20 January Sir George was authorised to offer a global figure of £450 to £475 million to complete the development, pre-production and production of 100 aircraft. This was soon rejected by the Ministry as too high, as it put the total cost of the project at £670 million (including the cost of the engine and avionics), whereas the Ministry's maximum, if the project was to be saved, was put at £604 million, requiring a saving on the aircraft of £66 million.

Further meetings were quickly held at BAC, at which strong objections were expressed by Sir Charles Dunphie, now chairman of Vickers, that they could not accept any 'open-ended' liability. As a result, a new formula of profit and loss sharing with the Ministry was arrived at. Accordingly, on 27 January, Sir George wrote to Sir Richard Way, Permanent Secretary at the Ministry of Aviation, making a final offer of £430 million. He spelled out the great risk to BAC in making such a proposal. 'The company is prepared, if costs exceeded expectation, to contribute to the excess the whole of their profit, which would be a maximum of around £46 million under the above arrangement and incur a loss of a further £9 million – a total of £55 million. This obviously contains an enormous incentive to contain the costs on the project,' he stated.

It was too late. The political die had effectively been cast two weeks earlier, on 15 January, at a Defence and Overseas Policy Committee, when Healey had presented what he called his 'aircraft purge'. According to Edward Pearce, his plan 'seems to have been cheerfully received', Mountbatten calling it 'excellent, first class, splendid'. By 25 January Healey was conferring with Henry

Hardman and Sam Elworthy, after which he wrote: 'Sam at last agreed Air Staff now prefer TFX to TSR.2 on *military* [Healey's italics] grounds.'

Healey, however, did not enjoy total support in Cabinet, and several members were concerned about unemployment and the effect on the British industry. Roy Jenkins, in his autobiography, summed up what many felt. He wrote: 'I did not think we should keep it going, although I was not convinced that the automatic alternative was to buy the F-111. My scepticism about a continuing British East of Suez role predisposed me in favour of doing without either. This divided me from Healey, who was determined to buy the American 'plane.'

In early February 1965 the Defence Minister announced the cancellation of the two Hawker projects, the P.1154 and the HS.681, but because of the political sensitivities pronounced a postponement on TSR.2. It occasioned Sir George to issue a final 'rallying call to the troops', while the project was still alive. But the stay of execution was short-lived, although it took two Cabinet meetings and a midnight resolution to strike the final blow.

In his memoirs, Harold Wilson describes the lead-up to the decision, which had to be made at the Cabinet meeting on 31 March before the Chancellor opened his budget speech the following Tuesday. 'Parliamentary pressures were formidable – and those of industry no less so,' he wrote. The Cabinet 'most unusually' failed to reach a decision in the normal allotted time, and a second late-night meeting was convened. Wilson writes: 'By midnight I had to resolve a difficulty – indeed I think in all our time a unique situation. The Cabinet was split three ways: some favoured continuing with TSR.2; some favoured its outright cancellation, with no replacement; and the third group supported by the Defence Secretary's view that TSR.2 should go but that its military role should be taken over by an order for American Phantoms, together with one for a number of F-111As.'

The Prime Minister recorded: 'There was not, in fact, a clear Cabinet majority for any one of the three propositions. I summed up, and this was accepted, that a clear majority was for cancelling TSR.2. The question of a replacement, if any, should be further examined in the Defence committee, subject to final Cabinet approval.'

Edward Pearce wrote, 'The thing had been done after interminable unstable debate, a tribute to Wilson's conduct of his government. But it had been done, and after a modest military and civil celebration with Hardman, Cooper, Nairne and Elworthy, the minister [Healey] got to bed at 1.30am.'

Unusually, it had been agreed that the decision would not be announced until the Chancellor's budget speech on 6 April. Sir George, with Portal and Verdon-

Smith, were among a small gathering summoned to the House of Commons, where they were met by Roy Jenkins. He told them that the cancellation of TSR.2 was to be announced in the budget speech, but he wanted them to know before it became public knowledge. Because of this, Jenkins hoped they would understand that they were not in a position to leave until after the budget speech was over. 'We were virtually locked in the room so we couldn't blow the gaff,' says Sir George. This annoyed him because he was unable to let BAC employees know, as was the custom, before they read it in the newspapers. He was also very unhappy about it. 'Once more I knew that I was right and they were wrong, and that subsequent events would prove it,' he says, adding: 'I think of all the blood and sweat that I and my chaps had put into it, being carelessly thrown away by some chap making a speech in the Commons.'

The figures used in the following debate to justify the cancellation have long been a matter of argument. Healey quoted £750 million as the total cost of TSR.2 and a unit cost of £5 million for 150 aircraft, rising to £6 million for 110. He claimed that the purchase of an equal number of F-111s would save at least £300 million, including the write-off money for TSR.2. Charles Gardner, in his BAC history, stated that it later became clear that Healey had used 'programme costs' for TSR.2, which included maintenance, training and operating over a period of time. He wrote: 'It was, however, never quite clear to many MPs when like was being compared with like.' To which Sir George says: 'I would not be surprised at that. I had no time for the way Healey went about things at all. He seemed to be out to do the industry harm.'

Healey also claimed that the manufacturers had been offered a fixed price which they could not manage, so there was 'no assurance that Her Majesty's Government's ultimate financial liability would have been limited'. This assertion was disputed by BAC. In a notice to employees, approved by Sir George, the company stated that BAC had made every effort to give satisfactory assurances on cost, deliveries and performance, and had put forward a target price for its part in the development and production of a fixed number of aircraft. The notice stated: 'In order to provide the government with maximum assurances a formula was proposed for sharing profits and losses up to a maximum loss to the Corporation of £9 million.'

What Healey did not divulge was a damning report on the F-111 compiled by a team of government experts led by Handel Davies, and presented to him early in 1965. In it the team concluded that the F-111 was in deep technical trouble, which would cost a lot of money and a lot of time to cure. In his Hinton lecture to the Fellowship of Engineering in 1982, Sir George said: 'The F-111 was clearly full of problems, but there was a touching belief that the Americans would always get a job right regardless of how much trouble it was in. I must say that over the years they have given themselves plenty of practice.'

At the time of cancellation, TSR.2 development aeroplane XR219 had completed twenty flights, having been moved to Warton, much to the pleasure of Freddie Page. It had proved all the parameters set for it, from great stability at low level to supersonic dash at altitude. But to the anguish of the brilliant technical team, and others responsible for the project, the government flatly refused to allow any further development flying, which at comparatively low cost (£2 million was quoted) would have been of great benefit to British aviation, especially to engine development.

Orders were also issued to break up the airframes and destroy all the jigs. It had long been held that these orders came from Denis Healey, but he subsequently flatly denied this. George Edwards, in retrospect, could not be sure when and how the orders came, although he had some sympathy for such a move, recalling his decision to break up the V1000 jigs 'so as not to leave dead corpses lying around'. There is some credence, therefore, to the belief that Sir George, if he was not the instigator of the order, gave some support for it.

Thus ended TSR.2, but not the debate, which still rumbles on nearly fifty years later. There are those, both inside and outside the company, who have been critical of Sir George, claiming particularly that he did not, or could not, devote enough time to the project. In a note written in January 1964, the Assistant Chief of Air Staff (OR), Air-Vice Marshal Denis Smallwood, stated: 'The real problem is, of course, that Sir George Edwards is the only man who can make anything of the mediocrity at his disposal, and he has not the time. The VC10, the BAC One-Eleven and now the Concorde are much more worrying and important to BAC and in particular to Weybridge than TSR.2. These are the aeroplanes which are going to pay the shareholders, and BAC is not in sight of the break-even point on any of them.'

Freddie Page adopted a similar theme, saying: 'Sir George Edwards necessarily had been much occupied with the setting-up of BAC and the Vanguard, the Super VC10 and the BAC One-Eleven programmes, but near the end of 1964 intervened to put me in charge of the TSR.2 programme. This was a doubtful honour, as it was then clear that a new Labour government, aided by several powerful figures behind the scenes in Whitehall, were determined to cancel the project.'

Sir Frederick also believed that the 'premature announcement' of the TSR.2 contract in the first place on a fifty-fifty workshare basis 'only served to prevent the formation of a properly balanced project team and led to delays and increased costs. . . . Vickers had clearly won the battle in Whitehall, and the uncompromising terms of the January 1959 announcement, followed by the award of all subsequent contracts to Vickers only, even after the formal incorporation of BAC, inevitably meant that all definitive aspects of the project were controlled by Vickers men.'

Freddie Page's remarks reflected some deeply felt resentment at Warton over the original selection of Vickers, of which Sir George was fully aware. However, there is no doubt that a combination of his leadership and the weapons-system approach won the day, and there is also no doubt in the minds of all those close to Edwards that nobody could have fought longer or harder for its survival than he did.

But if English Electric was, in Page's words, 'firmly treated as a subcontractor', the programme did have one beneficial side-effect, which, he said, 'was to outlast TSR.2'. This was the transfer of responsibility from the Preston factory to English Electric Aviation in early 1963, as recommended by Page and supported by Sir George and Lord Caldecote to avoid further production delays. 'This was a key TSR.2 achievement and the foundation of the successful Military Aircraft Division of BAe (British Aerospace) at Warton and Samlesbury,' he said.

The TSR.2 chapters should not be concluded without recording that its demise in 1965 did not bring a credible US alternative. Three years later Harold Wilson cancelled the options on F-111, although he confirmed an order for McDonnell Douglas Phantoms, but with Rolls-Royce Spey engines. These were supplied to both the RAF and Royal Navy with varying degrees of success. Ironically, much of the conversion work was done at the Preston factory.

CHAPTER TWENTY-TWO

Life After Death, but Only Just

The immediate aftermath of the cancellation of TSR.2 virtually brought BAC to its knees. For Sir George Edwards it was the most traumatic and worrying period in his whole career. 'It knocked the stuffing out of BAC,' he said at the time. Not only had the company lost a huge slice of its workload and half of its expected profits, but, equally grievously, it had lost out to an American rival on questionable technical and financial grounds (as later proved to be the case), depriving Britain of a hard-earned but easily destroyed technical capability. Now it would lose precious jobs and its international reputation, and its very survival was at risk.

Compounding this dire outlook, the government was deferring payment of rightful TSR.2 cancellation 'hardship' charges and dragging its feet on normal launch aid for the new versions of the One-Eleven, in which BAC had already invested substantial sums. To make matters worse, export chances for the VC10 were irrevocably damaged by Sir Giles Guthrie, chairman of BOAC, who was attempting, very publicly, to breach the airline's contracts on the highly bespoke aircraft, having altered the specification no fewer than three times in seven years.

'There was a general attitude you couldn't avoid noticing, that everybody thought that the aircraft industry were a lot of wastrels who spent money at a rate of knots,' Sir George says.

Although neither the Ministry of Aviation (Jenkins) nor the MoD (Healey) wished to see the company go under, both believed the industry should be smaller, and reorganised, with the government owning a minority share. To this end the Wilson administration, within two months of taking office, established the Plowden Committee to report and recommend on its future. The Committee itself comprised many eminent men, but only one, Lord Penney, the atomic scientist, had any experience of the problems of advanced technology. That the committee was set up at the height of the TSR.2 debate by a government whose leader described the industry as 'a monster' left little to the imagination as to its likely findings, with the inevitable call for a reduction in size and capability. For the moment, however, it provided a useful excuse for the government not to act or respond to the BAC dilemma.

Sir George now found himself under extreme pressure, not only in making decisions under the duress of a vacillating government, but from the worried parent companies. Vickers stood to lose substantial amounts of private capital on the Vanguard and VC10 'old account' aircraft, while English Electric, although less exposed financially, blamed him for the loss of TSR.2. 'The Vickers view was a bit jaundiced, and the English Electric view was also, because they knew only about military aeroplanes like the Canberra and Lightning. They could not understand why I had been spending money on civil aircraft,' says Edwards. 'So the tales that went around that they weren't mad keen on the way things were going weren't far out.'

In facing up to such criticism, Sir George found great comfort in the support he received from Lord Portal. Sir Reginald Verdon-Smith, who succeeded him as chairman in 1968, referred to it in Portal's biography. He wrote: 'Vickers were somewhat disenchanted with Edwards at this time – they had been let in for a huge bill for the VC10 and sales of the Vanguard were not doing at all well. Edwards was by no means the doyen of the industry that he is today. English Electric, too, suspected civil aviation as a money loser. Portal had a delicate job inside the Corporation building up the authority of George Edwards, and this he did successfully through his own strong personality.' Sir Reginald added: 'Whether or not Portal pursued a conscious policy of this kind, Edwards certainly emerged as one of the two leading figures of the industry. His relationship with Portal was marked throughout by the warmest feelings of admiration and friendship on both sides.'

Portal's support for his managing director showed itself in a practical way during 1963/4, when Sir George's hand was considerably strengthened by major organisational changes within BAC. It was decided that enough progress had been made on unifying the company to drop the old company names and transfer the business previously carried out by its operating subsidiaries into a newly formed and tightly knit British Aircraft Corporation (Operating) Ltd. Sir George was appointed chairman and managing director, and the businesses were formed into four divisions: Filton (Bristol), Preston, Weybridge and the Guided Weapons Division. (These were later reduced to three: Military Aircraft, Commercial Aircraft and Guided Weapons.) To represent the shareholders'

interest, a new overseeing Holdings Board was created, of which Lord Portal
was chairman and Edwards a member.

But the most pressing matter facing Sir George and the company in April
1965 was to fill the production hole left by TSR.2 and reduce the overheads
substantially. This meant unavoidable redundancies, especially in the northern
factories centred on Preston, and at Weybridge in the south. This amounted to
a 15 per cent reduction in the workforce, affecting over 4,000 BAC employees.
Asked later how he had gone about conveying the bad news, Sir George said
they were told 'eyeball-to-eyeball'. He told the factory managers, and they told
the chaps personally. 'One of the harsh parts about a decision like this is that,
as so often happens, in order to do what in the interests of the company as a
whole is the right thing, poor souls who had nothing to do with it got hurt.'

This remark applied particularly to the second problem, reorganising work
to fill the gaps, which was bound to bring the threat of factory closure. 'English
Electric became a distressed area, and Preston and Samlesbury [its 'daughter'
factory] suddenly became devoid of work. Something had to be done about it,
because the design capability and the gang at Warton had to be preserved,'
Edwards says. Logically it might have been expected that one of the former
English Electric sites most heavily involved in TSR.2 would be shut down. But
Sir George could not let this happen. Instead, the axe was raised against the
small and thoroughly excellent former Hunting factory at Luton, which was
successfully building the Jet Provost trainer for the RAF and a growing number
of overseas customers.

'I was confronted with the job of keeping Preston Division afloat, and I did it
by the simple process of shutting Huntings down and transferring the chaps
and the work – and that was the thing [the work] – up there,' says Sir George.
'Everybody got suitably tearful about this because the Hunting outfit at Luton
wasn't bad. Summers [W.A. Summers, the general manager] ran it well. He
was pretty grievous about it, but I was faced with no alternative and I just had
to shut the place down.' The factory was subsequently sold to Vauxhall Motors,
and Summers moved to manage, very successfully, the Hurn plant.

With the blood-letting thus temporarily staunched, senior BAC management,
led by Sir George and Lord Portal, together with the chairmen of the parent
companies, became engaged in a long, tedious and largely unrewarding
dialogue with Whitehall for TSR.2 compensation in the shadow of Plowden,
which was not due to be published until the end of the year. The only good
news to come out of this was the confirmation of two major new military
collaborative programmes with the French. Both had been negotiated by Denis

Healey, supported by Jenkins, during the previous year, so the predictable plight of the industry post-TSR.2 had not been entirely ignored.

But this was in the future, and although it gave immediate and very welcome work to preserve the design teams at Warton, the most pressing problem was to secure promised funds to keep the company afloat. This became Sir George's priority, and he was spending more and more time in Whitehall 'pedalling up and down so fast that my feet were a blur'. By October 1965 he was telling Sir Richard Way at the Ministry of Aviation that BAC had an immediate need for £20 million, either for TSR.2 compensation or for expected launch aid for developing the new One-Eleven. The situation, he said, was 'desperate'.

At one time it appeared the Ministry had agreed to a compensation and launch aid package, but this did not materialise, provoking a strong letter from Lord Portal to Roy Jenkins. Portal stated that the BAC claims had been properly examined by the Ministry accountants but payment was still being deferred. In the absence of substantial payments, he said, they would have to take drastic action, and this would be carried out within the next week or ten days unless some understanding could be reached.

At last Jenkins yielded, and he agreed to a support package amounting to £6.75 million. But the government (the Treasury) did not agree. In a break with tradition they turned down the request. Some believed this was a cynical move to drive down the value of the company at a time when they were contemplating its acquisition. Then, at the worst possible time for the company and the negotiations, Roy Jenkins was moved from aviation to become Home Secretary. He was replaced by Fred Mulley and, as he was a new Minister, BAC would now have to start all over again.

In December 1965 the Plowden Committee finally published its report. Its findings were, as expected, disappointing, negative and defeatist. As Charles Gardner noted: 'It was very strong on analysis of past mistakes . . . and weak on what ought to be done.' It suggested that the industry should be reduced in size, needed no more support than was given to comparable industries, and offered little prospect of substantially increasing sales of purely British products. The committee declared the industry must now look to collaboration with other countries in Europe, which, of course, BAC was doing already.

Plowden's view on ownership was no surprise either. It suggested the government might take a shareholding in BAC and Hawkers, but came to no firm decision as to whether there should be one or two airframe companies. The only positive and helpful proposal to emerge was a recommendation to increase to ten years the standard period for Export Credits Guarantee Department insurance cover, which would help export sales of civil aircraft, particularly the One-Eleven.

In achieving very little the Plowden Committee occupied an inordinate amount of the BAC top management's time and effort in preparing documentation and providing evidence (mostly in written form) at a time when more pressing matters, like staying in business, were on their minds. A comprehensive document, based largely on Sir George's letters to Roy Jenkins on the adverse effect of the cancellation of TSR.2, was submitted by Lord Portal and largely ignored by the committee.

The crux of BAC's argument was that the company had been formed 'specifically, and with government encouragement, to provide a balanced aircraft unit with the right mixture of civil and military work'. Lord Portal referred to the worldwide evidence that civil aircraft projects had not been viable on their own, and that all their competitors operated with an extensive background of military work. He said that BAC required 'a new alignment' with government, in which the industry was recognised as a national enterprise and was brought under 'one unified direction'. This did not mean nationalisation, but the realisation that they were so surrounded by government influence that decision-making on commercial grounds had become impossible.

Giving oral evidence to the committee in July 1965, Sir George was able to give examples of this and have a swipe at the government's policy of buying the cheapest in the market (the F-111) at the expense of the wider implications for the British industry. He referred to the huge advantage the Americans had in having long production runs; F-111 production would be in the order of 1,500 aircraft, against an initial requirement of 110 TSR.2s.

'The position between the American and British industry,' he stated, 'was like David and Goliath.' Hitherto he had been comforted by the outcome of that particular conflict, but now the government had 'removed his pile of stones and was giving them to Goliath'. As far as the French were concerned, he envied the way they were supported by their government. This was in sharp contrast to the way BOAC and the government had handled the VC10. 'It was a harrowing experience to be asked by overseas customers why they should buy British if their own airline and government did not do so,' he said.

Sir George had also been incensed by an earlier remark by Roy Jenkins in the TSR.2 parliamentary debate. The Minister had said it was the government's wish to reduce the size of the industry and transfer the technology into other fields that included the design of modern cutlery and Swedish-type furniture. Edwards responded: 'You would have to export a hell of a lot of three-piece suites to get in foreign currency the value of just one VC10.'

In January 1966, following the publication of the Plowden Report, Lord Portal, Sir George and Willie Masterton met Fred Mulley to discuss its findings, and particularly the government's wish to establish just one airframe company. According to the contemporaneous minute it was clearly an acrimonious meeting, at which Portal pressed first for the outstanding compensation claim on TSR.2 to be settled, especially as the previous Minister had agreed it was morally justified. The refusal of the Minister's colleagues (the Treasury) to agree to it had destroyed mutual confidence between them, he said. Until confidence was re-established, there would be no point in negotiation, and he therefore felt 'unable to have a substantive discussion with the Minister on the implementation of the Plowden Report'.

Fred Mulley retorted that, although he would do his best to persuade his colleagues to accept the claim, he would not go beyond that. He was bound to tell Lord Portal frankly that if other ministers were told that BAC was not willing to discuss Plowden unless the TSR.2 hardship claim was settled first, his colleagues were bound to feel that BAC was attempting to 'hold a pistol at the government's head', which would have the very worst effect, and almost certainly lead to summary dismissal of BAC's claim. Portal responded by stating it was the government who were exercising duress, and not the other way round. In his view the government were 'trying to ruin the corporation so as to acquire their assets cheaply'.

Sir George told the Minister of the damage to confidence in the British industry that Plowden was causing, especially with the French, and expressed his concern at the committee's view that the UK should also turn to the USA for big projects. Britain, he said, had 'the ingenuity and the ingredients' to do any aeronautical jobs, and the real problem affecting the industry was the frequency of cancellations.

But it was left to the Minister to fire the most destructive salvo, when he said that, in forming one airframe company, the government were no longer talking about a minority shareholding in BAC, as previously stated, but were now considering a majority shareholding. To this Lord Portal said the government would then be obliged to acquire 100 per cent of the BAC shares.

Effectively, a stalemate was reached. This was to last for nearly two years, with the BAC parent companies resisting government attempts to merge the corporation with Hawker Siddeley to form one airframe company on a minority basis for BAC (30 per cent) on a valuation assessment which was far too low, and which the government proposed to acquire. English Electric also made it clear that in these circumstances it would retain the GW Division. Sir George took the view that the government estimates on value were wrong. The longer negotiations went on to include compensation for old-account aircraft, 'the more wrong the government would get its sums', he said.

In an attempt to win BAC round to a merger, Sir James Mackay, who had taken over as the Permanent Secretary at the Ministry of Aviation, suggested to Sir George that he was likely to be asked to run the new outfit. He received short shrift. Sir George said that, if it went ahead, he and many senior members of his team, many of whom were vital to the continuation of government programmes such as Concorde, would leave the industry.

Matters came to a head in November 1968 when, in a surprise move, Mulley announced in parliament that the national interest would best be served by a merger of the airframe interests of BAC and Hawker Siddeley into one company, in which it was the government's intention to take a minority interest. This would be the 30 per cent which would come from their total ownership of BAC. The employees of BAC were quickly advised by Lord Portal that, although the company would examine the Minister's proposals, it was likely that 'we shall be in prolonged discussions and the conclusions are, at this time, difficult to foresee'. He added: 'There will probably be a great deal of speculation on all sides and in the press. I hope you will treat with caution anything you read or hear which does not come specifically either from the corporation or the Minister.'

Sir George and the Board members all knew that the sticking point would be in reaching agreement with the parent companies on the government's valuation of BAC, which would obviously be much lower than theirs. Since the government did not have a mandate to nationalise the industry or take ownership, they could not just confiscate the shares or, as one observer put it, 'send in the Brigade of Guards'. Inevitably this led to further meetings with the parent companies at which more proposals and counter-proposals were made. Sir George said that the clear way to meet the situation was 'to play it slow'. Sooner or later the government would have to settle the TSR.2 claim and provide launching aid for the One-Eleven, for which an order from BEA was in the offing. This would be at the expense (for a change) of an American buy.

By this time things were improving within the company. Despite all the uncertainty and financial constraint, orders were being received from abroad. Sales of military aircraft, led by the new Preston Division, included reorders for the Canberra and new orders for both the Lightning and Strikemaster (the strike derivative of the Jet Provost). Of particular significance were the orders received from Saudi Arabia, which were to be the foundation of the enormous and lasting defence contracts (still extant) with that country. Furthermore, work on the two new Anglo-French programmes was keeping the talented design teams occupied, and there were long-term production prospects.

The GW Division, under the direction of Lord Caldecote and the very able George Jefferson, was recovering from the serious loss of two major programmes, PT.428 and *Blue Water*, as predicted by Edwards in his 'anguished' note to Lord Portal in 1962. This had led to the closure of the GW factory at Luton and the loss of 1,000 jobs. Other weapons systems were, however, now winning orders overseas. But the most promising prospect was the successor to PT.428, destined to become known as the world-famous Rapier low-level air defence system. In addition, two anti-tank weapons, Vigilant and Swingfire, together with new space products, were finding lucrative export markets.

On the civil side, the principal hope lay with the BAC One-Eleven. Hitherto it had offered little financial return pending launch-aid subventions, but with a new £32 million order for a developed version from BEA in 1967 the government reluctantly were left with little option but to fund 100 per cent development costs to the extent of £9 million.

Then, in September 1967, after two years of patient negotiation, Jimmy Armitage, the BAC comptroller, announced a final settlement of £13.25 million for the TSR.2, which greatly increased BAC's viability. As the obvious value of the company went up, the government interest went down. Anthony Wedgwood Benn as he was then known, who as Minister of Technology had taken over the aircraft merger/acquisition problem, was cooling to the task for various reasons. He was now receiving ever-strengthening ripostes from BAC, who pointed out the uncertainty and damage that was being caused as negotiations dragged on.

Matters were finally resolved in December 1967, when, propelled by the effect of the devaluation of the pound, Wedgwood Benn finally and irrevocably relented, and sent a telex to the company effectively calling it all off. He stated they were conducting a re-examination of their existing policies, and it would not be possible to proceed for the time being with negotiations to implement their policy on mergers. He added that it was still the government's view that a merger of the two companies 'was desirable'.

In a Christmas message to all employees, Lord Portal stated that it was their intention to continue the progressive development of the corporation as an independent private-enterprise company. It was to the credit of all those who worked for BAC that, during the prolonged period of uncertainty, they had maintained and exceeded their performance of 1966, for which they had won the Queen's Award to Industry. During the last three years they had continuously increased export values, which totalled £152 million, and the current figure of £68 million represented over 50 per cent of total output. By any yardstick, even given the most favourable conditions, this was an impressive performance.

Sir George's comment at the end of it all was typical of his whole outlook, even when the odds were stacked against him: 'Never give up. I used to beat them over the head with it – press on, never give up.'

CHAPTER TWENTY-THREE

Concorde – the Beginnings

On 27 July 2000, at the time of the Farnborough Air Show, a chartered Air France Concorde crashed in flames shortly after take-off from Paris Charles de Gaulle Airport. It was the first and only total loss of a Concorde after over thirty years of flying, and cost the lives of every soul on board. George Edwards, who watched the sad events on television at home, sensed that, whatever the cause, it was likely to mark the end of the SST era. It was also a personal blow, for he alone had been deeply involved from the very first days of its conception to handing it over for airline service, as leader of the British Concorde team, in 1975.

It all began for Sir George on 1 October 1956, when Sir Cyril Musgrave, Permanent Secretary at the MoS, who had been so supportive of the Viscount, called a high-level meeting of industry, airline and government representatives to consider the possibility of a supersonic transport. This was based on work carried out by the RAE at Farnborough, which had shown that economic operation at supersonic speeds 'might well be a practicable possibility'.

Edwards attended the meeting, and although many others were sceptical he 'stuck out' and insisted that they 'get into the act'. The outcome was the setting-up of a special committee, the Supersonic Transport Aircraft Committee (STAC), drawn from industry and government and sharing resources. It was chaired by Morien Morgan, then the RAE's Deputy Director. Morgan had also been attached to the Farren Mission in 1945 and, like Sir George, had collected valuable information on high-speed wing design during the tour of German industrial and research establishments. Since then he had overseen and encouraged the continuing and original work at Farnborough, much of it inspired by German scientists and aerodynamicists. They included particularly Dr Kuchemann and Dr Doetsch, who, as previously noted, had been recruited in Germany and had now settled in

England. Today, most people in the industry regard Morgan, for his foresight and leadership, to be the true father of Britain's SST programme.

Sir George, who did not sit on the STAC himself, but supported its establishment and was party to its findings, says: 'It was a joint government committee, which was quite unique. It actually worked jolly well, largely because the technical people involved all got on, and I got on well with Morien. Out of it emerged how not to do a thing with a W-shaped wing (the structural problems would have been horrendous), and we gradually worked our way through to a slender delta; the shape you have today.' Later this was attributed largely to their work.

After three years, a very short time considering the immensity of the task, the STAC recommended in 1959 that the development of SSTs 'should be pressed forward without delay'. It proposed two alternative designs: a medium-range aircraft cruising at Mach 1.2 (about 800mph), which was quickly dropped, and a more realistic long-range transatlantic aircraft, carrying about 150 passengers and cruising at speeds not less than Mach 1.8 (about 1,200mph). Both could be built of conventional alloys, whereas higher speeds up to Mach 3 (three times the speed of sound) would require new and untried materials to withstand the effects of kinetic heating (caused by air friction) of up to 300° centigrade. A range of development costs was given rather over-enthusiastically, ranging from £50 million for the medium-range aircraft to £95 million for the longer-range version.

In arriving at a basic feasible design, the designers had to resolve the conflicting aerodynamic demands of supersonic and subsonic performance. Sir George explains: 'The ideal shape to fly at Mach 2 was a slender delta, just a narrow triangle where you were pretty free of shock waves. Unfortunately the aspect ratio was very nearly zero, with virtually no span or length. So you had to increase the aspect ratio to get the subsonic performance, and increase the span at the back end. Then you have another compromise, so you didn't overdo it and damage the supersonic cruise.' He adds: 'What you got was this fancy wing shape which everybody thinks we did to make it look pretty, but the only reason for it was you couldn't do it any other way.'

Of vital importance to this approach was the brilliant work of Dr Dietrich Kuchemann and his team at Farnborough. Kuchemann demonstrated that an arrow-shaped wing generated large vortices (circular air currents) off the leading edge, which rolled into a pair of very stable conical air currents over the wing, providing added lift and lateral stability at critical low speeds. This was a revolutionary approach, for up to that time aerodynamicists had tried to achieve an uninterrupted airflow that passed smoothly over the wing. Now they were proposing the opposite, and depending on the vortices for a proportion of the lifting force.

The government duly accepted the STAC report and funded two feasibility studies, of which the most promising was for an SST with a slender delta wing and a conventional discrete fuselage. The contract was awarded to Bristol Aircraft under the leadership of Dr Archibald Russell (later Sir Archibald), the chief designer, and the company proposed an aircraft of 380,0000lb take-off weight to cruise at Mach 2 and carry up to 132 passengers on transatlantic routes. Designated the Bristol Type 198, it was to be powered by six turbojets.

At this point, in 1960, Bristol was merged into BAC, and Sir George Edwards inherited ultimate responsibility for the project he had followed so closely for so long. His enthusiasm for an SST was infectious, and there could have been nobody better placed to encourage its development. Indeed, two years earlier, as president of the RAeS, an honour of which he was extremely proud, Sir George, in a visionary and much-quoted presidential address, had foreseen the coming of the supersonic age and had demonstrated its advantages, especially to world trade. To do this he plotted the impact of speed from the stagecoach to the present day. He showed that, once two places became within 12hr of each other, trade and population grew rapidly and very considerably. 'When we do get a supersonic jet we get with it the ability to bring practically the whole world within reach of the 12hr journey time,' he stated, adding: 'I am convinced that nothing will stop the ultimate operation of long-range supersonic aeroplanes.'

It was unfortunate, therefore, that the SST project brought him into immediate conflict with Dr Russell on the design of the Bristol aircraft, which required six engines. Sir George says: 'I always said that the only contribution I made that was worth making was that I took two engines out. I just banged on the table and said the operational costs of the aeroplane were not dependent on the power of the engine, but were dependent on the number of engines. No airline could stand such complications and costs.'

Sir George says: 'Russell waved his arms about and said I didn't know anything about it, and the only way you could get the power you needed was to put in six engines. There was a hell of a set-to in convincing everybody that there wasn't an airline in the world that would have settled for it.' Edwards continues: 'The smart thing to do was devote time and energy in making four engines have enough power.' In time, that was what happened, resulting in a lighter aircraft of 250,000lb with four engines and carrying 100 passengers.

In pursuing the SST programme the government had made it clear that Britain would be unable to bear the cost of development on its own, and that collaborative partnerships should be sought either in the USA, then the preferred option, or in France. Sir George was asked by the Minister, Julian Amery, to sound out the Americans. He met with the officials, including Federal Aviation Authority (FAA) Administrator Najeeb Halaby, who had set up a Supersonic Transport Advisory Group and had recommended an early commitment to an SST to President Kennedy 'as a national objective'.

'An immense argument went on, all revolving around the difference between Mach 2 and Mach 3,' says Sir George. 'The Americans weren't going to join in to something so antique as Mach 2, and were hell-bent on pressing on with Mach 3. For this we had built this all-steel research aeroplane down at Bristol, the T.188 [to explore the effects of kinetic heat beyond Mach 2]. It was only a little aeroplane, but it drove everybody mad trying to make it. Although it cost a lot to do, it was cheap in the end, because it headed off any serious attempt at building a Mach 3 aircraft.'

The French, however, through Sud-Aviation, were more amenable than the Americans. They had been developing a medium-range Mach 1-plus aircraft, the Super Caravelle, and exploratory discussions had already taken place at Filton with Dr Russell's team. Although the French were devoted to a medium-range aircraft, the two teams found many areas of commonality, notably the adoption of a slim delta shape, using the same powerplant, the Bristol Siddeley Olympus 593 turbojet. This engine, of course, had been chosen (and mostly paid for) by the government for TSR.2. It was not only a practical choice, although further development would cost much more, but, most of all, it was available.

Both the British and French teams accordingly recommended further joint technical study into all aspects, and, with government encouragement, more-formal discussions continued through 1961 to seek common ground between the two concepts. Russell and chief engineer Dr William Strang were convinced that a Mach 2 aeroplane for the 'blue riband' London–New York route, offering a flight time just above 3hr, was the way to go. Furthermore, it was over the sea, minimising the effect of the supersonic boom created by shock waves when an aircraft flies beyond the sound barrier.

The French, however, having spent much time and government money on their medium-range aircraft, designed to replace their own very successful Caravelle, were not prepared to abandon it. They also argued that the

Americans would inevitably join the supersonic race and eventually dominate the long-haul routes at the expense of the British proposal.

Despite these differences, both sides realised that they must seek a uniform approach if they were to secure further government funding. However, matters were not enhanced by the first top-level formal meeting at Weybridge in July 1961, between Sir George and his opposite number in Sud-Aviation, Georges Hereil. Hereil was a forceful and unyielding character, and Sir George was 'not wildly enthusiastic' about collaboration with the French at the time. It was hardly surprising that the two did not get on. 'With Hereil on one side and me at the other end, I thought this was never going to come to pass,' Sir George says. Geoffrey Knight, who was to become chairman of BAC's Commercial Aircraft Division, wrote: 'Sir George Edwards and Georges Hereil knew each other perfectly well. They were both too strong and determined to find it easy to share a common approach.'

But within a few months there came a change that altered the whole perspective of the project. Georges Hereil resigned, to be replaced by Gen André Puget. In Sir George's view the change was of the greatest importance to the future of the SST. The move was precipitated, he believes, by 'diplomatic intervention' instigated by BAC's Paris agent, Baron de Longlade. He was a man of influence, and was fully aware of the difficulties between the two industry leaders. 'I think he talked to his friends and relatives in high places, and they put him [Hereil] in charge of Simca [the French car manufacturer],' says Sir George.

Unlike Hereil, who was a trained lawyer, Puget was a pilot and an anglophile, having commanded the Free French bomber squadrons in England during the war. Not only did both men like each other, they trusted each other's judgement and were mutually supportive. 'He knew what a funny lot of buggers we were,' says Sir George, who earlier had placed substantial subcontract work for the VC10 with Sud-Aviation 'as a gesture of goodwill'.

In November 1962 sufficient progress had been made to allow the signing in London of the historic treaty between Britain and France for the joint design, development and manufacture of a supersonic airliner. Julian Amery, the Aviation Minister, signed for Britain, and the French Ambassador, M de Courcel, signed for France. Although both parties would continue to pursue their respective proposals, they agreed to have two common prototypes, followed by two pre-production aircraft that would develop each country's respective concepts. In this case France would build the first prototype, predicated for medium-range, and BAC would build the first pre-production aircraft, designed for long-haul routes. Many areas of commonality were also identified, including the critical engine intake and nozzle designs, and aircraft systems, interiors and cockpit layout. Cost estimates up to 1969 were put at £135.2 million, of which £39.9 million would be for engine development.

With the government-to-government agreement came, inevitably, a complex management arrangement, with a central directing committee, made up mainly of civil servants and their advisers, under which there were two key committees of directors, one for the engine and one for the airframe. The chairmanship of these was to alternate annually between the two nations. The first chairman of the airframe group was Gen Puget, with Sir George as his deputy, a position that would reverse the following year.

For Sir George, who was then 'up to his eyes' in TSR.2 Whitehall bureaucracy, the complexity of the Concorde administration was familiar but unwelcome ground, except that it was now compounded by duplicating everything between two design concepts, two companies and two nations speaking different languages. 'These are not usually taken to be the ingredients of success,' Sir George said in an extended interview with Ken Owen for his excellent book *Concorde – a New Shape in the Sky*. As a personal example of commitment to an unwieldy arrangement, Sir George decided to take French-language lessons from a local teacher. This was not only a courtesy to Puget, who spoke English well, but, as with his flying activities, he wanted to be able to understand the situation better and make sure he could express his point of view correctly to the French.

The cost of the SST was now coming under public scrutiny, especially as estimates continued to be exceeded. Sir George attributed part of this to not having direct competitive pressures, either through the threat of war, as was the case with the Valiant, or through direct commercial opposition from the USA, which was still only at a preliminary stage with its Mach 3 aeroplane. He told Ken Owen: 'It was a combination of the fact that we were starting from a comparatively low state-of-the-art in what we were trying to do, and we had lots of time in which to do it. It was absolutely inevitable that there were going to be progressive improvements all the way through the programme. And that made it take longer, it made it cost more, but at the end of the day they really did make it better.'

To add to the difficulties, there followed a prolonged period of wrangling and disagreement between the two technical teams, who were determined to preserve their own design proposals and their own methods of working. Talking about the difference of approach to crucial weight measurement, Sir George said: 'It was a difference of attitude and temperament. The French thought that if you aimed for a low weight and you presented the low weight as something you were going to achieve, then you stood a much better chance of achieving it. . . . That's a bit naïve when you are dealing with Isaac Newton.'

Relationships, even between Edwards and Puget, were sometimes strained. Ken Owen quoted Sir George as saying: 'Every now and then there used to be an absolute confrontation, and I remember one occasion especially, at Toulouse. This involved Puget and Pierre Satre, his technical director, and Lucien Servanty, Satre's chief designer, who was a very good man. . . . We had a tremendous battle, but in the spirit of our relationship, the next time Puget and I met it was all over and done with.'

Geoffrey Knight, in his book *Concorde – the Inside Story*, remembered the early 'interminable' committee meetings and the parts played by Puget, 'a splendid chairman', and Edwards, who 'was not a Montgomery to Puget's Eisenhower'. Sir George, he said, had taken enormous care to see that he did nothing to erode Puget's authority, although in terms of sheer experience and engineering skill he was the dominating personality. Of his style, Knight wrote: 'Sir George had a very quiet way of operating and would never indulge in a knock-down, drag-out altercation at a committee meeting. If a difficulty cropped up, and I remember there was an early serious difference of opinion about the shape of the wing, he would go down personally to Toulouse to work out the problem, often in the company of Archibald Russell, and persuade them that the BAC solution was the right one. When the matter came up at the next Board meeting there was usually little further argument.'

Knight added: 'I don't think I ever heard him [Sir George] raise his voice. His greatest quality was his ability to convince people of the utter sound common sense of what he was saying. He also had an original turn of phrase, which was sometimes difficult to put across in French. One of the most remarkable men that the British aircraft industry has produced, the part that he played in our long travail cannot be exaggerated.'

In 1963 Pan American Airways, then the trend-setting airline for the world, took options on six long-range SSTs, with early delivery positions. Other major airlines quickly followed suit. The French at last capitulated 'reluctantly' on their Super Caravelle, and all efforts were concentrated on the transatlantic aeroplane. Sir George says: 'There is only one range to fly the aeroplane, and that is across the Atlantic. I had a hell of a dogfight, but I got Julian Amery on my side and finally the French conceded. Once we got that done it was a working proposition.'

Both design teams were now free to explore and exploit the transatlantic aircraft, and it resulted in a virtual redesign. Russell had always envisaged a larger aeroplane of around 380,000lb all-up weight, to guarantee true transatlantic range carrying a full payload. The fuselage was lengthened by 14ft, the wing area increased by 15 per cent and the weight increased to 367,000lb. A year later a further 6ft extension was added to the fuselage, and the passenger cabin was reconfigured to accommodate a maximum of 140 economy-class seats.

Power increases were now available at up to 40,000lb rating from the Olympus. Its characteristics were, of course, very familiar to Sir George, and although the engine was troubled by early technical problems, he still recognised its potential and later described it as 'a pretty satisfactory engine'. Many of the improvements were attributed to intake and nozzle design. The variable-geometry ramp intakes controlled the airflow, which had to be slowed to subsonic speed to be accepted into the engine when flying supersonically. The necessary reverse effect was achieved by convergent–divergent (narrowing–widening) nozzles on the jet exhaust, to achieve maximum efficiency. Astonishingly, the intakes and nozzles contribute 90 per cent of the thrust at cruising speed and at cruising altitudes up to 60,000ft.

But most of all, as the Olympus designers confirmed, the use of military-style reheat 'came to our rescue'. Originally this method of relighting the excess fuel in the jetpipe to give added thrust was not envisaged for the aircraft, but as the weights increased for the longer-range aeroplane the engine was virtually redesigned. Reheat was incorporated and developed progressively for use both for take-off and for added impetus to push through the 'sound barrier'.

As to the complexity of the design that now emerged, and the narrowness of the technical margins within which the two teams had to work, Sir George said famously (with deference to Mr Micawber): 'An aeroplane like this only survives if you've got about a half per cent five times on the right side. Then you're doing all right. If you've got a half per cent five times on the wrong side it's a splash off Gander [Newfoundland].'

By now the SST had been named Concord(e), the result of a company competition at Filton that was won by the undergraduate son of the publicity manager, F.G. 'Nobby' Clark. The true story over the disputed 'e' is told in Charles Gardner's book. Gardner had received the suggestion from Filton and laid it before Sir George, who liked it, but asked whether it should be with or without the 'e'. 'The author thought it looked better and more attractive to the eye with the "e" and Sir George said it would also give pleasure to André Puget.' The proposal was put to Sud, who accepted it. Brian Cookson, who was company secretary at BAC, was particularly pleased. 'The "e" did make the registration of the name as a trademark etc. much simpler,' he says. Unfortunately, as far as Gardner knew, it was not submitted to any government committee, and 'Julian Amery protested strongly at not being consulted'.

It was only later that the 'e' was officially removed from the British side by Macmillan as a response to de Gaulle's Common Market rebuff. It was not reinstated until the roll-out of prototype 001 in Toulouse in 1967 by Technology Minister Tony Benn.

CHAPTER TWENTY-FOUR

'She Flies'

Just as things began to look up for Concorde, two near-mortal blows were delivered from both sides of the English Channel. In Britain, the newly elected Labour government of 1964 were intent on unilateral cancellation. In France, where they were equally anxious about rising costs, they sacked André Puget, replacing him with a suspected and later convicted war criminal. The departure of Gen Puget and the arrival of Maurice Papon, then the Paris Prefect of Police, threatened future working relationships, but if the British government got its way there would be no further working relationships.

Predictably, the new Wilson administration would have no love for a very expensive airliner that was likely to be the preserve of the privileged. In an emergency White Paper on the economic position, produced within days of being elected, they confirmed their 'disposition to cancel' Concorde. According to the new Minister of Aviation, Roy Jenkins, in his autobiography, he had been unaware of this intent. and asked to attend the subsequent Cabinet meeting to argue against it. This was not because Jenkins supported the project, for which he now estimated the cost at £10 million per unit, but because the Anglo-French treaty, although 'unwisely drawn', was, in his words, 'indisputably binding'.

Jenkins recorded that, at the Cabinet meeting, he had to have three goes at deploying a coherent argument, but none of them had made any difference to the outcome. 'Teeth were bared, swords were girded, resolution, not rationality, was the order of the day,' he wrote. He was then deputed to tell the manufacturers of their intentions, before the White Paper was published, and to tell the French government later that week.

The subsequent meetings with Sir George and Sir Reginald Verdon-Smith 'were not exactly joyous occasions', Jenkins wrote. 'Dealing with a new minister who was their paymaster for most of their other projects, they had little alternative but to accept the news with dismayed resignation.' He added:

'The dismay was genuine but the resignation was feigned, for they had every intention, as was reasonable from their point of view, of organising as much opposition as they could muster and shrewdly saw that, given the style and nature of the Wilson government, the unions with whom they normally battled and the press offered the best foci.'

Two days later Jenkins received a formal letter from Sir George, who, as predicted, set out the effect of cancellation on employment and relationships with the French, and outlined the current situation. 'The result of cancellation must therefore lead to an immediate redundancy of 2,300 (of which 2,000 would be at Filton), building up to 6,000 by the end of 1965', he wrote. 'In addition, because of the lack of new aircraft projects, this could lead to a reduction of about 1,000 design staff. I need hardly elaborate on the effect this would have on the corporation's design strength and the attractiveness of this class of employment to those who remained.'

Sir George continued: 'When we started work with the French three years ago, our biggest difficulty was to overcome the natural suspicion with which they viewed anything that the British were doing. During the years, by a long and painful process of perseverance and the forging of many close friendships, we have succeeded in removing those doubts.' In his view they had now reached a degree of collaboration which 'compares favourably with anything that has been achieved between the two countries on the diplomatic front'.

Sir George was aware that the Minister was shortly to meet his French counterpart. As a final 'shot across the bows' he told Jenkins that the reaction he had already received from French colleagues left him in no doubt of the 'difficulty which will confront anyone in this country who tries to promote any further Anglo-French ventures'.

On 17 November Jenkins snapped back, requesting Sir George to let him know, if Concorde were to continue, 'the best financial contribution your company would feel able to make'. As an alternative, he invited Sir George to respond to a suggestion of a modified programme for the production of only two prototypes, with a slightly longer timescale, a proposal that had been made to Jenkins's predecessor in February of that year.

Edwards replied on 23 November, pointing out that they were still only working on an extension of the original design-study contract, pending negotiation of a full design and development contract, of which one of the terms was the level of contribution from BAC. The company and the equipment suppliers had already invested privately in the programme, he said, and would expect to spend more as it built up. 'We require a clear picture before we can agree with you the level of contribution, and we regard 5 per cent as a maximum with a provision for subsequent recovery,' he wrote.

That the Concorde programme survived had absolutely nothing to do with Sir George's letter, or with the expressed dismay of the industry in general. Roy Jenkins, having received a French response which he described as 'not nearly as bad as I feared . . . but gave absolutely nothing away', was being advised that the Treaty was as binding as he feared. Jenkins said the French 'played their cards brilliantly' by reacting 'more in sorrow than anger', but always 'kept in hand' the threat of suing them at the Hague Court of International Justice. The advice that he was getting from the Law Officers was that, if they did, the British would lose, and the government might face damages in the order of £200 million (well over £2 billion in today's prices).

The outcome was finally settled in January 1966, when a Cabinet Committee received the third formal note from the French, 'which sounded as firm as could be', wrote Jenkins. Since they were on the point of cancelling the Hawker Siddeley P.1154 'supersonic Harrier' and the HS.681 tactical transport, with a 'much bigger' cancellation of TSR.2 'lurking in the background', he concluded that, taken in conjunction with the Law Officers' advice, this 'was sufficient to tip the balance and secure a reversal of the ill-judged October pronouncement'. It was only later that Jenkins discovered that, had the British persisted, the French might well have accepted that the project was dead and agreed to its cancellation.

Now that the programme had survived the government axe, the removal of Gen Puget took centre stage for the BAC team. Puget's going was provoked by what Geoffrey Knight called 'the general alarm' caused by the estimated development cost doubling to £500 million. 'Curiously enough this caused relatively less uproar in the British parliament . . . the more serious rumblings came from France,' he wrote. The result was that the French Ministry of Finance became highly critical of the cost escalation, which undermined André Puget's position. In an unexpected move, Puget was appointed French Ambassador to Sweden and replaced by the shadowy figure of Maurice Papon.

During the Second World War Papon had been in Bordeaux as Secretary General of the Department of Gironde. It later transpired at his trial that, during his term of office, he had deported more than 1,500 Jews to Auschwitz. After the liberation he handed the prefecture to the Resistance and, according to newspaper reports, 'soared through the ranks of the French State'. Despite demands for action from the families concerned, it was not until 1998 that he was brought to trial and convicted, although three years later he was released on medical grounds.

The appointment of Papon in succession to Puget as the chairman of Sud-Aviation, and head of the French Concorde effort, was itself shrouded in mystery. That a police chief should be qualified to head France's most prestigious civil project was at least surprising and, at worst, conspiratorial. Sir George believes that Papon had information damaging to the re-election chances of President de Gaulle. Consequently, 'to keep his mouth shut', he was offered the chairmanship of Sud. He learned of all this from Puget, who had asked to meet him at Brown's, Sir George's favourite London hotel, and have a chat about the problem.

'Papon was put in charge of where Puget had been. His English was non-existent and his technical knowledge was non-existent,' says Sir George. 'So at these great inter-governmental meetings, before anything was settled, I had the interesting job of trying to explain the technical words in both languages at the same time.' But losing Puget was 'serious', he says. 'Fortunately de Gaulle was determined that the thing should not be cancelled, although the financiers in France were at him all the time to cancel, because it was costing too much.'

As it happened, Papon did not last long. He was replaced less than two years later by Gen Henri Ziegler who, like Puget, was a military pilot, had served in London during the war, and afterwards became general manager of Air France, where Edwards first met him and 'sold him half-a-dozen Viscounts'. He was, Sir George says, 'an orthodox Frenchmen who got on well with Geoffrey Knight'.

Looking back on the formative Concorde years, Sir George always felt that, in addition to the technology and cost problems of 'tackling the unknown', they were also disadvantaged by the technical superiority of the French officials. 'One of the differences between the two governments was that the French senior civil servants were drawn from chaps who had been put through the l'Ecole Polytechnique system. The result was you got on one side British Greek scholars de luxe who were absolutely ace on what I would describe as public school and Oxford projects, whereas, on the French side, you had chaps who knew what a pound per square inch was.'

Sir George, who campaigned continuously for more technically qualified people to be at senior level within the Civil Service, says he once got cross while trying to explain something to a Permanent Secretary. 'I did my outfit a bit of no good by saying: "Look, I don't expect you to understand what I am saying, but I wish I thought you recognised the words I was using!"'

That Concorde technically 'worked out all right', Edwards attributes to the 'quality of the chaps' responsible for it. 'The aerodynamicists were real aerodynamicists and no mucking about,' he says. 'It was a bloody strong team.

Russell flashed about a bit, driving everybody up the wall with his off-the-cuff remarks, but at the end of the day it all came together, for which he must take credit. You had got the occasional bloke like Mick Wilde [later to become Concorde project director], who could really understand an aeroplane, and Bill Strang, who never really got the recognition for what he did.' On the French side, Sir George had the highest regard for Lucien Servanty, who 'not only knew what he was up to, but was a jolly nice chap'.

In December 1967 the first Concorde prototype, 001, was rolled out with great ceremony on a freezing day in Toulouse. Sales options now stood at seventy-four from sixteen airlines, and there was an air of optimism. Tony Benn, the Technology Minister, headed the British delegation and made a speech in which he formally replaced the 'e' in the Concorde name. He said, to warm applause, that the 'e' stood for excellence, for England and for 'entente Concordiale'.

Sir George got on quite well with Benn, who, as a local Bristol MP, was very supportive of Concorde. 'I used to be Benn's bag boy,' he says. 'I used to get a signal that the Minister was addressing an impartial meeting at Filton. I knew what that would mean. I would be put on a little chair up on the stage while he made an impassioned speech saying how marvellous Concorde was. He would then introduce me to help him on the way, and underline the validity of what he had been talking about.' Edwards adds: 'I got on with him all right; you bloody well had to, it was no good being at war with the Minister.'

Nine months later the British prototype was unveiled at Filton, but without similar French-style ceremony, which infuriated Mr Benn, who was in the area at the time and was not even invited to attend. Benn was now coming under pressure from his civil servants, led by his aviation permanent secretary, Ronnie Melville, to cancel the aircraft because it was 'not economic'. Benn, in his diary, retorted: 'Of course, it never had been,' and adroitly avoided the issue. But within four years, after a Labour victory at the polls in 1974, he was to be severely challenged on the Concorde issue again.

All eyes were now on the first flights, which were predicted for late 1968 or early 1969. It was a shock to them all when Russia's rival Tupolev Tu-144 beat them to it and became the world's first SST to fly, on the very last day of 1968, three months ahead of Concorde. Unlike the Russian event, however, 001's first flight was witnessed by millions on television, with Raymond Baxter in France and Cliff Michelmore in London (both friends of Sir George) providing the commentary. A film by BAC's Jack de Coninck and famous aviation photographer Arthur Gibson, entitled *She Flies*, was later released on the cinema circuits, capturing Baxter's euphoric description as the wheels lifted off the Toulouse runway.

The atmosphere was still full of excitement, although less pronounced, when in April the British Concorde, 002, followed suit. Tony Benn described the occasion on BBC radio in a broadcast in 2003, sadly to mark the end of the supersonic era. 'It was a hilarious day, like a village cricket match. People shouted "Good old Trubby" [Brian Trubshaw was now the British Concorde chief pilot], as if he was going in to bat, and Sir George Edwards was walking about with a pork pie hat like a vicar hoping it wouldn't rain. . . . It was typically British and tremendously exciting.'

Brian Trubshaw, in his book *Test Pilot*, recalled the flight, and how the loss of the radio altimeters on landing was 'definitely unfriendly'. Without the altimeters the pilots (John Cochrane was copilot) had to judge the distance to the runway by eyesight and instinct alone, a difficult task, as the pilot's eyes were 38ft off the ground because of the aircraft's high nose-up attitude. They did so with consummate skill and then received 'a warm welcome' from Sir George and other BAC and government officials. 'There was the usual sea of photographers,' wrote Trubshaw, 'but there was not too much for them to become excited about, because the flight had gone very well with the exception of the radio altimeters.'

With both prototypes successfully in the air and beginning to 'explore the envelope', Sir George became the first non-member of the flight-test team actually to fly Concorde. As a qualified private pilot he had made a point of flying every aircraft for which he was responsible since the Viscount in 1953. This time, dressed in the obligatory flying suit and parachute, he took the controls for a time under the command of Brian Trubshaw, who was accompanied by his opposite number in France, André Turcat.

In his log book Edwards simply recorded a flight time of 1hr 45min, during which he occupied the pilot's seat for a time as 'P2', second pilot. But the experience privately thrilled him and continued to do so. He remembered the 'thump in the back' as reheat was selected for the four Olympus engines as speeds nearing 200mph are reached along the runway before lift-off; the 'slight shudder' as reheat was applied again to carry the aircraft, still climbing, through the sound barrier to reach cruising height at 50,000ft, where the earth's curvature can be seen; the 'rumble' as fuel was transferred first from front to back and returned again to balance the aircraft as it slowed down; and the 'creaks and groans' of the fuselage at it expanded and contracted by nearly a foot, the effects of kinetic heat. But, above all, he recalled the sheer normality of it all, while being whisked along at the speed of a rifle bullet.

Pilots soon came to love the aircraft, and their response was graphically summed up by George Edwards's old friend, the late Capt Brian Calvert, who did so much later for the introduction of Concorde into the British Airways fleet. Calvert wrote: 'Concorde was a lady, climbing like a lovesick angel. Pilots wanted to fly her and see her at the same time. She expanded and contracted, flexed like a fly-fishing rod and flew at Mach 2.'

As the Concorde programme gathered pace, with both prototypes attaining Mach 2 by November 1970, so did the anti-Concorde campaign. Sir George was only too painfully aware of the protest movements and the damage they could do. Many of those who protested against TSR.2 now had Concorde in their sights. Added to this group were the environmentalists. They were convinced that an SST flying so high would damage the protective ozone layer, shatter eardrums and property around the airports, and cause untold damage to wildlife and anything else that was exposed to its sonic booms.

'I don't think we appreciated that part of it when we were rushing around trying to sell to the airlines,' says Sir George. 'I think we were sort of carried away with operating costs, or whether or not to land at Gander. I don't think we really understood what an impact the sonic boom was going to have on millions of people, and the power they would have in stopping it.'

Sir George realised that the USA, even though it was a supersonic rival, could be a most potent ally. 'I wanted the Americans to go on with their supersonic aircraft because that would put the backing into the British government to make sure we got one as well,' he says. He visited Washington and met President Nixon in the White House. The President was also under pressure to scrap the Mach 3 aircraft, which was attracting the same kind of environmental and cost protests as Concorde. The President told Edwards he personally thought it was a pity they had not done a Concorde themselves. Sir George replied: 'I said your lot were insistent on doing a Mach 3, which the rest of us knew was virtually impossible.'

For political reasons, Edwards did at one stage seriously suggest that there could be a joint programme with the Americans for the development of SSTs. In lectures and through the press he outlined his idea in some detail. In an address to the Washington Aero Club in 1967 he stated: 'Viewed against the general background of the American SST with the attendant costs and technical problems of producing it, it could well be that a joint manufacturing programme on Concorde is set up between Europe and the USA. At a later date, when the longer-term American SST appears, the reciprocal arrangement for that to be built in Europe would be equally sensible.'

He carried his theme to the influential Newcomen Society, of which he was a member, in New York in 1969, to the Economics Club in Chicago and to the American Chamber of Commerce in London in 1971. To them he referred to his previous attempts to encourage some form of supersonic partnership. 'But these were listened to with polite attention, to which I had become accustomed, and some members of the US Administration reacted visibly. But it was clear that all the time there was on the one hand a chance of the American SST being built, and on the other hand a chance that Concorde might not go forward, no one took me very seriously.'

For the present, however, the priority was to encourage the Americans to keep going with their programme. Nixon had appointed a former Lockheed test pilot and engineer, Bill Magruder, director of SST development, and located him nearby in the White House so that he could be informed on progress. Magruder had kept in touch with his supersonic ally, Sir George. 'He used to ring me up and ask if I had got any tit-bits or helpful information for him to go in to bat with to persuade the Americans to continue with their own programme. We were in the lunatic situation of me sitting on the telephone giving him material with which to build a supersonic transport that would inevitably compete with Concorde. But I knew enough about Mach 3 to know the Americans weren't good enough to do it then, so I kept old Magruder going with enough to write his report.'

Magruder's efforts were unrewarded, and in March 1971 the US Congress voted against the SST programme on grounds of cost and environmental fears. To many in Britain and France it was good news, leaving the way clear for Concorde. To Sir George it was a huge blow. 'We were now all on our own,' he says.

The American pull-out unfortunately coincided with (or was a result of) a severe international economic downturn, with massively rising fuel prices that were not conducive to Concorde's commercial prospects. This especially applied to the aircraft, as it was described as a 'voracious gas guzzler', needing to carry nearly half its all-up weight in fuel. The advent of the 'environmentally friendly' subsonic Boeing 747, offering large-capacity 'wide-body' comfort and better seat-mile costs, was a much safer and appealing bet for the world's airlines, which generally like to stick together.

Furthermore, many carriers had mortgaged themselves to the hilt to acquire the 747, which, to be profitable in service, still depended on its first- and business-class passengers. It was estimated that they represented some 15 per cent of a typical 747 passenger load, but contributed more than 70 per cent of the flight's revenue. Concorde, therefore, presented a real threat for the airlines, which could see it creaming off the crucial 747 premium passengers, a situation they could not allow to happen, and which conditioned American and airline thinking in the years to come.

'They were dead set against it,' Sir George said at the time. 'The airlines didn't want it because at that stage they had neither the money nor the will to get involved in a great new programme like this.' He added: 'There had been an air of respectability about the project all the time the American SST was under way. . . . The odds were now stacked against Concorde.'

In the summer of 1972 BOAC reluctantly, and suitably 'encouraged' by the government, signed contracts for five Concordes, while Air France signed for four. The value of the BOAC order was put at £115 million by Sir Keith Granville, the chairman, who exchanged contracts with Sir George Edwards in a much-publicised ceremony. Shortly afterwards both prototypes set out on long-distance sales tours. Britain's 002 headed to the Far East and Australia, giving demonstrations in the Middle East and India on the way. The French aimed at South America.

Sir George, who joined the Concorde team in the Philippines, was privately not over-enthusiastic about the tour, as it exposed a prototype to a gruelling 50,000-mile schedule on which every falter, every blemish, would be reported in detail, while its achievements would be less noticed. Even so, a sales and demonstration mission of this kind was desperately needed to encourage airline confidence, and it was heavily backed by the now Conservative government and the new Aerospace Minister, Michael Heseltine.

As it transpired, Concorde 002 behaved perfectly throughout its six-week tour. It got off to a good start by picking up orders from Iranair, while other commitments were received, including preliminary purchase agreements from China. The aeroplane was able to demonstrate the true advantage of speed by halving journey times on key international routes, while exposing its passengers for the first time to 'shirt-sleeve' high-altitude supersonic flight. Hitherto this had been experienced only by military pilots wearing protective flying suits, crash helmets and oxygen masks, while sitting on a rocket-powered ejection seat.

On the down side, the demonstration tour, which was financed by the government, played very much into the hands of the environmentalists. Concorde's smoky engines (the new smoke-free combustion chambers had not yet been introduced), its airfield noise and supersonic boom, were exploited by the protest movement. This was especially so in Australia, where Concorde made a series of proving flights along a special overland corridor from Darwin to Melbourne, having been refused permission to land in Sydney. Although the tour was an outstanding technical achievement, it was also, as Sir George feared, a catalyst for protest, which did not go unnoticed by politicians and airline officials.

Worse was to follow, because the BOAC and Air France orders triggered off an option arrangement with Pan American, negotiated by the French against Sir George's will. This meant that, in order to retain its early delivery positions to be competitive with the two national carriers, PanAm was now obliged to confirm or cancel the order.

The whole option system had been introduced in 1963, as a spur to the world's airlines to 'join the club' and an encouragement to the sponsoring governments. But, as Sir George predicted, all it did was to encourage airlines to make 'phoney orders' by placing returnable deposits to reserve production positions. 'I reckoned that if you were going to lay out a lot of money for a production programme you wanted to be pretty certain they really were going to be built; an old-fashioned attitude,' he says. Geoffrey Knight wrote: 'All this tended to prove that Sir George Edwards, who had an uncanny prescience about this sort of thing, was absolutely right in his unwillingness to enter into the option arrangement in the first place.'

And so it proved. For, unknown to the Concorde team, Pan American was on the verge of bankruptcy and in no position to convert its options into orders. Frantic efforts to renegotiate the timescale were made by the BAC team, led by Geoffrey Knight, who was joined in New York by George Edwards. But they were of no avail, and on 31 January 1973 Pan American announced it was withdrawing its options, as did TWA at the same time.

Bob Gladwell, who was now in charge of the American sales effort for BAC, remembers a gloomy gathering in Geoffrey Knight's suite at the St Pierre Hotel in New York, after they had been informed of Pan Am's decision and its plan to announce it the following day. Gladwell says the telephone rang, and it was Michael Heseltine, who wanted to speak to Sir George. Heseltine wanted to know what had happened, and said it might be better after the announcement if Sir George talked to the press. Edwards responded by suggesting it might be better if the Minister talked to parliament.

On the following day, 1 February, three press conferences were called, in New York, Paris and London, in an effort to re-establish confidence in the programme. Sir George returned to London, where he presided at the conference. 'I used sloppy phrases like "We shall just have to roll down the production line," by which I meant the rate at which the options should be taken up were slowed down,' he says. Although he talked as optimistically as he could, it was 'a crucial blow', and during the following months most of the options and commitments were withdrawn.

Matters were not enhanced when, at the 1973 Paris Air Show, the rival Tu-144 crashed shortly after a spectacular demonstration of a French Concorde flown by test pilot Jean Franchi. The press wanted to know if it could happen to Concorde, and public confidence again took a knock. Although Sir George was horrified at the loss of the aircraft and everybody on board, he was not altogether surprised, for he had first-hand knowledge of the Russian aircraft. In 1967, as a member of a high-powered delegation to Russia led by the then Aviation Minister John Stonehouse (who later 'disappeared' in spectacular fashion after bathing in the sea), he met up again with the Tupolevs, father and son, who had offered him a job in 1956. They were now keen to show off their supersonic aircraft.

'When I was shown the Tu-144 by the young Tupolev, I said to him: "You've got the engines in the wrong place, underneath the fuselage with a long intake." I said: "You will have hellish trouble getting the air down it, and the right place for the engines is under the wing." By the time of the Paris Air Show Sir George had noted that the most significant change was that the engines had been repositioned under the wing, without a long intake and similar to Concorde. This 'was no light achievement', he says.

However, he attributes the Paris crash to the Russian weakness in power controls. 'They were never any good, and they didn't know how to design them.' He dismissed other speculation as to its cause, although he had no particular insight. He believed that the Russians had been outmanoeuvred by the Concorde, and that the Russian pilot 'over-controlled the aeroplane, and the control system gave up the struggle'. Nevertheless, it was another blow.

In March 1974, with the return of a Labour government, Tony Benn was appointed Secretary of State for Industry. Whereas his determination to nationalise the aircraft industry was to bring him into conflict with Sir George, his continued support for Concorde averted another serious attempt to cancel it. In his diaries Benn tells of a meeting with David de le B. Jones, Deputy Secretary in the department, and Ken Binning, Under Secretary, later to become Concorde Director General. They told him there was 'unanimous official advice now throughout Whitehall for the cancellation of Concorde, and they had agreed it was unsaleable in its present form'. Benn noted: 'My own view is that we should continue with the present Concorde programme. This is one of the most difficult problems I have to tackle, and I will have to fight it with tremendous care because it could be a disaster politically for me both in Bristol and personally.'

By now, development costs had risen again, though mainly as a result of the 'galloping inflation' of the time. The current estimates were now put at £1,000 million, spent over 14 years and shared equally between the partners. But Benn's dogged and skilful defence of the programme again brought a reprieve. In July he made a statement to the House, confirming the continuation of Concorde. He wrote: 'It was really exciting: I have saved Concorde and that is now off my chest.'

In December 1975 Concorde received its British C of A (the French certificated the aircraft in October), but by now only British Airways (BA, as BOAC had become) and Air France were left as customers. Upon formally receiving the C of A Sir George was reported as saying: 'This is probably the most expensive piece of paper ever written.'

Scheduled services began a month later, on 21 January 1976, with Concorde now configured with a 100 first-class seats for which passengers would pay an extra 15 per cent premium on the fare. Concordes belonging to both airlines took off simultaneously from London and Paris, the Air France aircraft heading for Rio via Dakar, and BA going to Bahrain. Sir George, although in his first month of retirement, was an invited BA passenger.

But flights to the USA, especially New York, for which the aircraft was designed, were still barred by the Americans, who wished to enact a long and costly Environmental Impact Study. In a deliberately prolonged process, involving public hearings in Washington, they delayed the New York services by nearly two years, until a series of proving trials totally vindicated the manufacturer's claims in meeting required airport standards. At last Concorde was able to operate across the Atlantic, and did so successfully until October 2003, when it was withdrawn from service following the Paris crash and the 'Nine-Eleven' terrorist attacks on New York, which had a devastating effect on airline services everywhere.

Why did Concorde attract such hostility? Sir George says there were many reasons, which might have been joined together. 'The first one is it is too expensive for the ordinary person to go and buy tickets. It's not just a case of doing without a couple of bottles of beer or whatever, it is just out of reach. That also gives the incentive to what you might call the "do-gooders" when it comes to ground noise. I'm not just talking about supersonic booms, although that is part of it. The aeroplane is pretty bloody noisy within reach of a major airport. So you have what you might call an old-fashioned arrangement. It brings up a great "anti" against a few people who fly in it because they are so rich, and they are doing it at the expense of those on the ground.'

As to its technical achievement, Ken Owen summed this up by recalling the inaugural flight to Bahrain, when a fellow passenger remarked to Sir George that flying at Mach 2 felt no different. 'Yes,' said Sir George, 'that was the difficult bit.'

CHAPTER TWENTY-FIVE

Trouble with the French

Although Concorde, the first major Anglo-French collaborative programme, was to have a controversial and rocky economic ride, it did demonstrate the power of a binding agreement. It also offered the means of sharing development costs and doubling the order, especially if applied to a military aircraft for which there was a joint requirement. The announcement by Denis Healey in 1965, immediately in the aftermath of TSR.2, that he had successfully negotiated two new joint military aircraft programmes with the French, was therefore widely welcomed by the industry. This was especially so for BAC, struggling to survive after the loss of TSR.2, which would be the major benefactor of the new deal. For Healey it was a politically astute move.

On the face of it the new proposals offered everything Sir George had long advocated. The two new military aircraft would serve both countries, thus providing large production runs to rival the US industry, and the economies of scale would reduce the unit price to an attractive level, especially in the export market. Above all, because it would take two parties to break the agreement, it should prevent the government 'Placing thumping great orders followed by thumping great cancellations', as Sir George once stated.

Unfortunately, things did not work out quite as either he or the Minister had hoped. On the table were two aircraft. One was to be an outstanding success; the other, a swing-wing fighter known as the Anglo-French Variable-Geometry (AFVG), was to be short-lived, the victim of what many would say was 'French chicanery'.

The AFVG was a new multi-role, multi-service Mach 2-plus aircraft. It would be the first example in Britain of a technology invented by Barnes Wallis and now successfully adopted by the North Americans for the F-111. The advantage of 'swing-wings' was that, by moving the wings fore and aft in flight, maximum efficiency could be achieved by reconciling the conflicting aerodynamic requirements for high speed (fully swept wings) and slow speeds and landing (intermediate setting and straight wings).

Sir George says that Wallis had been 'fiddling about' with flying models for some time, and the theory was fairly well established. 'It was just the mechanics of making it do it that was the problem; it involved a hell of a lot of work.'

Although there was some conflict in requirements between the two partners, the flexibility of design for AFVG allowed for compromise, although it is said the French were only lukewarm from the outset because they were preparing to develop their own version. Essentially, the French wanted a tactical strike aircraft within the European theatre, while for the British, the accent was more on the fighter role.

The other aircraft in the package was the less-glamorous Ecole de Combat et d'Appui Tactique (ECAT), an advanced fighter/trainer with added ground-attack capability. A basic design from the Louis Breguet company had already been chosen by the French at the expense of a Dassault design, something that Dassault never forgot and never forgave.

In May 1965 inter-government agreements to proceed were signed by the two countries. Crucially, it was stipulated that the British, with their variable-geometry experience, would have the lead on AFVG, while the French would take the lead role on ECAT. A similar arrangement was made on engine supply, but, as with Concorde, the leadership positions were reversed.

At the time, relationships between Britain and France were at an all-time low. De Gaulle's rejection of British entry into the European Economic Community, and the perceived French dominance in all joint aircraft developments, had riled the British. The French saw the Labour government's attempts to cancel Concorde and then place orders with the USA in excess of £1,000 million for the F-111, the Lockheed C-130 transport and the McDonnell Douglas Phantom, which had been ordered by Healey to replace TSR.2 in the fighter role, as nothing more than a destabilising plot. Sir George Edwards was quoted at the time as saying: 'The only Englishmen who were still speaking to the French were the engineers on Concorde.'

But for Healey and the new Wilson administration there was now good reason, both politically and industrially, to seek easement in relationships between the two countries. The warning by Sir George and others of the grievous effect the US procurements would have on relationships with the French on future joint projects had not gone unnoticed, although neither Healey nor Jenkins wanted to see Britain lose its indigenous capability in both civil and military projects. It was also necessary to try to encourage the French to remain within NATO (an aspiration not fulfilled when they pulled out a year later). New high-profile Anglo-French aircraft projects of the kind now being proposed would, therefore, suit both purposes. In Healey's biography, Edward Pearce wrote that getting on terms with the French in the early days of the Labour government was important in itself. 'Healey was accordingly an Anglo-Saxon bearing gifts.'

Crucially for BAC, the advent of the AFVG under BAC leadership would keep the design teams together and occupied within the Preston Division. But it did not solve the immediate factory shortages. For, despite the work Sir George had transferred to the north, together with government contracts to convert the Phantoms to RAF and Royal Navy specifications, which would be carried out at Preston, there was still a production shortfall across the company.

To fill the gap, BAC proposed a new private joint venture with the French, to build a developed Dassault Mirage IV with Rolls-Royce Spey engines. The team at Warton had been working on such a concept for some time as a better alternative to the F-111 if TSR.2 was cancelled. Performance projections suggested that the Spey Mirage, as it was known, had exceptional promise, and would keep the Preston Division occupied until the new programmes came on stream.

The idea, however, was short-lived. Healey saw it both as a threat to the F-111, on which his reputation stood, and to the AFVG. Edwards and his team argued that this was not the case, that the F-111 was already in trouble, and an alternative should be considered, while the AFVG was not comparable or in the same timeframe. But it was of no avail, and, according to Charles Gardner, 'Denis Healey lost his temper' and even threatened to take the AFVG and ECAT work away from BAC and give it to Hawkers. Gardner added: 'The better the Spey Mirage looked, the angrier grew the Minister and the Ministry of Defence.' Such argument with the company's largest customer was, in Sir George's words, 'unrewarding', and the proposal was dropped, causing further irritation to the French.

But as time went on, and to add to Healey's disgruntlement and BAC's concern, growing rumours suggested that, after less than a year, France wanted to pull out of AFVG. Sir George warned Healey personally of this, and put forward a suggestion for an all-British variable-geometry programme, which was pursued for a time. The crux of the matter was that Dassault, having extracted as much British know-how on variable geometry as necessary for its own (but concealed) variable-geometry aircraft, would no longer accept British design leadership.

Jack Gee, in his book *Mirage*, wrote: 'It soon became clear that Dassault balked at playing second string to BAC in the new AFVG programme.' He recalled the visit by Sir George Edwards to Paris in April 1967 for a 'showdown' with Marcel Dassault, the eponymous and autocratic founder of the firm. 'For half an hour the two men sat in Dassault's splendid office at the Hotel de Mory. The summit meeting ended in total deadlock. Dassault refused to yield control of the swing-wing project to the British.'

George Edwards remembers meeting Dassault. 'He used to spend his Saturday mornings in the drawing office, and he wasn't going to be done out of that. It was one of his forms of amusement to poke about with the design of the latest device that was there. He knew jolly well that if I were put in charge of the AFVG design, he would be thrown out, so that came to a grinding halt.' As to the purpose of the Paris meeting, Sir George said afterwards: 'I wanted no misunderstanding on this one [technical leadership], otherwise I could foresee endless argument. . . . It became quite clear to me that the old man was never going to accept this. Considering the power he had in France, I read the eventual doom of the AFVG in that one conversation.'

Charles Gardner, in his BAC book, relates the farcical situation that arose at subsequent meetings between the British and French, when the French tried to disguise the fact that they were building their own aircraft, the Mirage G. They admitted to it only when it became apparent that the British knew of the development. Jack Gee wrote that, at the Edwards meeting in Paris, Dassault spoke from a position of strength, for he knew that the first test flight of his own aircraft was only a few months away. 'Exchanges of designs and ideas between the British and French companies had strengthened the confidence of Dassault engineers in their own prototype. . . . The same confidence inspired the French government. De Gaulle was eager to see the new Mirage G in the air before reneging on the partnership with Britain.'

In June 1967 French Defence Minister Pierre Messmer flew to London to tell Healey the bad news that they were pulling out 'through lack of funds'; no doubt they were now absorbed in their own project. On 5 July Healey was forced to make a statement confirming that the French government had, 'for budgetary reasons', decided to withdraw from the programme.

If the AFVG were to suffer a political and nationalistic fate, the ECAT, soon to be named 'Jaguar', did not. This was mainly because the British did not argue over the agreement that the French should lead on the airframe design. After all, its basic concept was already in existence, and both companies needed the work. Furthermore, the Breguet company, led by the aforementioned Henri

Ziegler (before his Concorde involvement), was much more amenable and internationally minded. Moreover, an advanced jet trainer of this kind did not ring any patriotic, public or political bells.

Again the requirements differed, but this was overcome by development proposals by the British to give added lethality and supersonic performance to the original Breguet design, which had been essentially for a transonic advanced jet trainer. These improvements would meet the RAF need to replace its Folland Gnat trainers, for which the Jaguar was inherently well suited, and also its Hawker Hunters in the ground-attack role. An upgrade was thus necessary to provide a sophisticated navigation/attack system and a greater and more varied weapons-carrying capability. Additionally, a more powerful version of the chosen Rolls-Royce/Snecma Adour engine with reheat was selected.

The developments were quickly agreed. In all, five variants were produced, covering both single-seat and two-seat aircraft, matched to the differing specifications of the two air forces. A French naval version, which successfully carried out seaborne trials, was eventually dropped after pressure from Dassault to replace it with its own Etendard aircraft. Under the agreement, both countries would have separate assembly lines, but this added cost was significantly counteracted by an initial order of 300 aircraft (150 for each country), which was quickly increased to 400 under the same terms.

Unlike Concorde, which was managed by a series of government and industry committees, a much more businesslike arrangement was set up for Jaguar. A single company, the Société Européene de Production de l'Avion d'Ecole de Combat et d'Appui Tactique (SEPECAT), registered in Paris and populated by appropriate directors from both companies, was established to control the programme. A similar arrangement was made for the Adour engine, with Rolls-Royce taking the lead with Snecma. The workload was split fifty-fifty, although, importantly, the proceeds of third-country sales would be to the advantage of the supplying company responsible for final assembly, something that would be of special benefit to Britain in the years to come.

Development progressed smoothly, and even the choice of the name Jaguar was settled by one phone call from Zeigler to Edwards without any reference (as was usual) to the Services. There were no subsequent objections from that quarter, and the Jaguar car company quickly gave approval.

In his 1973 Wright Brothers Memorial Lecture to the RAeS, 'Looking Ahead with Hindsight', Sir George referred particularly to the Jaguar as an example and 'message of hope' for the real benefits of international collaboration. He said that, having suffered for years 'at the mercy of a short-term political situation', the business had 'changed dramatically for the better, and we have already shown that this new pattern can be made to work'. He added: 'The great thing about the Jaguar programme is that it gives us the chance to work from an initial order base of 400 aeroplanes for the two sponsoring countries, and thus provide the opportunity to go on to sell off the thin end of the learning curve instead of the more usual thick end. Our inability to do this in the past has always been our Achilles' heel of single-nation programmes, but with these international collaborative efforts, that is now removed.'

Through the years there was only one real (and enduring) threat to the project. That came from within France, from Dassault, which first acquired a majority shareholding in the Breguet company and then completed the takeover in 1971. From then on, working from a position of inside knowledge, Dassault rolled every stone in the way of Jaguar progress, particularly in the international sales arena, and even, as it later transpired, to its own disadvantage.

For although the French were content to take the pickings from the large initial orders for their own air force and RAF, they were not prepared to develop the Jaguar, or promote it, at the expense of their own aircraft. As frustrating as this was, it also presented an opportunity not lost on the BAC Jaguar project teams, led by chief designer Ollie Heath and project director Ivan Yates (later to become divisional and group managing director). They uprated the aircraft again to an international standard, providing more power, enhanced systems and range/load-carrying capability.

These efforts led to important sales in the Middle East, South America and especially in India, where a huge and continuing contract was eventually won against fierce opposition, especially from the new 'partner', Dassault, giving the British team a certain satisfaction. This arose because, during the negotiations, Dassault mistakenly had discounted Jaguar's strike potential, which was what the Indians wanted, in favour of its own Mirage F.1, essentially a fighter. Nevertheless, it prolonged and frustrated the Indian sales campaign, which began in the early 1970s under Sir George's jurisdiction, and was led initially by Jeffrey Quill. It was not until both men had retired that the Indian government finally announced, in 1978, that Jaguar was the winner.

Under the agreement with India, negotiated by Freddie Page, then chairman of the Military Aircraft Division, and Dick Evans, who was the commercial director, the first batch of aircraft was to be built by BAC and the work would then be progressively transferred to India. When told in the year 2000 that the aircraft was still being built by the Indians, Sir George was truly amazed: 'How extraordinary, it really turned out to be a good aeroplane in the end,' he said.

Edwards's last direct involvement with the Jaguar was less happy. It occurred during what was called 'the sale of the century' in the early 1970s. This was a deal for the supply of new fighters to Belgium, Holland, Norway and Denmark, who collectively agreed to take the same aircraft type. The Jaguar, with its low-level ground-attack capability, was particularly suitable, especially to meet the designated NATO requirements for the two lead countries, Holland and Belgium.

The USA threw everything behind its submissions, with the General Dynamics F-16 emerging as the front runner. Dassault, however, refused any support for the more logical case for the Jaguar, again favouring its own F.1, and privately undermined the Jaguar wherever possible. The predictable result was a massive order for the F-16 and nothing for either the F.1 or Jaguar. Sir George was incensed, and spoke publicly of the 'French interpretation of the meaning of the word partnership'.

But perhaps the French 'go-it-alone' policy was providential, for it suffered from all the disadvantages of a one-nation, one-company approach that Edwards had warned against. For in the final reckoning, the Mirage G, which was developed into various prototype versions, came to nothing, while the AFVG cancellation led to the Multi-Role Combat Aircraft (MRCA), involving BAC, Messerschmitt-Bölkow-Blohm of Germany (the two major shareholders) and Aeritalia of Italy, in what was then the largest European aircraft collaboration, with nearly 1,000 aircraft being built.

CHAPTER TWENTY-SIX

Guided Weapons and Defence Contracts

Sir George Edwards always used to say that the strength of BAC came from what he called his 'three-legged stool'. The three legs referred to military aircraft, civil aircraft and guided weapons, the sum of the parts providing the technical and financial stability for the whole. It was a message of unity that he preached to all corners of the BAC empire, and particularly to the Guided Weapons Division, which was by far the smallest at the time of the company's formation.

As an example of such philosophy, within just fifteen years GW had risen from being Cinderella to Prince Charming. Such was its growth and success that, by the mid-1970s, its profits were helping to finance aircraft programmes, its workforce had increased to 10,000, and financial turnover was in the region of £200 million.

Unlike the military aircraft divisions, bonded initially by the TSR.2, the guided-weapons business was forced together by joining two rival outfits from Bristol and English Electric. Not only were they rivals in spirit, but they were rivals in the market too. Both had major competing products: the English Electric Thunderbird mobile anti-aircraft system for the Army, and the Bristol Bloodhound surface-to-air missile for the RAF for airfield protection. Both systems had reached second-stage development by the time of the formation of BAC in 1960, and both groups were in a bitter head-on clash for orders.

Adding to the difficulties was the perception by those in guided weapons that they were commanding much less attention from Portal and Edwards than was paid to aircraft matters. The full force of these problems landed on the plate of Lord Caldecote, who, as executive director at the start of operations, was responsible for GW and Sir George's opposite number. He had the unenviable task of bringing cohesion and recognition to the new set-up. As already noted,

Caldecote was critical of both Portal and Edwards, and complained that Edwards was 'not particularly interested in GW', and that Portal had not put the effort into defending guided weapons projects as he had into TSR.2.

The appointment just over a year later of Sir George as managing director, with Caldecote as his deputy, but with continuing responsibility for guided weapons, did little to alleviate the 'poor relation' syndrome.

Crisis came in 1962, when *Blue Water* and PT.428, both being developed within the old English Electric GW Division, were scrapped. The PT.428 low-level anti-aircraft system, of increasing importance, was cancelled in February with the loss of 150 jobs. The technology was, however, retained, leading to bigger and better things. Much more devastating was the abandonment, a few months later, of the high-priority *Blue Water* tactical ground-to-air missile. It brought, as Sir George had feared in his note to Portal, attendant factory closure and job losses.

At the time of the initial threat to these programmes, Sir George, as executive director for aircraft, was not heavily involved. He felt unable to make a personal contribution, 'knowing little of guided weapons'. He did, however, join Lord Caldecote in the fight with Whitehall to preserve PT.428, an effort which he described in his 1982 Hinton Lecture to the Fellowship of Engineering, of which Lord Caldecote was then president. Sir George said: 'I recall one great meeting at which ministers, civil servants and very high ranking army officers were present in force. One of the latter eloquently cried: "We really cannot do without this weapon, it is essential that we have PT.428. We'd sooner lose *Blue Water*!" Well, *Blue Water* was an artillery weapon a long way down the road into initial production. He reasonably thought it was sacred. But as we walked out of the room together I said to him [Caldecote] in order to cheer him up: "Well now Robin, I reckon we've lost both," and we jolly well had.'

The cancellation of *Blue Water* was in many ways as devastating to the fledgling guided weapons business as the loss of TSR.2 was later going to be to the aircraft divisions. That GW survived and prospered so quickly was a remarkable story in itself, which has been well told in Pat Adams's book *Good Company*. Much of the credit for this must go to George Jefferson (later Sir George), who was appointed chief executive and later took up full control as chairman and managing director when Lord Caldecote retired.

His appointment, which strengthened Caldecote's hand, was a welcome one for Sir George, who had always stated that guided weapons was a specialist job and should be run by a specialist. He felt that his responsibility was to see that the best man was selected to run it. Such ambition was amply rewarded by Jefferson, a former Royal Ordnance apprentice who joined the company in 1953 and rapidly rose through its ranks.

Edwards and Jefferson got on immediately. Both shared a similar educational and engineering background, Jefferson having gained a first-class honours degree in engineering, achieved, like Sir George, externally. Having served his apprenticeship at Woolwich, he was commissioned in the Royal Army Ordnance Corps and moved to English Electric at Luton, where he became chief engineer by 1960.

George Jefferson also had his own views about the early problems within GW, which Pat Adams quoted in his book. 'There was no clear nomination of a top executive for GW with real authority,' said Jefferson. 'Lord Caldecote was largely hamstrung in trying to exert real authority, in contrast to Sir George Edwards on the aircraft side. For the first two or three years it was really a question of internal politics in the corporation, with a good deal of in-fighting alongside the battle between the two parts of the GW organisation.' He added: 'Whenever you have a situation in which nobody is really the boss, then it naturally leads – particularly with a struggle for survival going on – to your being wide open to gamesmanship, political pressure and increasing acrimony in order to establish a position, which undoubtedly happened in those three years.'

In 1963 things changed when the rival Bristol and English Electric units were rolled into one Guided Weapons Division. Lord Caldecote was appointed managing director and G.R. Jefferson chief executive, the latter becoming the accepted leader of the combined organisation, with its headquarters at a new purpose-built factory at Stevenage, Hertfordshire. The changes did much to unify and pacify the business.

Although Sir George was not an expert in the new science and technology involved in guided weapons, he was fully aware of the growing demand and political impact it would bring. In his 1981 television broadcast he outlined his approach at the time. 'I said we must get away from these big strategic missiles which were very expensive and always likely to be cancelled. So we launched ourselves into a series of tactical weapons, anti-tank, low-altitude anti-aircraft like Rapier and a succession of tactical weapons which have a relatively low development cost.' He added: 'They are the things that most countries can afford, and they are the things that most countries need, because there are a lot of countries under danger of being attacked and they are defensive weapons.'

In saying this he was painfully aware of the high risks involved with large-scale guided weapons programmes, which he had witnessed at Weybridge, where a guided weapons unit was established by Vickers in the early 1950s. Several promising projects had been started, often as private ventures, had blossomed and then been cancelled. These included *Blue Boar*, an air-to-ground weapon, *Red Rapier*, a surface-to-air long-range missile, and, most significantly, *Red Dean*.

Red Dean was a highly sophisticated air-to-air weapon, and as managing director at Weybridge Sir George became ultimately responsible for it, but placed the project under the direct control of Henry Gardner, who was technical director. It was given high priority, which included test flying from Wisley. More than 800 people were employed at one time on its development before, inevitably, it was cancelled in 1957.

The *Red Dean* cancellation charges, however, were put to good use, financing a new anti-tank weapon called Vigilant. Vigilant was a man-portable wire-guided system, the brainchild of Col Harry Lacey, who Sir George took on as military adviser at Weybridge. But the British army was sceptical about such private-venture inventions, until a convincing firing demonstration at Larkhill, on Salisbury Plain, changed its mind and Vigilant became an important part of its inventory.

With the formation of BAC, Vigilant was transferred as a 'new-account' product to GW, providing it with important anti-tank capability that was soon to have impact in the export market. Vigilant was followed by the larger, vehicle-mounted Swingfire, for which design and development agreement had been reached with its originators, the Fairey Aviation Company. This too proved to be a highly effective weapon, and entered service with the British army in 1968.

But at the top of the newly formed Guided Weapons Division's list of promising products was the ET.316 low-level anti-aircraft system, designed to combat the ever-increasing threat of high-speed, low-level air attack. With its origins in PT.428, it was to become known as Rapier and, with added 'blindfire' capability, entered service with both the army and the RAF and subsequently sold throughout the world. Although its potential was unfulfilled at the time, the project did allow Jefferson, who had masterminded its steady progress, to make one significant and unifying decision: to move the work for the launcher and fire unit down to Bristol.

Sir George encouraged Rapier and allocated funds (£250,000) for its early development. These were not the actions of somebody who was 'not particularly interested in guided weapons'. Pat Adams tackled this suggestion in his book, and asked Jefferson for his opinion of Sir George's involvement.

Jefferson replied: 'I think he has been reasonably content to allow something which seemed to be going along fairly well to carry on without adding to his burden that was already pretty heavy.'

Adams wrote that this comment 'reflects equal credit on Sir George – who knew when he had got a good man producing successful results – and on Jefferson'. He also noted that Sir George had latterly 'seemed to have taken a great deal more interest in us – he came to Stevenage fairly regularly and his visits were always a tonic and delight to us all.' He added: 'Sir George retired at the end of 1975, and every part and particle of the corporation owes him an immense debt for his inspired leadership ever since its formation.'

By 1975 GW had built up a formidable capability in weapons for land, sea and air, space programmes and specialist products of all kinds, and Sir George promoted this at every available opportunity. 'The guided weapons and space part of our business has been a success story,' he said in his 1982 Hinton lecture. This was delivered shortly after the Falklands campaign, in which many GW products, such as Rapier and Sea Wolf, the naval anti-missile missile, were seen in action and had become 'household names'.

In retrospect, looking back on GW's contribution to BAC, Sir George says: 'The real ones that earned a living were Jefferson's lot at Stevenage. He made it work. As far as money was concerned, I was always pretty receptive and I could see there were one or two jobs they had got that, if properly supported, would make money, like Rapier.'

While GW was resurrecting itself after *Blue Water*, the Preston Division at Warton was developing, post-TSR.2, a new and highly rewarding export business: the provision of complete defence services and infrastructure to support its front-line equipment. This began in 1966 with the supply of ex-RAF Lightnings, Hunters and a Thunderbird battery to Saudi Arabia, under a government-backed scheme known as 'Magic Carpet'. This was an immediate response to a Saudi request for help to defend itself against bombing incursions from North Yemen, supported by the Egyptian air force.

British relationships had not been particularly good with the Saudis, who depended on the USA to provide their defensive needs. However, with the outbreak of desert hostilities the Saudi Air Force was unable to respond, as it was equipped only with a few decaying and unmaintained North American F-86 Sabres. By now it was already looking to Britain, thanks largely to the efforts of British businessman Geoffrey Edwards, a former RAF officer, who steered them towards the UK. As a result the Lightning had been convincingly demonstrated by Warton test pilot Jimmy Dell in Riyadh a year before, and negotiations with BAC had begun.

'Magic Carpet' was negotiated at government level by the wayward but effective Defence Minister John Stonehouse, whose later disappearance and feigned death captured the headlines. Sir George had got to know Stonehouse personally as a member of his British delegation during a fact-finding visit to the Soviet Union in 1967. Edwards liked Stonehouse for the energetic and enthusiastic way he carried out his official duties, but his abiding memory of the visit was playing conkers with the Minister in Red Square, presumably to confuse their Russian 'minders'.

There is no doubt that Stonehouse deserves credit for setting up the Saudi deal, and in May 1966 an order for forty new Lightnings and twenty-five Strikemaster trainers, valued at £65 million, was placed with BAC. In addition, in partnership with AEI (the electronics company that subsequently became part of GEC) and Airwork, a service and support business, BAC was tasked with providing the necessary modern defence infrastructure, including training, maintenance and construction. By 1973 the Saudis had enough confidence in BAC to ask it to take over the entire contract. This brought with it a further five-year extension, together with more orders for aircraft and spares, all of which came under a government-to-government Memorandum of Understanding. The total value was now assessed at over £500 million, the largest defence contract yet received in Britain.

Sir George saw the Saudi business, important as it was, in much the same way as he viewed GW. He was content and confident in delegating responsibility, but was available to provide the top-level clout when required. Sir Dick Evans, whose commercial acumen was instrumental in sustaining and expanding the contract to the present day, confirms that, at the time, Warton was not directly involved in the 'lobbying' or 'politicking' process in Whitehall. At English Electric this had been the preserve of Lord Nelson, father and son, and Lord Caldecote. Now, within the new BAC, Lord Portal and, particularly, George Edwards were the torch bearers.

Sir Dick, who was then a commercial contracts officer at Warton, recalls those days and his frequent visits to Weybridge accompanying his boss, Alec Atkin, which was when he first met Sir George. 'We were asked by the government if BAC çould take on the whole [Saudi] thing, but it was just too big for us in balance-sheet terms. There was a lot of to-ing and fro-ing to

Weybridge and dialogue with the government. We had to persuade them to take the contract up front, and we would back it up. There was a committee at Weybridge called the Contracts Advisory Committee, under the chairmanship of Tom Pritchard, and basically every contract had to go through them for risk analysis, etc. Alec and I were shuffling backwards and forwards, and that was when I first really came across Sir George. Alec and George got on very well.'

Edwards was impressed by Atkin, the director in charge of the Saudi business, a larger-than-life character who spent much time getting to know the Saudi royal family and hierarchy. 'Alec didn't just know which of the Saudi princes was the one to go to about the next order, he knew also what were the weak points that we had got to tackle,' says Sir George. 'Anybody who looked less like a traditional ambassador figure you could never find. He worked his way round and about and was a very handy bloke to have on the staff.'

In January 1975, shortly before his retirement, Sir George made a 'presidential-type' visit to Saudi Arabia, where there were now more than 2,000 expatriate BAC employees engaged in the work. By this time relationships between the two countries were very good and strong bonds of friendship and loyalty had been struck with the Royal Saudi Air Force. Ron Read, who was the chief executive of the BAC contingent in country, tells of the happy and successful visit in his privately published book *The Magic Carpet & the Plane-Makers*. He described Sir George as 'a real down-to-earth character who, although serious about business matters, had a great sense of humour and was able to talk to anybody on equal terms'. 'Of all the senior BAC officials,' he wrote, 'George Edwards was the most approachable, at least when he was on tour.'

During the ten-day visit Sir George, accompanied by Freddie Page and Alec Atkin, met King Faisal in a private audience. Then followed meetings with Prince Turki, the Vice-Minister of Defence, who was responsible for the contract, and the Commander-in-Chief of the Royal Saudi Air Force, Gen Zuhair. Read tells how Edwards 'got on like a house on fire' with Gen Zuhair, talking about cricket. 'To General Zuhair, cricket was probably more difficult to understand than Einstein's theory, but George spent 15min explaining the theory of bowling the "googly" out of the back of the hand, demonstrating the finger-hold with an orange. I never saw the general play cricket though.'

Ron Read also gave a glimpse of Sir George's personality and human touch on such occasions. He wrote: 'Whatever George's successes and failures, he was a warm-hearted man. It was my job during the tour to keep it all going on time. I had great difficulty, especially when he was talking to the wives, and sometimes I had to practically drag him by the arm to move on to the next person and venue. But everyone who met him felt warmed by his kindness and concern.'

At this time Sir George was particularly interested in the possibility of selling Concorde to the Saudis. 'He had high hopes because the Shah [of Persia] was about to order six for Iranian Airlines,' said Read, 'but we felt that there was a possibility that the Saudis would not like to trail behind the Iranians in this matter. George was hoping to get the ball rolling this visit.' There was talk of arranging a special demonstration in Saudi, for which they would commandeer a BA Concorde by diverting it from its regular run to Bahrain. There were, however, many logistical problems, not the least of which was that the demonstration could only be arranged in the afternoon, at the hottest time of day, when the aircraft would require the longest-possible take-off run. Ron Read wrote: 'George gave all this some thought, and finally said – you know Concorde is a funny old aircraft, the tyres have to be very narrow to fit in the wing, so the tyre temperatures rise quite a bit on take-off. We shall have to have her standing on the apron for an hour or more, so they will be quite hot before we start up. Thinking it over, I don't think we can take that sort of chance.'

Before departure Sir George and his colleagues met with Sir Lester Suffield, who was the head of MoD Defences Sales and, as such, under the government-to-government agreement, was BAC's paymaster. According to Read, Suffield took the opportunity to complain about progress on the construction programme. 'Your people at Warton are running the programme from there. They never let people here get on with things when they really should be doing so,' he said. 'George was surprised at this,' wrote Read, and after Lester left he called a meeting with Freddie and Alec. 'He told them quite firmly, that, as the man on the spot, I had to be in overall charge of the construction programme, and Warton should do all it could to assist me in trying to speed it up.' Read added: 'His [Suffield's] previous intervention hadn't changed things a lot, either. Atkin had carried on as before. But when George Edwards spoke, things were different.'

Later Sir George wrote to Ron Read to thank him for arranging the visit, which he believed had been 'such a success'. He had been pleased to see so many wives, and, as many were pretty cut off from home, he was glad to 'chat them up a bit'. Edwards believed they were all doing a jolly good job, and he would do all he could to make the contract get bigger and last longer.

In 1977 his hopes were amply rewarded. A further four-year extension was agreed, valued at an additional £500 million, leading to the next phase to what has become known as 'Al Yamamah 2'. This involved the supply of the new MRCA Tornado, the Hawk advanced trainer, and other communications and transport aircraft, plus the continued training, construction, maintenance and support, earning revenues assessed at many billion of pounds to the British economy.

Dick Evans says that Saudi became the 'bedrock' of the company and in later years saved British Aerospace. 'There is no doubt whatsoever that if it had not been for Al Yamamah, BAe would have gone under.'

CHAPTER TWENTY-SEVEN

His Last Aircraft

The last aeroplane to enter service bearing the distinctive design stamp of George Edwards was the BAC One-Eleven short/medium-range twin-jet airliner. It was also the last civil jet aircraft to be built by BAC, and the last but one to be built in Britain at all (the last being the BAe 146). Today's major British civil aircraft interests are maintained only by the design and manufacture of wings for the impressive Airbus programme.

That the One-Eleven ever saw the light of day in 1961 was little short of miraculous. At that time BAC's whole future was very much in the balance. Both TSR.2 and Concorde were coming under increasing and hostile scrutiny, BOAC was trying to cancel the VC10, and Vanguard sales had stalled. As far as Vickers, which was holding the financial ring for both the VC10 and Vanguard, was concerned, this might not be the time to launch another new civil product, a view shared by English Electric.

It was, therefore, a courageous BAC Board decision in May of that year to go ahead with the One-Eleven on the strength of just one confirmed order from one small British independent carrier British United Airways and a promising worldwide market survey. With the BUA order came indicated government start-up launch aid of £9.75 million, while the personality of, and confidence in, BUA's managing director, Freddie (later Sir Frederick) Laker lent credence to the decision.

This would not be the only time that Laker championed a British product. As an independent, unencumbered by political pressures, his view carried weight. Having started from scratch, Laker progressed rapidly in the airline business by shrewd judgement and business acumen. He became a thorn in the side of the bigger, government-protected flag carriers with his innovations and low-fare policies, often to their embarrassment. He was also able to attract a following in the City, something which did not go unnoticed by BAC's shareholders. If Laker thought it was a good aeroplane, then few would argue with him.

Even so, it says much for the persuasive powers of George Edwards that he gained Board support for the project. His trump card was the results of the market survey, which showed, as a result of consulting some 100 operators, that an aircraft of the specification of the One-Eleven would result in 'probable sales' of 144 and 'possible sales' of 1,000.

The One-Eleven originated in a Hunting Aircraft project, the H.107, acquired when Hunting was absorbed within the new BAC in 1960. The H.107 was a twin-engine jet with rear-mounted engines, a clean, swept wing and a cruciform tail, seating up to fifty-six passengers and powered by two Bristol Siddeley BS.75 fan engines of 7,000lb thrust. After a full assessment the Weybridge team concluded by 1961 that the project was viable in the short/medium-range sector, but that it would rival the four-engine VC11, on which work was then still continuing. Clearly it was not practical to build both, though the VC11, having been withdrawn from the BEA competition, had attracted some interest in North America.

In February 1961 Sir George decided to visit Canada and the USA 'to settle the VC11 position' and explore the potential of the H.107 with leading contender airlines. He met the presidents and senior officials of American, Braniff and Northeast Airlines, particularly to explore the prospects of the twin-jet. Additionally, he had talks with the VC11's two potential customer operators, TCA, for which Gordon McGregor had taken up options on fourteen aircraft, and his old sparring partner, Bob Six of Continental. Six's airline, Edwards said, was 'quite firm' that the VC11 was the best medium jet for its purpose but 'cannot place an order right now'.

During his three-week tour, which was clearly uncomfortable for he experienced 'the worst dislocation I have ever experienced due to weather and strikes', he found that in essence there was now an acceptance by American operators of a rear-mounted twin-jet. There had been resistance by the Americans to such aircraft on safety grounds, but favourable in-service experience of the French Caravelle had changed this attitude. The response to the H.107 was that it was a promising concept, but that it might be too small.

Sir George's perception was that it was. In a report for the Board he wrote: 'It became clear that at least thirteen seat rows would be needed, that equipment weights, including such things as built-in power units for starting, would force up the empty weight, and that the required payload/range configuration was outside the capacity of the original project.' He added: 'Carline [Hunting's chief designer] was therefore sent back to the UK to produce a specification to meet this need. This he did, and a new appraisal is being made by the team still in the US in conjunction with the engineers in Braniff, Continental and American Airlines.'

The new specification proposed an aircraft of the same basic shape but with an increased take-off weight of 65,000lb, thirteen seat rows, 980sq ft of wing and a bigger engine of around 10,000lb thrust. This was beyond the performance of the designated Bristol Siddeley engine, and the more powerful Rolls-Royce RB.163 Spey was selected. This engine had the added attraction of already being proven in both the DH.121 Trident and the RAF Buccaneer.

Edwards estimated the cost of the new aircraft at £660,000, half the cost of a Caravelle. He wrote: 'I am satisfied that aircraft generally to the revised specification will be bought by the US major domestic operators from somebody. There is as yet no firm proposal from any US manufacturers. A number of paper projects are floating about from McDonnell Douglas and Boeing, but I am fairly sure they are not being taken seriously by the operators. Hence the interest shown in our proposal.'

On his return to England, in March, Sir George wrote to Lord Portal ahead of a BAC Board meeting the following Monday. 'By then I shall have screwed up my courage to write a recommendation which I think is to cancel the VC11 and go with the 107 with the Rolls-Royce engine. At what I think is a competitive selling price we would break even, without government support, at about ninety aircraft, and with government support at about sixty.'

The Board agreed to Edwards's recommendation to cancel the VC11 and to approach the government for launch aid for the new project, which they defined as 50 per cent of the development bill and 50 per cent of the production commitments. After meetings with Peter Thorneycroft, the then Minister of Aviation, it was finally agreed that the government would transfer the £9.75 million originally earmarked for the VC11 to the new aircraft, now designated BAC One-Eleven.

Looking back on the history of the One-Eleven and its origins in the Hunting design, Sir George does not place too much weight on comparisons between the H.107 and the emerging One-Eleven. 'I wouldn't put too much significance between the two. The 107 had got that funny little Bristol engine that it was built around. The engine didn't really go on and nothing much came of it, whereas

Rolls was able to produce what became the Spey, with the right dimensions and weights, which were critical with the engines at the rear,' he says.

He adds: 'I don't think the 107 would have been much of a commercial proposition. It was the best that Hunting could do, but they were really frightened of building anything bigger. It was Hunting-run and to an extent a Hunting-financed operation. They took the simple view that the smaller you made it the less your loss, which wasn't far out.'

Sir George fully acknowledges, however, that it was the catalyst for the new aircraft. 'When we got our hooks on it, it became fairly obvious, with Derek Lambert [chief development engineer] and others, that there was a market for an aeroplane of that shape, but not of that size. We had got the Caravelle, which showed you could stuff the engines in the back and everybody was pretty pleased about that,' he says.

The revised project was finally defined as the BAC One-Eleven Series 200, with an all-up weight of 78,500lb, accommodating up to seventy-nine passengers at speeds in excess of 540mph, and having a range of 200–500 miles. The chosen Rolls-Royce Spey 506 would deliver 10,400lb static thrust, and the total basic package had risen to £709,000. To ensure continuity and experience from the original design, Hunting's technical director, Fred Pollicutt, and chief designer, A.J.K. Carline, who had drawn up the first revised specification, continued to work with Basil Stephenson, the Weybridge director of engineering, who had overall responsibility for the aircraft.

But to anyone at Weybridge the undisputed boss was George Edwards, and few in the design office would introduce any major proposals without his blessing. Indeed, despite his onerous duties in the early days of BAC, he moved his office from the administration block on Brooklands Road to the design offices within the factory complex. Thus nobody was left under any illusion as to the critical importance of the project to the company's well-being. His continual fight with various governments and aviation ministers to secure rightful and repayable development funding for progressive developments of the One-Eleven have already been noted, and without this BAC would have found it difficult to survive.

There can be little doubt that the One-Eleven helped rescue BAC at a critical time, and Sir George still attributes the real start to Freddie Laker, whose initial order for BUA set the ball rolling and guaranteed government development funding. 'There was a great deal of heartburning and anguish that we were going to start a brand new aeroplane on the back of a not very experienced operator, and not a very big airline,' he says. 'In fact it worked out all right.

Over the years I had a lot to do with Freddie Laker; he was a decent enough chap. He learnt his business on the Berlin Airlift. That picked him up a few bob, and also got him trained in the general business of running an airline.'

'In the early years,' Edwards continues, 'Laker was struggling, and my great aim was to do everything I could to see he didn't go bust. Therefore I did my best to see that chaps like Geoffrey Knight, who was pretty friendly with him, did what they could to make his operation with the One-Elevens as painless as it could be. You had to be a bit considerate in the way you handled him, and not too bloody-minded about terms and conditions under which you were going to sell him things.'

However, as the market survey suggested, and Sir George found out, the best prospects for the new airliner lay, as with the Viscount, in the USA. In the immediate frame was the Texas-based airline Braniff, which he had visited in March. 'You have got to start off with Chuck Beard [the president],' says Sir George. 'He's the chap, he was a classic example of what I have said about Gordon McGregor. If he and I hadn't got on all right there would have been no business. He could see that I was doing my best, apart from running BAC, to help him on his way.'

Edwards and Beard became family friends. 'I remember one night he said to Dinah: "I'm going to trust this husband of yours with a big order for a British aeroplane, and I have never done anything like this before"; and he meant it, too.'

So, coincident with the BUA contract in October 1961, Braniff announced an order for six One-Eleven Series 200 aircraft, with options on another six, an order that was later increased to fourteen. It was the first time a US operator had ordered a British aircraft 'off the drawing board'.

The gates to the North American market were now opening, and shortly afterwards Mohawk Airlines, an intercity carrier, announced that it, too, would join the One-Eleven club, ordering four aircraft, taking options on four more. The order was not without internal difficulty for its president, Bob Peach. He was challenged by the US Civil Aeronautics Board, which provided his airline with subsidy. The board queried the need for jets on local services, and the ability of the One-Eleven to make money on these routes.

Peach, who also became a personal friend of Sir George and a regular visitor to Weybridge, was not to be moved. He replied that the break-even load factor of the One-Eleven over typical 200-mile stage lengths was 46.5 per cent. This was 'satisfactorily below those of the most efficient short-haul transports now operational over the actual flight stage lengths proposed,' he told the Board. Permission to proceed was quickly given.

Then the biggest opportunity appeared in the shape of American Airlines, one of the 'big four' US carriers, whose boss was the legendary C.R. Smith. Edwards and Smith were old friends, having met during the Viscount days. Smith, like Edwards, was a self-made man, a Texan, whose autocratic style and closeness to several presidents of the United States, particularly Lyndon Johnson, made him both revered and respected.

The spur to the sale to American was the availability of an uprated Spey engine with increased thrust, which permitted an increase in weight to carry up to eighty-nine passengers over longer stage lengths. The British version was designated the Series 300, and in the USA, the Series 400. During 1962–3 the BAC sales teams, headed by Geoffrey Knight, virtually camped out in New York to stay close to the airline's headquarters, and Sir George made frequent visits to meet Smith and senior members of his staff.

During these visits, Edwards remembers Smith telling him about his outlook on such a deal. 'The thing about committing yourself to a pretty major project like this one, is that you are not mesmerised by a book-full of figures and a lot of young chaps buzzing around with what the thing will do,' he told Sir George. Smith added that getting all the figures was an essential part of the performance, but, he added: 'The thing that really counts at the end is whether you can trust the bloke that you are buying from.' Sir George had no difficulty with this attitude, and says: 'They well knew that if they paddled along to see me and launch a complaint, something would be done about it in pretty short order.'

In July 1963 BAC's perseverance paid off when American Airlines ordered fifteen One-Eleven Series 400s, the order eventually being increased to thirty. It was one of the biggest single dollar export contracts ever won by the UK, valued at £12 million ($40 million) and rivalling Capital Airlines' $45 million order for Viscounts some ten years before.

Sir George has always acknowledged the importance in securing the American Airlines contract of the BAC support facility in Arlington, Virginia, established to service Viscounts and now expanded to provide necessary local back-up for the One-Eleven. 'It was a hell of a set-up in the light of what we had got out there. The amount of aeroplanes which were sold or were likely to be sold didn't justify a big organisation, but we had to have one,' he says. He despatched his personal assistant, Bob Gladwell, to Washington to support Murry White, a former Supermarine engineer, who was in charge of the outfit. 'Murry was the front man to deal with the airlines, while Bob put his head down and got out his hammer and chisel. He did a good job,' he says.

In 1963, with American interest rising and further orders in the pipeline, tragedy struck. The prototype, having successfully completed fifty-two flights in less than two months, crashed near Cricklade in Wiltshire with the loss of all on board. Those killed were the pilot, Mike 'Lucky' Lithgow, who had captured the world speed record in the Swift in 1953, copilot Dickie Rymer, formerly BEA's chief Viscount training captain, and all five flight-test observers and engineers. 'It was one of the worst days in my life,' says Sir George.

The One-Eleven had been undergoing a series of stalling trials when, on the last test run, with 8° of wing flap and the centre of gravity in the furthest-aft position, it failed to recover from an induced deep stall. It hit the ground flat, in a horizontal attitude. The flight recorders were quickly recovered, and revealed that the aircraft had a very low forward speed and a high rate of descent up to the moment of impact.

The accident indicated the potential danger inherent in all T-tailed, rear-engine aircraft. In a high, nose-up attitude, at certain speeds, the aircraft can stall when the wings blanket the airflow to the engines and over the tailplane. On this occasion, for certification purposes, the crew were exploring the extremes of the flight envelope, and the aircraft would never have been flown at such an extreme attitude during normal airline operations.

Sir George was in his office when news came through. 'It is one of those things you have to live with: breaking aeroplanes, particularly when you know the people who were killed, because you have made a balls of it,' he says. His grief was shared by Lord Portal, who arrived to offer help and comfort. 'He plonked himself down in the outer office, ready to lend any assistance required. The old boy could see it was all a bit dramatic and that I needed a bit of help. But I didn't want anybody's shoulder to cry on, I just wanted someone to give me a shake of the hand and a pat on the back; that was all. I always appreciated that of old Peter, it was a real Air Marshal's effort, and I thought it was good because he understood.'

As far as the cause of the accident was concerned, Sir George says that the rate at which they entered into the stall was critical. 'If you ran the aeroplane up into the stall too far, then the inertia would be such that the wash over the tailplane did the effectiveness of the elevator a bit of no good. High tailplanes are pretty sensitive to this.'

The 'fix' was quickly incorporated once the Weybridge design team and the Accident Investigation Branch experts had examined the wreckage. This entailed design modifications to the wing leading edge to give more downward pitch at the stall, and the fitting of fully powered elevator controls and an electro-pneumatic stick pusher for the pilot. As an additional safety measure a tail parachute, which could be deployed in the event of an in-flight emergency, was provided for the other test aircraft. This would drag the tail down and bring the nose up to re-establish effective forward momentum.

Brian Trubshaw, who had the unenviable task of telling Mike Lithgow's wife of the loss of her husband, wrote in his biography: 'It was no good pretending that we had not had an accident. It had been seen by all the world. It seemed to me that one of the main things to do was to prevent anyone else making a similar mistake. After talking to Sir George and Jock Bryce, it was agreed that Ken Lawson, chief aerodynamicist, and myself should go to the United States armed with the traces and other data to talk to Boeing, Douglas, Lockheed and Lear [all of whom were producing T-tail rear-engined aircraft].'

Sir George also insisted that the flight-test reports be circulated to all relevant manufacturers, including to Tupolev in Russia. 'I remember their chief pilot was all bothered,' he says. 'I sent him all the flight test reports. . . . He was a decent chap, and I didn't want to be responsible for him killing himself because I hadn't told him what not to do.'

The effect of the crash and its attendant publicity was viewed as serious at the time, but not life-threatening to the programme, given the circumstances. In retrospect, however, it probably cost the One-Eleven the early mass penetration into the short-haul market that it deserved. The inevitable damage to its reputation played into the hands of Douglas with its DC-9 and Boeing with its 737, both of which were later but much more successful entrants into the market.

Matters were not helped by two more accidents, neither attributable to an aircraft fault. The third one, at Wisley, caused by a pilot-induced oscillation on landing, occurred as Sir George was at a meeting with Alitalia, the Italian airline. He recalls: 'While I was there with the president, telling him what a wonderful aeroplane it was, a telephone call came through to say that the pilot had broken it.' Alitalia did not buy the aircraft, but later opted for the DC-9.

With the coming of the new Labour government in 1964, and the probable cancellation of TSR.2, the One-Eleven faced a fresh challenge, which Sir George took pains to point out to the Aviation Minister, Roy Jenkins, with whom he was in negotiation for additional development funding for later versions of the aircraft. In a letter dated 30 December 1964 he wrote: 'The inevitable increase in cost brought about by higher overheads attendant upon TSR.2 cancellation could not be passed on to the One-Eleven purchaser, and certainly not be allowed to reduce the margin between cost and selling price, which is already too small.'

Sir George also took issue with the Minister over his claims that BAC was always willing to ask the government for funds for major projects, and not so willing to invest its own money. He estimated that the company's contribution to launching the One-Eleven was in the order of £17 million, together with a further £20 million for production. 'It will be many years before this can be recovered in the further sales of the aircraft,' he said. The project was a major contributor to exports, and firm orders at the time stood at seventy-four, with twenty on option, the bulk for American customers. 'Those dollars, incidentally, amount to nearly $200 million,' he pointed out. This was in sharp contrast to spending precious UK dollar reserves on buying the American TFX/F-111.

A month later Sir George was having further worries as it became more apparent that they had failed to secure TSR.2, and rumours were spreading among One-Eleven customers that the company might become bankrupt. This coincided with a planned visit to the assembly plant at Hurn by American Airlines, which by now had ordered thirty aircraft. It had been arranged that during the visit the airline's new president, Marion Sadler, and other senior executives, would meet the Minister.

Edwards again wrote to Jenkins in February 1965: 'I have had great concern expressed to me by a number of future customers as to the effect which the much-publicised government policy for the British aircraft industry will have on BAC. There is no doubt that the American manufacturing companies have been making great play on the lack of substance which BAC is likely to have with the TSR.2 removed from it, and certain operators, such as American Airlines, who took a very courageous decision in buying a British aeroplane, are feeling rather apprehensive.'

He added: 'I know this is very much on Sadler's mind, and I think he may make some reference to it when you meet him. Even if he does not, I would be most grateful if you could make a special point to him that it is the government's policy to maintain a strong and healthy industry, and that he need have no fears on the count that BAC will not be able to meet its commitments. I would specially like you to stress that we shall be able to build aeroplanes for him as and when he requires them, because we know that the ultimate requirement of One-Elevens for this airline will be much larger than the thirty they have currently ordered.'

Whatever Jenkins said to the American Airlines chiefs, it convinced them not to cancel their order, but the potential of further orders was not realised.

Similarly, the prospect of a big order from Eastern Airlines, which the Weybridge team had been pursuing with great vigour, was lost, and no further penetration into the major US carriers was made.

In 1966 a new and vital home-grown opportunity arose from BEA, which now needed to replace its Viscounts, Vanguards and Comets. The airline, which hitherto had been an all-British operator, was now proposing to follow BOAC by favouring a bulk buy of Boeing 727s and smaller 737s. Fred Mulley, then Minister of Aviation, sensitive over TSR.2 job losses and remembering the VC10 fiasco, refused them permission and insisted on a British solution.

At the time Sir George and the team had been pressing Rolls-Royce to produce more power from the Spey. It was now available with an uprating to 12,000lb static thrust, enabling BAC to offer an enlarged new Series 500 aircraft. This would have a 13ft stretch in the fuselage, extended wingtips and carry up to ninety-nine passengers over 950-mile stage lengths. Most important of all, BAC was able to offer 15 per cent lower seat-mile costs compared with earlier versions. It was the kind of natural development that Edwards, mindful of the Viscount experience, had sought from the earliest days of the One-Eleven programme.

Spud Boorer, who was now chief project engineer in the Weybridge design office, tells of the BEA development. 'Prior to a meeting with Sir Anthony Milward, I had briefed Sir George on a three-seat-row stretch of the aircraft. The following morning I was called in by GRE and told: "I have sold your aircraft, Spud, but it's got to have four extra seat rows. So go and tell your mates to find that bit they have up their sleeves for wife and family!" That turned out to be the 500.'

On 27 January 1967 Sir George and Sir Anthony Milward, chairman of BEA, signed a £32 million contract for eighteen of the new Series 500 aircraft, for which the government agreed to pay £9 million for development costs. Sir Reginald Verdon-Smith later described the contract as a 'turning point' for BAC, which not only strengthened the company's depleting finances but helped convince the parent companies at a time of government intervention and take-over threats that the company 'was worth fighting for'.

At that point, major progress on the One-Eleven virtually stuck, hamstrung by any further significant increases in engine thrust. The One-Eleven was now being outclassed by the Pratt & Whitney-powered DC-9 (to become the revamped McDonnell Douglas MD-80), and the Boeing 737, which retained the same cabin width as the manufacturer's 707 and 727, giving it added appeal to the vast number of Boeing operators.

'I had some difficulty getting Rolls-Royce off the pot as the years went by to get the right sort of power,' says Sir George. 'The performance of the One-Eleven with the Spey just hadn't got the power that the American airlines really needed, although there was a plot to put in Pratt & Whitney engines.' But Edwards knew that such a move was full of risk, both technically and financially, especially as it would probably require designing a new beefed-up wing. And by then, new alternative projects were in the offing, such as the projected larger BAC Two-Eleven.

Although restricted by the Spey engine's performance, other One-Elevens of various varieties continued to be built and sold. This included a smaller short-field version, the 475, which was based on the 400 fuselage with the 500 wing and engines. But by 1975 activities were eventually curtailed. The final total of 234 sold was below expectations, but its value to the company at a critical time, and to the nation's economy in terms of earned dollars, was not. Sir George emphasised the point at every conceivable opportunity. He put total value of sales at more than £383 million, of which two-thirds were for export, making it, in monetary terms, Britain's biggest-ever export-earning civil aircraft.

With the coming of nationalisation in 1977, the Labour administration, led by Tony Benn, favoured the once-discarded all-new four-engine Hawker Siddeley HS.146. The project was supported by the unions, which encouraged Benn to choose it in preference to further One-Eleven development, of which there were now several larger, re-engined proposals on the table. Benn says he is 'very proud' of the HS.146, which over a twenty-year period was to do well, achieving significant sales of over 350, mostly to overseas operators.

The HS.146 was, unfortunately, to meet a slump in the airline business in the 1990s, and production was prematurely curtailed in 2001. Sir Dick Evans, who was very much against the original decision to proceed with the HS.146, says it cost the company £3 billion, 'the true cost to the shareholders'. He adds: 'I suspect that the regional aircraft today that could have dominated the world market would have been a redesigned, re-cockpited version of the One-Eleven – without a shadow of doubt, when you think of all the DC-9s that were built [over 2,000] after we canned the One-Eleven.'

CHAPTER TWENTY-EIGHT

Enter the Wide-Bodies

'I think the great unrecognised story about George Edwards and his team is Airbus. People today forget that the originators of Airbus were the Concorde partners, BAC and Aerospatiale.' So says Sir Dick Evans, looking back at a ten-year period between 1967 and 1977, when Britain's contribution to the civil aircraft market was redefined.

It was in July 1964 that the seeds of the fabulously successful Airbus programme were sown. With the active encouragement of George Edwards and André Puget, two teams met in Paris to discuss a joint approach to a new short-range, high-density airliner in the 180–200-seat class. It would be powered by two as yet unspecified engines in the 30,000–35,000lb thrust class, and have a range of up to 1,000 miles. It was aimed initially at the two 'home' airlines, Air France and an enthusiastic BEA, which were seeking to replace their Comets and Tridents.

The first meeting in Paris between BAC and Aerospatiale resulted in the establishment of a technical evaluation team headed by Ernie Marshall, project director at Weybridge, and his opposite number in Toulouse, Lucien Servanty, who particularly impressed Sir George. Codenamed *Galion*, the team set about defining the new aircraft, but as time went by the French progressively began to favour a larger wide-body 300-seat version designated A300. In the opinion of Sir George, his Weybridge colleagues, BEA and every market survey, this was too big for the market. What was needed was a 200-seater.

By 1966, with growing BAC disenchantment with the enlarged Airbus, which was attracting no serious customer interest, Sir George and BEA chairman Sir Anthony Milward began a dialogue on a new proposal, the twin-engine BAC Two-Eleven. This would seat some 203 passengers on sectors up to 1,000 miles, and be powered by the proposed new Rolls-Royce RB.211 engine of 30,000lb thrust. The aircraft would be narrow-bodied, with engines mounted at the rear. It shared much design commonality and drew much experience from the One-Eleven, so Sir George and the team could rely on experience – the 'thick end of the learning curve' – to offer an aircraft which would fly further, more quietly and, most importantly, more cheaply than the rival Boeing 727.

There was criticism that it was narrow-bodied at a time when it was fashionable to embrace the wide-body concept, even though the value of wide-bodies would best be realised initially on long-haul routes. This helped fuel an 'Airbus versus Two-Eleven' controversy, which occupied both political and public attention through 1966–7. It was clear, however, that the government favoured a European solution, a view strengthened when Sir George found himself sitting opposite Harold Wilson at an industry lunch. Edwards told the Prime Minister that, if the Airbus was selected, it would be competing head-on with US projects, which would seriously reduce sales prospects, whereas BAC was certain it could sell many more Two-Elevens. Wilson replied that the Cabinet attitude to the British industry was 'very anti', and they thought the UK was 'just no good at aircraft'.

Although he was disappointed at such a negative response, Sir George, supported by Tony Milward, went on the offensive and launched a very public campaign in favour of the Two-Eleven. He was armed with market surveys indicating overwhelming acceptance of the British aircraft, against little interest in the Airbus A300. In August 1967 Edwards wrote an open letter to Milward designed to put pressure on the government. He wrote: 'In order to ensure that BEA, who have consistently supported the project since its inception, have a fleet of BAC Two-Elevens for operation in the summer of 1972, BAC are, pending a final decision, continuing to work on the programme at their own expense.'

Sir George also wished to press the government into launching the RB.211 engine with the necessary development funding. 'When BAC knows that the Rolls-Royce RB.211 engine is to be available,' he wrote, 'then they will be prepared to discuss with the government the best method by which the project can proceed and BEA can have the aeroplane they want.' The latter comment was aimed at the Ministry, who were suggesting that BAC was reluctant to carry its share of development funding.

BEA, through Milward, was equally public in its support. In December, when the die was almost cast, Milward told the BEA staff in a New Year message: 'The Two-Eleven was, in my view, the finest and most advanced aircraft which this country could produce.' He added: 'It grieves me very much that the government should shy away from the project like a startled horse – because we cannot afford it. If we cannot afford the best, can we afford second best?'

But Tony Benn and his advisers in the Ministry of Technology were quite convinced by the European dimension of Airbus, which meant the sharing of risk and cost. Although Sir George was convinced by the principle, he could see little virtue in doing so with a product unlikely to attract sufficient sales. Nevertheless, the government ploughed on, and opted for the A300. In September 1967 a formal partnership was agreed which saw Britain and France take a 37.5 per cent equal share in it, with Germany entering the programme with 25 per cent. In view of BAC's preoccupation with the Two-Eleven, the British airframe design and manufacturing interest was entrusted to Hawker Siddeley, and Rolls-Royce was tasked with the development of its large 50,000lb-thrust engine, the RB.207, which had now been selected.

Without the prospect of additional launch aid for the Two-Eleven, Sir George reluctantly drew a line under the project. He says: 'There was great regret it didn't get built, and the general opinion was that we might sell a few. It was all a bit muddy, especially as Milward was pretty stuck over it. He really threw his hat in the ring over the Two-Eleven and infuriated quite a few chaps in BEA for the support he openly gave it.'

In announcing their preference for the A300, the government sensibly made an important proviso that a final decision was dependent on Airbus receiving orders for at least seventy-five before launching aid would be granted, amounting to £130 million for the airframe and £60 million for the engine. Final project definition was to be confirmed by June 1968.

It was a bitter irony for Sir George and the team that, within a year, following various redesigns of the Airbus, no significant orders had been placed. Tony Benn was thus obliged to announce to the House of Commons in December 1968 the government's effective withdrawal from the project. 'The response of world airlines to the revised proposals had not been encouraging, and the prospects of an economic return both to the firms and the government were not sufficiently good.' Mr Benn said that the firms concerned now wished to put forward proposals for a scaled-down version. 'In these circumstances the cost of developing the RB.207 could be saved and Rolls-Royce are stopping work in this application.'

Mr Benn added: 'The withdrawal of the A300 design presents the three governments with a new situation which they will have to consider. As far as Her Majesty's government is concerned, I must make it absolutely clear that I cannot in any way commit the government to give financial support to any new proposals which may be brought forward by the consortium. In this new situation we shall judge these or any other proposals on their merits against the stringent economic criteria which we apply when government launching aid is sought, including the assurance of a firm market . . .'

So the A300, by mutual agreement, was abandoned in favour of a revised smaller design with 250-seat capacity, designated Airbus A300B. It could be powered by the now revived RB.211, which had been in abeyance since the cancellation of the Two-Eleven and the selection of the RB.207 for the A300. But, again, the A300B did not attract early orders as hoped, and consequently successive British governments decided not to rejoin the consortium as equal partners with the French. Hawker Siddeley retained its interest on a private-venture basis, being responsible for the design and construction of the wings.

George Edwards and the Weybridge team, encouraged by the Minister's statement that the government were prepared to consider 'any other proposals', decided to put forward their own alternative Airbus, the BAC Three-Eleven. With the increasing uncertainty over the Airbus future, the design office had been working for some time on a 'big twin' wide-body of around 250 seats, which closely matched current airline requirements. It would be powered by two rear-mounted RB.211s, now reinstated and uprated to 50,000lb thrust.

With BEA's continued support the Three-Eleven was unveiled and intensive marketing campaigns initiated, while the application process for government launching aid was begun. Lord Portal, at the time of his retirement in 1968, said the Three-Eleven was necessary to BAC if it were to face the next decade 'competitively armed at all points of our technology'.

The Three-Eleven campaign was to be Sir George's last effort to retain a major civil aircraft design and manufacturing capability within the company. The Weybridge team threw every bit of experience and flair into the design, which incorporated the structural integrity of earlier aircraft and the latest aerodynamic advances, particularly in the Farnborough-inspired high-lift wing concepts. With the booming inclusive tour (IT) market in mind, the aircraft was to be offered in two basic versions: a 245-seat eight-abreast configuration aimed at the major carriers, and a 270-seat nine-abreast version with a maximum range of up to 1,500 miles for IT operators.

Although the Three-Eleven was predicated on winning substantial orders from home and abroad, the initial battle would be political, in securing the government launching aid that had been on offer to the Airbus consortium. With this in mind Sir George, in a paper delivered in London and published in

Flight International, spelt out the economic advantages to Britain of having a vibrant aircraft industry and the benefits that would accrue from programmes such as the Three-Eleven.

In the last 20 years the British aerospace industry has earned for the nation over £2,000 million in exports. During the same period it had supplied a further £4,000 million-plus worth of essential equipment to the United Kingdom's airlines and to the defence forces of this country. If our industry had not supplied these goods they would have had to have been purchased abroad – mostly from the USA. These we call frustrated imports. The total beneficial effect on balance of payments of our industry in the past twenty years has, in fact, been about £6,500 million.

Sir George then compared these returns with government investment in research and development costs to launch the products. He estimated this at £1,400 million, of which £400 million had been wasted for policy reasons beyond the control of industry. 'The effective government R&D investment over twenty years has been £1,000 million. This is an average of £50 million a year towards a benefit in balance of payments approaching £350 million a year, a ratio of about 7:1.'

His message was not wasted on Tony Benn, who had not endeared himself to the British aircraft industry when, in a speech at the SBAC annual dinner in 1967, he likened their absorption of public funds to that of the Great Train Robbers. Now, two years later, at the same SBAC dinner, Mr Benn changed his tune as the industry announced that production for the year had risen to £535 million, of which £280 million was for export. 'If every industry in the country exported half of its production, we would have no problems at all. Nobody who has anything to do with the aerospace industry can fail to be excited by it or infected by the enthusiasm of those who work in it,' he stated.

In retrospect, as far as his 'Train Robbers' speech was concerned, Tony Benn admits to being annoyed by the attitude shown to him by the SBAC, and with the industry in general, because of their continual demands for public money. But, like Sir George, he was determined to preserve Britain's aircraft capability. 'It seems to me that Britain's industrial strength and its agricultural strength are basic national interests, full stop. You just have to defend them,' he says.

Therefore Benn was not ill-disposed towards the Three-Eleven, having received both a compelling market analysis and an interesting alternative financial proposal to cover launch costs. As far as projected sales were concerned, surveys indicated a total market of some 1,140 aircraft, of which the Three-Eleven was expected to capture some 241 sales by 1984, with starting orders for forty-three, of which twenty would be for BEA. The BEA order, if confirmed, would make the aircraft eligible for government launch aid, for which BAC put forward two proposals.

The first was a conventional request for a 50 per cent loan to cover development costs estimated at £150 million, which would be recovered by the government over 250 aircraft on an increasing scale of levies. A further £30 million was asked to cover half the production costs and repayable at 5½ per cent. The second scheme was more elaborate and on a loan basis to cover 85 per cent of net capital employed on both development and production to a maximum £120 million over the years 1975 and 1976. Under a complicated financial formula, the government would guarantee the loan with recourse to BAC and insure the company for recovery of 50 per cent of development costs if fewer than 250 aircraft were sold. The maximum government liability would be the same £75 million as under the conventional aid package.

However, it was not the viability of the Three-Eleven that stalled progress, but government concern over the financial state of BAC and its ability to undertake such a project. They indicated that the company would need a substantial injection of capital to sustain it. For the first six months of 1970 Sir George, his colleagues and the shareholding companies were engaged in serious debate with the Ministry over Three-Eleven financing. For the first time this 'powerfully involved' Sir Arnold Weinstock and his GEC company, which had successfully taken over English Electric in late 1968 and thus become a 40 per cent shareholder in BAC.

The arrival of Sir Arnold, who was not a natural ally of Sir George, was to have a profound effect, and his influence was decisive in putting forward a revised financial proposition. A plan was conceived whereby the government would increase the launch aid to 60 per cent if BAC increased its share capital from £30 million to £50 million, including the issue of £12 million in convertible loan stock, thus including the City in the venture.

The Minister also insisted that BAC share the work and risk by bringing in other partners on the basis that they finance their own R&D and tooling costs. Companies both at home and abroad were duly lined up, and talks even began with Boeing. At the most senior level, activity was concentrated on the City, which was not unreceptive. All those involved were convinced that these new measures, which would share responsibility between government and the private sector, would see the project through and secure Cabinet approval.

But once again matters outside the control of the company dealt a decisive blow when Labour was defeated in the general election of 1970. Charles Gardner, in his BAC book, wrote: 'There is little doubt in Sir George Edwards' mind that if the General Election of June 1970 had not intervened, or had the Labour Party not lost it, the Three-Eleven would have been given the go-ahead.' As it was, the Labour administration was swept from power by the Conservatives led by Edward Heath, and the whole process had to begin again with a new Minister of Technology and a new Minister of Aviation.

Sir George and the BAC hierarchy immediately reacquainted the new government with the project. Through the Permanent Secretary at the Ministry of Technology, now presided over by John Davies, they confirmed that the shareholders were willing to increase their equity holdings to £40 million and would raise the required additional £10 million in the City.

But the Ministry procrastinated and no clear decision was forthcoming. By now BAC had spent nearly £2 million of its own money on the project, at a time when sales of the One-Eleven had dropped and more uncertainty hung over Concorde. Sir Arnold Weinstock became increasingly alarmed at the Ministry delay, and 'let rip', as Charles Gardner described it, in a memorandum intended as much for outside consumption as for inside consideration. 'The continued inertia in the handling of this project,' he wrote, 'has given rise to a situation in which it will either come to a stop or fail commercially as a result of the simple efflux of time.' He could not believe that the Ministry was holding up a decision for the sake of BAC raising £10 million in the City for a £150 million project.

Despite such misgivings, and unaware of the serious situation building up over the viability of Rolls-Royce, in the words of Sir George, 'we pressed on', confident the Three-Eleven was a winner. He went to see the new Prime Minister to promote the case, as he recalled for his 1981 *All Our Working Lives* broadcast. 'He was jolly reasonable about it. I explained to him the virtues of the Three-Eleven and what a good thing it would be for the British to go forward in this field in which we'd been pretty successful with the Concorde and One-Eleven. He was reasonable and understanding, but at the end said: "You know there is only a certain amount of money that we can invest in these programmes, and we are already investing heavily in Concorde. I don't see that the money can go into both, there really isn't enough for both."'

The debate was curtailed by the financial crisis at Rolls-Royce. It now became apparent that the company had severely overreached itself with the development of the RB.211. As a result, in December 1970, Fred Corfield,

Minister of Aviation, announced that there were no funds available for either the Three-Eleven or re-entry into Airbus because Rolls-Royce had absorbed it all. A few weeks later Rolls-Royce was declared bankrupt. Owing to the company's 20 per cent shareholding in BAC, inherited when Rolls-Royce took over the Bristol company, this was to have further repercussions.

At Weybridge, the effect of the cancellation was profound and lasting. A full-scale wooden mock-up of the Three-Eleven's interior had been completed, together with a fuselage and many other components. The company was so confident of going ahead with the Three-Eleven that a recruitment drive had already been initiated. Instead, a large-scale redundancy was declared in which nearly 1,000 people, many of them experienced and trained engineers, lost their jobs, and Britain lost a capability that has never been properly recovered.

With the benefit of hindsight, Sir George now reckons that it might have been a blessing in disguise not proceeding with the Three-Eleven, as he explained in his 1981 broadcast. 'It was a great disappointment, but we could have been in trouble because the airlines went into such a state of depression. On the other hand, we would have shoved out the 1011 [the Lockheed L-1011 TriStar], which was eventually and so controversially acquired by British Airways.'

CHAPTER TWENTY-NINE

Changes at the Top

At the end of 1968 Lord Portal stood down as chairman of BAC after eight years in office. From the beginning, his close relationship with George Edwards had brought a combination of wisdom and strength to the new company that was, in the opinion of those involved, the foundation on which its success was truly laid.

In his biography of Portal, Denis Richards wrote: 'This happy and harmonious relationship between chairman and managing director was undoubtedly one of the keys to BAC growth into a properly integrated concern and its predominately successful record during the years 1960–8. The esteem was completely mutual . . .'

Charles Gardner, who worked closely with both men during this period, wrote in his BAC history: 'That BAC owed much of its success to the Portal–Edwards axis is certain. Portal, who had known so many great men, rated Edwards highly as a leader and as a man; Edwards, for his part, admired Portal to the point of veneration.' Gardner added: 'Some have said that GRE manipulated Portal into support for all the Edwardian ideas – which is a ludicrous suggestion. When Portal supported Edwards it was because, on careful analysis, he believed Edwards to be right – just as when CAS he had supported Harris and Tedder. He also realised that Edwards was much more than a gifted engineer and designer, but a man destined to stand out among his fellows in any walk of life he chose to follow.'

It says much for their partnership that, by 1968, despite the traumas of TSR.2 and numerous political setbacks and takeover threats, BAC was now at its strongest since its formation. It employed 36,000 people in three divisions, with annual sales reaching a record £191 million, of which 75 per cent were for export (also a record percentage). The order book in all business areas was robust, particularly for military aircraft and guided weapons. In his farewell message, Lord Portal wrote: 'During the eight years of my chairmanship I have seen BAC develop from a number of previously autonomous units into a unified company which can truly claim to be the most powerful force in European aerospace.'

Of Portal, Sir George says: 'He was a big man. There was no argument, whether he had been chief of the air force or head of the navy, he would have been a big man. He carried a hell of a burden and a great responsibility during the war. People respected Peter. I did to the day they buried him. I helped write the insignia on the plaque in the church. So far as my standing was concerned, I was just a rough old mechanic who had worked his way up through the drawing office, and was always there to see that the rivets were put in the right place.'

Lord Portal died in 1971, and in a published personal tribute Sir George wrote: 'He was always there to listen sympathetically to one's troubles. . . . when a strong position had to be taken, or when it was necessary for plain words to be spoken at some highly important meeting, his words were few, dignified and mightily to the point. One never lacked his support. But if he thought that we had got it wrong, the opening remark "Are you sure?" could soon leave us in no doubt as to where he stood.'

A statue to Lord Portal stands today in the Victoria Embankment gardens close to the MoD. It was unveiled by Harold Macmillan.

The chosen successor to Lord Portal was Sir Reginald Verdon-Smith, a barrister and businessman, who was a descendent of the founding family of the Bristol Aeroplane Company and had been a director of BAC since its foundation. With such background he was considered a fairly neutral but experienced observer, wedged between the more powerful Vickers and English Electric/GEC representatives.

Verdon-Smith and Edwards did not share the same close accord of the previous relationship, but the two men held huge respect for each other. Indeed, Sir George was a powerful proponent for the nomination of Verdon-Smith as chairman, despite political and public controversy over his appointment. This followed claims that his Bristol Siddeley engine company had made excessive profits on a government maintenance contract, much to the displeasure of the Ministry of Technology.

Although most people within the industry, particularly in BAC, considered the allegations unfounded and unfair for various reasons, the predictable

Ministry of Technology response was decidedly unfriendly, as Sir George described following a meeting he and Lord Portal had with the Permanent Secretary, Sir Ronald Melville, who was by no means an ally of the company.

It was decided by the BAC Board that Peter and I were authorised to go to the Ministry in the form of Ronnie Melville. So we craved an appointment. Portal was interesting at a small meeting like that, and had got every word he was going to say written on a bit of paper tucked away in his pocket. There was to be no free speech was Peter's idea of how to handle the thing with a senior civil servant. Ronnie was sitting in his chair and we were the other side of the desk. Peter, like he was still the Chief of Air Staff, said: 'My Board wish me, as a compliment, to tell you it is their intention that when I resign as chairman they propose to appoint Sir Reginald Verdon-Smith in my place.'

This was not well received. Sir George continues:

Poor old Ronnie couldn't hear at the best of times, but when he didn't want to hear anything he didn't like, he switched off. I could hear him mumbling away and saying: 'Unbelievable, incredible, it can't be true!' Then he got himself into a bit of a flap, and leant down and pulled out his desk drawers and shut them again, still mumbling, in a sort of draw-shutting accompaniment to his sonata. Peter put up with this for a bit, and then decided that as a former CAS he wasn't going to be handled any more like this. The old boy sat up in his chair, straight as a ramrod, and said: 'Speak up, man, I can't hear what you are saying!' And that was that. That was the great momentous meeting deciding the fate of god knows how many people. But as far as Portal was concerned it had gone far enough.

Portal and Edwards went back to BAC and told the Board that they (the Ministry) did not think it was a very good idea. 'So it was a question of what we were going to do about it. Did we really think Reggie Verdon-Smith was the bloke for the job, or were there others who were better? It was what you might call an anxious time,' says Sir George.

While BAC and others were considering their position, Edwards took action himself. 'Being in a moderately key position, I used to go round peddling V-S's wares, and she [Lady Verdon-Smith] was very touched that I was doing a "Verdon-Smith for BAC" exercise. Then, as things tend to happen, in the fullness of time, we got there and gave Reggie the job.'

Sir George says he considered Verdon-Smith 'a decent chap' who had plenty of influence in the City and long experience of the aircraft, guided weapons and aero-engine industry. 'When BAC was formed he was the Bristol element in the merger, and he knew what was going on. He and I used to prod at one another over this and that, but we got on all right.' At the time of the announcement Edwards stated: 'Appointing Verdon-Smith to succeed Peter Portal was a mark of our confidence in V-S, who had been badly treated and made a scapegoat for others.'

For his part, Sir Reginald, according to Denis Richards, was not always enthusiastic about what some called 'Edwardian persuasiveness'. Richards wrote: 'If treated to one of Edwards's more extravagant statements he was not above saying – Now come off it George!' He was nonetheless fully appreciative of his managing director's exceptional powers and enjoyed 'a comfortable relationship' with him. Verdon-Smith's approach, however, was different to that of Portal, as Charles Gardner observed. 'He had always been involved in the battle rather than above it. He approached problems with the logic of counsel approaching a brief, and at all times kept a sharp eye on the attitude of the City towards the company and its financial position.'

Two other events of 1968 were to have far-reaching bearing on BAC. The first was a top-level internal reorganisation made at the behest of Sir George. This effectively transferred executive responsibility from the old main 'shareholders' Board to a reconstituted BAC Ltd Board to include the senior executives of all three divisions. The second was the arrival of Sir Arnold Weinstock, following the take-over of English Electric by his GEC company.

The Board changes arose from a memorandum written by Sir George early 1968, following the Benn statement in December 1967 that any takeover or nationalisation plans had been postponed. It was unlikely that such ideas could be resurrected quickly and, given some breathing space, now was the time to look ahead. Edwards proposed a change in the name of the company from British Aircraft Corporation Ltd to British Aircraft Corporation (Holdings) Ltd, while the old BAC (Operating) Ltd was to become BAC Ltd, with executive responsibility to run the company.

The point of the change was to ensure what Sir George wanted, that the future of the company lay firmly in the hands of those directly responsible for designing, making and selling its products. The full burden of company affairs would now rest with the BAC Ltd Board, presided over by an executive chairman, while the shareholders would retain a watching brief and ultimate control through the Holdings Board, which would meet less regularly than in the past. The chairman of the Holdings Board, Sir George said, 'must be of the same stature' as the present chairman, Lord Portal.

As far as his own position was concerned, Sir George was already chairman and managing director of the old Operating Board, and managing director of the main 'shareholders' Board. He was, therefore, expected to assume the chairmanship of the reconstituted BAC Ltd, in addition to being managing director. Edwards wrote at the time: 'If I were invited to take up that position, I would regard, as an essential part of my remaining term, the selection and preparation of my successor.' He added: 'A secondary advantage of the change is the removal of the present mental barrier, which I know a number of divisional directors have about their chances of ever becoming a director of BAC.'

In August 1968 the changes came into force, and to nobody's surprise Sir George was appointed chairman and managing director of BAC Ltd. His main line of authority rested with the chairman of the Holdings Board and the senior representatives of the parent companies, which were soon to include Sir Arnold Weinstock, managing director of GEC, although Lord Nelson, as chairman of GEC, retained his position on the Holdings Board.

Sir Arnold Weinstock's entry into the aviation arena was not propitious. His background lay in the supply of electrical goods through Radio & Allied Industries, of which his father-in-law, Sir Michael Sobell, was chairman, and in which he had worked his way to the top. The BAC involvement was therefore only through the acquisition of English Electric. Apart from the possible merger of BAC's Guided Weapons Division with its own subsidiary, Marconi Ltd, he had little interest in aviation, and really wanted out of the business.

Weinstock's concern over the prolonged and money-wasting fight for the Three-Eleven has already been noted. He now cast his eye over the entire civil aircraft prospects of the company, and particularly the future of the One-Eleven, of which there were some fourteen unallocated aircraft in production. He proposed an end to the One-Eleven and the closure of at least one of the civil aircraft factories, Weybridge, Hurn or Filton, as the airliner market fell into depression.

Sir Arnold also became increasingly unhappy with the company's financial position, primarily due to the demise of the Three-Eleven and the lack of a viable replacement project in the civil aircraft business. Sales, exports and profits all fell in 1970, a downward trend that was maintained the following year. As a result, Weinstock recommended that no dividend should be paid in

1971, although this was strongly (but unsuccessfully) resisted by Vickers, which feared it would lead to a loss of customer confidence in the company.

Adding to the complications was the 1971 bankruptcy of Rolls-Royce, which had already impacted so damagingly on BAC by absorbing all available government funds for launch aid. Rolls-Royce, which had previously acquired Bristol Aircraft holdings for its aero-engine company, had also assumed ownership of the airframe business, thus inheriting a 20 per cent shareholding in BAC. These shares were now held by the official receiver, and GEC was unenthusiastic in acquiring them. Negotiations dragged on, and it was not until 1972 that both Vickers and GEC agreed to take them up on an equal basis at a price of £6.25 million. Thus the two companies became the sole and equal shareholders in BAC.

Sir George took no part in these painful early deliberations. He was at home, recuperating from a stomach operation which had near-fatal complications, the aftermath of which was to trouble him for the rest of his life. But by the summer of that year he was back in harness. He was, of course, perfectly aware of Weinstock's outlook. 'His whole history was devoted to getting things done as cheaply as he could; that was where the profits came from,' Sir George says. 'When he came to London as an immigrant he had got in his system that money had to be taken care of. When he got into a position of running GEC, that stayed with him. It wasn't any good chaps trying fancy larks on him – be it some great new device, whether it be an aeroplane or an electrical system – unless they could show, without any doubt, that they were going to make some money with it.'

Sir George remembers many meetings with Sir Arnold in those days, when the topic was always financial matters. 'I remember spending time in Weinstock's office, with him bashing me over the head because I was spending too much in the factory, making things too expensively. Something had to be done about reducing costs. He made a speech once in which he said that one thing I could rely on was that he would walk out, and take no notice of what I was saying, unless matters improved. And that wasn't far out either.' Sir George adds: 'There was conflict between us. I wouldn't say it was bloody-minded, but when I needed some money to do something to an aeroplane, Arnold, as a matter of principle, tried to persuade me that I didn't need it. But our personal relationships were all right; we never fought.'

By 1972 the health of the company was beginning to improve. The threatened closure of one of the civil aircraft plants had been averted, but at a cost of some 2,000 redundancies across the civil aircraft factories. Sales of the

One-Eleven were picking up, and the government had now thrown its full weight behind the Concorde programme, with the SST scheduled to enter service in 1975/6. Military aircraft business was most encouraging. Strikemaster strike/trainers were being sold around the world, the first Jaguar deliveries had begun, and BAC had successfully established, with its German and Italian counterparts, the joint company Panavia, registered in Munich, to be responsible for the new MRCA. The initial requirement for MRCA was for more than 700 aircraft in various roles for all three countries, making it by far the largest military aircraft programme in Europe.

The guided weapons business, too, was doing well. Spearheaded by Rapier, it was now offering sophisticated systems for land, sea and air. The Seawolf ship-borne defence system against air attack was so good that it was even capable of engaging a shell from a gun. At Bristol, a new space facility had been established, working on advanced satellite and rocketry projects, while a range of special 'high-tech' by-products and test equipment was finding new markets.

Relationships between Sir George and Sir Arnold eased, and Sir George supported a new money-saving scheme introduced by Weinstock, which compelled every senior manager to fill in a weekly financial management control questionnaire, which had to be returned to his office. 'I agreed to co-operate with Arnold on these magical sheets showing what we had done in the way of cash flow for the preceding week,' says Sir George. 'It was a bloody tight arrangement, and chaps' eyes in BAC got focused on money more than they had done before. It was not to see if you had made, by some great invention, improvements in speed or performance to an aeroplane, but if you had made something a bit cheaper.'

Edwards adds: 'I used to encourage my lot to take them seriously, and I could see what Weinstock was at. The success as far as he was concerned was to see what money was coming in, compared with what money was going out. I think, and I can say it now because it is far enough away, it probably sharpened up many blokes in the outfit, like me if you like, whose life had been dominated by pursuing Isaac Newton and keeping him out of the way.'

There is no doubt in the history of BAC that Weinstock's influence greatly strengthened the company, as Sir George acknowledges. 'I used to sit in his funny little office and although he didn't necessarily agree with the rate at which I was spending dough, he never questioned how I was spending it. There was support for what I was up to. I was in that job and as far as he was concerned I should put my head down and get on with it.' Charles Gardner wrote: 'By the mid-1970s Weinstock, at first seen at Warton, Weybridge and

Filton as the dreaded axe-wielder, had become, behind the scenes, a tower of strength to BAC.'

In January 1972, with sales for the previous year slightly up to just under £159 million and the order intake also increased, Sir Reginald Verdon-Smith stepped down as the chairman of the Holdings Board. It was decided not to replace him, especially as Sir George Edwards was the acknowledged leader of the company and his BAC Ltd Board now had full control over the company's affairs. To retain a proper link with the Holdings Board, Sir George was also appointed managing director, with a direct line to the shareholders represented by Lord Robens (who had become chairman of Vickers) and Lord Nelson, chairman of GEC (with Weinstock ever-present). As to his stated intention to find and prepare his successor, Sir George nominated his long-time colleague from Weybridge, Allen Greenwood, who became deputy chairman and eventually succeeded him.

Greenwood had joined Vickers-Armstrongs in 1940, and worked briefly in the experimental department at the time when George Edwards was taking over as manager. He left shortly afterwards to join the Fleet Air Arm, and when he returned after the war, in 1946, he went to see Edwards, the newly appointed chief designer, to ask what job he could do. He was told that BEA was about to receive its first Vikings, and that he could best be employed looking after the airline and seeing it was properly supported, so that Edwards 'didn't get any complaints'. Greenwood rose rapidly through the ranks, making a name for himself in the service and support areas, for which he was later given directorial responsibility. He was also committed to European collaboration, and it was his high-level diplomatic skill that had helped forge the successful collaborative military aircraft programmes with France, Germany and Italy that became the foundation of BAC's and the British industry's future.

During this period, in 1971, Sir George received his greatest and most treasured honour when he was appointed to the Order of Merit (OM). The Order is restricted to twenty-four members, and is in the personal gift of the Sovereign. Its members comprise the most distinguished men and women of the time, drawn from the arts, politics, science and the military. Because the OM is beyond political or civil service direct influence it is much prized. On receiving the award Sir George said at the time that he needed 'all the power to his elbow', to fight the battles that still lay before the company.

At a celebration party with colleagues at 100 Pall Mall, Sir Reginald Verdon-Smith paid glowing tribute to Sir George which he reinforced at the prestigious RAeS Barnwell Memorial Lecture, delivered in 1974. He described Sir George as 'BAC's unquestionable leader', and stated, 'without his breadth of vision BAC might never have survived'.

It was also a time of 'moving on' for Sir George and his family. After twenty-five happy years at Durleston they decided to move to a larger house in White Lane on Albury Downs, near Guildford. The family had become well known and well liked in Bookham, and Sir George's regular 'thinking' walks with his beloved dog Rex had become a familiar sight in the area on most Sunday afternoons. His daughter Dingle had gone to school locally, and Dinah had made many friends there.

The new home, Albury Heights, built in 1926, was a large 'between-the-wars' two-storey house with a spacious attic area (later to be converted into Sir George's painting studio) and a generous cellar, in which he installed a billiards table. Sir George maintains it was not built as soundly as Durleston, but offered much more room, especially for housing relatives and later, in retirement, his long-time driver Archie Shields, his mother and his wife Rene. The property had a sizeable sloping garden, at the bottom of which Sir George laid out a tennis court. It had magnificent views of the surrounding countryside, and from his living room he could see the ancient church of St Martha's on the Hill, which was to play an important part in his future life. Albury Heights was to be his home for the rest of his life.

CHAPTER THIRTY

'Merger-itis' and Nationalisation

Sir George Edwards would have liked his last few years in office to have been less stressful than his first. He had every reason to believe they would be so when he took up the ultimate responsibility as executive chairman in 1968. The company's finances had been turned round, the military programmes were going well, and a Tory government appeared more sympathetic to industry needs. They supported Concorde, and were more realistic in their attitude to overseas defence sales, particularly to friendly Middle East countries. The main issue would be the impact on the aerospace industry of Britain joining the EEC, but this held no particular worry for BAC, which had pioneered European partnership with a string of major collaborative programmes. But any hopes for a calmer, more settled future, were ill-founded.

In 1972 a bright new Minister of Aerospace, Michael Heseltine, came to office and set out with enthusiasm to seek a resolution to the future size and shape of the British aircraft industry, particularly its position and relationship with Europe. A staunch European, he sought consultation with its leaders, and in April wrote to Sir George in order that, 'I may have the opportunity of listening – may I emphasise that word – to your views about the problems facing the industry'.

There followed a series of meetings and informal symposiums attended by Sir George and held at the Minister's own house in London, to which the other industry leaders were invited, including Sir Arnold Hall, chairman of Hawker Siddeley Aviation, and Sir Arnold Weinstock. The discussion centred on what was described as, 'developing a European strategy and the prospect of establishing a common procurement policy, both military and civil, and a strong European home market to rival the Americans'.

A note prepared by the Ministry to support the Minister's second symposium in November 1972 outlined what were seen as the next steps towards the development of 'closer co-ordination of European aircraft requirements and procurement policies and a more integrated manufacturing capability'. It stated: 'Discussions at both Ministerial and official level over the past few months have created a good general atmosphere in which these exchanges can continue (although there is still some way to go with the French).'

Of particular concern to Sir George was the suggestion that there be 'a more integrated manufacturing capability', which could only mean more industry mergers, and mergers probably on a European scale. An earlier Ministry discussion document had reinforced the point, stating: 'Economic necessity is already impelling a pattern of collaboration between national industries on an ad hoc basis. But collaboration alone is unlikely to provided the strength to withstand American competition or an environment in which the long production runs can be secured; the solution seems clearly to be in some form of European integration of the industry.'

Although Sir George was fully supportive of the idea of European collaboration, he believed it should be pursued on an individual product basis against an established market. There was no necessity to make wholesale and unwanted changes at home just to satisfy a European ideal. 'There is no earthly reason for building aeroplanes for their own sake, and for Europe to do so just for political reasons would be economic madness,' he said. Furthermore, there was no legal provision at the time to merge individual companies within the EEC.

He was also wary of Britain's role being diminished by such European association. In a contemporary lecture he told the students at the RAF Staff College at Bracknell that, although collaboration 'rightly used' was the key to the future of aerospace in Britain, it could not do without a strong, broadly based British aircraft industry. 'To strengthen Europe we must give away some of our knowledge and competitive position. But what I will never concede is that we must be permanently cast in a junior role.'

Following the November symposium, Sir George wrote to Heseltine, stating: 'I have worked towards European collaboration more than anyone else in the industry. I have always seen the eventual outcome as real commercial unions between companies across frontiers. The area where you and I may differ is in the matter of timing.'

One opportunity within Europe for which Sir George thought the timing was right was the prospect of building a new civil airliner that would fit below the larger Airbus family, and for which he was convinced there was a market. This would preserve the Weybridge expertise, which in engineering and marketing was considered to be world-class, especially in this category of short/medium-haul aircraft.

Several attempts were made with both European and British partners. The most promising of these was the Europlane Quiet Take-Off and Landing (QTOL) aircraft seating 180–200 passengers, to be developed with German, Swedish and Spanish partners. But after much intensive work this was abandoned in September 1973, as was a new proposal to build a 200-seater. For this, BAC and a group of six participating companies, including Hawker Siddeley Aviation and Dassault of France, had worked together on a design specification. A conflict on nationalistic lines (the French would only pursue their own concept) and the eventual advent of nationalisation, ended such ambition, even if a viable market could have been found.

During this time, almost inevitably, talk resumed of a merger between BAC and Hawker Siddeley. In the early months of 1973 Sir George came under increasing Ministry pressure and media speculation over what he called 'merger-itis'. He responded in a similar manner to his reaction to the earlier Benn proposals. He pointed out the healthy financial position of the company and the growing order book, which guaranteed long-term work. The BAC official line to press enquiries was: 'BAC does not want a merger with Hawker and, as far as it knows, Hawkers hold much the same view.'

In June Edwards wrote a personal letter on the subject to the Secretary (Aerospace) in the Department of Trade and Industry. 'What I find difficult in the present attitude towards British mergers in the aerospace field, is the insistence that it has to be done because there is an inevitable decline in the amount of work.' He pointed out that the BAC order book stood at over £600 million, of which two-thirds was for export. 'This is the highest figure since BAC was formed, and when one considers future programmes of Jaguars and MRCA, which are not included, does not to me suggest that whatever may be happening to the rest of the British industry, BAC is in a decline.'

Sir Arnold Weinstock, however, supported by the MoD, had a different approach to the merger possibility. For a time he saw advantage in 'hiving off' the BAC Guided Weapons Division, combining it with the Hawker Siddeley Dynamics business and merging it with his own Marconi company. Sir George was very much against the idea. After meeting Weinstock he sent him a considered statement on the disadvantages of such a move.

Sir George wrote: 'The most powerful companies with the greatest marketing success cover the whole spectrum of civil aircraft, military aircraft, weapons and space. The integration of these closely related activities in a single organisation gives a degree of technical and financial strength and stability plus international negotiating status which is not possessed by more specialist companies.'

As far as relationships with the MoD were concerned, he pointed out that, after years of having separate controllers for aircraft and guided weapons, the Ministry had now combined the job under one single controller. 'It would seem strange – to say the least – if at this moment industry decided to split its own guided weapons and aircraft work.'

Sir George then touched on the merger possibilities. 'There may be much to be said for the creation of a larger British organisation which would be of equivalent size and international status to the major United States companies. This has been one of the major arguments advanced by the government for such a change. It is essential, however, for such a group to be a match for its competitors. It must include all forms of aerospace activity.'

If this statement appeared contradictory to public pronouncements about merging with Hawker Siddeley, it was because Edwards by now felt that some form of merger was inevitable. If that were to be the case, a fragmented, larger company, along the lines proposed by Weinstock, would weaken it. Sir George continued: 'The financial progress of BAC can be largely attributed to the broad spread of its products and markets. It therefore would make sense for a further restructuring of the British industry to be built around BAC in its present form. The problems of managing such a large organisation would be formidable. It would demand the same effective divisional structure that had always existed in BAC and is only now being established by Aerospatiale [the new combined French aerospace company]. Meanwhile the right solution is to leave BAC as it is,' he told Weinstock.

Sir Arnold was, for the time being, persuaded to leave BAC alone. No doubt Sir George's objections, supported by Vickers, had their effect, although the excellent financial returns and the even better forecast would probably have had more impact. Any further debate was, however, interrupted by the fuel crisis and the 'three-day week', which was to precipitate a general election in February 1974. This saw the Heath government removed from office and a new Labour administration, carrying with it a belief in nationalisation, put in power. Tony Benn was reinstated as Secretary of State for Industry, and this time he was mandated to do it.

For Sir George and BAC, Benn's return was to have an immediate benefit. As previously recorded, Benn saw off a further effort by senior civil servants to cancel Concorde, despite contracts having been signed with British Airways and Air France.

But Tony Benn's view on nationalisation was equally uncompromising. It was now in the manifesto to bring into public ownership the aircraft and shipbuilding industries. The essential reasoning was the claim that, because the aircraft industry relied so heavily on public expenditure, it should be owned by the public. Sir George, who, as already noted, had disputed this on numerous occasions, said the government got back from the industry either in cash or in goods far more than it had put in. To lump it in with shipbuilding was misleading, as that industry was virtually on its knees and required government intervention if it were to be saved. Overall, Sir George said the nationalisation proposals were 'irrelevant to the problems of the industry'.

Interestingly, both Benn and Edwards believed in the importance of sustaining a strong aerospace industry in Britain, but they were coming at it from very different directions. Benn says: 'I was very fond of him [Sir George], I liked all these guys even if they thought I was a dangerous revolutionary. I liked them because we had this one common interest in seeing that Britain didn't lose. These industrial bosses used to make speeches at the weekend, denouncing government intervention in industry, and then turn up on Monday asking for millions of pounds. I didn't mind, but I thought that if we were going to invest it ought to be on the basis of a shareholder so we benefited from the success. And there was a bit of tension there.'

Benn adds: 'But it was a very close relationship [with Sir George], in the sense that we both had one thing in common; we wanted British industry to succeed against the Treasury, who didn't give a damn. Denis Healey tried to cancel everything.'

At first there was little clear government indication as to how, in what form, and when nationalisation would take place, or what would be the relationship it would have to the National Enterprise Board, through which British companies would be taken into public ownership. Furthermore, with only a slim majority, it was very possible that the government would not last long enough to see it through. Indeed, this proved to be the case when, in October 1974, the Labour administration went to the country and was returned to office, but only with the slimmest majority.

The interregnum, however, allowed for nationalisation matters to be formalised, and on the Labour government's return, in the Queen's Speech, it was confirmed that legislation would be introduced in the new session to bring the aircraft industry into public ownership as part of the government's general industrial policy.

In January Benn produced a consultative document which set out in more detail their nationalisation intentions. However, the speed and lack of clarity in the document were quickly rounded upon from all quarters of the industry. In a formal BAC response, Sir George stated: 'We found it lacking in precision and self-contradictory on a number of fundamental questions. We believe it fails to do justice to the very complex problems implicit in such a radical change of an industry so vitally important as aerospace.'

Among many queries listed by Sir George arising from the document were the lack of indicated timescales, the meaning of the introduction of 'industrial democracy' into the new company, the definition of 'fair compensation', the failure to include the space business, and the need for definite financial proposals. 'In order to achieve success in the world markets, would require a management structure at political and industrial levels of great flexibility. It follows that there must be a minimum of direction and interference by government,' he wrote.

The consultative paper even suggested a name for the new company: 'The Aircraft Corporation of Great Britain'. Sensing this was another indication of a split between aircraft and guided weapons, Sir George quickly pointed out that this did not take into account the GW business, even though it was included in the proposals. One piece of good news, however, was confirmation that the new company would not have to report through the National Enterprise Board (NEB). The NEB's role was already the subject of controversy and dispute between Tony Benn and his senior civil servant, Sir Anthony Part.

In the build-up to nationalisation, some observers have suggested that Sir George's attitude was 'collaborative'. This stemmed from the contents of Sir George's handwritten note to Benn, sent while he was on holiday in Cornwall immediately after the Queen's Speech. In it, Edwards said that, whatever views he might have about the desirability of nationalisation, 'I am determined to do what I can to make the industry in its new form a success.'

Part of this note was read out by Tony Benn at his press conference to launch the consultative document. In fact, Edwards had consistently attacked nationalisation of the industry from its inception, but throughout its implementation he had responded point by point to individual proposals in an effort to make the new company as viable as possible. As Charles Gardner records: 'From the time of the election, Sir George was privately convinced that Benn would push through nationalisation early in the new government's life, and that it would become law. It was not a subject on which the public felt deeply, and certainly not one which would bring people out in a procession of banners down Whitehall.'

Gardner adds: 'In any event the Conservative alternative, if Heseltine's seeming views were to prevail, was to split the UK industry into three separate lumps and Europeanise it in some unspecified way, with the British components as the only profitable ones. Of two bad proposals, Sir George preferred Benn's which he believed could be made to work if it was given the right management structure . . .'

At Tony Benn's request, in February 1975, Sir George wrote to the Minister and provided a detailed account of BAC's activities and healthy financial situation. This showed the firm order book at £849 million, of which £627 million was for export, which guaranteed at least four years of certain work. He noted future prospects including 'assumed' orders, such as those for the Jaguar and MRCA, which were not in the order book. He outlined the Concorde situation, for which a variable-rate production programme had been initiated which would 'enable us to retain the ability to build Concordes at the time when the airlines of the world are in a position to buy them'.

Referring to the many speculative sales prospects, notably air-defence systems in the Middle East, Sir George wrote: 'These orders, firm and potential, will provide many years of work for BAC, but they carry with them great responsibilities in countries whose relationship with the United Kingdom is politically sensitive. You will understand therefore why I say it is vital that the company which emerges after nationalisation must be able fully to meet the commitments undertaken by BAC.' He added, with Weinstock intentions still in mind: 'It is not my intention to use this letter as part of the debate about guided weapons being absorbed into the electronics industry. It must, however, be realised that an important reason for our successes with these large Middle East contracts has been our ability to offer complete integrated systems of weapons and aircraft as prime contractor in both.'

Sir George also warned Benn about reducing the size of the industry. 'It would be irresponsible for anyone arbitrarily to use the forthcoming nationalisation as a convenient opportunity to reduce the size of the aerospace industry in this country. There are very large commitments, existing and imminent, which demand a certain level of support in order that they shall be carried out within the terms of the contracts. They alone will set the minimum size of the industry.'

Finally, Edwards returned to his long-term theme. He wrote: 'I hope this will help to dispel the gloom through which Whitehall seems permanently to view the industry's future. A point worth making is that BAC has operated profitably since its formation.'

A month later Sir George led a senior BAC delegation to see the Minister. Mr Benn recorded in his diary entry for 17 March 1975: 'George Edwards said our main concern is that management should be allowed to manage, management should get its instructions from the Board and not from the government, we want to preserve the company in the meanwhile and what about bank guarantees?' Mr Benn also noted the comments of Allen Greenwood, who wanted 'greater clarification on primary objectives'. Greenwood was worried about the powers of the Secretary of State. 'We want to get the words right in the Bill; what about the capital structure and the method of financing?' he asked the Minister.

But if there was goodwill over Concorde, it was soon to evaporate when the meaning of industrial democracy was discussed at the meeting. 'It was like talking to some medieval people,' Benn stated, and the role of defence brought greater divide. Benn wrote: 'I was terribly courteous and polite and I didn't cause any offence, but I have no intention of letting those people continue to manage the industry, and I did say that there were a lot of people who felt that nationalisation just meant a new nameplate on the door.'

Sir George, much exercised by Benn's views on defence matters and particularly his attitude to defence sales, tackled the Secretary of State for Defence, Roy Mason, to whom he wrote in July. He pointed out the value of British defence exports, of the need for government support to compete with rival countries, and the importance of the role of the government's own defence sales organisation. Having outlined the many prospects, especially in the Middle East, where 'Saudi Arabia is the key', he wrote: 'The government says the balance of payments situation is important. If this is so, I think they should have clearly in their mind that the present methods they are adopting may well lose a substantial part of this valuable market to other countries whose methods are more direct.'

His challenge to nationalisation was not confined to letters to ministers, and Sir George took every available opportunity to express his views. In April, as the guest speaker at the RAF Central Flying School, he told them that this was likely to be his last appearance 'doing the job I'm doing' because there were those who thought the way to improve the industry was by nationalisation. 'A lesser civil servant than me it would be difficult to find,' he quipped. He added: 'I've had a pretty exciting sort of existence one way and another, fighting the powers of darkness, creeping up and down the corridors of power vainly searching signs of government policy.'

Sir George's response to nationalisation, and his attendance at some further meetings with the Ministry, were effectively his last executive actions as chairman. In the early summer of 1975 he entered hospital and underwent two further operations, in which half his intestine was removed. For most of the rest of the year he was either in hospital or recuperating at home. He returned to the office only at the beginning of December, three weeks before his retirement. Allen Greenwood, who had been 'holding the ring', took over officially as the chairman on 1 January 1976.

In the preceeding September the Aircraft and Shipbuilding Industries Bill had been given its first formal reading, and in December 1975 the second reading and debate was introduced by the new Secretary of State, Eric Varley. Varley replaced Benn, who had been moved to the Energy department, having fallen foul of Harold Wilson following his opposition to remaining in the Common Market. By now the acceptable name 'British Aerospace' had been adopted, and Scottish Aviation had been included with BAC and Hawker Siddeley Aircraft and Dynamics in the new organisation.

For a variety of reasons the committee stage dragged on until May 1976, to be followed by a further and almost successful Conservative legal challenge that claimed the Bill was hybrid because of the exclusion of a related ship repair business. It was not until March 1977 that the Bill finally received Royal Assent, and on 1 April 1977 (an appropriate day to some) the new British Aerospace formally came into being, with Vesting Day (on which trading could begin) set at 29 April 1977.

Sir George watched these events from the sidelines. He was not to be an entirely silent witness.

CHAPTER THIRTY-ONE

Into Retirement

Few people in BAC or in the industry wanted George Edwards to retire in December 1975. Although he was now 67 years old and was suffering a period of serious ill health, he had lost none of his intellectual powers, nor his acclaimed foresight. Sir Arnold Weinstock and the Vickers hierarchy wanted him to stay on until he was 72. He was still the outstanding and most-respected figure in the British industry, and his leadership was never more needed than now, in the face of the uncertainty nationalisation would bring.

Sir George, however, had no doubt about what he should do. The immediate and lasting effect of his operations had physically debilitated him and, as he says: 'I was flat on my back and in a bit of trouble. So my mind was focused on not leaving Dinah a widow. Work had become a bit secondary.' He adds: 'It was made abundantly clear that I had got to ease the throttles off a bit from the lunatic life I had been leading. Banging my brains out, trying to run this great outfit, had got to stop. So stop it did.'

His health problem, which deprived the industry of a few more years of his stewardship, had begun when he was only 10 years old, in 1918, when he was admitted to the London Hospital to undergo an operation for suspected peritonitis. Sir George still maintains it was in fact 'a plain straightforward appendix'. Unfortunately, during the operation, tiny grains of talcum powder were left inside his stomach, which turned into small growths. Eventually, after Sir George had suffered stomach pains for many years, his family doctor and friend, Dr John Morgan, referred him to the Queen's surgeon, Eddie (later Sir Edward) Tuckwell. Tuckwell discovered the growths and carried out a series of operations to remove them, both in Leatherhead hospital and later, after complications, at the Royal Masonic Hospital in London.

There is little doubt that such treatment kept Sir George alive until he was nearly 95, but it had a lasting effect that was to worry him and restrict his movements for the rest of his life. Edwards described his condition most succinctly, and in his own style, in a letter to a colleague. He wrote: 'My interior control system is as unstable as my early aeroplanes were always reckoned to be.'

Despite his illness, and with the prospect of his recovery, Sir George was still viewed as the prominent candidate for the chairmanship of the new nationalised aircraft industry. In fact, Sir George maintains he was not asked. 'I never received what I would regard as anything like a formal offer,' he says. He had, of course, made his anti-nationalisation views quite clear to those who counted, but his offer of support to the new organisation, as quoted by Tony Benn, led to further speculation. 'For some reason there were members of the Labour party who thought I could be persuaded. There was a sort of "Well, old George really believes that we ought to be nationalised, but he won't say so" attitude,' he recalls.

Although Edwards had no intention of taking on the chairmanship, he was consulted over the selection of the new man. 'I was called into various ministers' and civil servants' offices and quizzed about who we should have,' he says. The most serious nominees from industry were Sir Arnold Hall and Sir John Lidbury from the Hawker Siddeley Group, but both indicated that they were non-starters. Sir George's preference was a surprising one. He favoured Sir Anthony Part, the Permanent Secretary in the Industry Department.

Such a choice would seem inconsistent with his well-known criticisms of the civil service because of their lack of expertise in technical departments. However, he had got to know Sir Anthony personally, and respected his judgement on industry matters, which were in many cases at odds with those of his boss, Tony Benn. Sir George clearly felt that Part would have a moderating effect on some of Benn's more extreme proposals in the formative years of the new company. But, most of all, Sir Anthony was a member of that exclusive club of permanent secretaries who understood better than anyone the intricacies of decision making in Whitehall. Such insight could modify and mould a government's intention into more moderate and acceptable conclusions.

But Tony Benn would have none of it. 'I would die rather than appoint him,' he wrote in his diary. His reaction was not surprising, judging by his policy disputes with Sir Anthony, particularly over the NEB. His entry in his diary in December 1974, following a meeting with Sir George, was predictable. Benn wrote: 'He said he had been thinking about the chairmanship and he'd come to the conclusion that a civil servant was necessary. Guess who he thought would be best – Sir Anthony Part. Later Part asked how I got on with George Edwards and I said, oh fine, it was very interesting. He obviously wanted me to comment on the possibility that he might be Chairman. I'd rather be seen dead than do that.'

The 'pro-Part' campaign even reached the Prime Minister, who thought that Sir Anthony should be considered for the job. 'Of course, that came from George Edwards and from the Treasury and from my department, and I'm glad it is a suggestion from him because I will not have it,' Benn recorded.

The choice fell on Lord Beswick, a junior minister in the Industry Department, whom Tony Benn had long advocated. Frank Beswick certainly had appropriate qualifications. He had served in the RAF, had held several air-related government appointments, had been MP for Uxbridge and had even worked for BAC for a short time while Labour was out of office. Sir George, of course, knew him well, having offered him the job as a special adviser at Weybridge. He even sent Beswick a handwritten note while convalescing, to tell him of his impending retirement, which concluded: 'You know that I don't accept the need for nationalisation and in the present state of affairs I think it is lunatic to go on with it.'

As a first step towards nationalisation Lord Beswick was appointed chairman of an organising committee, who would in due course become the Board members of the new enterprise. Of Beswick himself, Sir George says: 'I think he was all right, but he wasn't really able to stand up there, with his uniform on, and give the order to the troops as to what to do, because he had no experience.'

So, in December 1975, after 40 years' service, Sir George severed all formal connections with the aircraft industry. Letters and tributes came from all over the world. The BAC house newspaper, *Airframe*, published a special four-page supplement in which the words of the Duke of Edinburgh occupied the centre of the front page. Prince Philip, who had been a personal friend since Viscount days, wrote: 'Sir George Edwards is one of those exceptional men who have stamped their genius on the course of human events. His achievements have earned him a place among the great company of pioneers and innovators in civil aviation.'

Prince Philip was also a special guest at a glittering farewell dinner at Claridge's in London for Sir George and Lady Edwards, organised by Lord Nelson, chairman of GEC, and Lord Robens, chairman of Vickers. The guest list read like a *Who's Who* of British aviation. It included all the principal heads, past and present, of the aircraft industry, including Sir Kenneth Keith of

Rolls-Royce, Sir Arnold Hall from Hawkers, Sir Basil Smallpeice from BOAC, Sir Anthony Milward and Henry Marking from BEA, Sir Morien Morgan from the RAE, and Sir Peter Masefield, who helped launch the Viscount.

Among his many colleagues were Sir Arnold Weinstock, Lord Caldecote, Sir Peter Matthews (managing director of Vickers), Sir Reginald Verdon-Smith, Sir Dermot Boyle and Sir Charles Dunphie. The RAF was represented by the present CAS, Sir Andrew Humphrey, and many other former chiefs and notable airmen. Among those from Whitehall were Lord Boyd-Carpenter, chairman of the Civil Aviation Authority, Lord Zuckerman, Harold Wilson's scientific adviser, and Sir Anthony Part. Allen Greenwood, Freddie Page, George Jefferson and Sir Geoffrey Tuttle represented the present BAC company.

Lord Nelson, who like his father had played such an influential part in the moulding of BAC, spoke of Sir George's 'determination and courage to see the job through', and his essential human approach to the problems involved. 'Your unique style had the facility to relieve tension or to emphasise a point by a pithy and original phrase,' he said. He could not remember any other occasion of such size and importance where so many people could record 'so many memories and so many exciting events that have involved them with the guest of honour'. He concluded: 'The company he has led over the years, he now leaves in first-class order. With the orderbook at over £900 million, of which 70 per cent is in the export market, what better tribute can be made to the man at the helm than these figures demonstrate?'

Lord Robens remembered Sir George 'in glimpses'. They were both closely associated with the development of the University of Surrey. They would meet up there on open days, when the parents arrived to meet the lecturers and officers of the University. 'George, at the beginning, would always have one or two young chaps around him, but the crowd grew bigger and bigger until there was no one left on my side of the room!' he said.

Robens spoke also of Sir George's courage, which was well demonstrated when he visited him in Leatherhead hospital after an operation. Although he was in real agony, he refused to show it in front of Dinah, so she would not worry and could continue a planned visit to friends in London. 'Shortly after she left he was back on the operating table.' He added: 'My experience of George has been in such glimpses, which has shown courage, integrity and plain straightforward talking when there have been problems. He has this tremendous ability to understand how to handle people. He can kick somebody's bottom and they will thank him! I've seen him do it from time to time, and I suspect I have also had my own bottom kicked!'

Responding, Sir George, before he became 'engulfed in the inevitable waves of my own verbosity', said that nothing like this had ever happened to him before. He told of the days when he had just started at Vickers at 5 guineas a week, and of the years in between, which had 'not really been a bed of roses'. He spoke of past trials and tribulations and battles they had won, and of some they had lost. 'I always reckoned that, after one of my battles, when I got off the ground covered in blood, I should be sure it wasn't all mine and hopefully somebody else's.'

On a more serious note, speaking of the tensions, anxieties and worries of his responsibilities, he said: 'The worst was knowing that you are doing something that is really being done for the first time, and you are taking on Isaac Newton on his grounds. If you make a mess of it, chaps are going to be killed.'

Would he do it all over again? 'Yes, but I need one or two conditions: The first is I would need Dinah there, I wouldn't want to do it without her. The second was I would need the help and support and encouragement of all of you here tonight.'

Although Sir George relinquished all his executive responsibilities at the end of 1975, there were some residual duties to perform. The first, and most enjoyable, was to fly as a guest on the inaugural BA Concorde flight from London to Bahrain, on 21 January 1976. Among the guests on the flight were the Duke of Kent, Lord Boyd Carpenter, Eric Varley and Peter Shore, Secretary of State for Trade. Tony Benn had not been invited, despite a suggestion by Sir George that he should, because 'he saved Concorde'. While BA headed east, Air France also inaugurated its first Concorde services, by flying west to Rio de Janeiro. By agreement, the two aircraft made well-rehearsed simultaneous take-offs from Charles de Gaulle Airport in Paris and London Heathrow.

The second and equally pleasing duty for Sir George was to oversee BAC's final financial accounts for the year 1975, to be published in March 1976. These showed excellent results, with sales up to £307 million, the bulk being for military aircraft and guided weapons products. Trading profit had risen to £25.4 million and, most reassuringly, a growing order book was now estimated to be in the region of £1,300 million.

As the year progressed Sir George followed closely the progress, or lack of it, of the Nationalisation Bill, particularly concerning compensation to the parent companies. In this connection he became involved in an exchange of letters with GEC, when asked to comment on a draft document prepared by the merchant bank commissioned to give an opinion on the value of BAC. In typically robust fashion, he was not over-impressed by their first efforts, and wrote: 'It is so verbose that I could not read enough at one time to leave any clear impression in my mind what the case really was.'

Sir George also took action over his concern that there was a lack of government support for overseas defence sales. He wrote to the Prime Minister 'to make a special plea', for their 'continued and increased support for their activities in the military export field, especially in the Middle East'. Referring to his visit to Saudi Arabia in early 1975 and his meeting with King Faisal, he said: 'I was left in no doubt from what he and members of his government said that Britain is held in high regard in that country. . . . I believe there are still greater prizes to be won in the Middle East, but it will need the strongest possible support from all departments of the British government to bring it about.'

On a personal note, he thanked Harold Wilson 'for the numerous kindnesses you have shown me'. He added: 'My time in the aircraft industry has not been easy, but I would cheerfully go through it all again.'

Sir George now settled into a life of retirement, which, although severely hampered by ill health, was to be in many ways as rich and rewarding as his career. Was he ever tempted to return in some way? 'No, not really,' he says, 'I can't recall getting into it at all. One reason was, apart from my having the guts-ache, and Dinah not being very well either, was that I had no great enthusiasm for taking in somebody else's washing.'

CHAPTER THIRTY-TWO

Pastimes, Painting and 'Cricket, Lovely Cricket'

It was only through sheer willpower that George Edwards was able to pursue his many and varied interests in his retirement. He did so with the same passion and zeal that he had brought to designing aeroplanes and running the company. Unhappily, for the rest of his life he was to suffer the consequences of his many operations, which restricted his activities. He was even forced to abandon a much-anticipated 'farewell' world tour to say goodbye to his many friends and colleagues, which he and Dinah were to have made in the spring of 1976.

His daughter Angela Jeffreys, or 'Dingle', as she is known, explains that the series of operations through 1975 were necessitated by recurring growths in his stomach, the effect of which was so serious that they very nearly lost him. 'It was so sad really, for if ever a man deserved a happy and relaxed retirement, he did. And of course he wasn't able to do a lot of the things he wanted to do because of the uncertainty of his innards.'

Nevertheless, undaunted and true to his belief 'never give up', he learned to live with his problem and was able to respond to the many demands placed upon him, dividing his time between the academic world, particularly the University of Surrey, and his artistic and sporting aspirations. The most enduring of these was an obsession with cricket. 'Sheer love of the game is one of the greatest things in my life,' he once wrote. 'I was immersed in cricket, its beauty and subtleness, from an early age.'

Edwards had been brought up to love the game. His uncle played for the police and his cousin, Bob Gregory, was a well-known professional cricketer for Surrey who had received international honours. 'So there was a collection of bits of reflected glory around the place,' he says, remembering his childhood. Bob Gregory was a frequent visitor to his home at Highams Park. 'He regarded it as part of his duties to the young to keep them out of the gutter as best he could. He used to come down at weekends, and we would creep out the back where we had about 25 yards of ash and mud to play on. The thing about Bob was he was always encouraging, whatever you were doing.'

The young Edwards began playing organised cricket while he was at technical college. He joined the local Hale End Cricket Club, where he became captain and later turned out for Highams Park. 'I played serious cricket then, and we had some county players among us. I used to bat and bowl a bit,' he says. When he moved to Vickers in 1935 almost the first thing he did was to find a new club to join. 'I was quite determined to go on playing cricket, and I poked about a bit to get sight of the clubs I might join. It ended up with me playing for Woking. I was given a sort of trial and put on to bowl. There were two hulking great brutes fielding in the slips with hands like sacks and hearts of gold; they were Alec and Eric Bedser.'

Sir George's friendship with the famous Bedser twins was to last all his life. In their young days he remembers how their mum used to make the teas ('she was a good 'un') and how later they all played at the prestigious Guildford Cricket Club, which was, and still is, a nursery for Surrey county players. The bowling attack of Alec Bedser's 'seamers' and George Edwards with his leg breaks became a potent force, and they took a lot of wickets together until the twins went on to play for Surrey, and Alec (later Sir Alec) for England. Alec remembers Edwards the bowler was 'a pretty good club cricketer, but he didn't play enough'.

At Guildford George Edwards achieved what he described as 'one of the greatest moments in my life', when he bowled out brilliant West Indies test cricketer Learie (later Sir Learie) Constantine. This was in a match against a Commonwealth XI in which Constantine was the star. Sir George can remember every moment of his triumph, which followed being hit for successive straight fours. 'As I ran up again, my mind thought of reverse thrust, and as I delivered the ball I ran my finger back down the seam, but disguised my action so that Learie thought I was delivering exactly the same as the previous balls. His eyes lit up, and I watched him shape to hit this one out of the ground; obviously I was a young pup who needed teaching a lesson. I held my breath as I waited anxiously to see what would happen. The ball pitched and held up, and he was through the shot fractionally too soon. The ball took out his middle stump and I had bowled him. The ball behaved exactly as I had hoped, and I was ecstatic,' he says. As delighted as he was, it did not go down too well with the large crowd who had come to see Constantine bat, and not Edwards bowl. 'It made me mildly unpopular for a bit,' he remembers.

If cricket was a rewarding pastime, it had also served as an effective means of fostering better business relationships during his working life. Sir George loved the challenge of explaining the intricacies of the game to unsuspecting customers, particularly those from North America. His good friend Gordon McGregor, president of TCA, recalled such an occurrence in detail in his book, and how cricket smoothed the path to a better understanding between them after they had spent the day arguing over specifications for the first TCA Viscounts. Both negotiating teams adjourned for dinner at the Mayflower Hotel.

McGregor wrote:

George Edwards and I were sitting beside each other at one end of the table. Here a heated argument developed, with a solid bank of Canadian opinion in almost violent disagreement with an equally firm phalanx of British opinion across the table. The subject of debate this time was not technical aircraft design, but whether or not a thrown ball could be made to curve in flight. At about this time *Life* magazine had come up with a series of photographs of the apparent path traced by a baseball ejected from a pitching machine; these purported to prove that the curve of a pitched baseball was an optical illusion.

To this the cricketers along one side of the table, and including George Edwards, who was himself a cricketer of repute, took violent objection. This was the type of fruitless argument that could only be settled in one way, and George volunteered to prove his point with a tennis ball. The management, with more regard for its fixtures than for the scientific point at issue, reported that it was unable to produce a tennis ball and, due to the fact that technical agreement had been reached during the day, greatly assisted by the excellence of the dinner in both the solid and liquid departments, the gathering broke up in a spirit of camaraderie that I would have not believed possible earlier in the day.

But this was not the end of the story. The following day at the hotel, TCA's Dave Tennant produced a brand-new cricket ball, which he gave to Sir George with apologies for its 'frivolous' ox-blood-red colour, which 'greatly amused' the British contingent. McGregor continued:

George proceeded out into the long but not too wide hotel corridor and, standing Dave at the far end, bowled in classic form down the length of it. Nobody was able to see whether the ball curved in flight, but on touching the carpet about six feet in front of Dave it broke sharply and he only saved his life by stepping nimbly aside and allowed the ball to crash into the door of a guest's bedroom. Since we did not want to get ejected before our lunch, it was hastily agreed to call the argument a draw, but the red cricket ball was autographed by the Canadian team and for years thereafter had a place of honour in George Edwards's office.

As well as playing a part in the TCA negotiations, cricket also became an instrument of diplomacy and customer relations with the RAF. As a sporting gesture, Sir George had for many years challenged the Air Staff to a game at Byfleet. This became an annual fixture that endured for 30 years, but one in which the BAC team were always mindful of the damage they could cause by beating their most important customer. Several talented BAC players, such as test pilots Jeffrey Quill and Brian Trubshaw, were briefed by Sir George to 'go easy' on the air marshals.

So it was both memorable and embarrassing when Sir George, on his very last appearance, achieved a lifelong ambition by taking a hat trick with his leg breaks. He later described it as 'his most damaging performance'. He added: 'The umbrage that was felt by the team I was shortly to leave, at such lunatic treatment of their chief customer, was considerable. But as far as I know no Jaguars were cancelled as a result.' To show there were no real hard feelings, Frank Denning, a regular BAC team member who was then running the Weybridge factory, had the hat-trick ball preserved and mounted, and presented it to Sir George on his retirement. It became a treasured possession at his home.

During the early 1970s George Edwards also became officially involved with cricket administration with the Surrey County Cricket Club. This association, which was to sustain him throughout his retirement, came about when he was asked to provide the BAC ground in Byfleet for Surrey to play a Sunday league match. The club secretary rang Sir George's office to make the request, and left a message to that effect. He was more than surprised to receive a personal return call from Sir George, agreeing to the proposition. Bernie Coleman, a long-serving committee member, says that at the time they had wanted to take the game out into the county. 'But every time we moved away [from the Oval] it cost us money. But Sir George arranged for us to use the BAC ground, and the company paid all the costs.'

Later, Sir George was invited to serve on the committee, and following a year as vice-president he became president in 1979, an honour and commitment he took very seriously. Bernie Coleman remembers early meetings with him. 'He would refer to himself as an extinct volcano. But he would sum up a situation so clearly and so effectively that you realised you were with somebody who had a great genius, which one didn't meet very often; they were wonderful times.'

He adds: 'He often used to go and talk with the players. You would see him put his arm around their shoulder and walk them round the ground. He would do this because they might have had some sort of problem. But he was never pushy, and although the age gap was enormous they respected him. . . . That was his great ability, to make you feel important.'

The great English test batsman and Surrey player, Raman Subba Row, who was the chairman of the cricket committee, also recalls those meetings. 'Without being nasty or spiteful he would talk about people and their level of competence, which was lovely to listen to.' Derek Newton, also to become president of the club, has memories of the practical help Sir George gave at difficult times, and how he had visited his own City company. 'One of his best sayings was "Never make a decision until you have to",' he says. 'The other saying he was always using was Drake's verse, which read: "There must be a beginning of any great matter, but the continuing unto the end until it be thoroughly finished yields the true glory."' It was a quotation used regularly by Sir George, particularly when addressing students and younger people.

On the lighter side, Derek also remembers how Sir George would ring up from the Oval committee room Sir John Mason, head of the Meteorological Office, to get an accurate weather forecast for the day's play. Sir John was a good friend and a fellow member of the Council of the University of Surrey.

Sir George cherished his days at the Oval, and at Guildford, where Surrey always played an annual festival match. As a past president he remained a regular visitor at both, making his last appearance at Guildford in 2002 during their festival week. He enjoyed mixing and meeting cricketers and cricket lovers such as Mickey Stewart, the England batsman and coach, who became a family friend, and John Major, the former prime minister. It was Mr (later Sir John) Major, also a president of the club and a passionate Surrey supporter, who recalled on television Sir George's contribution to Surrey cricket. He also remembered him for introducing back-spin to make the 'dambuster' bombs bounce, something he had learned from playing cricket.

As an aircraft designer, fully versed in the laws of aerodynamics, it is hardly surprising that Sir George became embroiled in the age-old mystery of why a cricket ball swings in flight, as Gordon McGregor had found out. He even wrote a thesis on the subject for Sir Alec Bedser's biography, and would bend the ear of any colleague who asked him for an explanation. During a discussion on the topic with the Bedser twins at his home in 2001, Sir George quoted an aerodynamic coefficient known as the Reynolds Number, which would give the optimum speed and range band for maximum effect. This was much to the amusement of Alec, probably this country's greatest exponent of the art, who still has no idea as to why a cricket ball swings. Remembering his previous role as chairman of the test selectors, he added: 'I would like to get hold of this Reynolds!'

The last word on cricket, which sums up his true feeling for the game and his own 'Englishness' comes from Sir George himself, who wrote: 'As a fervent believer that the British are a decent, fair-minded and compassionate race, I cling on to the grace, dignity and above all the discipline of cricket, as the remaining and non-besmirched outward and visible sign of this.'

Whereas cricket had been a preoccupation since his childhood, George Edwards came to painting comparatively late in life. In 1963 he became ill with glandular fever, and was advised by his doctors to rest for several months. 'I really had a fit at that,' he says. 'Dinah said I had always wanted to try my hand at painting, and now was my chance. So I sent a message to the works: send for Moon!'

Bryan Moon, to whom the call came, worked in the Vickers publicity department and was known to be a talented artist. Undaunted by the challenge of teaching the boss how to paint, he readily agreed to do it, especially as he knew Sir George, with his background in design engineering, was a good draughtsman. But he might have guessed that his mission would have a twist in the tail.

'I am going to Torquay at the end of the week, and you have a week to turn me into a painter,' Sir George told Moon, adding, 'I will do my best, but the important thing is I don't want you wasting your time if you can see that I am no bloody good at it and never will be.' At the end of an intensive week, the crucial question was asked, and reassurance was given. 'I was told I would be all right if I spent time at it. So I sloped off to Torquay, and some of my earliest efforts are of the Torquay scene and the villages around there,' says Sir George.

Bryan Moon continued as tutor for a time, before he left the company to join an American airline. He was replaced by Roger Steel, a personnel manager at Weybridge and friend of Moon since they began working together at Supermarine. Roger was also an acclaimed artist, and a founder member of the

Guild of Aviation Artists, of which he was the first chairman. 'Roger stepped into the breach. He was pretty special and really turned me into a painter,' Sir George says.

Steel remembers his first meeting with the great man in his office at Weybridge. 'I was a bit overawed, but Bryan told me not to worry, and Sir George told me he was just an ordinary chap with dirt under his fingernails.' Steel added: 'He would give me a shout now and then, and I would go up and see him. He had a little changing room at the back of his office where he had set up his easel. Later I would go up to his house, where his studio was upstairs.'

At first Edwards was heavily influenced by the work of the Dutch artist van Ruisdael and the English painter Sisley, both of whom painted landscapes and skies, but in very different styles. 'He was struggling to know which of the two artists to follow, and I realised this was a problem he had mentally,' Roger says. 'I told him he had got to stop painting like either, and start painting like Edwards. And that is what he did.'

Sir George applied himself as usual. He painted mainly in oils, and his subjects ranged from landscapes, seascapes and Scottish lochs to cricket scenes and views of his beloved Surrey countryside. In later life he turned his attention to horses and dogs. He explained: 'These days I do dogs, this place is infested with them. I can make them laugh, I get on with them, I know I'm potty.' Steel recalls the house being filled with dogs, which belonged to his helpers, or to Dingle or his grandchildren. 'He started to paint them, and similarly horses, because of his granddaughter's interest.' He adds: 'Nothing was too difficult or too daunting. He once painted New York at night from his hotel bedroom – extraordinary. He painted mountains, the Lake District, cattle of all sorts, but he didn't like close-ups of people.'

Nor, in his formative years, did he like painting aeroplanes. Roger Steel says he didn't begin until 1980, after he had accepted his invitation to become patron of the Guild of Aviation Artists. Steel remembers receiving a note from Sir George, who was on holiday in Keswick, to the effect that he was considering submitting a patron's picture to the Guild, and reckoned it should be of an appropriate subject. It read: 'It occurred to me that, with the credentials of the Kennington Oval established [he had already completed a painting of the famous ground], suppose I paint in a small Concorde to give it an aviation flavour – you may think I'm daft.' Roger didn't think he was daft, and the resulting large oil painting of a packed Oval with a Concorde passing serenely over on its way to Heathrow is one of his best works. It was exhibited at one of the Guild's annual summer exhibitions, and now hangs in Derek

Newton's home in Surrey. It was the first of several aircraft paintings, which included a Viscount, which he gave to Sir Peter Masefield, Valiant, VC10, Tornado and Harrier, the last being given to his neighbour and friend, the distinguished Hawker test pilot Duncan Simpson.

Painting was also to be a means of personal exchanges with members of the Royal family. Prince Philip, whose friendship Sir George had greatly valued through the years, presented him with his picture of St Kitts, painted from the deck of the royal yacht *Britannia*. In doing so he suggested they swap paintings. In response, Sir George presented the Duke with a painting of a tin mine in Cornwall. He also produced an impression of the Prince driving his famous racing carriage, with four horses thrashing through the waves across a beach. The picture had special meaning for Sir George, who, years before, had engaged Weybridge expertise in designing and building special light-alloy wheels for the carriage, the full story of which will be told later.

A further 'painting experience' was with the Queen, but in reverse circumstances. It is the custom for every person awarded the OM to have their portraits commissioned by Her Majesty and hung in a dedicated gallery at Windsor Castle. Sir George's portrait, however, was not to the liking of the Queen, who discussed it with him. 'She didn't like it, nor did I, and a second one was done,' he says.

The Duke of Kent, too, became an admirer of his work and personal friend, through their mutual association with the University of Surrey. The Duke accepted an invitation to open Sir George's first one-man show, to commemorate the opening of the university's new art gallery, which was to be named after him. Before agreeing to exhibit his paintings, which he considered a 'signal honour', Sir George had doubts about his work being up to standard. He wrote to the chairman of the university arts committee, who had invited him, and stated: 'I am not sure (a) if my work is good enough (b) if there is enough of it and (c) if there is enough time to fit into your programme.' It was only after lengthy discussion and encouragement from Roger Steel that he went ahead.

Twenty years later, on his nintieth birthday, Sir George was persuaded, for only the second time, to mount another exhibition of his paintings at the university, at which the Duke of Kent was again the guest of honour. At a celebration lunch afterwards for more than 100 friends, the Duke paid glowing tribute to Sir George's life, career and paintings. He had been particularly impressed with their variety and quality, and he especially admired his horses and dogs. In response, Sir George greatly amused his guests with a description of how to paint them: 'You start with a blob, which is the nose, and when you have got that right you fill in the other bits,' he said.

In these later years George Edwards found great solace in his painting, which absorbed more and more of his time. Although he was now much troubled by cataracts, which on bad days prevented him from working at all, he was still able to maintain an astonishing output. It kept his mind active and his ambitions alive, the most compelling of which was to have a painting accepted for the Royal Academy summer exhibition. For 30 years he had striven to get a picture accepted. He took immense trouble to select his best paintings, a process taking many months. 'This became an annual ritual,' says Roger Steel. A private selection panel was set up, which included the portrait painter Jane Allison, who was now helping him with his work, friend and art lover Charles Bone, and Steel himself. 'But most of all it was up to me and him and, mostly, in the end, up to him,' Roger adds.

It was not until the year 2000, at the age of 92, that he finally succeeded, with a small picture of a dog with a log in its mouth. He called the painting *Ben the Log Carrier*, and says: 'I think the selection committee might have said to one another: "That's a saucy sort of title."' That year he had submitted three paintings, and he remembers vividly receiving the formal reply cards. Two were rejects and the third had an 'e' for exhibition marked on it.

'It was a joyous day when he actually made it on the wall, and he threw a party for everyone who was involved,' says Roger. Later he visited the Royal Academy to see his work displayed, and was very pleased to be given special treatment by Roberta Stansfield and Tessa Abineri, staff members at the Academy. Afterwards he received a personal note of congratulation from the president.

Sir George, however, was always very modest and amusingly critical of his own work. Lord Robens, at the famous retirement banquet in 1976, recalled this in his speech, describing how he had once been taken to the studio at the top of the house to look at his paintings. 'George screwed up his face and said: "I can't do rivers, you know. Skies; I'm very good at skies because I've spent so much time there. Clouds, I can close my eyes and paint clouds anytime, but rivers; I can't get rivers because the damned light keeps changing!"'

While painting and cricket were passions, George Edwards enjoyed other interests, but viewed them more as hobbies. He collected antique maps, and played golf regularly until ill health forced him to retire. He took up yachting until he and

Dinah were nearly drowned in the Solent when their new boat developed a leak, though he retained a small boat on the Wey canal for the family. And from the age of 15 he was a 'hi-fi' addict. He built much of his own equipment, on which he played his favourite brass-band music and Gilbert and Sullivan operettas. 'I strung together a lot of bits and pieces that produced an amplifier that provided a bloody good sound, the like of which you never get in a shop,' he says. 'People used to come and listen because the quality was pretty outstanding.' He admits, however, that 'to get the quality you need a lot of volume', a fact that worried his family, who feared complaints from the neighbours.

But of all his hobbies, he loved fishing the most. As a youngster, he fished for roach in nearby rivers and ponds in Huntingdonshire during the school holidays with his uncle. When he moved to Surrey he explored the local water, and would go on fishing holidays to Ireland, Scotland and the West Country. 'There is a six-pound tench up at Busbridge [a lake near Guildford] that has my name and address on its back,' he says. 'I've pulled out a few fish in my time, but this one I really want.'

His six-pound tench, which as a bottom-feeder was difficult to catch, was one of two remaining ambitions. 'I've got my picture in the Royal Academy, and I've caught a five-and-half-pound tench, which now leaves the six-pounder,' he says. Unfortunately it was one ambition that was unfulfilled.

CHAPTER THIRTY-THREE

The University of Surrey and a Personal Crusade

From its foundation in 1966, George Edwards was devoted to the University of Surrey at Guildford. He was its first Pro-Chancellor, its first Pro-Chancellor Emeritus, and one of a small band of people who helped shape its history and character. Prof Patrick Dowling, until recently the Vice-Chancellor, says of him: 'He made a seminal contribution from the outset. He had a clear vision of what he wanted the University of Surrey to do. He wanted Surrey to be a place to train engineers and scientists who were very much in demand, and still are very much needed.'

Prof Dowling, who rates Sir George as 'one of the great heroes of engineering and science in this country', added: 'He wanted engineers and scientists to be trained in such a way that they were not narrow. He wanted depth, but he also wanted breadth, and that has shaped his whole life.' It was a theme Sir George was to repeat on every conceivable occasion, and one which the university still reflects with its maxim, 'Understanding the Real World'.

George Edwards's interest in the University of Surrey began with its predecessor, the Battersea College of Advanced Technology, in South London, in the late 1950s. As a product of a technical college himself, he took a keen interest in Battersea and was pleased to confer the diplomas one year. There he met Lord Robens, then chairman of the National Coal Board and an influential figure at the college. Robens shared a similar interest in promoting higher technical education, and they formed an association that was to lead to greater things, both in business and in the academic world.

At this time, in the early 1960s, the government was looking at ways to create more universities, especially by elevating technical colleges for the purpose. Battersea, with an excellent reputation, was an obvious candidate, but was a college in search of a campus. At the same time, Guildford was a county town looking for a university. In September 1966 the match was made, and a Royal Charter was granted to elevate Battersea to establish the University of Surrey at Guildford. It was to occupy a new site on Stag Hill, overlooked by Guildford Cathedral.

To preserve the scientific and technological reputation of Battersea, Surrey called upon many of its tutorial staff, officers and patrons. They included both Lord Robens and Sir George, who were invited to take high office in the new university: Robens as Chancellor and Edwards as Pro-Chancellor. They also appointed the former principal at Battersea, Dr Peter Leggett, Vice-Chancellor. Sir George remembers Dr Leggett visiting him in his office at Weybridge to ask him to take the job. 'I was asked to accept, which I did. I had seen quite a lot of Battersea, and it had the right base to form a technical university,' he says.

Sir George recalled those early days and their collective ambition to create a great technical university. Writing in an official history of the University of Surrey, published to commemorate its thirty-fifth anniversary, he stated: 'He [Dr Leggett], Alf Robens and I, had several discussions about the University, and Peter Leggett persuaded me that I could play an important part. He was keen to ensure that the university produced the best engineers and technologists who could grasp the detail essential to successful design and innovation. I thought the way the university planned to tackle this, especially with a year's practical experience in industry, was the right one.'

Prof Dowling says Sir George believed firmly in work experience, which originated at Battersea. 'He was sure that after students had served a year in industry they would be much more suited for the real world.' He added: 'This was one of the most valuable traditions which has continued to this day and, in turn, was accountable for the very high employment rate the University always had. We are invariably in the top three.'

Lord Robens shared Edwards's view, but there were differences between the two. 'While Lord Robens always argued that universities should produce rounded individuals, Sir George would stress the importance of producing the best engineers in the country,' Dr Leggett noted in the official history. To which Sir George added: 'I did tend to emphasise the importance of knowing your trade, but it is important to remember that the detail is the heart and soul of what you are doing as an engineer. This was partly to counter Alf Robens's slightly less practical emphasis, but also to encourage Peter Leggett to take on the best staff and encourage them in turn to pursue their own research.'

Not everybody in Guildford was at first enamoured with the prospect of having a university in the town, particularly those at the cathedral. The official history reveals that Sir George, who knew the Bishop and the Dean well, was asked to help. 'At first the Cathedral authorities were understandably a little concerned about the plans for a new university to be built right on their doorstep on Stag Hill. I was able to reassure people about the character of the university, although again it was Peter Leggett who really built the strong relationship between the University and the Cathedral,' Sir George wrote.

One month after receiving the Royal Charter in October 1966, the university really came into being with the installation of the Chancellor at a ceremony at the Civic Hall, attended by representatives from forty-one universities and colleges. It was a celebrated day for the town, which began with a special service in the cathedral and ended with a luncheon at the Royal Grammar School, at which Sir George was a speaker.

In his address, Sir George reverted to his favourite theme: 'The university was not to be simply a factory for turning out technologists, but citizens capable of making a contribution to the nation's welfare.' In an interview with the local *Surrey Advertiser*, which had campaigned hard for the university, he stated: 'There is a lack of awareness in the circles in this country that take important decisions, that Britain's future depends on high-powered technologists. This is at the root of the whole situation in this country. Surrey University will change this if I have anything to do with it.'

To this end, George Edwards did have something to do with it. He embarked on a vigorous educational campaign, which he pursued for the rest of his life. But first, together with those most closely associated with Surrey, the most pressing problem was raising a substantial sum to secure the site and construct the buildings. The government had provided half of the total expenditure, and despite a £1 million contribution from the Surrey County Council there was a shortfall of nearly £4 million.

A major appeal was launched in 1968, involving Sir George; Sir William Mullins, the first treasurer; Lord Nugent, MP for Guildford; and Col Wells, chairman of the County Council. In just three years some £3.75 million was raised, and the early commitments were sufficient to secure the university's future. In the words of Peter Leggett, this was an 'outstanding' effort, and in October 1968 the first students were progressively transferred from Battersea to Guildford. By the early 1990s numbers had risen to over 4,000, and today, with the development of many new facilities, there are over 11,000 students on campus.

With the foundations now firmly established, Sir George responded to the longer-term objectives of bringing university and industry closer together by establishing the Managing Directors Club. As the chairman, he invited his counterparts from local companies to join and to meet monthly in a forum to discuss the best way to do this. Before he retired, the club had more than 100 members, who contributed not only by supporting the 'year in industry' scheme, but by providing a basis for continuing fund-raising activities.

From the beginning it was apparent to Sir George and others that the university could not survive on government funding alone. 'He correctly envisaged that the money would not just come from the government or the taxpayer to do the sort of things he had in mind. We had to earn our own money, to earn our own bread,' says Prof Dowling. The opening of the Surrey Research Park, which 'transformed' both the finances and academic standing of the university from the mid-1980s, has been a major contributor. 'We are one of the universities – probably in the top six – that is least dependent on government money,' says Dowling.

Today the university enjoys a reputation for scientific discovery and endeavour. It is noted for its world-class research work, particularly in the field of satellite development, led by Dr Martin Sweeting, a former student at Surrey. Prof Dowling recalls how Sir George reacted to the announcement that Dr Sweeting had received a knighthood in the Queen's Birthday Honours in 2001. Edwards sent a congratulatory message, reading: 'From the oldest of our knights to the youngest'. Dowling adds: 'Even Martin, who is normally a very controlled person emotionally, was moved when I read those words out to him.'

Throughout his long association with Surrey, George Edwards made a point of engaging in the life of the university and keeping in close touch with its staff and pupils. He was a popular figure on the campus, and his understanding of what was going on was much appreciated by the staff. Patrick Dowling says: 'It was an easy way in for our management of the university because he listened to people.' Much of his social contact with the students and staff came from sport, and particularly cricket. He started an annual cricket match between his team, which he usually captained, and one selected by the Vice-Chancellor. In the process he became president of the staff cricket club. As an encouragement to the furtherance of the game, he presented two trophies, one for the Southern Universities tournament and the other for the winner of his annual fixture.

It was, in fact, in such a game that Sir George made his last appearance on a cricket field, when he was already in his seventies. He had gone to Guildford as a spectator, but when he found his team to be one man short he volunteered to play. This was strictly against the promises he had made to Dinah. Almost inevitably, he tripped over and severely damaged his Achilles tendon, which ended his playing career. 'Mum was absolutely furious,' says daughter Dingle.

In 1977 Lord Robens, having completed ten years as Chancellor, stepped down and was succeeded by the Duke of Kent. His appointment was greatly influenced by George Edwards, who knew and had great respect for the Duke. Sir George recalls how it came about, following several conversations he had had with the Duchess. 'She pulled me to one side more than once and said: "You are involved in all sorts of things, and I don't think the Duke is being used properly. I would like to see him given the opportunity of doing something more worthwhile."'

With the appointment of a new Chancellor at Surrey in the offing, Edwards 'sounded out' one or two people at the university and then went to see the Duke. 'I said there was a vacancy at Surrey for the Chancellor in which I am involved, and I think it is the sort of job you would enjoy doing. I then had to work on his wife, who was slightly suspicious of universities in general. But I finally got away with it, and I got him in. I think he has been pretty good ever since,' he says.

Prof Dowling is in no doubt about the royal appointment. 'It was through George's influence that we attracted His Royal Highness to be Chancellor. If you want to mark down one outstanding contribution he has made, that is the one. The Duke of Kent has been remarkably good, and has put his whole weight behind the university. We have benefited from this involvement, and that is to the credit of George.'

Sir George was also due to retire along with Lord Robens, after ten years in office, but with the arrival of the Duke of Kent he was 'easily persuaded' to continue for another three years to support the new Chancellor. When he finally retired, in 1979, the university honoured him by conferring the title of Pro-Chancellor Emeritus on him and awarding him the honorary degree of Doctor of the University. For this he was formally presented by his successor, the industrialist Sir Monty Finniston, at a ceremony at Guildford Cathedral. Sir Monty said: 'Sir George is in the line of the great engineers in this country. Their minds are in the clouds while their feet are on the ground.'

In 1981 the university bestowed a further honour by naming the library after him, for which Sir George unveiled a plaque recording his achievements both as an aeronautical engineer and at the university. In 1985 a portrait sculpture, donated by British Aerospace, was placed in the library and unveiled by the Duke of Kent. And in 2004, as a posthumous recognition of his contribution to the aircraft industry, the university created a Sir George Edwards Chair in aerospace engineering, the first recipient being Dr Martin Gillan, who was principal operational aerodynamicist for the Jaguar Formula One racing team.

Although poor health curtailed his visits in later years, Sir George continued to monitor academic progress of the university. 'The bit I always look at is Surrey's record in getting jobs for its graduates. You don't need to be any more fancy than that. If you are producing chaps who the engineering industry are prepared to take, and pay, then you are not doing badly.'

Sir George was succeeded as Pro-Chancellor by Sir Austin Pearce, who was an original Board member of British Aerospace and became chairman when Lord Beswick retired.

George Edwards's contribution to higher education was not confined to the University of Surrey. From the early 1960s through to the 1980s he pursued his personal crusade to attract more students into science and engineering and excite them in the new technologies that were now available. He did so by taking every opportunity his health would allow of accepting many of the numerous invitations to speak as guest of honour, or to confer degrees or give out the prizes at schools, technical colleges, universities and training establishments. He particularly enjoyed talking to young people, and once told the students of an Essex technical college: 'The ravages of time have never quite extinguished the spark of adventure and wide-eyed innocence in me, so happily I may still claim some identity with youth.'

Sir George was an experienced and natural speaker, with the gift of self-expression in his own colloquial but laconic style. He possessed an acute sense of timing and mood, while his humorous asides and use of quotation and parody endeared him to his audiences. Over his career he delivered more than 100 formal lectures and speeches, and once said: 'When I have something to say I have a knack of saying it,' adding, 'I am also absolutely confident that nobody will take the slightest bit of notice.' Of course people did take notice, especially in his offerings to youngsters.

In 1970 Sir George was presented with an ideal platform to convey his message when he accepted the appointment of President of the Association of Colleges of Higher and Further Education. In his presidential address he spelled out his enduring theme, one which is as relevant today as it was then. 'In the public eye industry carries the wrong image,' he stated. 'Engineering is still regarded as a dirty word, and because of this too many good-quality boys are creamed off into the arts stream. We cannot afford to let this state of affairs continue. Our national prosperity depends to a large extent on our ability to turn raw material into exportable goods. The engineer is a man who can convert an idea into something useful.'

Sir George coupled these concerns with his long-held worry about the lack of technically qualified civil servants in the highest echelons of Whitehall. 'I think a number of our problems, notably those involving technical matters, would be better resolved if the decision-making set-up was changed. The Fulton Report [which had been undertaken for this very purpose] had unlocked the door for getting young men from the technical universities into the top layer of the civil service. I'm not suggesting for one minute that there is a takeover by engineers and scientists, but I certainly am suggesting that there is a strong case to be made for a leavening of high-powered technologists to be put into the ranks of permanent secretaries,' he said.

At the University of Oxford that same year he delivered the first Maurice Lubbock Memorial Lecture to the School of Engineering Science. Although his subject was the advantages of partnerships in major technological projects, he could not resist diverting from his main theme to promote his education campaign. 'In this great seat of learning there is a need to have a realisation of the importance of high technology. I am an engineer, and I feel it right at the outset to tackle one of our great problems right here in the home of many causes. In a sense I am opening up the possibility of a new partnership between the great liberal universities and the people in them who shape the current attitudes to technology.' He added: 'The problem was the status and social prestige of the engineer in society, which was bottom of the preferred list of professions.'

Of all his speaking engagements, Sir George especially liked talking to the young men and women of the RAF. 'All my working life in the aviation business I have been mixed up with the RAF; I have got RAF roundels right through me like the lettering on Blackpool rock,' he once said. To the graduate engineering officers at RAF Henlow he stated: 'Aerospace is the spearhead technology which represents generations of man-skill investment, built up on a wealth of achievement of an earlier area of profitable technology. We are in a position to do things which many other countries require to be done, yet would find it difficult, expensive, and unprofitable to do themselves. Therefore we have access to a market where the customer is prepared to pay (often in oil) for the goods we produce. But if as a nation we downgrade our level of applied technology by choosing to do the easy things, the competition increases rapidly and the market recedes.'

From the beginning, and well into retirement, Sir George's addresses would always encourage youngsters to value quality, integrity and loyalty, and urge them 'never to give up', and not to be too narrow in their outlook. 'In your leisure, for goodness sake do something, and do it fit to bust,' he would say. To pupils at a well-known school in Surrey he said: 'To those of you who will become heads of great companies, or high officials in government, I give you one piece of advice – never forget that it is you who owe loyalty to those who work with and around you.'

And for students at his old technical college, now called Waltham Forest Technical College, he had some homespun advice: 'The principal threat as I see it which faces young people today is that of early disillusionment and cynicism – euphemisms for bitter and twisted. If you are already suffering from this malignant contagion, let me suggest to you some overkill therapy. If you try hard enough, and have an adequate imagination, you will soon have to admit, if you are honest, that no one and nothing in the real world is ever as bad as you imagine. Within a short while you will become cautiously optimistic, even graduating to being downright enthusiastic, and that is what is really needed in the world today.'

For Sir George, his speaking campaign over twenty-five years was nothing more than 'a duty'. He never forgot his own background, and how grateful he had been for a system that allowed him to receive some inspired teaching and to gain a university degree which set him on his way. Nor had he any doubt of the importance to Britain of maintaining its technological capability. It was, perhaps, a reflection of his efforts, not only as a speaker but as a contributor to the technological wealth of the country, that no fewer than nine British universities conferred honorary degrees on him. They were the universities of Bristol, Stirling, the City of London, Cranfield, Salford, Southampton; he received a fellowship from the Manchester Institute of Science and Technology (UMIST) and the University of Surrey and, to his great delight, a doctorate of science (engineering) from his old university, the University of London, which was presented by the Queen Mother in 1970.

CHAPTER THIRTY-FOUR

'A Man of Absolute Rectitude'

George Edwards was unassuming, hated personal flamboyance, and always conducted himself in a correct and controlled manner. His dealings, both in public and private, reflected the values he was brought up to cherish: respect, integrity and compassion for others. His friend Sir Peter Masefield described him as 'a man of absolute rectitude'. His daughter Dingle says she never saw him lose his temper, although he could convey his displeasure with scathing and sometimes silent rebuke. His secretary for over fifty years, Mrs Joyce Brixey, confirms that he was not a man who showed emotion or stress, although she once saw him kick the radiator in frustration. His grandchildren 'loved him to bits', but were also wary of him and sometimes fearful when they had misbehaved.

For those who met Sir George, their lasting impression was of his courtesy, humour and huge intellect. He was of medium height, slightly built, slightly stooping (in older age), and without any semblance of fleshy excess. He possessed a large head with a prominent domed forehead with little hair, on which was usually perched, at a jaunty angle, his familiar pork-pie hat. He dressed soberly, preferring to wear what he called his old tweed 'ratting suit' to traditional pinstripes in the office. His only visible show of any personal indulgence was a coloured handkerchief, usually red, displayed in his breast pocket. According to Dingle he was always conscious and careful as to how he looked and how he was regarded by others.

Perhaps the most lasting description of him in his prime came earlier, from Gordon McGregor of TCA, who talked of his 'aquiline features', and 'a pair of eyes which radiated intelligence'. Joyce Brixey says that, as a young man, he was 'good looking in an aesthetic way' and was attractive to women. 'He would respond to them in a gentle, even flirtatious manner, but Lady Edwards never had any cause for anxiety, and found it rather amusing.'

In the office, Mrs Brixey says he disliked routine paperwork, and left her largely to deal with it and select the important items he needed to see. To those he would respond with a crisp note of instruction or advice, written in pen at the top of the page, and signed 'GRE', by which he was known throughout the company and the industry at large. When working he would sit at his large mahogany conference table, where he could spread his papers and drawings. 'I never saw him work at his desk,' she says.

Mrs Brixey was also entrusted with his household bills, and even administered his personal finances. This included managing his portfolio of investments, mainly in gilts, for which she kept a ledger recording every transaction she had been instructed to make. 'He did make some money,' she says, adding: 'He has always been, not obsessed by money, but unnecessarily anxious about it. Of course, he never had much in his younger days and he had to fight for it. He never reckoned they paid him enough, especially at Vickers.'

For his business dealings, Sir George preferred personal contact so he could judge better the correctness of advice or the strength of an argument by the demeanour of the person presenting it. Charles Gardner recalls his technique in his BAC book, and how both he and Lord Portal would ask the same key question on receiving an opinion from a subordinate: 'Are you sure?' Gardner says it was Sir George's habit to keep this question until last, and often until the person concerned was actually at the door and would have to return to answer, thus meeting GRE's eye-to-eye gaze. 'If there was the slightest hesitancy in the reply, or any drop of the eyes, the day was lost. Edwards had one more hurdle to erect. "All right," he would say, "have it your way. But when it goes wrong, don't forget I warned you." A pause, and then the Edwards grin, robbing the words of malice.'

Mrs Brixey says her boss had no difficulty making himself clear to others. 'He could be sarcastic and he could give a tongue lashing, but I never saw him do it, never in front of me,' she says. 'But like everybody else,' she adds, 'he had his shortcomings and overlooked quite a few of them in others, but he never lost that touch with people. It brought out the best in them, making the most of what they had to offer, and using it because it reflected glory on to them. I think it was his interaction with people that made him special.'

Norman Barfield, who worked with Sir George for many years, remembers his human side in a story that has been repeated many times. He recalls how he was once called to his office but met a senior member of the service staff coming out, looking 'ashen-faced'. When Barfield arrived 'in the presence', Sir George enquired how the chap looked, and, when told of his anguished expression, asked Norman to bring him back at lunchtime for 'bread and cheese' in his office. 'I don't want him to go home and fret over the weekend and upset his wife and kids', he said.

In his private life George Edwards practised the same self-imposed standards of traditional Victorian values as he applied in business, sometimes too rigorously for the liking of the younger members of the family. This was conditioned by a progressive and deep inner religious belief. When he and Dinah moved to Guildford they joined the congregation of the picturesque thirteenth-century hilltop chapel of St Martha's, which they could see from their home in White Lane. Sir George remembers being visited by a neighbour, Col Wigan, a church warden, who invited them to join. 'He suggested it, and I decided I would help the Lord up the hill,' he says, adding: 'If you lived here your "In-and-Out" place was St Martha's really.'

For the rest of their lives the Edwards family were regular worshippers. Sir George frequently read the lesson, a tradition continued to this day by his daughter. He became a member of the Parochial Church Council and took the chair at the Standing Committee, at which he insisted on business-like practice. 'I was sort of chairman, but I don't believe I was ever formally appointed,' he says. He declined the offer to become a church warden, preferring to be 'the plumber's mate'. But he did act as a steward at the popular Christmas midnight mass, when more people arrived than could be accommodated. He would stand outside the side door where they congregated and led them inside, like a cinema usherette, when space became available. 'They were almost hanging from the rafters; they were eager to come in and I used to swap them over,' he says.

His special contribution at Christmas, however, was to produce a seasonal painting that was reproduced as a Christmas calendar and sold to raise money for parish funds. One of the most memorable was his depiction of the floodlit church, painted in the year 2000. It had special meaning for the congregation, for Sir George, 'with a little help from Weybridge', had been responsible for reinstalling the floodlights. In pre-war days the illuminated church had been a local landmark, standing out like a beacon and seen and admired for miles around.

By instinct and nature George Edwards was a patriot, proud of his heritage, his country and his cockney roots, and fiercely loyal to the Sovereign. Outside his front door he erected a flagpole from which he flew the Union Jack. 'He was a great royalist, and he would have done anything for the Queen,' says Dingle. His prominence in the aircraft industry and his fellowship of learned societies under royal patronage, together with his duties as an OM, brought him, to his delight, special and privileged contact with the Royal Family.

His first recorded meeting was during the war, with the then Queen Elizabeth, when she agreed to the chopping down of a line of oak trees in Windsor Great Park to make way for a dispersed landing strip for Wellingtons. 'If it helps beat that man Hitler, cut them down,' she had said. After the war, in the early days of the Viscount, Sir George had got to know Prince Philip, who flew the new aircraft. 'He was, of course, jolly interested in aviation and has become a fair decent pilot. He was not a playboy pilot, and as an operator he knew what he was up to. We had a bit of luck having him up where he is,' he says.

It was from Prince Philip, some years later, that Edwards received what he reckoned to be 'a Royal Command', when he was asked if he could build special wheels for his famous horse-drawn racing buggy. The circumstances are best described by Sir George in his own characteristic way:

I was at a cocktail party at the Palace, and during the course of the evening Prince Philip talked to me about this truck of his, and how he could save weight. I said: 'Do you want to save weight on your carriage, or do you want to keep the weight down to make it more stable?' Then I got a sharp lecture on wagon stability, and on unsprung and sprung weight. He thought I wasn't trying hard enough, and then the Queen came pounding along and asked Prince Philip how he was getting on. He said he wasn't getting on at all. I thought: 'Blimey, the Tower of London awaits you,' so I took steps to say that I didn't say we wouldn't try, but I said it was difficult.

Some time later I got curt instructions to present myself at the stables at Windsor for a trial run on the buggy. He drove me around Windsor Park like a bloody lunatic, at least I thought it was, but I didn't know anything about it. So we went round and about, and I said to him that there was one thing about it, if we make it lighter, it won't hurt so much if you insist on keep pulling it on top of yourself!

Prince Philip also recalled the help he received for his racing wagon in his book *Thirty Years on and off the Box Seat*. He wrote: 'I got to know Sir George Edwards quite well. Aircraft engineers know all about light metals, so I thought I would ask his advice about some lightweight carriage wheels with tapered roller bearings and, above all, without hubs that stuck out some 10cm. He told me that his experimental workshop could handle the problem quite easily, and a short time later a splendid set of new wheels appeared and made all the difference to the suspension of the carriage.'

But most precious to Sir George was his contact with Queen Elizabeth II, the 'Sovereign' or 'Monarch', as he always called her. Through the regular meetings of the Order of Merit he was able to talk to her both formally and informally. His regard and admiration for her never wavered, and that there was rapport between them was confirmed by Dingle, who in later years escorted her father to the OM meetings. She remembers the Queen visiting the University of Surrey in 2002, and talking to her. 'The Queen reminded me of a conversation at Windsor Castle she had with dad, who told her his target was to be alive for the centenary of the Order to take place later that year. Nobody could have prompted her for remembering that, and, of course, he did make it, which was wonderful.'

In keeping with George Edwards's whole outlook to life, he was, in the words of his daughter, 'a devoted family man who took his responsibilities terribly seriously'. He was, however, strict in attitude, and Dingle admits that in her younger days, although he was 'a lovely dad', there were times when she was afraid of him. 'He was quite determined he was not going to spoil me. If I wanted something I had to go and ask for it and justify it, rather than just being handed it on a plate.' Her most cherished childhood memories are of her days out alone with her father. Every school holiday he would take a day off from work and they would go to a museum, or a show, or to the ballet. 'It would be our day, and they were very special days,' she says.

These outings were all the more enjoyable for Dingle because she did not see much of her father, who was so busy at work he seldom got home until late evening. But in retirement he had more time for the family, especially his two grandchildren, who by then had become, to use his own word, 'interesting'. His granddaughter Clair says they saw him regularly during holidays, and at other times during the week at his home. 'It was a lovely place to look forward to; it was as good as going overseas,' she says. When staying there, both she and her brother, Richard, would be taken off fishing, or down to the cellar to play billiards, or out to fly kites on Newlands Corner or to play cricket on the tennis court. It was always her grandfather who led these trips, but Clair says, 'Granny was the one who would give us a packed lunch and see we were wearing our coats and wellies. And when we came home we would find a lovely cooked meal awaiting us. . . . But the best bit was being picked up by the chauffeur, Mr Shields!'

Like her mother, Clair at a young age was also fearful of him. 'I just knew he was a great man, and, although he was very loving and there was lots of laughter, we always knew not to push it too far; it was utter respect.' She adds: 'I don't remember him actually having a go at me, he would just look, and his eyebrows would come down and you would get that dirty look and silence. I would think: "Oh my God, what have I done?"' As she got older, she says: 'the fear went, but the respect was always there. You always tried so hard to please him, whether it was exam results or riding my horse.'

Richard, recalling his childhood memories of his grandfather, says: 'He was one of those people you had got to walk around carefully.' But in later years they spent many enjoyable days together fishing on Busbridge Lake. 'He was right up there with me, he was on my level, we could communicate easily and have some jokes, which I never had with him before.' He also recalls his grandfather's mischievous humour. On one occasion he introduced him to two girlfriends who had volunteered to help him paint his boat, which he stored at Albury Heights. Shortly after they arrived Sir George appeared, bearing a tray with a bottle of wine and just three glasses: one for him, the other two for each of the girls. 'And that was the last I saw of them, it was two hours later before they came back. . . . His eyes lit up when these girls came up,' Richard says.

There were other times, too, when the fearsome grandfather became 'a mad grandad', such as when Richard took his new motorbike to the house. Clair says that, although he was well into his eighties, he wanted to ride it. 'He insisted on taking his jacket off, and in braces and trousers he drove it round a field at such speed that granny was about to phone for an ambulance.' And at her wedding 'he really let his hair down' at the reception. 'He was nearly 90 when he got up on the dance floor with myself, my bridesmaid Louise, and Richard, and was doing his stuff for the benefit of the rest of the marquee. He stole the show; you wouldn't have known whose wedding it was!' Clair adds.

All his life Sir George had liked a bet, and the family have fond memories of how he approached the subject with mathematical precision. Clair says he would make complicated combination bets and forecasts, and talked about 'the rule of probability'. She remembers the horseracing was on all the time, and how he preferred certain jockeys and trainers, such as Gordon Richards, and later 'took a fancy' to Mary Revely's horses. His biggest win was when he had a treble on Hello Dandy in the Grand National, from which he received £1,000, enough to buy a sit-on motor mower, which he appears to have driven as recklessly as Richard's motorbike. Dingle says he only bet in small amounts, and in the end he came out about 'even-stevens'. Clair still reckons the best bit was trying to explain to granny that you couldn't bet on 'bar'.

If Sir George sometimes had misgivings about the youngsters in the family, his response to the older members was unequivocal. When his ageing uncle Bill and aunt Sally, who had brought him up in Highams Park, retired and were in ill health, he acquired a bungalow in nearby Fetcham where he and Dinah could keep an eye on them. Later, he did the same for Dinah's mother and father, and when her father died he moved mother-in-law into Albury Heights. For a time there were six of them in the house, for not only did he care for his elderly relatives, but he continued to look after the 'wonderful' Archie Shields, his driver for so many years, his wife and his mother, who lived in a ground-floor flat he had converted for the purpose.

Outside the family, George Edwards did not gather around him too many close personal friends. According to his daughter the closest was Ernie Bass, chief engineer and technical manager of the Shell Aviation Petroleum Company. Bass was well known in the business for his pioneering work on aviation fuels, and had worked closely with Rolls-Royce and Vickers when propeller turbines were introduced on the Viscount. He and Edwards had struck up immediate accord, and became golfing partners at the RAC Club at Woodcote, Epsom. The bond was such that the two families always spent Boxing Day in each other's company.

Other special friends included the Bedser twins, several former colleagues such as Allen Greenwood and Sir Geoffrey Tuttle, Gordon McGregor from Canada, his doctor, Dr John Morgan, and his surgeon, Sir Edward Tuckwell. It was with Tuckwell that he became involved in fund-raising for the Phyllis Tuckwell Memorial Hospice in Farnham, named after his wife, who died of cancer. In later years his near neighbour and fellow worshipper at St Martha's, Duncan Simpson, became a valued companion on many formal outings and joined what Sir George called 'my praetorian guard'.

Throughout his married life George Edwards was wonderfully supported by his wife Dinah. True to the old adage, she was the rock on which he built his success, and although his daughter and grandchildren rarely saw visible signs of affection, he was completely devoted to her, and acknowledged the fact publicly many times. In 1985 they celebrated their golden wedding anniversary, a happy occasion that was reported in the local newspaper.

Sadly, shortly afterwards, Dinah became ill with the progressive Alzheimer's disease. Dingle says that, as her condition worsened, he was urged to put her into a nursing home, especially as he was in a fragile state himself, but he refused to do so. 'He was absolutely determined to look after her himself, and rejected all appeals to move her into a home. He was amazing really, he wanted to look after her because he felt it was his responsibility as her husband.'

In 1996 Dinah suffered a stroke and died at home. They had known each other all their adult lives, from the days when they were at college. Dingle says that her mother had found it hard to cope with the high society in which they suddenly found themselves, particularly as both had come from lowly backgrounds. 'He found it difficult, she struggled, but she was so wonderful because she braved it on and on, but she was never really comfortable with it.' She adds: 'She was such a support to dad; she devoted her life to him and to me.'

Dinah was buried at St Martha's, and for the rest of his life Sir George struggled up the hill every week, refusing any transport, to lay flowers on her grave.

CHAPTER THIRTY-FIVE

Last Overs

In the latter years of his retirement George Edwards remained occupied by both duty and interest in the large number of organisations with which he was associated. Although quiet contemplation at home with his painting and fishing were therapeutic, especially after the loss of his wife, his mind remained fertile and required stimulation from the world outside. For this there was ample opportunity, provided by continuing requests to perform official duties or attend and speak at numerous functions.

It is worth noting just how many associations there were, and how many honours and distinctions he had received. The list is long and impressive: Order of Merit (1971); Fellowship of the Royal Society and recipient of its gold medal in 1974 (an honour rarely given to an engineer); Honorary Fellowship and President of the Royal Aeronautical Society (1960), and holder of its Gold Medal for aeronautics (1952); recipient of the Albert Medal of the Royal Society of Arts (which he received from Prince Philip at a ceremony at Buckingham Palace in 1972); member of the Royal Institution (1972); and Honorary Fellowships in 1976 of both the Institution of Structural Engineers (which gave him his first professional qualifications) and the Fellowship of Engineering. In later years he was awarded the Diploma of the Royal Aero Club (1994) and made a Companion of the Air League (2000), and in 2002 he received the special Award of Honour from the Guild of Air Pilots and Navigators, of which he was a liveryman.

Added to this were continuing obligations to the church and university, together with those of civic duty. In 1981 he was appointed Deputy Lieutenant for the County of Surrey, in which capacity he represented the Queen at official events on several occasions. Of a more social nature were commitments as past president of Surrey County Cricket Club and Guildford Cricket Club, patron of the Guild of Aviation Artists and of Brooklands Museum.

In response to all this, health permitting, he would place his royal and civic duties first. He never missed an OM meeting, and by 2000 had become the senior member, even though it was now a physical strain to attend. He continued his duties as a Deputy Lieutenant to the end, and in 2002 carried out his last public engagement when he helped escort the Queen on her visit to the University of Surrey.

He still enjoyed his visits to the Oval, although they became less frequent, but insisted on turning up to the annual past presidents' lunch at Guildford Cricket Club during its Festival week. As past president and patron of the Guild of Aviation Artists he continued to submit his paintings and attend their annual exhibition in London, a ritual he much enjoyed.

Locally, he seldom missed regular reunions with his old work colleagues from the design office and the experimental department at Foxwarren. Spud Boorer records that these were joyous occasions, and he would always give his old staff a 'pep talk', referring to them as 'the best design team he could ever wish to have'. Many of them were members of the local Weybridge branch of the RAeS, of which Sir George was a founder member and past president. One of his last appearances was in 1998 to hear John Weston, then the newly appointed chief executive of British Aerospace, deliver the branch's main Rex Pierson Memorial Lecture, something he himself had done in 1967. As a sign of the times, Sir George remarked afterwards: 'He [Weston] didn't mention engineering once from start to finish, but only talked about systems.'

These meetings were held at the Brooklands Museum, now the only visible remains of the great Vickers factory at Weybridge. As patron he took a keen interest in the museum's progress and remained a regular visitor. His portrait by Jane Allison, who in later years became his tutor, now hangs in the members' club room. Outside has been gathered a unique and comprehensive collection of his aircraft, from the Viking to Concorde, the latter being the last to be allocated by BA for public display. The only missing examples are his favourite Valiant, of which only one remains and is exhibited at RAF Cosford, and TSR.2, though nose sections of both aircraft are retained by the museum. Complete examples of the TSR.2 are displayed as part of the Imperial War Museum's collection at Duxford Airfield in Cambridgeshire and at the RAF Museum, Cosford.

One other local commitment he held dear was the Byfleet Parish Day. As a former resident of West Byfleet, and with the factory on its boundaries, Sir George for years had offered his patronage to the local church and 'encouraged' the company to participate. He would invite personalities to open the show, including Barnes Wallis, the broadcaster Cliff Michelmore and his friend Bishop Reindorp, 'to give it a bit of respectability'. On one occasion a member of his publicity staff was hauled over the coals for not providing an adequate model aircraft display at Byfleet. Sir George was not impressed by the excuse that he and the department had been 'flat-out' preparing for the forthcoming Farnborough Air Show. 'Byfleet is far more important,' he said.

Perhaps the most enduring legacy of George Edwards's achievements is the vast collection of lectures and speeches that have been preserved. In November 1982, at the age of 74, he delivered what was to be his valedictory address to the Fellowship of Engineering (now the Royal Academy of Engineering). With the 'magic of hindsight' he pronounced on the progress of the industry since his retirement, and looked back particularly at the effects of the recently concluded (June 1982) Falklands conflict. On British Aerospace he reiterated his opposition to nationalisation, but noted that since then it had 'some good leadership and had prospered'. This was mainly due, he said, 'to the same people who had worked in the industry for years, and went on working in it, nationalised or not'. He added: 'The public has since become involved by the share offer of around half the equity; they got them for 150p each and are now sitting on a handsome profit.'

On the Falklands conflict he spoke of the success of guided weapons, particularly the Rapier air-defence system and the naval systems, such as the Sea Skua and Sea Wolf, all of which were in 'promising' development in his day. He had a special word for the Sea Harrier, 'without which there would not have been a Task Force', and quoted the RAF's CAS, who had complimented the industry for completing necessary modifications to aircraft in weeks. Sir George stated that, through the normal procurement system, this would have taken months, 'and probably years', which illustrated what he described as 'an archaic system'.

It would not have been a George Edwards lecture had it not contained at least one wisecrack at politicians' expense. For this he used his favourite Gilbert and Sullivan verse: 'But the privilege and the pleasure, that we treasure beyond measure, is to run little errands for the Minister of State'. He noted that, since 1945, on average they had no fewer than one new minister every eighteen months, and that they 'were not always going in the same direction'.

His parting shot, however, was upbeat: 'We have a great asset in our aerospace industry, but it needs nourishing. I no longer have any direct connection with it, but I have a very lively interest in the wellbeing of this country, and I am convinced that a healthy aerospace industry is not only a national asset, it is a national necessity.' He concluded: 'I end on an optimistic note; I only hope I am proved right.'

Twelve years later, in 1994, at the age of 85.9 (as he now described his age), George Edwards made the first of two last formal appearances before the aircraft industry at large. In March of that year he was the guest at a dinner in London to celebrate the twenty-fifth anniversary of the first flight of Concorde. Surrounded by Concorde pilots and Concorde people, Sir George felt very much at ease, and despite his advancing years was still able to sparkle and recall a few tales 'out of school'. Those who knew him knew they were in for a treat when he got up and began fiddling with the microphone: 'I don't like the look of it – it has a very unhealthy look about it – probably made in France!' he said.

Having described his earlier encounters with the Tupolevs in Russia, and how he told the younger one that he had got the engines of the Tu-144 in the wrong place, he spoke of the early days, and how the Anglo-French set-up 'didn't stand a cat in hell's chance' of working. 'If you put your mind to it to invent an organisation that couldn't front up, you couldn't have done better than the one we started with,' he said. 'A number of blokes had to be put into jobs according to their nationality. It didn't matter whether they thought two and two was something between four and five. We also had a rotating chairman, while the rest of us went round in circles!' Apart from his personal friendship with General Puget, 'the only thing that kept it on the road was Bill Strang and his mate Lucien Servanty.'

Six months later, at the Farnborough Air Show 'Flying Display' banquet, he made his positively last appearance when he received the award of the John Curtis Sword. The sword is given once every two years to honour the person who has made a significant contribution to Anglo-American aerospace. It is sponsored by the influential American magazine *Aviation Week and Space Technology*, whose publisher, Ken Gazzola, and editor, Don Fink, were on hand to make the presentation. Don Fink gave a resume of Sir George's career and achievements, and spoke of his 'key role' in the design of numerous aircraft leading up to the Concorde.

To many in the room, including leaders of the present industry and overseas customers, Sir George, now retired for twenty years, was not a familiar face. Any doubts they may have had about the quality of his contribution were soon erased, for Sir George, although looking fragile, was on cracking form. He was full of reminiscences of his many meetings with many great US designers and airline bosses since his first visit forty-five years before. 'I got to know the chaps in the aviation game and got to know them as men, good men, apart from the fact that they knew their job,' he said.

But his meeting with the legendary Kelly Johnson, chief research engineer at Lockheed, was less rewarding. 'He was a fairly tough citizen and not too warmly addicted to the British,' he said. 'He showed me one day this new fighter of his, the F-104. We trotted round it and I made the usual polite gurgling noises and then said, all innocently: "When are you going to put the wings on?" That, I have to say, didn't go down with too much of a swing!' He added: 'It didn't alter the fact that they sold a hell of a lot of them, so maybe wingless fighters are a good idea after all.'

But, most memorably for those who were there, on receiving the sword he brandished it over his head 'like some ageing St George about to slay the dragon'. He declared: 'I couldn't half have done with this a few years ago, when I was working my way up and down the corridors of power, trying to cut my way through the network and tangle of changes of policy, or changes of minister, or both. This would have been very handy then, and I shudder to think where that point would have ended up on one or two occasions!'

Following the dinner, at the request of Sir George, the sword was put on display at the RAF Museum with the Valiant, and remained there for two years.

Although Sir George did not perform again on the public platform, he was frequently called upon to speak on special occasions or at services of thanksgiving and funerals of revered colleagues and friends. In 1989 he was accorded the special honour of being invited to give the address at the service of thanksgiving at the RAF Church, St Clement Dane's in London for Sir Tom Sopwith, one of the immortal pioneers of British aviation. Sir George knew the great man well. He recalled how, years before, Sir Tom had presented the prizes at the Weybridge Apprentice School. 'The kids were enthralled with the clarity with which he talked of the old days at Brooklands, and how he talked to them as equals. I doubt if they realised how much of the freedom they took for granted they owed to him.'

A year earlier Sir George had taken part in Sopwith's memorable 100th birthday celebrations with a luncheon at Brooklands, organised by Sir Peter Masefield. The event was televised, as was Sir George's speech. 'To speak about a chap who has not only seen it happen from the Wright brothers to Camm's Harrier and Concorde – in fact uniquely everything – I feel a mere boy compared to this tremendous centenary we are celebrating today,' he said.

There were numerous other occasions when Sir George was called upon to speak about the lives of his 'mates' and colleagues. He did so with eloquence and sensitivity that inspired family and friends alike. Of Charles Gardner, the former BBC air correspondent and company colleague for more than twenty years, he said: 'There grew up between us one of the close personal relationships which I believe only exists in the world of aviation.' After the death of Sir Geoffrey Tuttle, who joined BAC after a distinguished career in the RAF, he spoke of his 'uncanny ability to be offering help before one knew it was needed'. And in tribute to his surgeon and friend Sir Eddie Tuckwell, he referred to him as 'one of the great surgeons of our time; his appointment to the Royal Household as Sergeant Surgeon to the Queen is evidence of that'. 'Above all,' he added, 'as a committed Christian he was steady as a rock.'

By the turn of the century, when he was into his ninetieth year, Sir George increasingly became confined to his home. But he continued to entertain his friends to tea or to take a 'drop of the green stuff', as he called his select white wine. He would still make a few visits outside, often driven by Len Pledger, whose father had helped him tow the 'Metal Mossie' to Farnborough during the war. A familiar figure at Albury Heights, Len assisted him in anything mechanical, from his lawnmower to the electric generator he had installed in his garage at the time of the power cuts in the 1960s. He made forays into Farncombe, near Godalming, to his favourite picture framers, run by his friends the Woods family, or went on unescorted walks, much to the horror of his daughter, as his frailty caused him to lose his balance and fall. He did manage to make a last visit to Brooklands for a lunch to discuss the prospect of this book, and with the help of Peter Daws, who had become another regular driver and friend, travelled to London on a few chosen occasions, such as the day he went to see his painting in the Royal Academy.

In July 2001 he was able to celebrate his birthday at a lunch hosted by Sir Dick Evans, who shared the same birth date. The lunch had become an annual fixture, organised by Dingle and Barbara Ferguson, who had worked for the company for many years, and who had joined the 'praetorian guard' that had done so much to keep Sir George going in latter years. Many of his old friends and colleagues attended, including Spud Boorer, Norman Barfield, Joyce Brixey, Brian Cookson, for many years company secretary, and Syd Gillibrand, a former British Aerospace director and county-class cricketer, who years earlier had been summoned down from Warton to play in Sir George's select cricket team.

The following year, as a consequence of another fall, Sir George was admitted to hospital, but struggled out again in time to fulfil his last ambition, to attend the Order of Merit centenary celebrations and lunch with the Queen at Windsor Castle. Shortly afterwards he re-entered Mount Alvernia Hospital in Guildford, as his overall condition had worsened. His family did not think he would re-emerge, but he did, and in early 2003 he returned home to be cared for by his 'heroic' Dingle, who by now was spending most of her time looking after the old man with the same compassion as he had shown for Dinah.

On 2 March 2003, at the age of 94, Sir George died, surrounded by his family at home. His last conscious acts were to recognise the mounted cricket ball with which he had taken a hat-trick playing at Byfleet, and the commemorative photograph of the OM gathering that had arrived a few days before his death, and in which he pointed out the Queen.

Many generous tributes and letters of condolence arrived from all over the country and from abroad. Half-page obituaries appeared in all the major national newspapers, the personally written contribution by Sir Peter Masefield being much appreciated by the family.

The little chapel of St Martha's was packed for the funeral service eight days later. Perhaps the most poignant moments came with the address by his grandson, Richard, who talked about all the days out they had together and said of his grandfather: 'How could we have asked for a greater role model to follow? Your generosity, your kindness, your warmth, your protection, your influence. To achieve only half of what you achieved would in itself be an achievement to be proud of.'

In June of that year a full and Royal Service of Thanksgiving was held at Guildford Cathedral, conducted by the Dean and Bishop of Guildford and attended by the Duke of Kent, who read a lesson. The RAF accorded military honours, with escort officers and many senior officers present. The Central Band of the RAF accompanied the procession and augmented the cathedral choir. Among a congregation of over 700 were many friends from his professional and social life, including former prime minister John Major and official royal and civic representatives. To express Sir George's diverse achievements, addresses were given by Sir Richard Evans, chairman of BAE

Systems, Sir Alec Bedser, and the Vice-Chancellor of the University of Surrey, Professor Patrick Dowling.

Sir Richard said that, when he first learned of the loss of George Edwards, there was a feeling of 'shock, sorrow and even disbelief' among his friends and colleagues. Having given a comprehensive account of his life and career, Sir Richard said: 'He was a great engineer and a great man who served his country well.' Sir Alec said he and his twin brother Eric had been friends of Sir George for sixty-eight years, since they first played cricket together at Woking when they were only 17. They had forged a 'lasting and wonderful' friendship. He recalled the days when Sir George had been 'a proud president' of Surrey County Cricket Club. 'As we would expect, he did a great job and his wise counsel was sought and respected by us all,' he said.

For the University of Surrey, whose high officers and many staff and students attended, Professor Dowling recaptured the scene on Stag Hill in 1967, where sheep still grazed on the northern slopes and the new University of Surrey had just been granted its Royal Charter. 'There was excitement in the air. Into the picture strides Sir George Edwards at the pinnacle of his career in the aircraft industry, in his characteristic pork-pie hat and wearing wellington boots. He is undertaking an early site visit with Lord Robens, our first Chancellor, and Dr Peter Leggett, our first Vice-Chancellor. There is a kind but firm determination in his eyes.'

A lasting, and to many an emotional moment, was the fly-over of a lone RAF VC10, which dipped low in salute over the cathedral just a few miles from where it was conceived and built by the man it had come to honour.

Sir George Robert Edwards OM, CBE, FRS, FR Eng DL is buried in the place of his choosing, alongside his wife Dinah, near the west door of St Martha's Church. His epitaph, drawn from his coat of arms, reads, '*Fermeté et Ténacité*'. It was the nearest the translators could get to 'Don't give up; press on'.

Envoi

By Sir Richard Evans, formerly Chairman of British Aerospace and BAE Systems

The working life of George Edwards covered the most productive, ambitious and sometimes politically wasteful period of aircraft design and development in Great Britain. During this time he became part of the fabric of British aviation, and his influence was, and continues to be, widely felt. His career began with the biplane and ended with Concorde, and in between were the highs and lows as the world struggled to come to terms with the technology revolution that rapid progress in the design of aircraft, systems and engines brought about.

When I first heard of Sir George's death, in March 2003, my feeling was of shock, sorrow and even disbelief. I had known him since the early 1970s, when I was 'a young hack' from Warton working on the Saudi Arabia defence contract. In later years, after his retirement, we were in regular contact, and every year since 1990 we celebrated our birthdays, which fell on the same day in July, with a special lunch. In speaking with George, and in sharing our similar experiences, I became aware of the debt of gratitude we owe him, particularly in the advancement of civil aviation, and for being a 'founding father' of the company which has now emerged as BAE Systems.

In assessing Sir George's contribution to Britain's aerospace industry there is little doubt that he was the dominating and driving personality from the early post-war years through to his retirement in the mid-1970s, and helped lay the foundations for the thriving international business we have today. As a chief designer and later managing director and chairman, he was both a brilliant engineer and leader; a rare combination which impressed the customers, particularly the Americans, when they discovered he was not only the boss of the outfit, but the designer of the aircraft as well.

When George Edwards left the industry as chairman of BAC at the end of 1975, he left behind a company that had become the most powerful of its kind in Europe. In technical and balance-sheet terms it was in a very healthy position, which was soon to be a key asset for the nationalised and then privatised British Aerospace. Although Sir George vigorously opposed nationalisation as 'irrelevant to the industry's needs', he offered full support for the new company, which survived and prospered because, as he said, it was still manned by good people who knew what they were doing. The merger in 1999 with Marconi Electronic Systems, whose parent company GEC had been a 50 per cent shareholder in BAC, completed an industrial circle with the formation of BAE Systems, which remains a major player in the world marketplace.

To me, probably the most important and lasting legacy of Sir George's era was his introduction and development of major international collaborative programmes. In doing this he realised very early on that, economically, the only way to launch and preserve a major aerospace project was with overseas partners, provided there was an identifiable and government-backed requirement.

This began with the hugely political Concorde programme, which, from my knowledge, was the first of its kind, where policy, design and production were carried out on an equal footing across national boundaries. This brought about a new kind of international politicking, which George Edwards and his team had the knowledge and diplomatic skill to carry out. In time this led not only to many great and extant European military collaborative programmes, such as Jaguar, Tornado and Eurofighter, but especially to the fabulously successful Airbus family of airliners. People forget that the Concorde partners, BAC and Aerospatiale, were the original founders of Airbus.

There was, of course, much more. His influence was strongly felt in Saudi Arabia, India, North America and the Middle East markets in general. I was personally involved from early on with the Saudi Arabian contract, for which we had to conduct our business through Sir George and 'that lot down south'. There was a huge amount of fear and respect for him, and we considered George Edwards and his team to be demigods. We all knew that, if you wanted political influence with the government, you had to go to Weybridge to organise it. In receiving his unstinting support we secured government backing and completed the Saudi business, which, through the Al Yamamah programme, became the bedrock of the company, and without which I doubt we would have survived in the lean years of the early 1990s.

For many people, however, Sir George will be remembered as a true pioneer of modern air travel. In 1948 he introduced the world's first turbine-powered airliner, the turboprop Viscount. He faced terrific opposition, but he was convinced that it would set new standards of passenger comfort and airline efficiency. His faith was to be fully vindicated when the Viscount became Britain's best-selling airliner, and the first successfully to break into the highly protective North American market.

Had there been more airline and political support at home, George would also have been first with a true transatlantic jet transport, the V1000, ahead of both the Boeing 707 and the Douglas DC-8, which subsequently dominated all the lucrative long-haul routes. It was a combination of intransigence and political vacillation that led to the V1000 cancellation, six months before first flight, which he always considered to be 'the biggest blunder of all'.

Sir George faced similar problems with the VC10, which severely curtailed its progress, although enough were built to prove it to be by far the best long-range airliner of its day, and, of course, it is still operating with the RAF. The later BAC One-Eleven, which he developed and sold – almost personally – to the USA, was, like the Viscount, to advance air travel. It was the first to introduce jet services on many regional routes, while in Britain it became the chosen aircraft to lead the Inclusive Tour revolution, bringing fast jet services to the sun spots of the Mediterranean for the benefit of almost everybody.

For Concorde, George gave his heart and soul from its very beginnings, as far back as 1956. With the formation of BAC in 1960 he became leader of the British team, and was again faced with a barrage of hostile protest and criticism. To his everlasting credit it did not deflect him or his colleagues from meeting a supreme technical challenge by introducing the world's only successful supersonic airliner.

In military aircraft, his greatest achievement was the Valiant, Britain's first V-bomber. Again, he was breaching the bounds of known technology, but he was still able to deliver the aircraft in an incredibly short time, with a performance above specification, to time, to cost. Recently, it was brought to my attention that new evidence of the Russian assessment of Britain's V-bomber force had placed the Valiant as the aircraft they most feared.

But people from my part of the world, at Warton, will remember George Edwards most for the TSR.2, and his leadership in the bitter battle to preserve the aircraft against the most outrageous odds. We did not always see eye-to-eye with him, and many felt he was more engaged in developing his civil aircraft at Weybridge than in understanding the complexity of the most advanced military aircraft of its time. I do not believe this to be the case, and his decision to preserve 'at all costs' the northern factories involved after the cancellation gives credence to that belief. Needless to say, the military aircraft business now centred on Warton has become Europe's most productive facility.

Throughout his career George Edwards had to fight, and fight hard, against those with limited knowledge or with a contrary political agenda. He, like many of his contemporaries, such as Freddie Page, who sadly died recently, bore enormous scars from such tribulations. But George did so with such fortitude, and utter belief that what he was doing was right, that he usually won the day. It is my belief that, had he been operating at the highest level in wartime, and if his aircraft had been measured against winning the war, instead of winning the peace, his name would be as familiar today as those other great British engineers and designers, such as Mitchell, Chadwick, Wallis and Whittle.

I trust his story, now told, will do much to enhance that belief.

APPENDIX ONE

Abbreviations

A&AEE	Aeroplane and Armament Experimental Establishment
AFVG	Anglo-French Variable-Geometry (aircraft)
AI	airborne interception (radar)
BA	British Airways
BAC	British Aircraft Corporation
BEA	British European Airways
BOAC	British Overseas Airways Corporation
BUA	British United Airways
CAS	Chief of the Air Staff
C of A	Certificate of Airworthiness
ECAT	Ecole de Combat et d'Appui Tactique
FAA	Federal Aviation Authority (USA)
GRU	General Reconnaissance Unit
GW	BAC Guided Weapons Division
HSA	Hawker Siddeley Aviation
IT	inclusive tour
ITP	Instruction to Proceed
MAP	Ministry of Aircraft Production
MoD	Ministry of Defence
MoS	Ministry of Supply
MRCA	Multi-Role Combat Aircraft
NEB	National Enterprise Board
OR	Operational Requirement(s)
PPL	Private Pilot's Licence
QTOL	Quiet Take-Off and Landing
RAAF	Royal Australian Air Force
RAE	Royal Aircraft Establishment
RAeS	Royal Aeronautical Society
SAC	Strategic Air Command
SBAC	Society of British Aircraft Constructors

SEPECAT	Société Européene de Production de l'Avion d'Ecole de Combat et d'Appui Tactique
SST	Supersonic Transport
STAC	Supersonic Transport Aircraft Committee
STOL	Short Take-off and Landing
TCA	Trans-Canada Airlines
USAAF	United States Army Air Force
USAF	United States Air Force
V/STOL	Vertical/Short Take-off and Landing
VTOL	Vertical Take-off and Landing

Chronology

EDUCATIONAL AND ENGINEERING BACKGROUND

1928–35　Walthamstow Engineering and Trade School (subsequently the Waltham Forest Technical College and the South West Essex Technical College). Civil engineering in the London Docks. Part-time external University of London BSc(Eng) degree course. Degree awarded in 1935. Associate Membership of the Institution of Structural Engineers

AVIATION CAREER

1935　Joined design staff of Vickers (Aviation) Ltd at Weybridge, Surrey

1938　Postgraduate course in experimental structures, University of London

1940　Experimental Manager, Vickers-Armstrongs Ltd, Weybridge, Surrey

1940–1　Part-time secondment to the Ministry of Aircraft Production under Lord Beaverbrook to accelerate the development of new aircraft types in other aircraft factories

1945　Member of the Farren Mission to Germany to sequestrate advanced aeronautical research information

1945–53　Chief Designer, Vickers-Armstrongs, Weybridge

1948–53　Special Director of Vickers-Armstrongs, Weybridge

1953　Director, General Manager and Chief Engineer, Vickers-Armstrongs Aviation Section; and then Managing Director

1955–67　Director, Vickers Ltd

1958–60   Director, Vickers Research Ltd

1959–61   Member of the UK Government Committee on Management Research

1960–1   Executive Director – Aircraft, British Aircraft Corporation Ltd

1961–8   Chairman and Managing Director, British Aircraft Corporation (Operating) Ltd

1968–75   Chairman and Managing Director, British Aircraft Corporation Ltd

1975   Retired 31 December 1975 after 40 years in the aviation industry

OTHER NOTEWORTHY APPOINTMENTS

1950–3   Vice-President of the Royal Aeronautical Society

1958–61   Vice-President of the Royal Society of Arts

1957–8   President of the Royal Aeronautical Society

1966–79   Pro-Chancellor of the University of Surrey

1970–1   President of the Association of Technical Institutions

1970   President of the Association of Colleges of Further Education and Higher Education

1970–2003   Patron of the Guild of Aviation Artists

1974   Vice-President of Surrey County Cricket Club

1976–83   Trustee of the Royal Air Force Museum

1979–80   President of Surrey County Cricket Club

1979–2003   Pro-Chancellor Emeritus of the University of Surrey

1981–2003   Deputy Lieutenant of the County of Surrey

1987–2003   Patron of the Brooklands Museum Trust

HONOURS AND AWARDS

1945   Member of the Order of the British Empire

1949   Royal Aeronautical Society George Taylor Medal

1952   Commander of the Order of the British Empire

1952   Royal Aeronautical Society British Gold Medal for Aeronautics

1957   Created Knight Bachelor

1959   Honorary Fellowship of the American Institute of Aeronautical
Sciences (now the American Institute of Aeronautics and
Astronautics)

1959   Daniel Guggenheim Medal

1960   Honorary Fellowship of the Royal Aeronautical Society

1968   Fellowship of the Royal Society

1968   Air League Founders Medal

1969   Membership of the Newcomen Society of North America

1971   Appointed to the Order of Merit by HM Queen Elizabeth II

1972   Albert Medal of the Royal Society of Arts

1972   Member of the Royal Institution

1974   Royal Medal of the Royal Society

1974   Silver Jubilee Medal of the Institute of Sheet Metal Engineering

1975   Honorary Fellowship of the Institution of Mechanical Engineers

1976   Fellowship of Engineering (now the Royal Academy of Engineering)

1994   Awarded John Curtis Sword by the American magazine *Aviation
Week and Space Technology* for his 'distinguished contribution to
Anglo-American relations'

1994   Diploma of the Royal Aero Club

1996   Companion of the Air League of Great Britain

2000   Special Award of Honour by the Guild of Air Pilots and Air Navigators

2002   Service and lunch with HM The Queen in celebration of the
centenary of the foundation of the Order of Merit and in Her
Majesty's Golden Jubilee Year celebrations

PRINCIPAL LECTURES AND SPEECHES

1949   'Problems in the Development of a New Aeroplane', Royal Aeronautical Society, London. Published in the *Journal of the RAeS*, March 1949

1949   'Turbine-Engined Transport Aircraft', Second Joint Anglo-American Conference – Royal Aeronautical Society and American Institute of Aeronautical Sciences, New York, 24 May 1949

1951   'Flight Experience with the Vickers Viscount Turbopropeller Airliner', Society of Automotive Engineers, New York, September 1951. (Repeated at the SAE National Aeronautic Meeting in Los Angeles on 6 October 1951, and published in the *SAE Quarterly Transactions*, April 1952, Vol. 6 No. 2)

1958   'The Influence of Speed on Transport', presidential address to the Royal Aeronautical Society, London, 26 February 1958. Published in the *Journal of the RAeS*, April 1958

1960   'A Dip into the Future', Third Trenchard Memorial Lecture, School of Technical Training, RAF Halton, May 1960

1960   'National and International Aspects of the Aircraft Business', Institute of Directors Annual Conference, October 1960

1962   'Defence and the Aircraft Industry', Fourth Wakefield Memorial Lecture, College of Aeronautical and Automobile Engineering, London, May 1962

1963   'Evolution in Air Transport', R.J. Mitchell Memorial Lecture, Stoke-on-Trent Association of Engineers

1964   'Progress with the Concord Supersonic Transport', Twenty-first Branker Memorial Lecture to the Institute of Transport, London, 10 February 1964. Published in *Flight International*, 20 February 1964

1966   'Anglo-French Collaboration – The Present and Some Thoughts for the Future', Royal Aeronautical Society Centenary Congress in conjunction with the Fifth Congress of the International Council of the Aeronautical Sciences, London, September 1966

1968   'The Impact of Speed on Transport', inaugural address to the Dublin Branch of the Royal Aeronautical Society, 28 May 1968

1969   'The First Sixty Years' (of BAC and its predecessors), address to the Newcomen Society, New York

1970   Presidential Address to the Association of Colleges of Further Education and Higher Education, the Institution of Electrical Engineers, London

1970   'Air Transport – A Changing Scene', Institute of Metals, London

1970   'Partnership in Major Technological Projects', Seventh Maurice Lubbock Memorial Lecture, University of Oxford

1970   'Some Thoughts on the Future of the British Aerospace Industry', speech to the Economic Club of Chicago, USA, 29 October 1970

1971   'Collaboration in Aerospace Projects. A Discourse', the Royal Institution, London

1971   'UK Aerospace – A Personal View', Sixth Henry Tizard Memorial Lecture, Royal Aeronautical Society, Boscombe Down Branch, Wiltshire

1973   'The Technical Aspects of Supersonic Civil Transport Aircraft', Review Lecture to the Royal Society, 29 March 1973

1973   'Looking Ahead with Hindsight', Sixty-second Wilbur and Orville Wright Memorial Lecture, Royal Aeronautical Society, London, 6 December 1973, commemorating the seventieth anniversary of the Wrights' first powered manned flight in December 1903; largely autobiographical. Published in the *RAeS Journal*, April 1974

1974   'The Aerospace Industry – A National Asset', Silver Jubilee Lecture, Institute of Sheet Metal Engineering, London

1974   'Supersonic Transport – Some of the Problems', lecture at the Franklyn Institute, New York

1982   'The British Aerospace Industry – A National Asset', the second Christopher Hinton Lecture, Fellowship of Engineering (now the Royal Academy of Engineering), London, 29 November 1982; largely autobiographical

Bibliography

SIR GEORGE EDWARDS'S (GRE) PERSONAL PAPERS

School Reports, Walthamstow Junior Technical College, 1922–6
Correspondence, the Ocean Accident & Guarantee Corporation, London, 3 October 1933
Certificate of Associate Membership of Institution of Structural Engineers, London, 8 November 1930
Personal diaries, 9 July 1945 to 26 July 1945
Extracts from unexpurgated script of recordings for BBC Television programme *All Our Working Lives*, dated 18 November 1981, for broadcast in 1982
Correspondence with Roy Jenkins, Minister of Aviation, 2 February 1965
Recording by Sir Geoffrey Tuttle of personal reminiscences, 1975
Air Ministry brief on visit to Russia, 1956
Memoranda to Lord Portal of Hungerford, 4 December 1961
Memorandum on meeting with Peter Thorneycroft, Minister of Aviation, 28 November 1961
Memorandum to Lord Nelson, 23 September 1961
Memorandum to Lord Portal, 5 August 1962
Correspondence with Peter Thorneycroft, 17 April 1962, 1 June 1962
Correspondence with Roy Jenkins, Minister of Aviation, 21 December 1964, 30 December 1964, 12 January 1965
Notes on meeting with Prime Minister Harold Wilson, 15 January 1965
Letter to Sir Richard Way, Permanent Secretary, Ministry of Aviation, 27 January 1965
Extracts from BAC Board Minutes, 11 January 1965, 20 January 1965, 26 January 1965, 27 January 1965
Notice to Employees, 9 April 1965
Extracts from BAC Board Minutes regarding meeting with Aviation Minister Fred Mulley, 4 November 1966
Correspondence with Roy Jenkins, 28 October 1964, 17 November 1964, 23 November 1964
Letter to Denis Healey, Secretary of State for Defence, 19 January 1967

Memorandum to Lord Portal, and BAC Board Report on sales visit to North
America, 3 March 1961
Notes on meeting with Peter Thorneycroft, 14 March 1961
Correspondence with Roy Jenkins, 30 January 1964, 2 February 1965
Tribute to Lord Portal published in BAC house newspaper *Airframe*, May 1971
Extracts from BAC Board Minutes, 8 October 1968
Correspondence with Michael Heseltine, Minister for Aerospace, 10 April 1972,
22 May 1972, 2 June 1972, 8 November 1972, 15 November 1972,
22 November 1972
Letter to R.E. Thornton, Secretary (Aerospace), DTI, 5 June 1973
Letter to Arnold Weinstock, managing director GEC, 26 November1973
Letter to Tony Benn, Secretary of State for Industry, 25 November 1974
Letter to Roy Mason, Secretary of State for Defence, 14 July 1975
Letter to Lord Beswick, 22 September 1975
Correspondence with GEC, 11 March 1976, 22 March 1976
Letter to Harold Wilson, 8 January 1976
Letter to Prof T.R. Lee, University of Surrey (chairman of the Arts Committee),
25 October 1981
Extracts from recorded addresses at GRE retirement dinner, Claridge's, London,
13 April 1976
Informal address at Concorde reunion dinner, London, 4 March 1994
Tributes at Sir Tom Sopwith's 100th birthday lunch, Brooklands, 18 January
1988, and at Thanksgiving Service, London, 12 April 1989
Recorded address at funeral of Charles Gardner, Leatherhead, 8 June 1983
Undated notes of tribute to Sir Geoffrey Tuttle and Sir Edward Tuckwell

SIR GEORGE EDWARDS'S LECTURES AND SPEECHES

These are presented in chronological order.

'Problems in the Development of a New Aeroplane', Lecture to the Royal
Aeronautical Society, London, 2 December 1948
'Turbine-Engined Transport Aircraft', Lecture to the American Institute of
Aeronautical Sciences/Royal Aeronautical Society Joint Anglo-American
Conference, New York, 24 May 1949
'The Influence of Speed on Transport', Presidential Address, Royal Aeronautical
Society, London, 26 February 1958
Acceptance address at the Daniel Guggenheim Medal Award Ceremony, New York,
7 April 1960
'A Dip into the Future', Lecture to the RAF School of Technical Training, RAF
Halton, 22 May 1960
Address to the Air League, Mansion House, London, 8 November 1960

Address to the Business Economists Group, London, 16 February 1965

Address to the Aero Club of America, Washington, DC, 25 July 1967

'Some Joint Anglo-European Aircraft', lecture to the Society of Automotive Engineers, New York, 1 May 1968

'Things are Looking Up', lecture to private club, reproduced in *Flight* magazine, 13 February 1969

'The First Sixty Years', lecture to the Newcomen Society, New York, 16 October 1969

Presidential address to the Association of Colleges of Higher Further Education, 6 April 1970

'Partnership in Major Technological Projects', seventh Maurice Lubbock Memorial Lecture, University of Oxford, 14 May 1970

Address to Economics Club, Chicago, 29 October 1970

'The Technical Aspects of Supersonic Civil Transport Aircraft', review lecture, the Royal Society, London, 29 March 1973

'Looking Ahead with Hindsight', sixty-second Wilbur and Orville Wright Memorial Lecture, Royal Aeronautical Society, London, 6 December 1973

Address to Waltham Forest Technical College, 30 September 1974

Address to RAF Central Flying School, 13 June 1975

'The British Aerospace Industry – A National Asset', second Christopher Hinton Lecture, Fellowship of Engineering (now the Royal Academy of Engineering), London, 29 November 1982 (largely autobiographical)

Address at SBAC Farnborough Air Show Dinner on receipt of the Curtis Award, London, 7 September 1994

OTHER SOURCES

BAC Press Statements, 11 June 1966, 2 September 1966

Bedser, Sir Alec, Dowling, Prof Patrick and Evans, Sir Richard, extracts from addresses delivered at GRE Service of Thanksgiving, Guildford Cathedral, 16 June 2003

Benn, Tony, unpublished extracts from his diary from 4 January 1968 to 22 January 1976

Boorer, N.W., 'Sir George Edwards OM, CBE, FRS', lecture to Royal Aeronautical Society, Weybridge Branch, 25 February 2004

Cookson, Brian, correspondence relating to BAC Ltd, 10 March 2004, 11 August 2004, 25 February 2005

Dunphie, Sir Charles, letter to Lord Portal, 26 January 1965

Edwards, Grant, history of the Edwards family, 23 October 2002

Farren Mission, National Archives AVIA 10/411

Finniston, Monty, address to the University of Surrey, 30 November 1979

Jeffreys, Richard, address at GRE funeral, Guildford, 10 March 2003

Luther, Philip, description of GRE dismissal of Learie Constantine, 21 January 2004

McLean, Sir Robert, letter to Air Vice-Marshal Dowding, 5 July 1935
McClen, Don, correspondence relating to Saudi Arabia contract, 2005
Motum, John, various correspondence, 2004/5
Pugsley, Sir Alfred and Rowe, N.E., 'Barnes Neville Wallis', biographical paper for the Royal Society, London, November 1981
University of Surrey Notices 20 June 1981, 12 July 1985
Verdon-Smith, Sir Reginald, 'British Aircraft Corporation – The First Twelve Years', Barnwell Memorial Lecture, Royal Aeronautical Society, Bristol, 28 March 1972

BOOKS

Adams, A.R., *Good Company*, British Aircraft Corporation, Stevenage, GW Division, 1976
Andrews, C.F. and Morgan, E.B., *Supermarine Aircraft since 1914*, London, Putnam, 1981
Andrews, C.F., *Vickers Aircraft Since 1908*, London, Putnam, 1969
Barfield, Dr N., *Vickers Aircraft*, Chalford, Chalford Publishing, 1997
Benn, T., *Diaries 1968–72, 1973–76*, London, Hutchinson, 1988
Cairncross, Sir Alec, *Planning in Wartime*, Oxford, Oxford University Press, Macmillan Series, 1991
Calvert, B., *Flying Concorde*, London, Fontana Books, 1981
Churchill, W.S., *The Second World War*, vol. 1, London, Cassell, 1948
Curtis, D., *The Most Secret Squadron*, Wimborne, Skitten Books, 1995
Donald, D. (gen. ed.), *Encyclopedia of All the World's Aircraft*, Leicester, Orbis Publishing/Aerospace Publishing, 1997
Flower, S., *Barnes Wallis' Bombs*, Stroud, Tempus, 2002
Gardner, C., *British Aircraft Corporation*, London, Batsford, 1981
Gee, J., *Mirage*, London, Macdonald, 1971
Hunter, Air Vice-Marshal A.F.C. (ed.), *TSR.2 with Hindsight*, London, RAF Historical Society, 1998
Jane's All the World's Aircraft (various eds), London, Sampson Low/Jane's Publishing, annual editions, 1935 to 1976–7
Jenkins, R., *A Life at the Centre*, London, Macmillan, 1991
Knight, G., *Concorde – The Inside Story*, Weidenfeld & Nicolson, London, 1976
McGregor, G., *The Adolescence of an Airline*, Montreal, Air Canada, 1980
Masefield, Sir Peter and Gunston, W., *Flight Path*, Shrewsbury, Airlife, 2002
Owen, K., *Concorde – A New Shape in the Sky*, London, Jane's, in co-operation with the Science Museum, 1982
Pearce, E., *Denis Healey, A Life In Our Times*, London, Little Brown Book/Time Warner, 2002
Pick, C., *Understanding the Real World – A Visual History of the University of Surrey*, Guildford, University of Surrey Press, 2002

Pilkington, L., *Surrey Airfields in the Second World War*, Newbury, Countryside Books, 1998

Prince Philip, H.R.H., *Thirty Years On and Off the Box Seat*, J.A. Allen, London, 2004

Read, R.A., *The Magic Carpet*, privately published, Alcantara, San Pedro, 1999

Rummell, R., *Howard Hughes and TWA*, Washington, DC, Smithsonian History of Aviation Series, Smithsonian Institution Press, 1991

Richards, D., *Portal of Hungerford*, London, Heinemann, 1977

Scott, J.D., *Vickers – A History*, London, Weidenfeld & Nicolson, 1963

Sharman, S., *Sir James Martin*, Sparkford, Patrick Stephens, 1996

Trubshaw, B. and Edmondson, S., *Test Pilot*, Stroud, Sutton Publishing, 1998

Turnill, R. and Reed, A., *Farnborough – The Story of the RAE*, London, Robert Hale, 1980

Wilson, H., *The Labour Government 1964–70*, London, Weidenfeld & Nicolson, 1971

Wood, D., *Project Cancelled*, London, Macdonald & Jane's, 1975

NEWSPAPER AND MAGAZINE ARTICLES

Anon., 'A Capital Occasion', *Aeroplane*, 27 June 1955

——, 'Capital's Troubles', *Flight*, 10 January 1958

——, 'First in the Air Again', *Daily Graphic*, 21 September 1949

——, 'Papon', *Daily Telegraph*, 19 September 2002

——, 'The English Electric Division', *Aeroplane*, 3 June 1949

——, 'The Pro-Chancellor', *Surrey Advertiser*, 29 October 1966

——, 'The Saudi Arabian Deal', *Flight*, 19 June 1966

——, 'The Vanguard', *Flight*, 9 January 1959

——, 'Three Men Staked Their Lives Against Ice', *Sunday Empire News*, 9 March 1947

——, 'Tushino Revelations', *Flight*, 29 June 1956

Barfield, Dr N., 'The Valiant', *Air International*, September 1992

Bolt, Rear Admiral A.S., 'Minesweeping Wellingtons', *Air Pictorial*, April 1969

Bryce, G.R. 'Jock', *Sunday Express*, 2 July 1978

Edwards, Sir George, 'The VC 10 – Personal Overview and Perspective', *Putnam Aeronautical Review*, May 1989

Masefield, Sir Peter, 'The Story of the Viscount', *Flight*, 15 July 1955

Mellberg, W., 'The Vickers Vanguard', *Airliners* (USA), Autumn 1993

——, 'Vickers Viscount – Rolls-Royce of the Air', *Airliners* (USA), 1994

Serling, R., 'Bob Six and the Viscount', *Airline Magazine*, July/August 2004

——, 'Britain's Viscount – the Real Jet Age Pioneer', *Airways* (USA), June 2000

Taylor, H.A., 'The Viscount', *Air Enthusiast*, June 1965

Thorne, J., 'Letter to the Editor', *Airframe* (house newspaper of BAC), November 1975

INTERVIEWS WITH THE AUTHOR

Barfield, Dr Norman, numerous, 2004–5

Benn, Tony, interview 21 April 2004

Bedser, Sir Alec, and Eric, interview 27 April 2004

Boorer, N.W. 'Spud', interviews 19 and 26 October 2001

Brixey, Mrs Joyce, interview 18 July 2002

Brown, Capt Eric 'Winkle', conversations 1 July 2005, August 2005

Bryce, G.R. 'Jock', interview 17 April 2005

Coleman, Bernie, interview 22 May 2002

Dowling, Prof Patrick, interview 22 February 2002

Edwards, Sir George, interviews 2 November 1999, 10 November 1999, 7 December 1999, 17 December 1999, 13 January 2000, 25 January 2000, 10 February 2000, 16 March 2000, 13 April 2000, 27 April 2000, 9 May 2000, 1 June 2000, 27 June 2000, 11 July 2000, 17 August 2000, 12 September 2000, 19 October 2000, 23 November 2000, 4 January 2001, 6 February 2001, 15 February 2001, 1 March 2001, 8 March 2001, 29 March 2001, 23 October 2001, 29 November 2001, 12 March 2002, 20 June 2002

Evans, Sir Richard, interview 30 May 2002

Jeffreys, Angela 'Dingle' (GRE's daughter), interviews 3 June 2003, 11 June 2003

Jeffreys, Clair (GRE's granddaughter), interview 25 October 2004

Jeffreys, Richard (GRE's grandson), 25 October 2004

Newton, Derek, interview 22 May 2002

Steel, Roger, interview 3 December 2002

Simpson, Duncan, interview 29 November 2001

Subba Row, Raman, interview 22 May 2002

Thurgood, George (GRE's brother-in-law), interview 11 June 2003

Index

Note: aircraft and factories are listed under their manufacturer's names.